I ended up taking a long break after hurting my back.
I intend to keep working hard, so please keep up the
support!! Not being able to even sit in a chair for
about two weeks got me a bit worried. But I'll keep
going at my own pace!

— Takeshi Konomi, 2006

About Takeshi Konomi

Takeshi Konomi exploded onto the manga scene with the
incredible **THE PRINCE OF TENNIS**. His refined art style and
sleek character designs proved popular with **Weekly Shonen
Jump** readers, and **THE PRINCE OF TENNIS** became the
number one sports manga in Japan almost overnight. Its
cast of fascinating male tennis players attracted legions of
female readers even though it was originally intended to be
a boys' comic. The manga continues to be a success in
Japan and has inspired a hit anime series, as well as several
video games and mountains of merchandise.

THE PRINCE OF TENNIS
VOL. 35
SHONEN JUMP Manga Edition

STORY AND ART BY
TAKESHI KONOMI

Translation/Joe Yamazaki
Touch-up Art & Lettering/Vanessa Satone
Design/Sam Elzway
Editor/Leyla Aker

VP, Production/Alvin Lu
VP, Sales & Product Marketing/Gonzalo Ferreyra
VP, Creative/Linda Espinosa
Publisher/Hyoe Narita

Published by VIZ Media, LLC
P.O. Box 77010
San Francisco, CA 94107

10 9 8 7 6 5 4 3 2 1
First printing, January 2010

www.viz.com

RATED

PARENTAL ADVISORY
THE PRINCE OF TENNIS
is rated A and is suitable
for readers of all ages.
ratings.viz.com

THE WORLD'S
MOST POPULAR MANGA

www.shonenjump.com

SHONEN JUMP Manga

テニスの王子様

THE PRINCE OF TENNIS

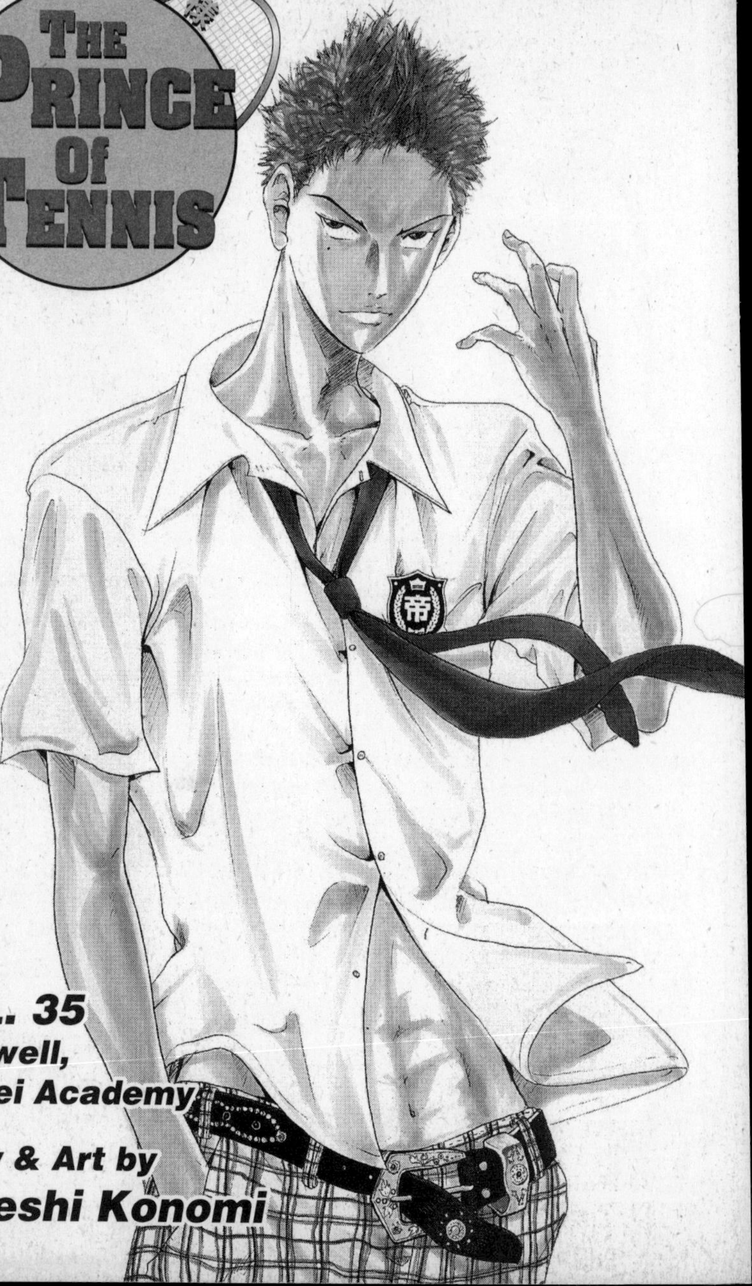

VOL. 35
Farewell, Hyotei Academy

Story & Art by
Takeshi Konomi

ENNIS CLUB

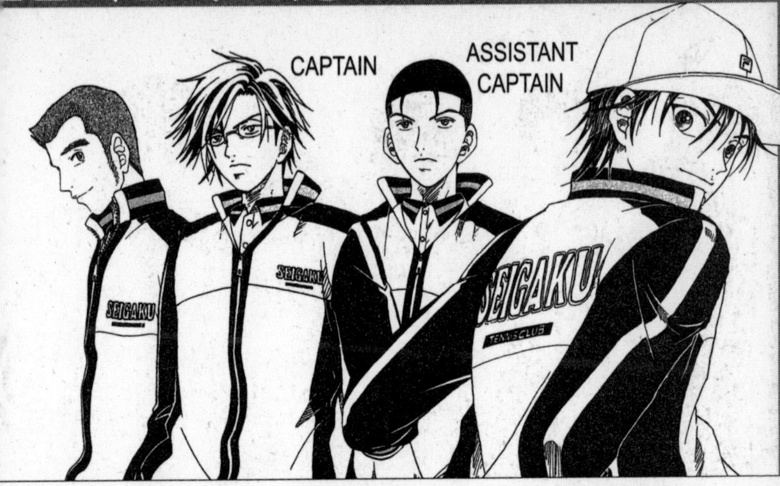
CAPTAIN
ASSISTANT CAPTAIN

• TAKASHI KAWAMURA • KUNIMITSU TEZUKA • SHUICHIRO OISHI • RYOMA ECHIZEN •

STORY &

Seishun Academy student Ryoma Echizen is a tennis prodigy, with wins in four consecutive U.S. Junior Tennis Tournaments under his belt. He became a starter as a 7th grader and led his team to the District Preliminaries! Despite a few mishaps, Seishun won the District Prelims and the City Tournament, and earned a ticket to the Kanto Tournament. The team came away victorious from its first-round matches, but captain Kunimitsu injured his shoulder and went to Kyushu for treatment. Despite losing Kunimitsu and assistant captain Shuichiro to injury, Seishun pulled together as a team, winning the Kanto Tournament and earning a slot at the Nationals!

With Kunimitsu recovered and back on the team, Seishun enter the Nationals with their strongest line up and defeat Okinawa's Higa Junior High in the opening round to face Hyotei Academy in the semifinals. Seishun and Hyotei play to a 2–all tie with only the No. 1 Singles match left to play. Now Ryoma and Keigo are squaring off against each other for the ticket to the semifinals! Ryoma counters Keigo's World of Ice with the Tezuka Zone, but can he stop Hyotei's captain?

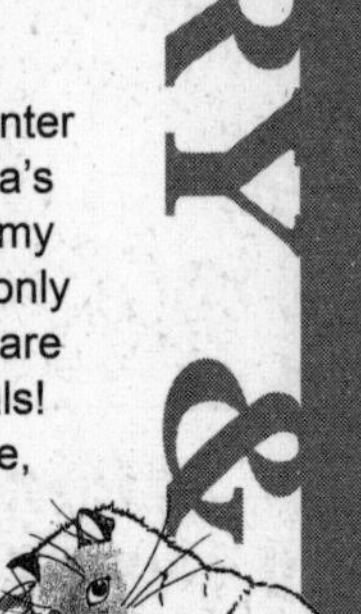

HARACTERS

SEIGAKU T

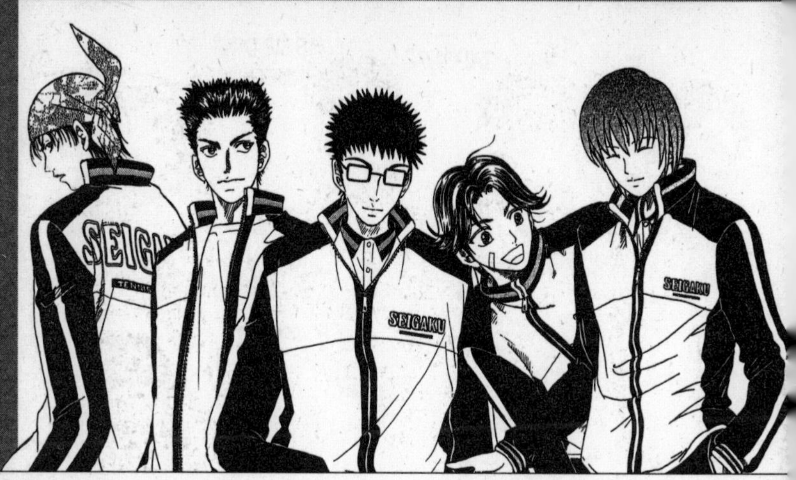

● KAORU KAIDO ● TAKESHI MOMOSHIRO ● SADAHARU INUI ● EIJI KIKUMARU ● SHUSUKE FUJI ●

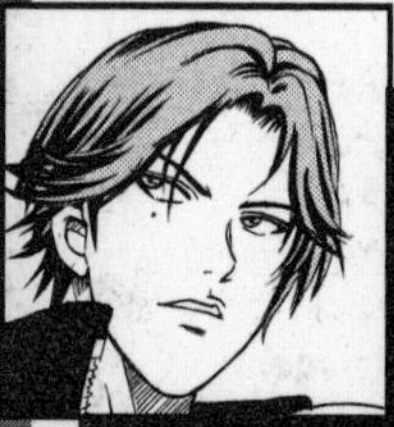

KEIGO ATOBE
HYOTEI ACADEMY

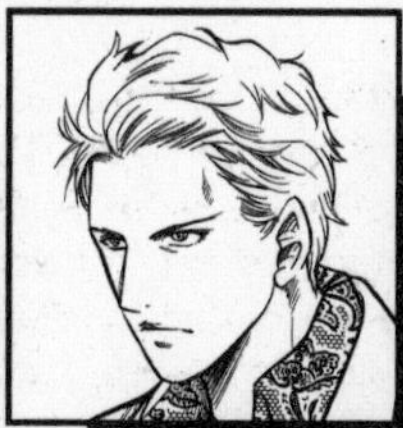

TARO SAKAKI
HYOTEI ACADEMY TENNIS COACH

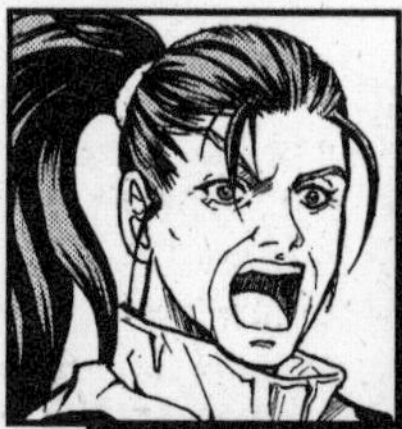

SUMIRE RYUZAKI
SEISHUN ACADEMY TENNIS COACH

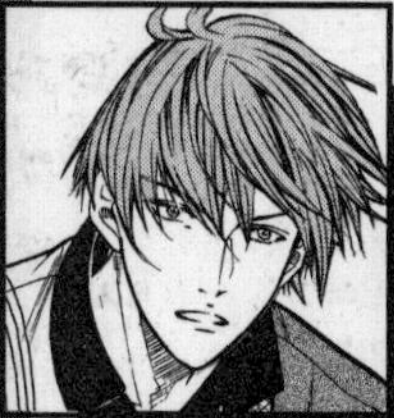

WAKASHI HIYOSHI
HYOTEI ACADEMY

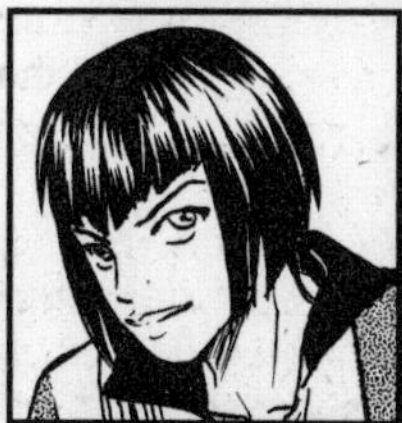

GAKUTO MUKAHI
HYOTEI ACADEMY

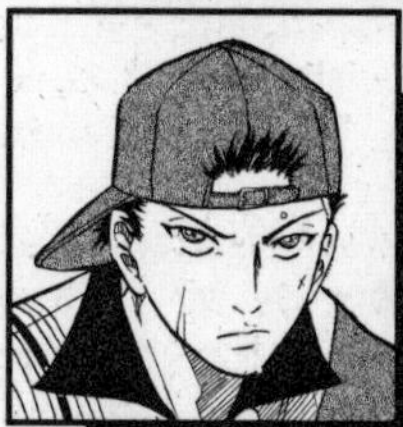

RYO SHISHIDO
HYOTEI ACADEMY

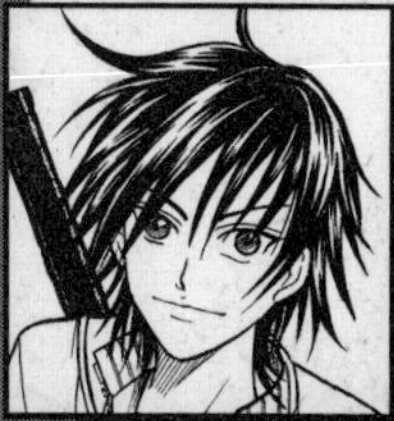

KINTARO TOYAMA
SHITENHOJI

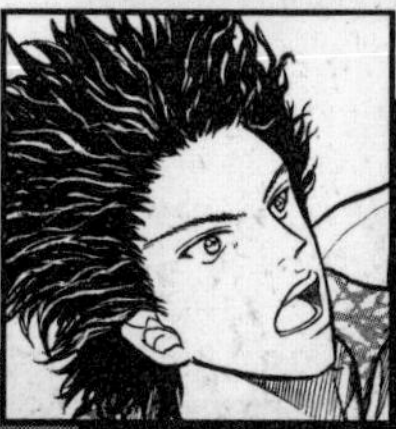

SENRI CHITOSE
SHITENHOJI

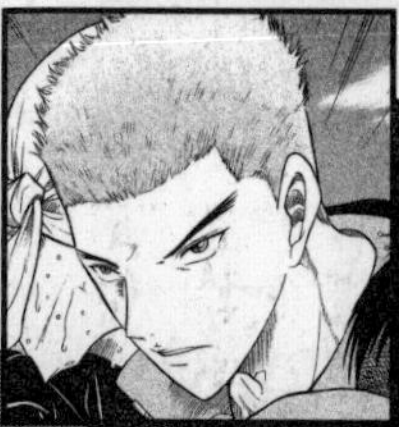

KIPPEI TACHIBANA
FUDOMINE

CONTENTS Vol. 35
Farewell, Hyotei Academy

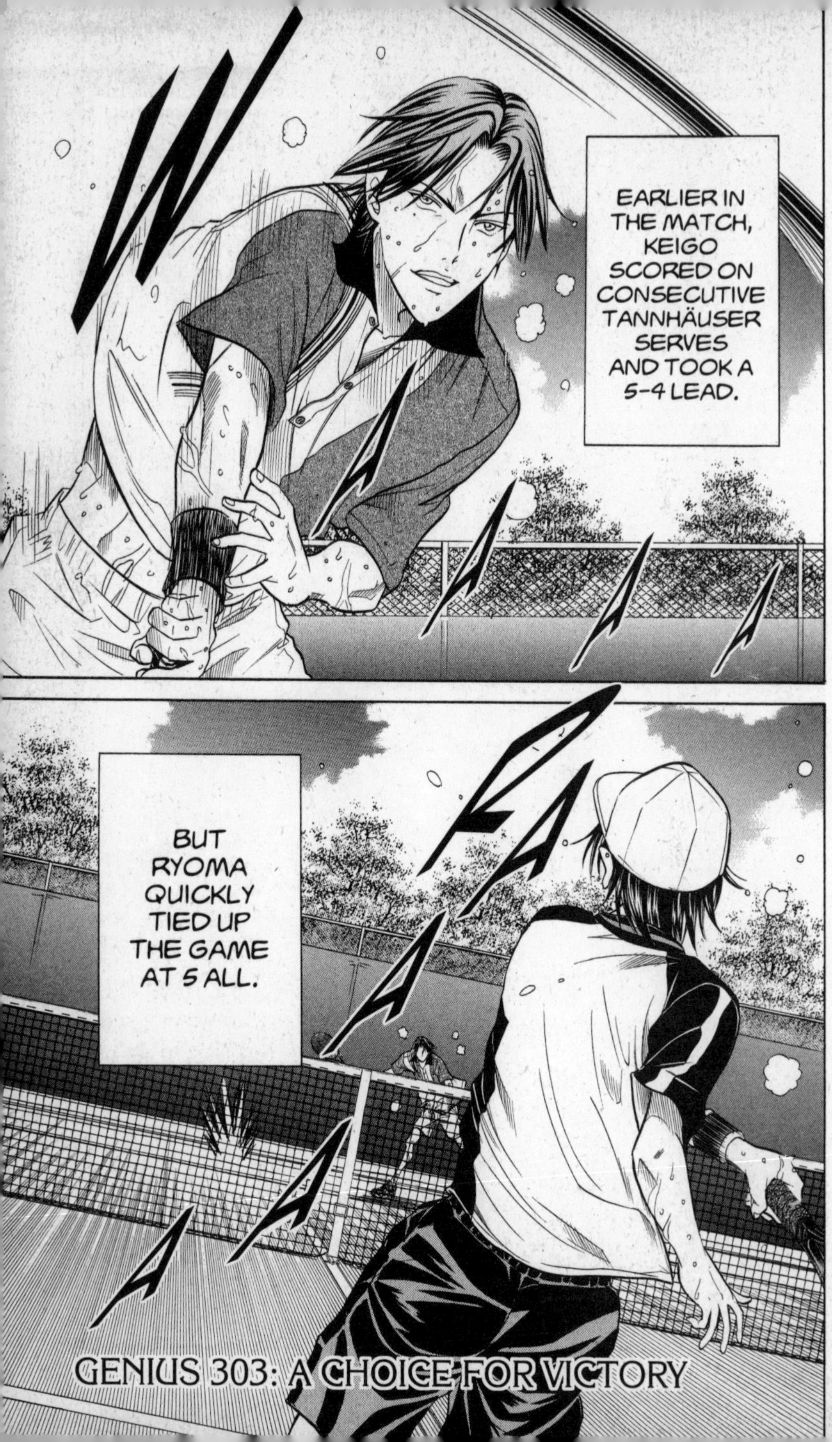
EARLIER IN THE MATCH, KEIGO SCORED ON CONSECUTIVE TANNHÄUSER SERVES AND TOOK A 5-4 LEAD.
BUT RYOMA QUICKLY TIED UP THE GAME AT 5 ALL.
GENIUS 303: A CHOICE FOR VICTORY

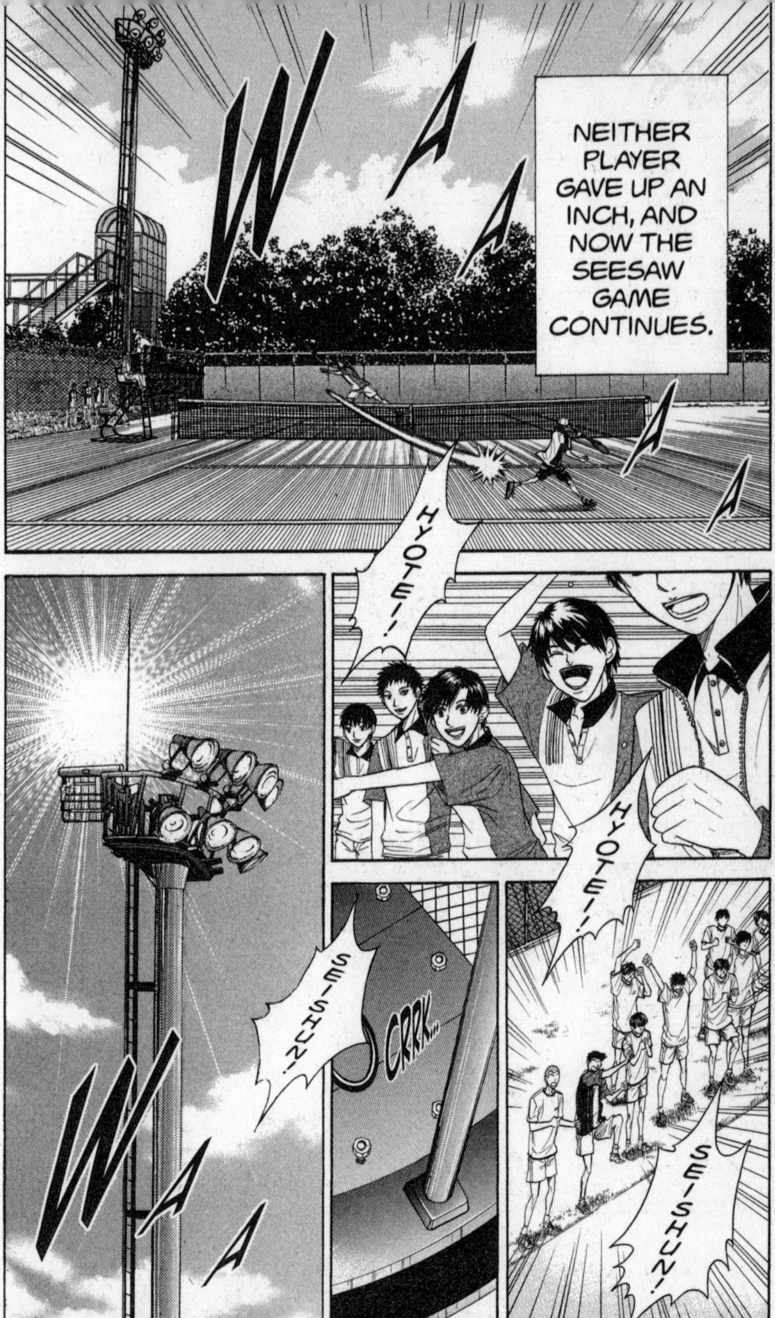
WAAAAA
NEITHER PLAYER GAVE UP AN INCH, AND NOW THE SEESAW GAME CONTINUES.
HYOTEI!!
HYOTEI!!
SEISHUN!
SEISHUN!
CRRK...
WAA

READ THIS WAY

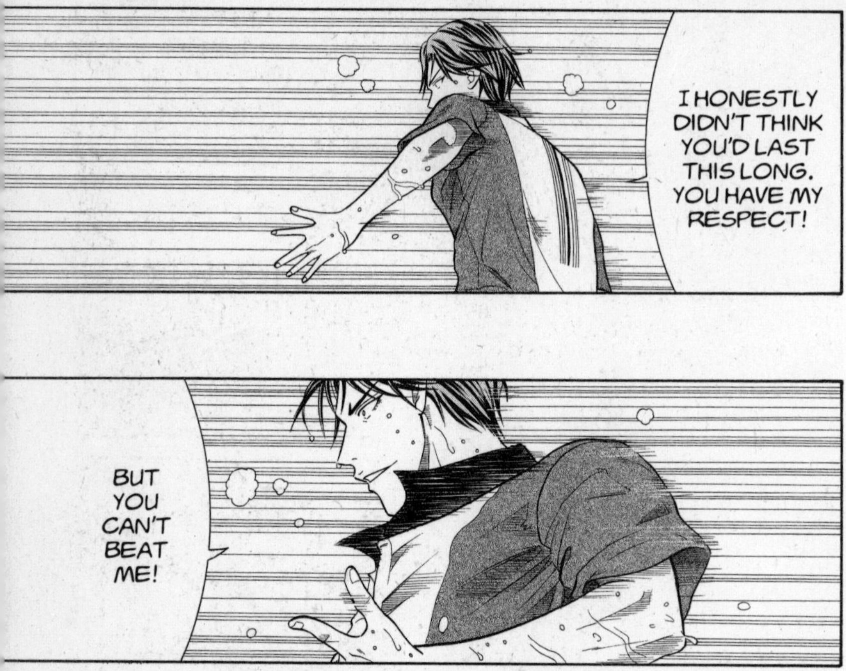
I HONESTLY DIDN'T THINK YOU'D LAST THIS LONG. YOU HAVE MY RESPECT!
BUT YOU CAN'T BEAT ME!

GENIUS 303:

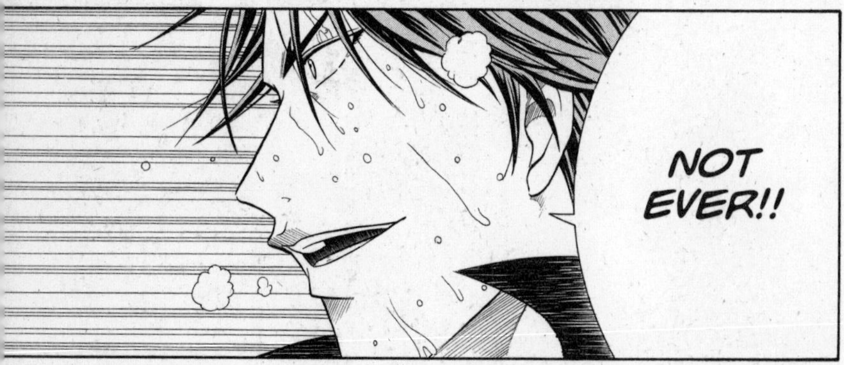
NOT EVER!!

A CHOICE FOR VICTORY

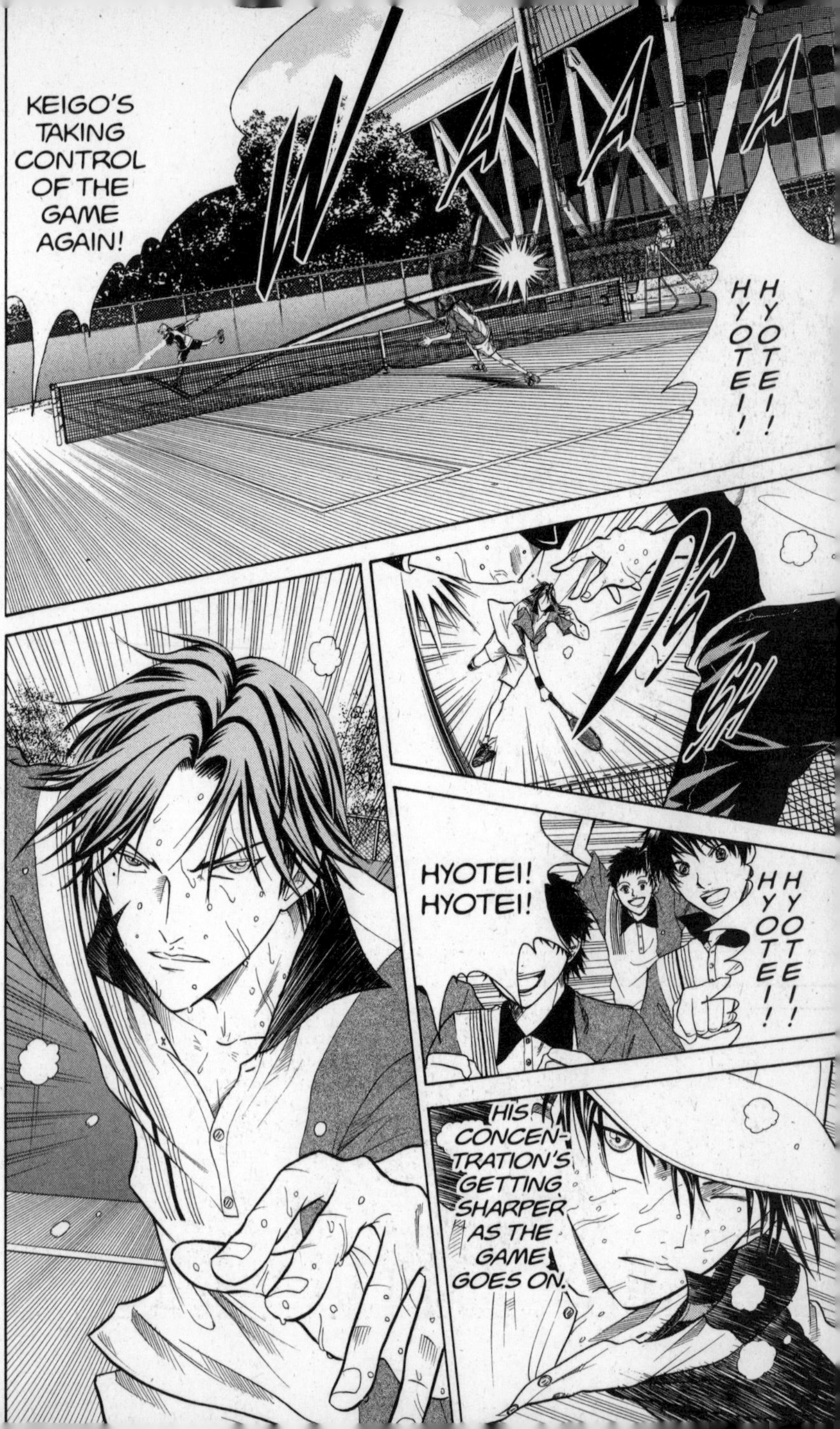
HYOTEI!
HYOTEI!
WAAAA
KEIGO'S TAKING CONTROL OF THE GAME AGAIN!
HYOTEI! HYOTEI!
HYOTEI!
HYOTEI!
HIS CONCENTRATION'S GETTING SHARPER AS THE GAME GOES ON.

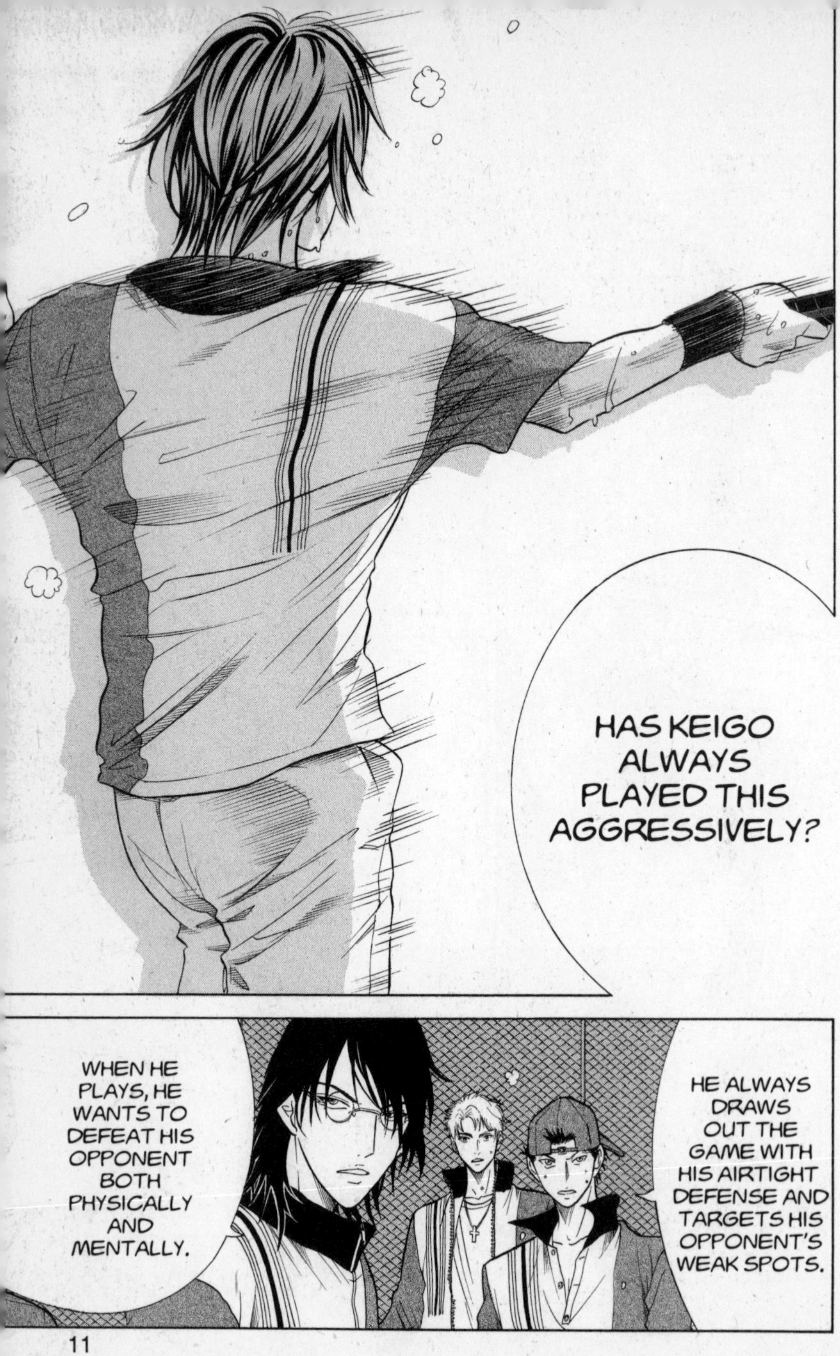
HAS KEIGO ALWAYS PLAYED THIS AGGRESSIVELY?
HE ALWAYS DRAWS OUT THE GAME WITH HIS AIRTIGHT DEFENSE AND TARGETS HIS OPPONENT'S WEAK SPOTS.
WHEN HE PLAYS, HE WANTS TO DEFEAT HIS OPPONENT BOTH PHYSICALLY AND MENTALLY.

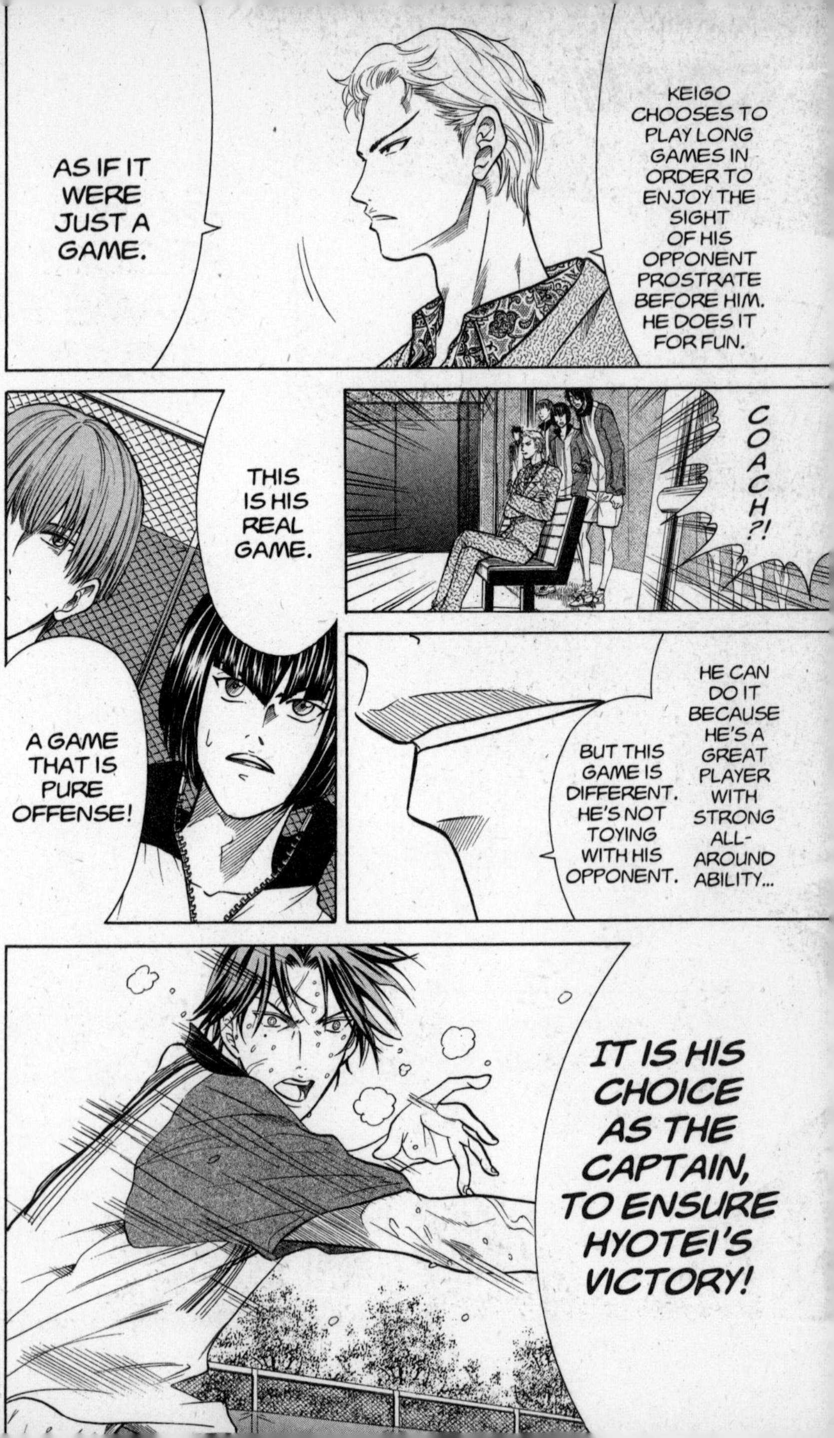
KEIGO CHOOSES TO PLAY LONG GAMES IN ORDER TO ENJOY THE SIGHT OF HIS OPPONENT PROSTRATE BEFORE HIM. HE DOES IT FOR FUN.
AS IF IT WERE JUST A GAME.
COACH?!
HE CAN DO IT BECAUSE HE'S A GREAT PLAYER WITH STRONG ALL-AROUND ABILITY...
BUT THIS GAME IS DIFFERENT. HE'S NOT TOYING WITH HIS OPPONENT.
THIS IS HIS REAL GAME.
A GAME THAT IS PURE OFFENSE!
IT IS HIS CHOICE AS THE CAPTAIN, TO ENSURE HYOTEI'S VICTORY!

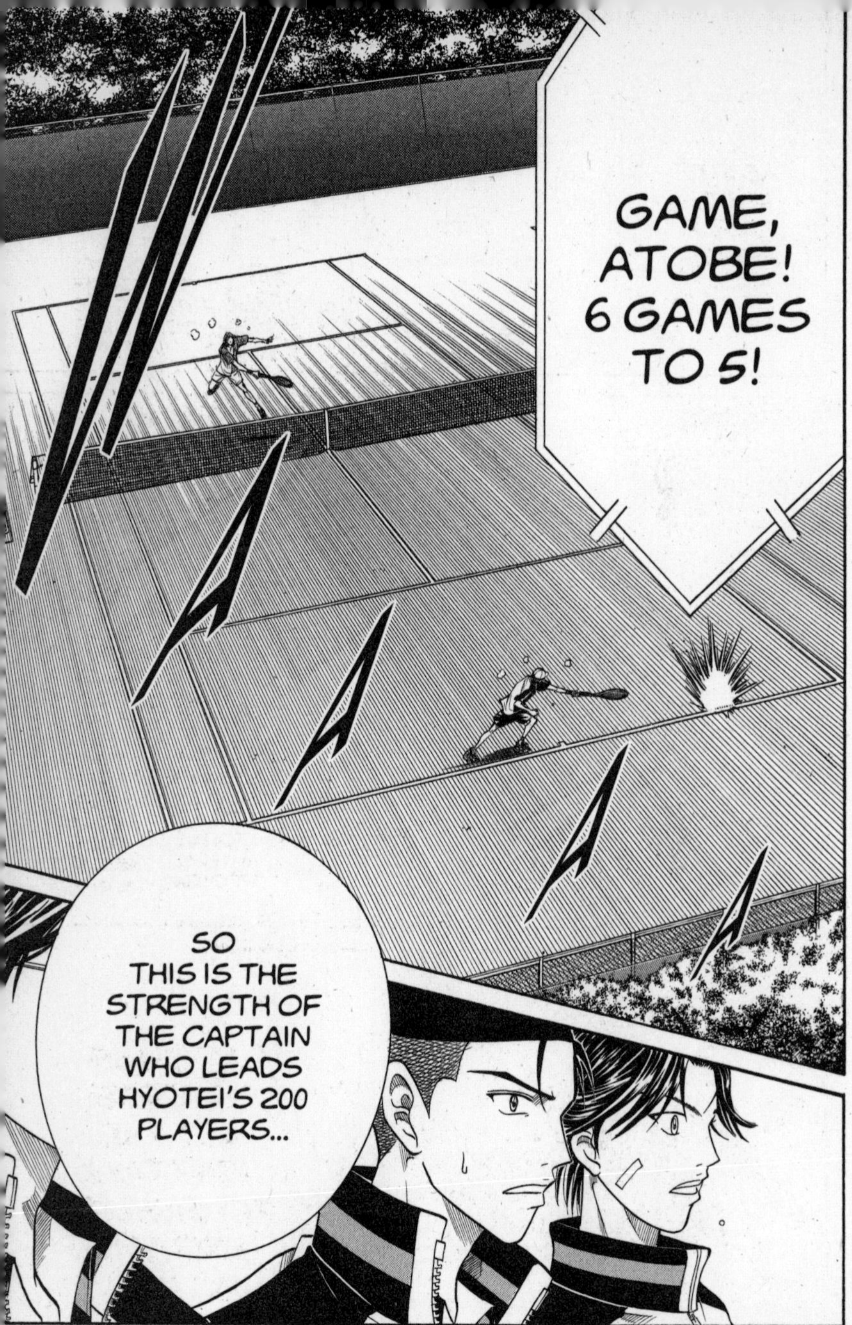
GAME, ATOBE! 6 GAMES TO 5!
SO THIS IS THE STRENGTH OF THE CAPTAIN WHO LEADS HYOTEI'S 200 PLAYERS...

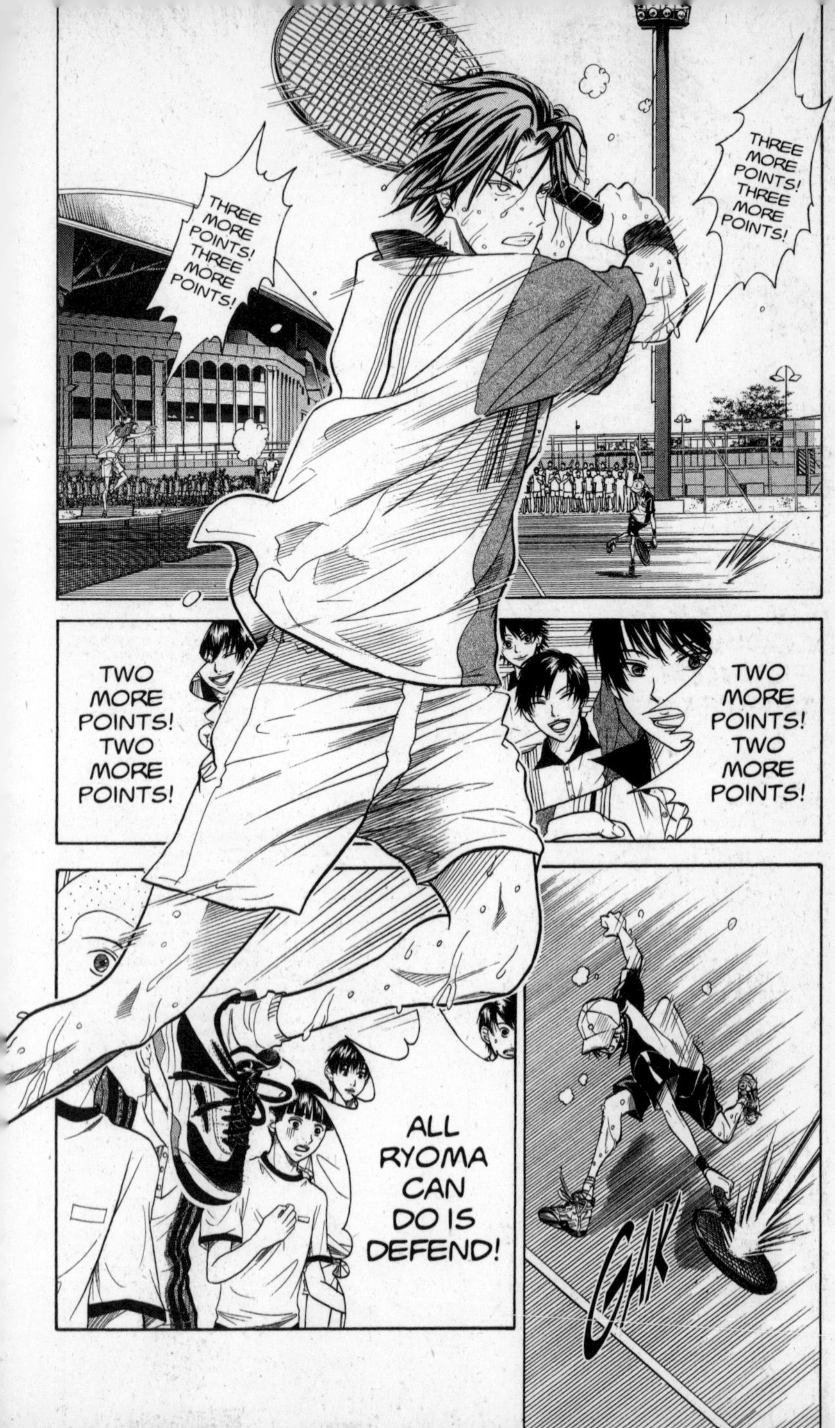
THREE MORE POINTS! THREE MORE POINTS!
THREE MORE POINTS! THREE MORE POINTS!
TWO MORE POINTS! TWO MORE POINTS!
TWO MORE POINTS! TWO MORE POINTS!
GAK
ALL RYOMA CAN DO IS DEFEND!

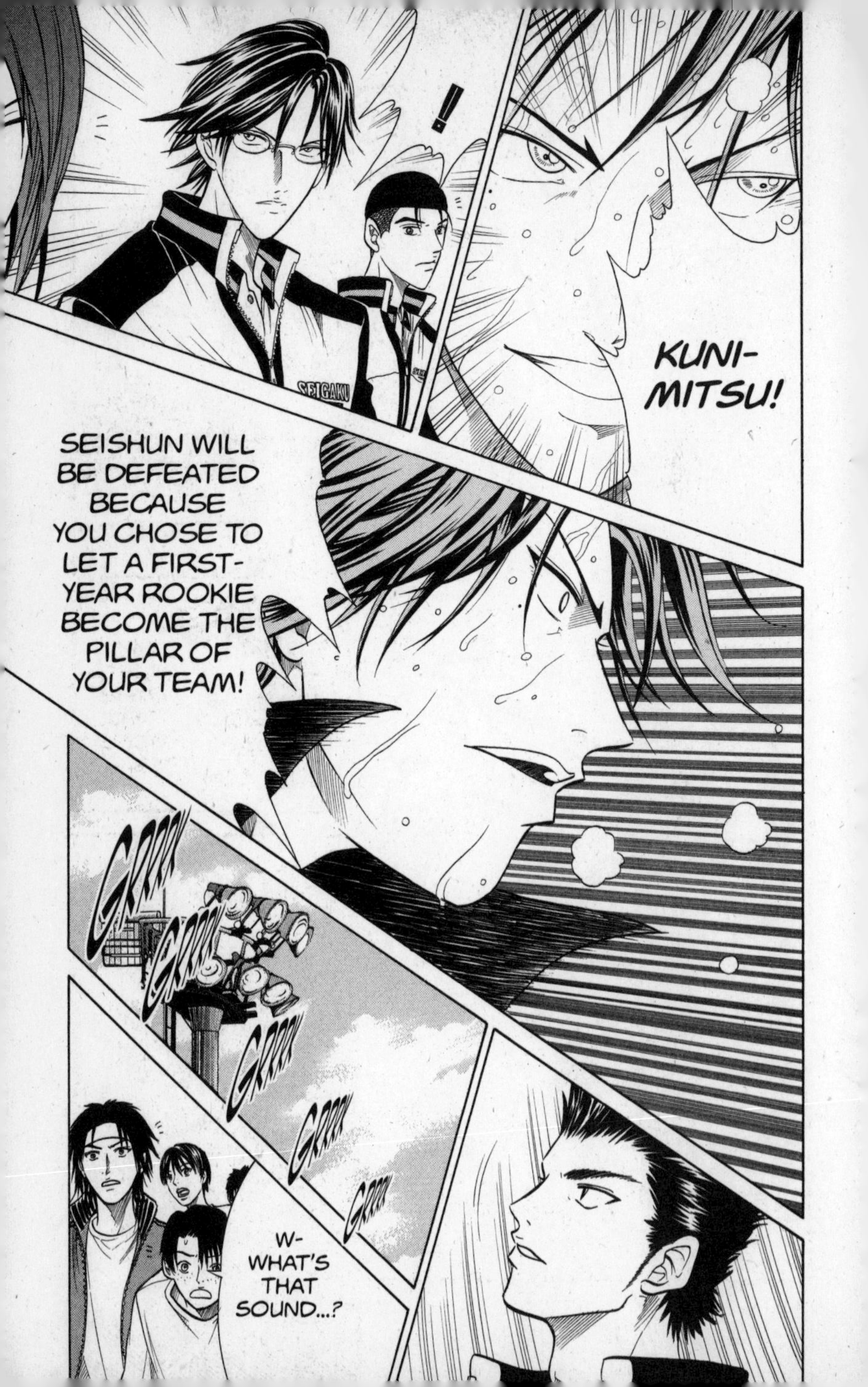
KUNI-
MITSU!
!
SEISHUN WILL BE DEFEATED BECAUSE YOU CHOSE TO LET A FIRST-YEAR ROOKIE BECOME THE PILLAR OF YOUR TEAM!
SEIGAKU
GRRR GRRR GRRR GRRR GRRR
W-WHAT'S THAT SOUND...?

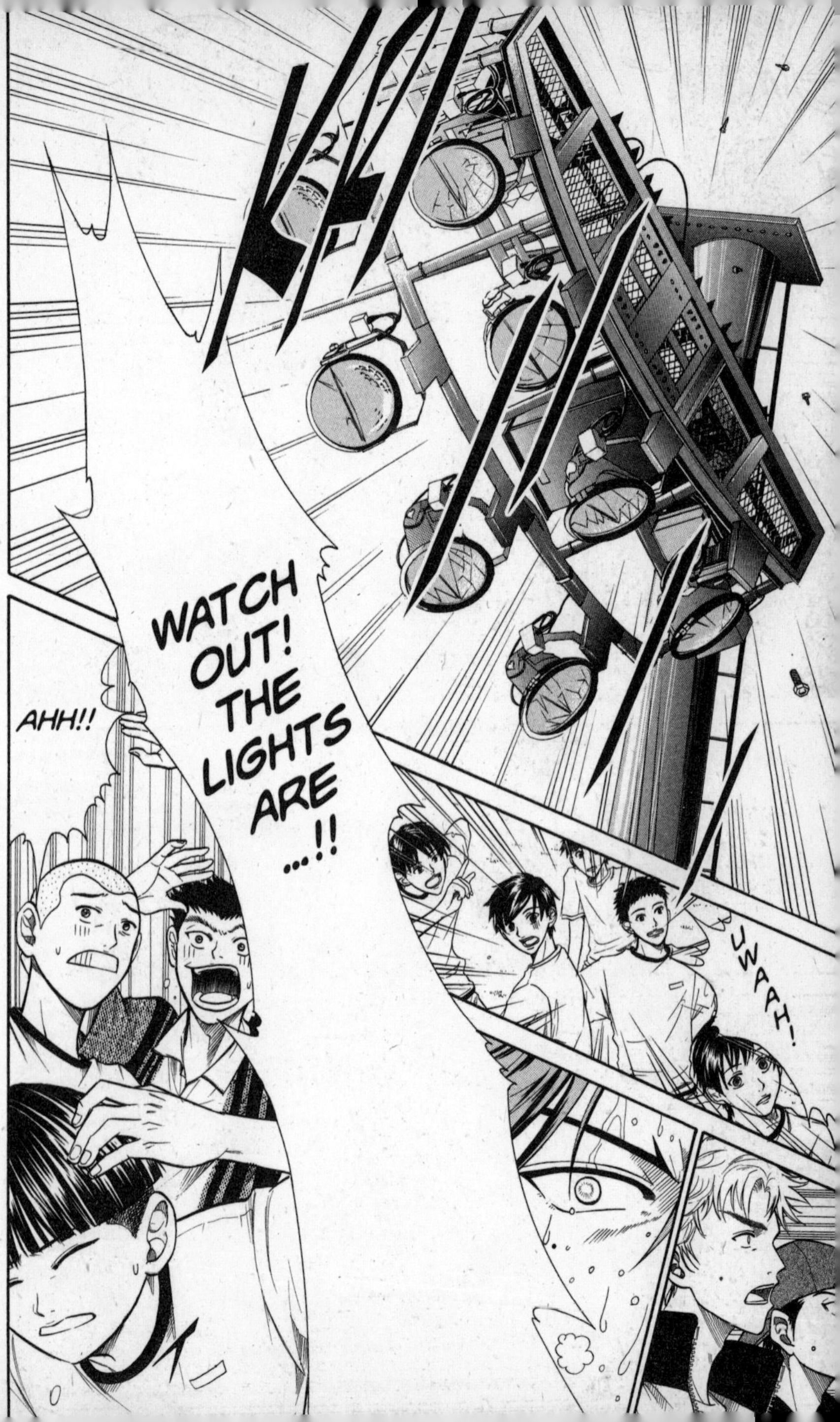
WATCH OUT! THE LIGHTS ARE ...!!
AHH!!
UWAAH!

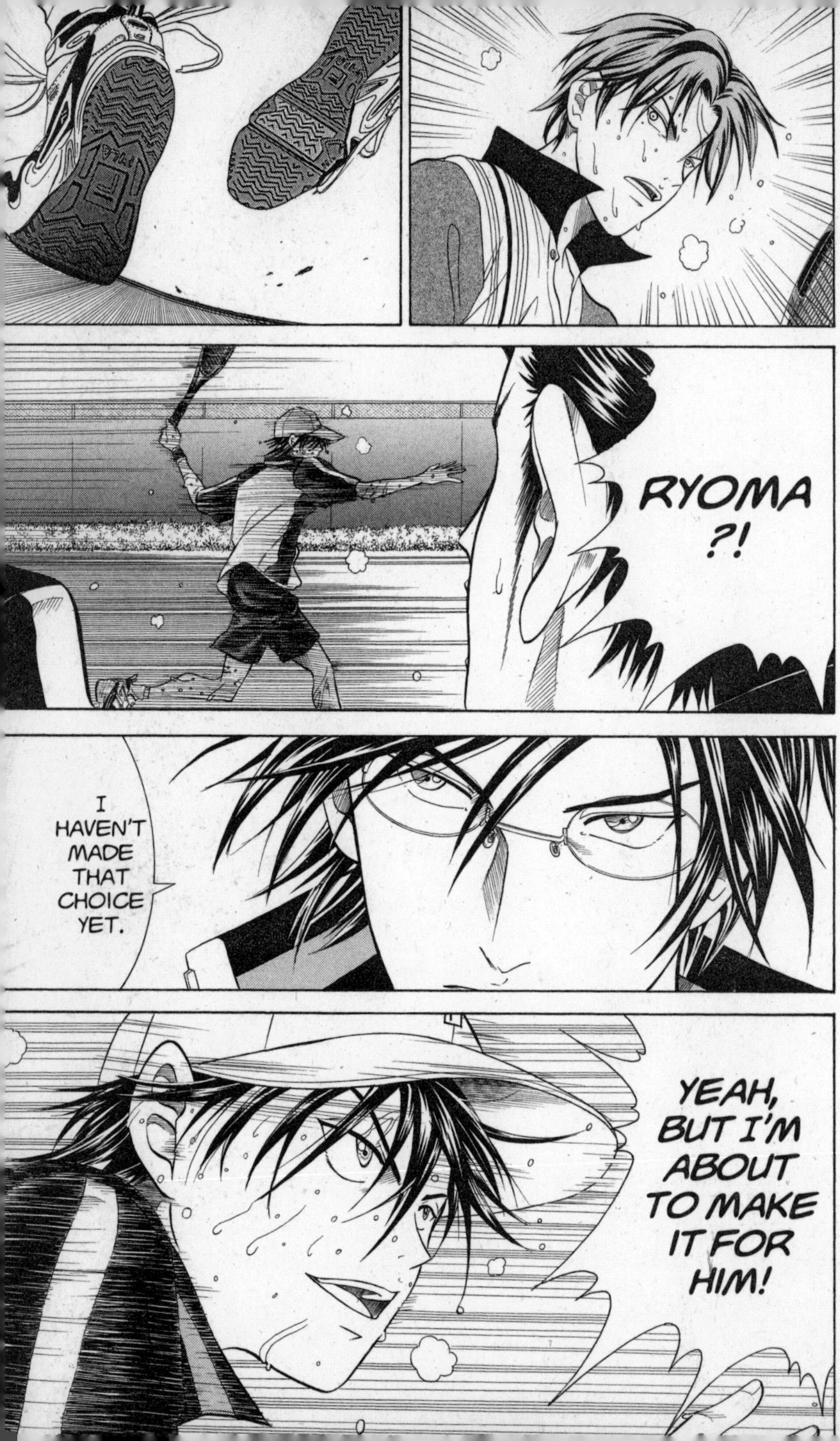
RYOMA ?!
I HAVEN'T MADE THAT CHOICE YET.
YEAH, BUT I'M ABOUT TO MAKE IT FOR HIM!

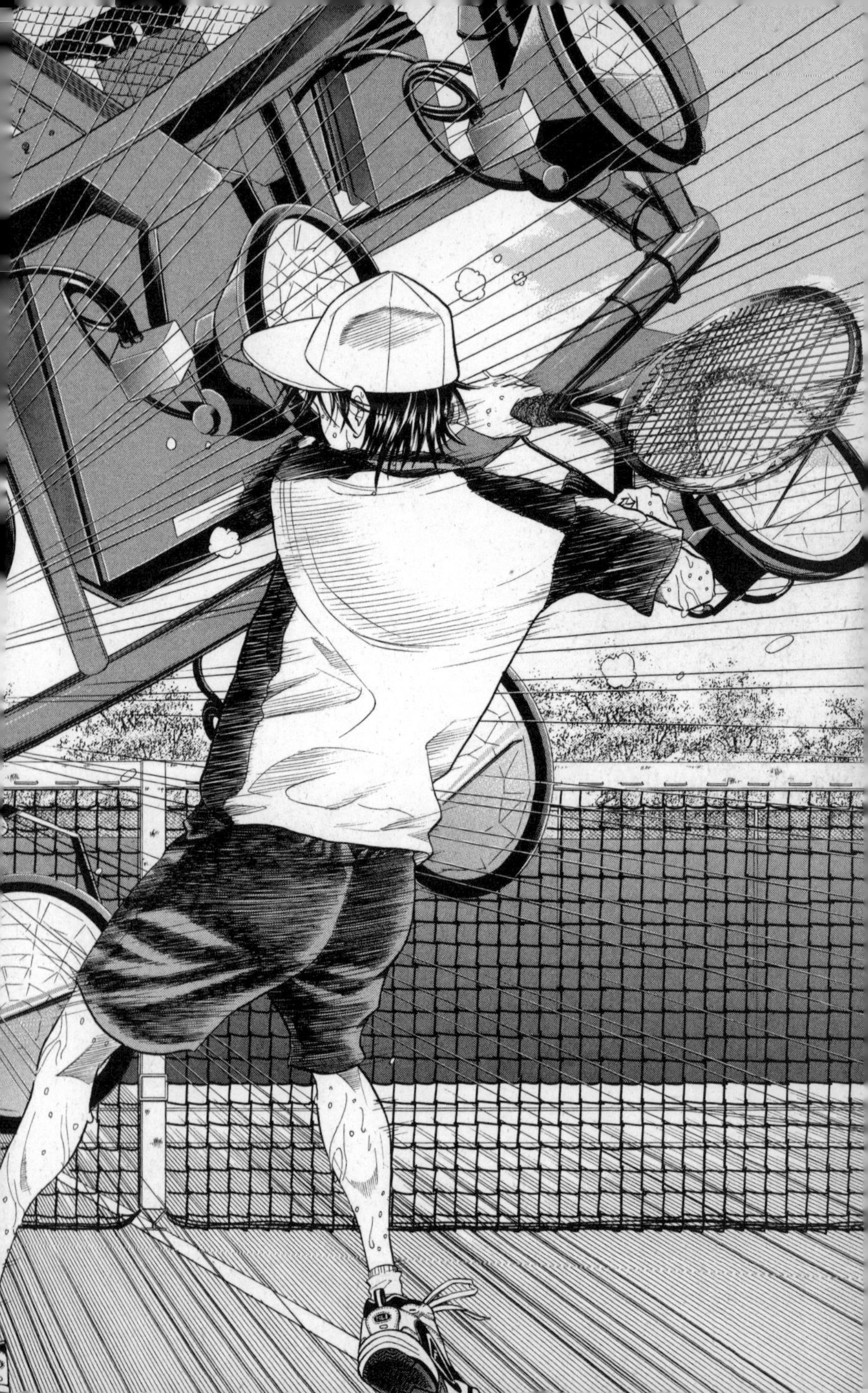

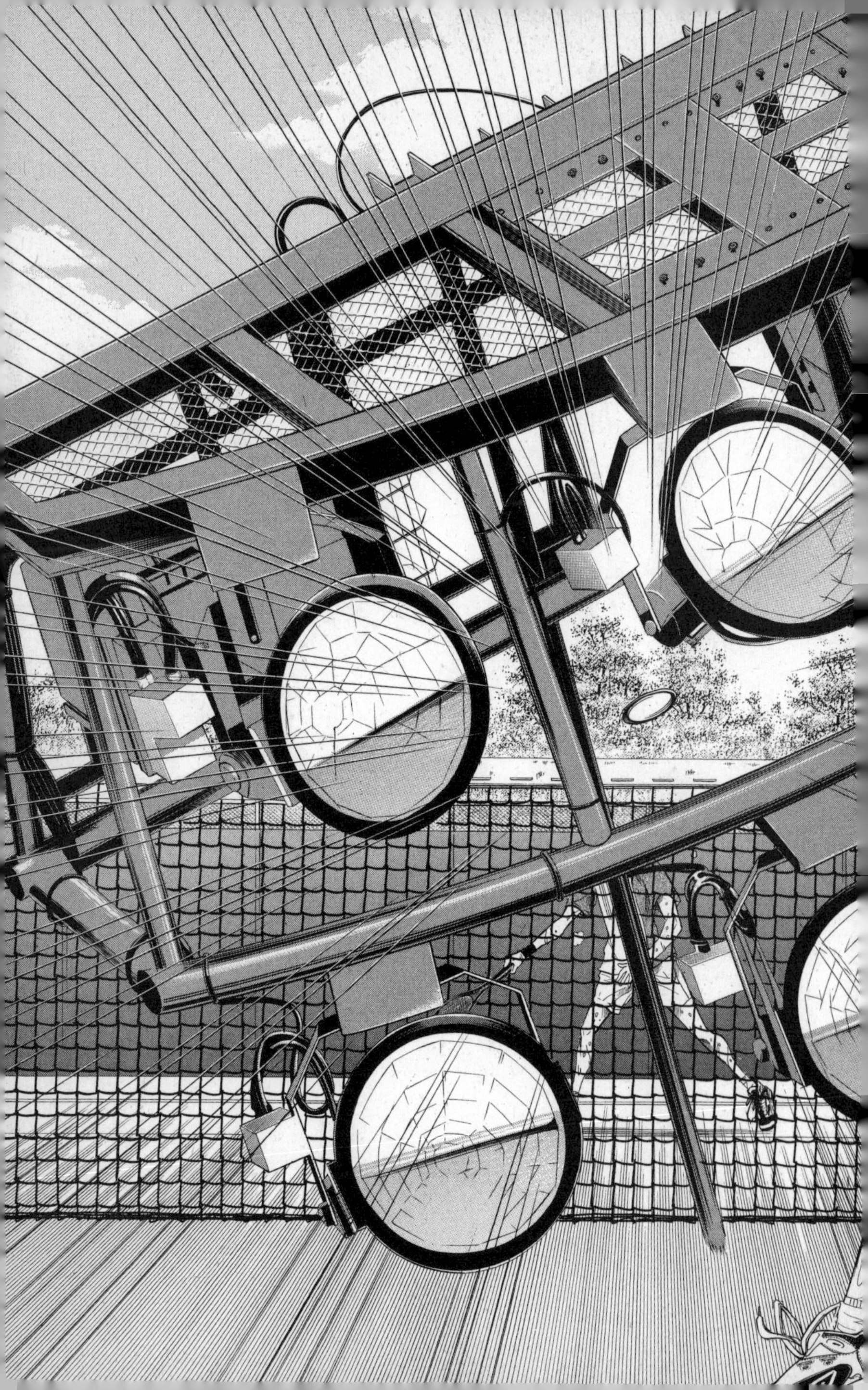

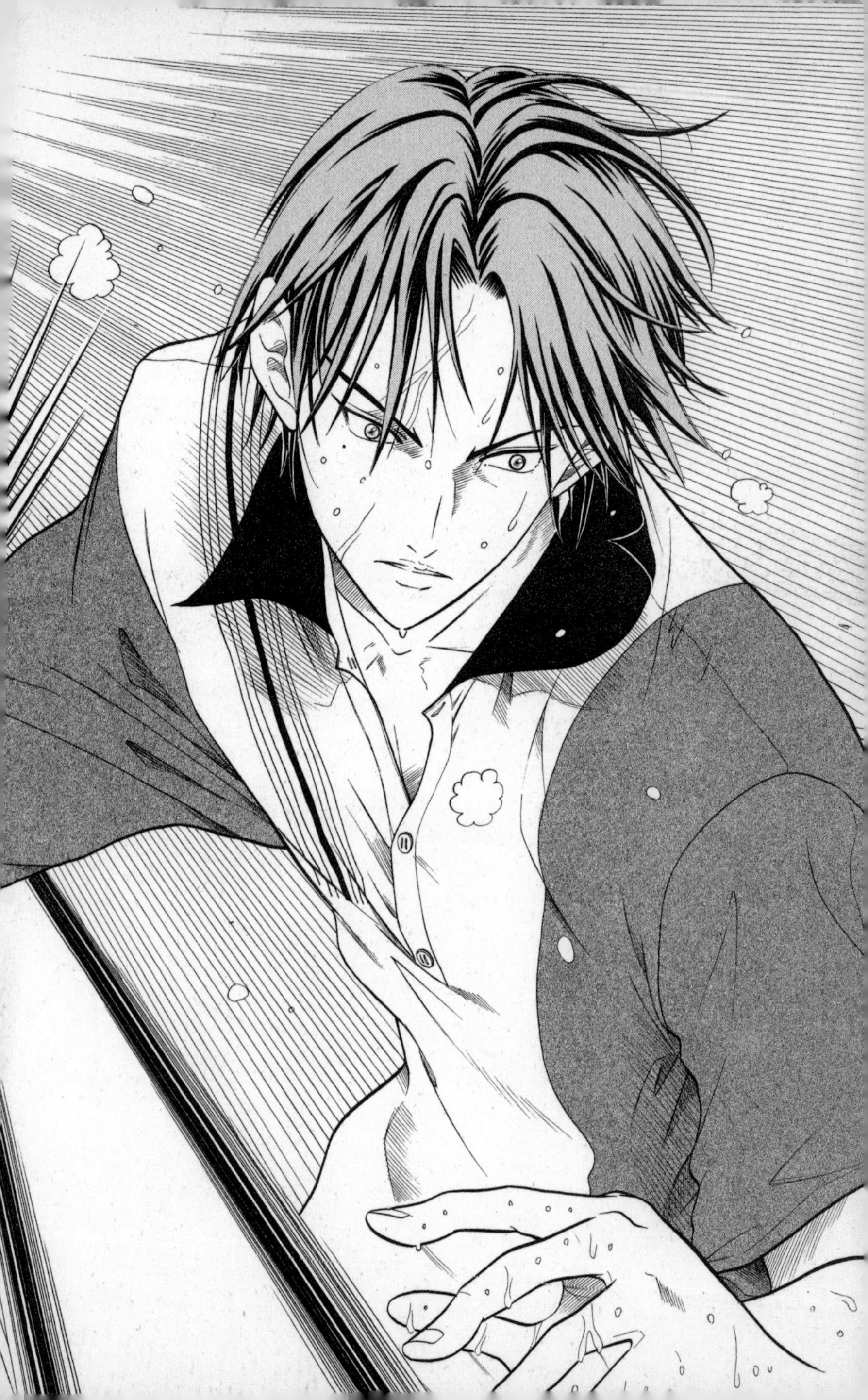

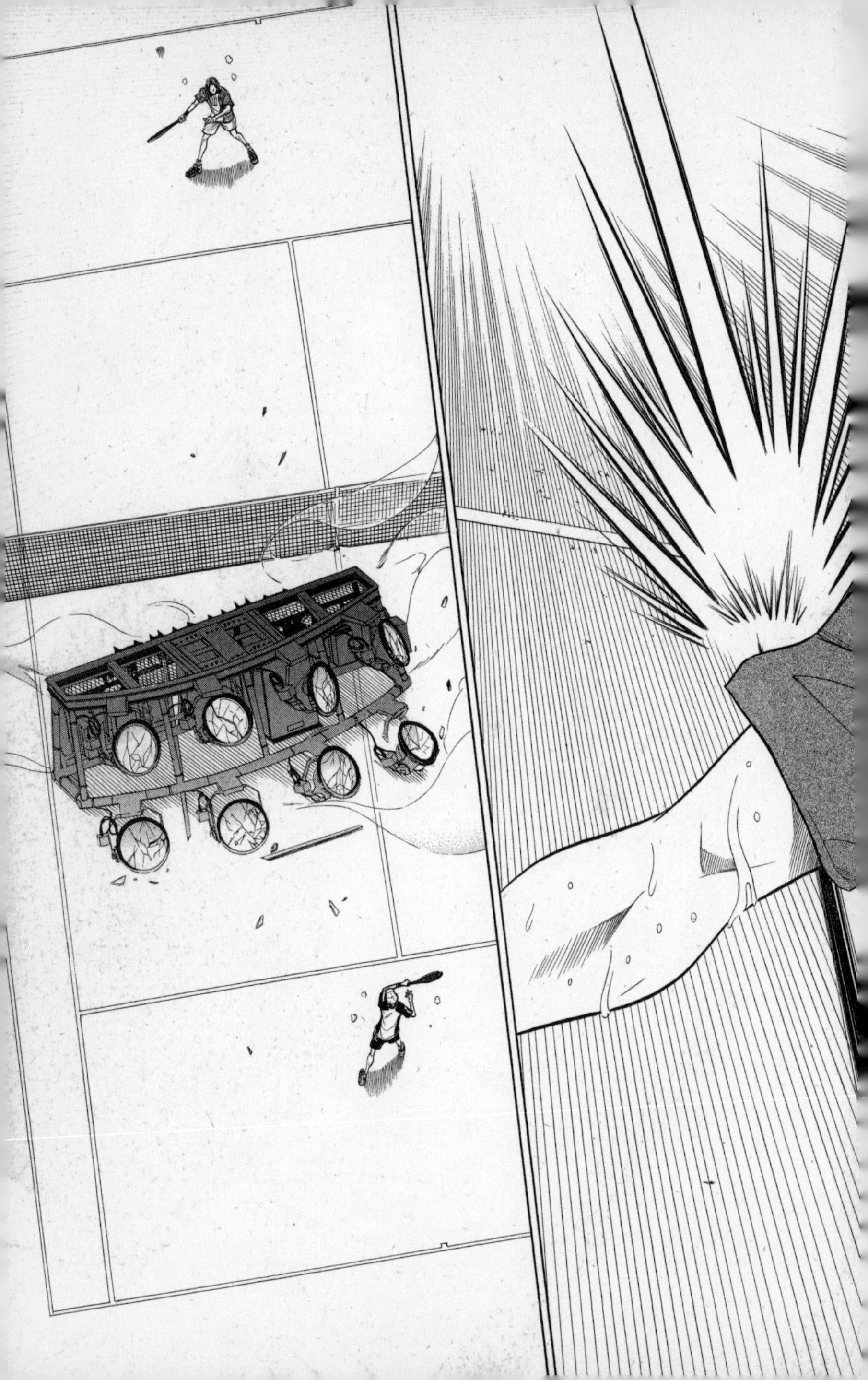

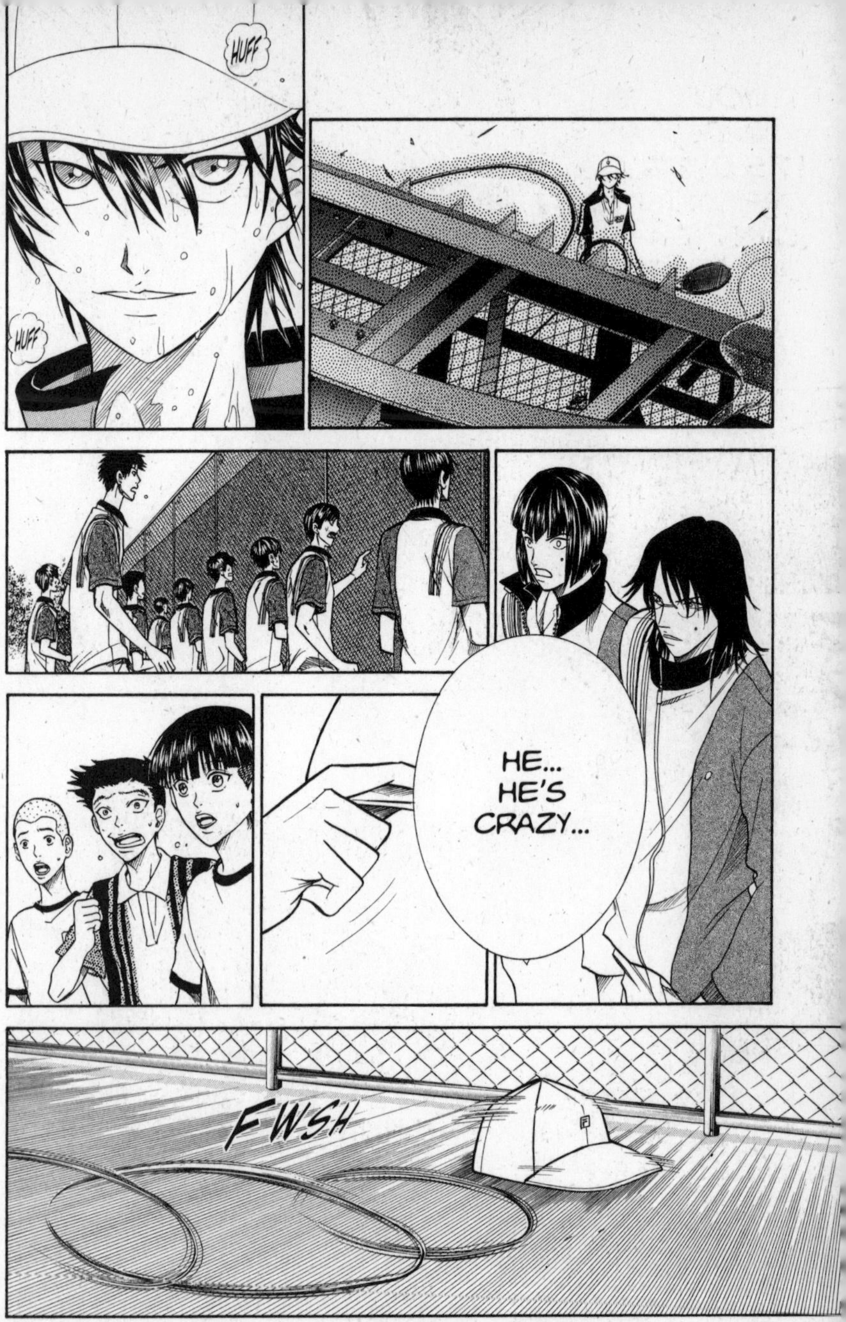
HUFF
HUFF
HE... HE'S CRAZY...
FWSH

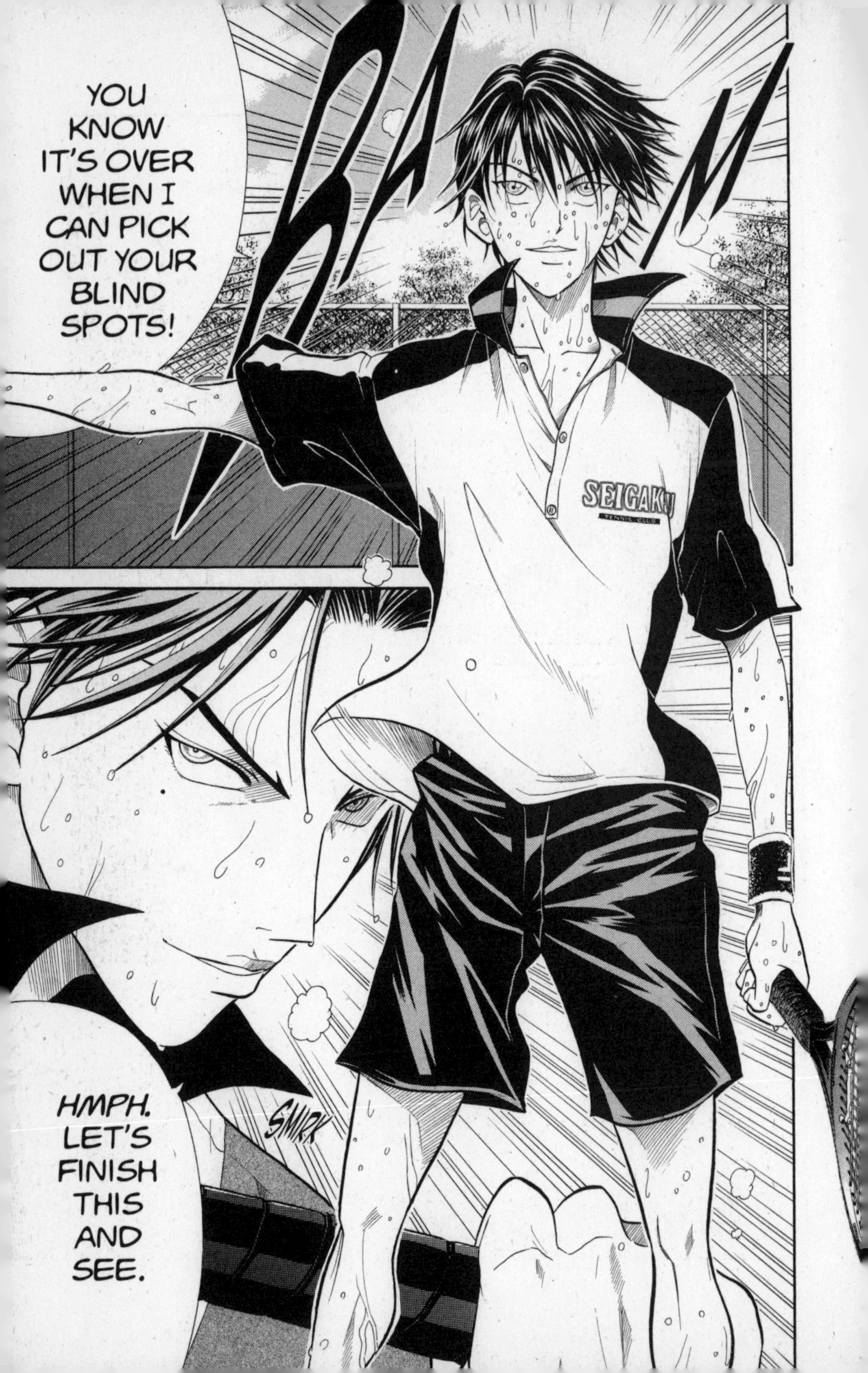
BAM
YOU KNOW IT'S OVER WHEN I CAN PICK OUT YOUR BLIND SPOTS!
SMIRK
HMPH. LET'S FINISH THIS AND SEE.

テニスの王子様

THE PRINCE OF TENNIS

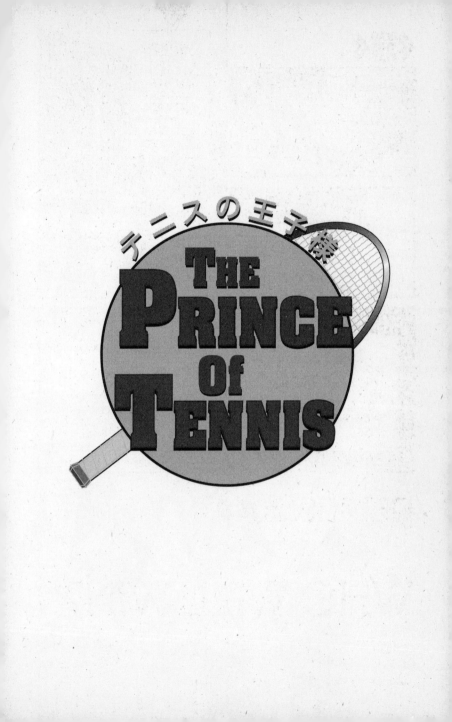

READ THIS WAY

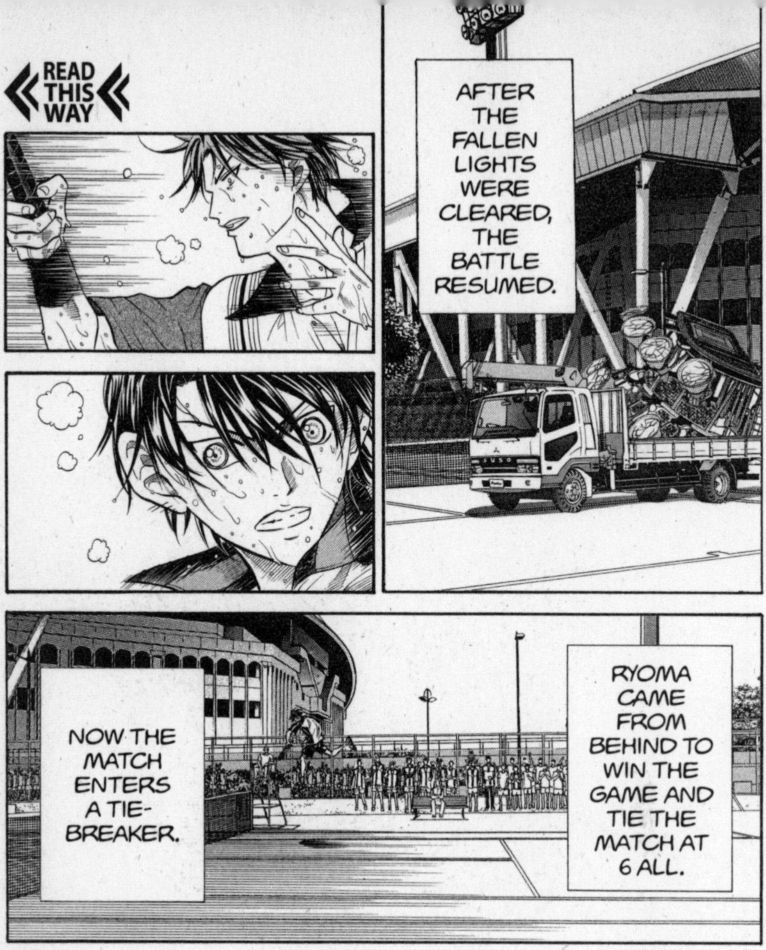
AFTER THE FALLEN LIGHTS WERE CLEARED, THE BATTLE RESUMED.
RYOMA CAME FROM BEHIND TO WIN THE GAME AND TIE THE MATCH AT 6 ALL.
NOW THE MATCH ENTERS A TIE-BREAKER.

GENIUS 304:

WHO WILL WIN?!

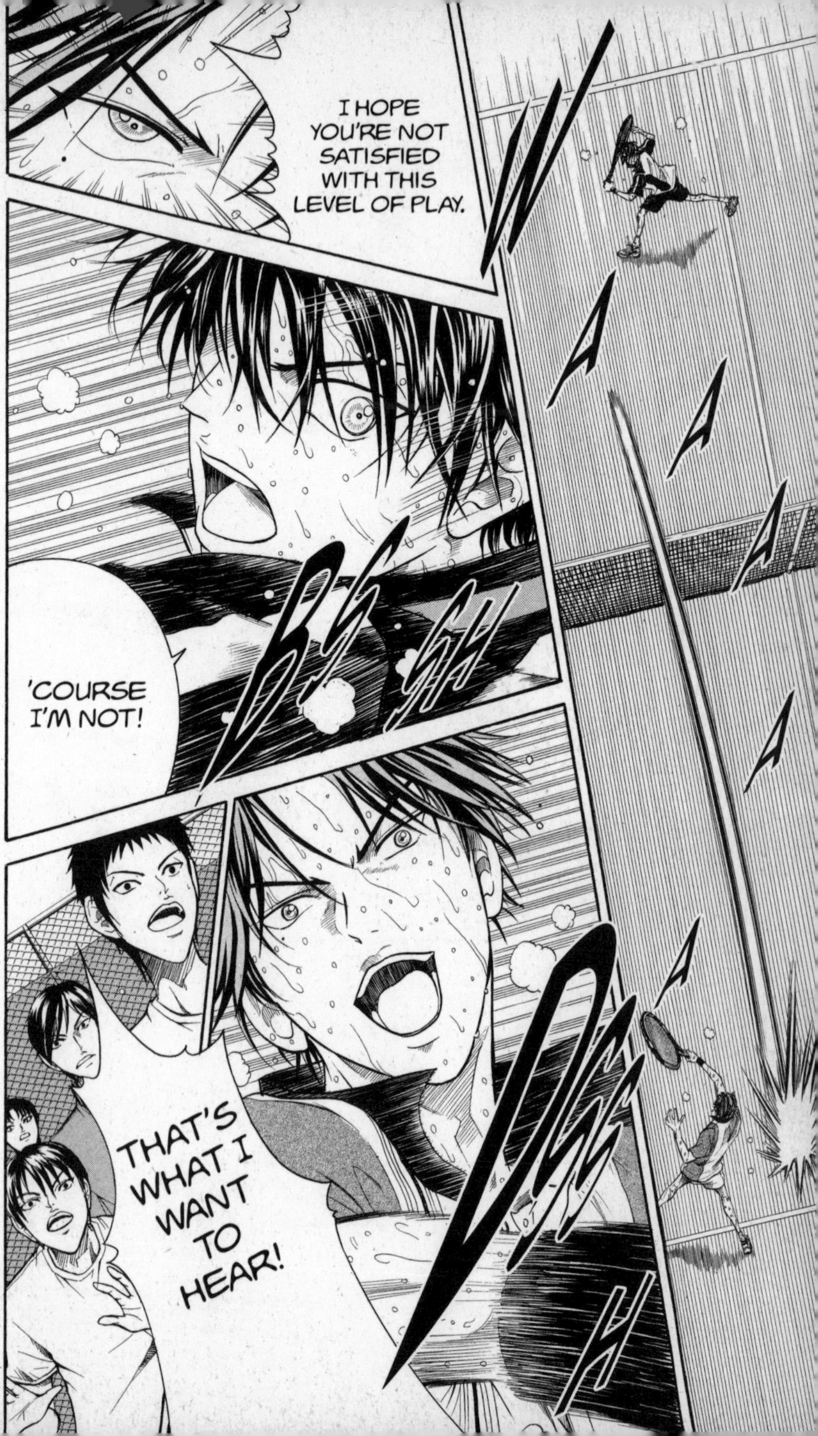
I HOPE YOU'RE NOT SATISFIED WITH THIS LEVEL OF PLAY.
'COURSE I'M NOT!
THAT'S WHAT I WANT TO HEAR!

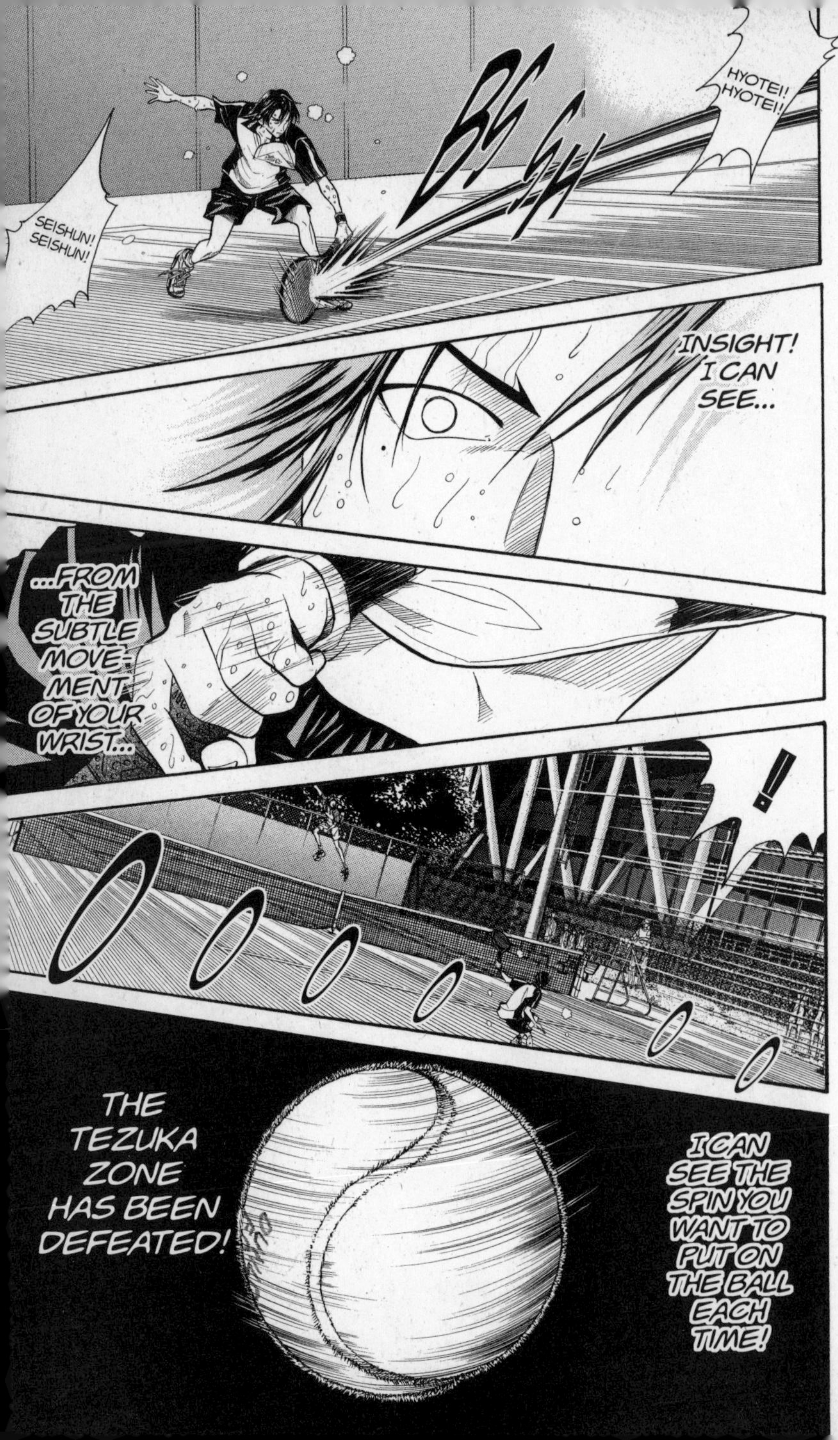
HYOTE!! HYOTE!!
BASH
SEISHUN! SEISHUN!
INSIGHT! I CAN SEE...
...FROM THE SUBTLE MOVEMENT OF YOUR WRIST...
!
I CAN SEE THE SPIN YOU WANT TO PUT ON THE BALL EACH TIME!
THE TEZUKA ZONE HAS BEEN DEFEATED!

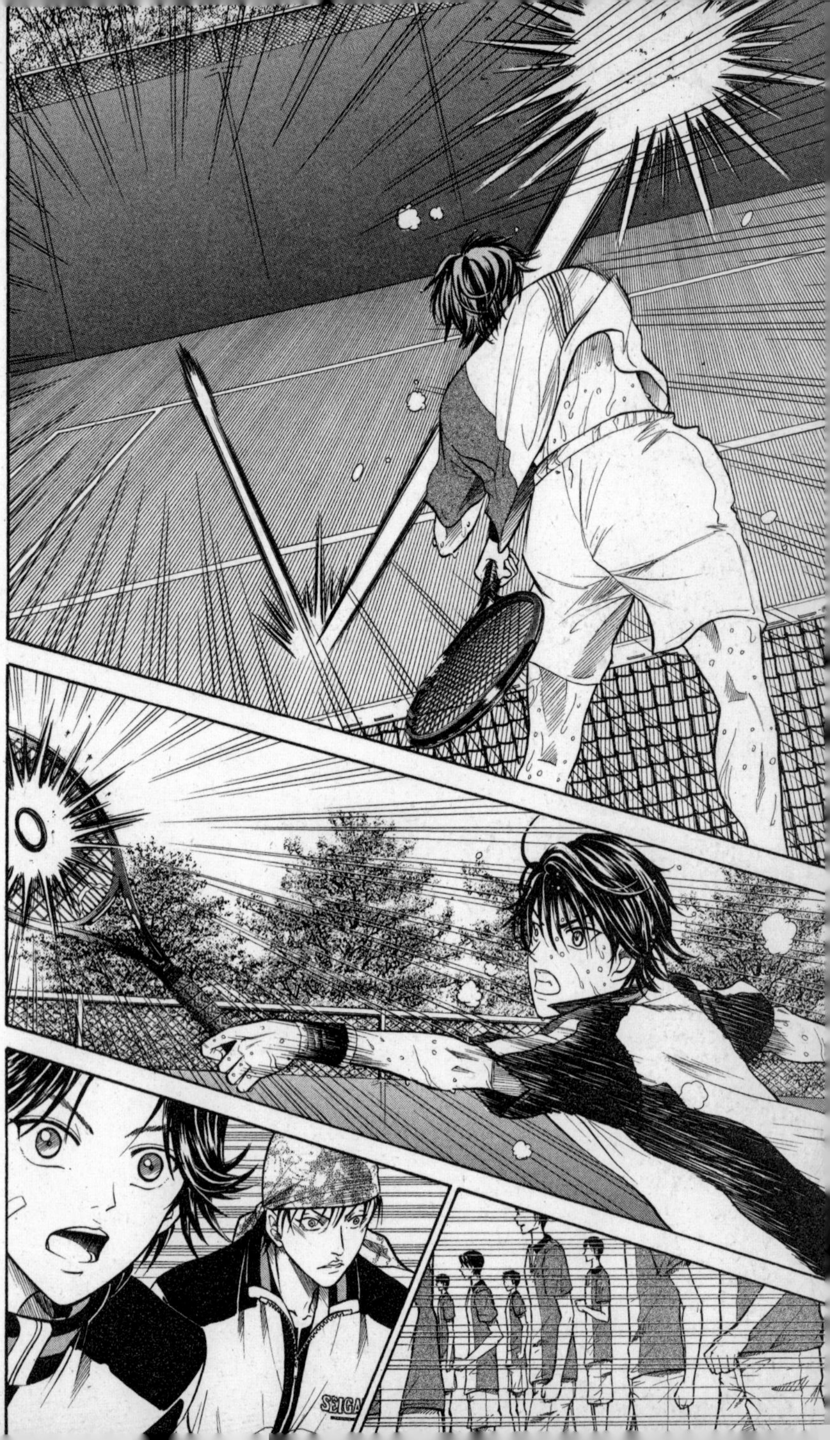
SEIGA

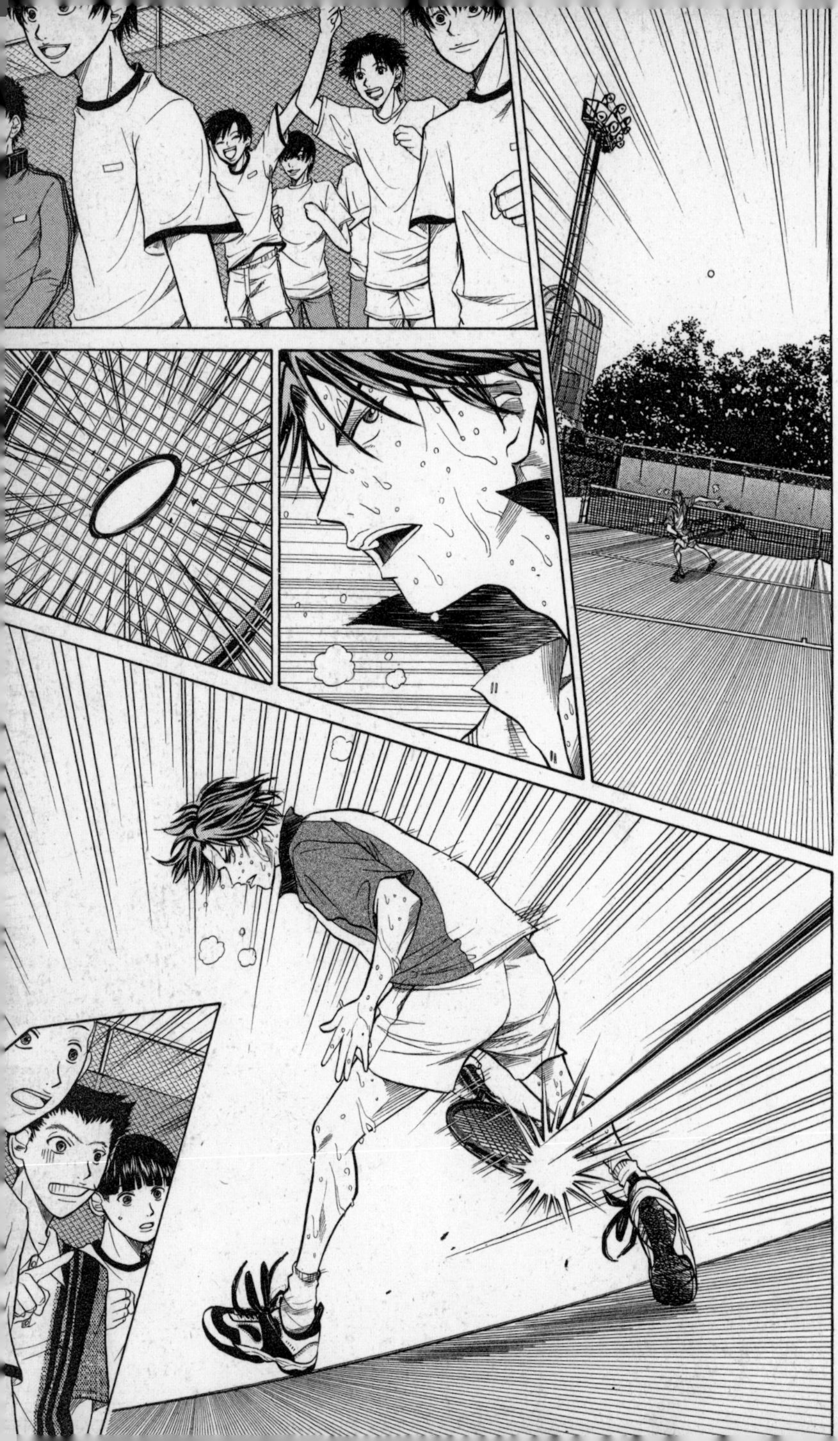

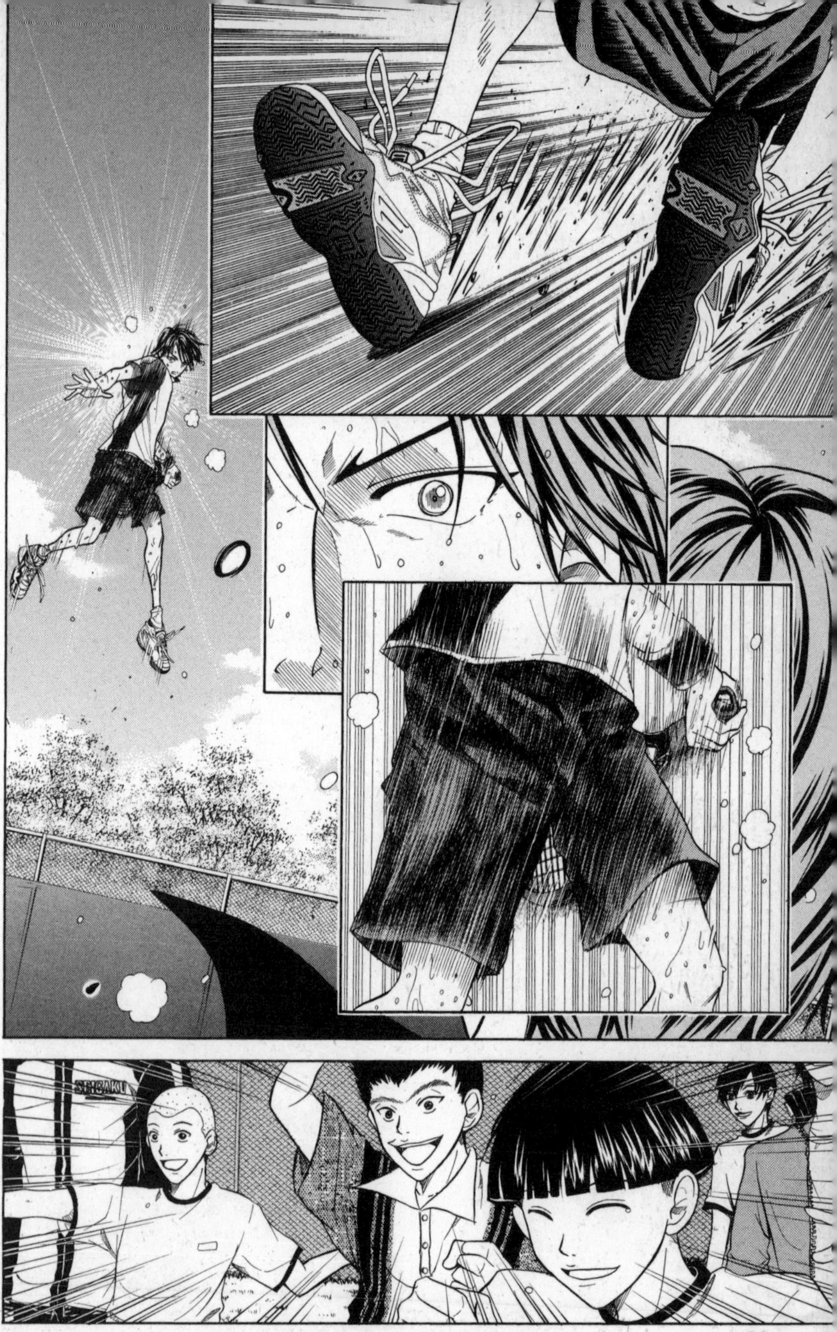

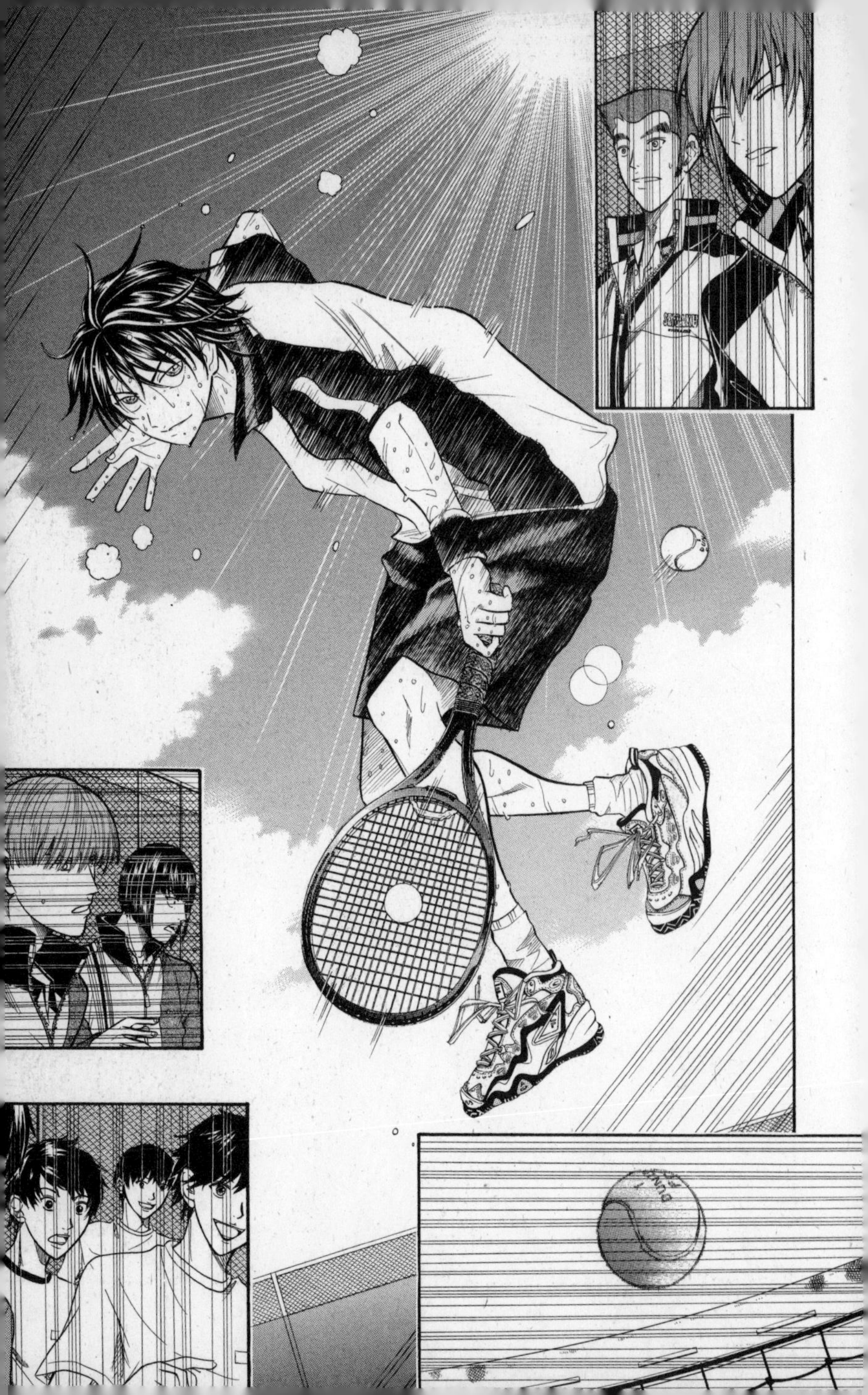

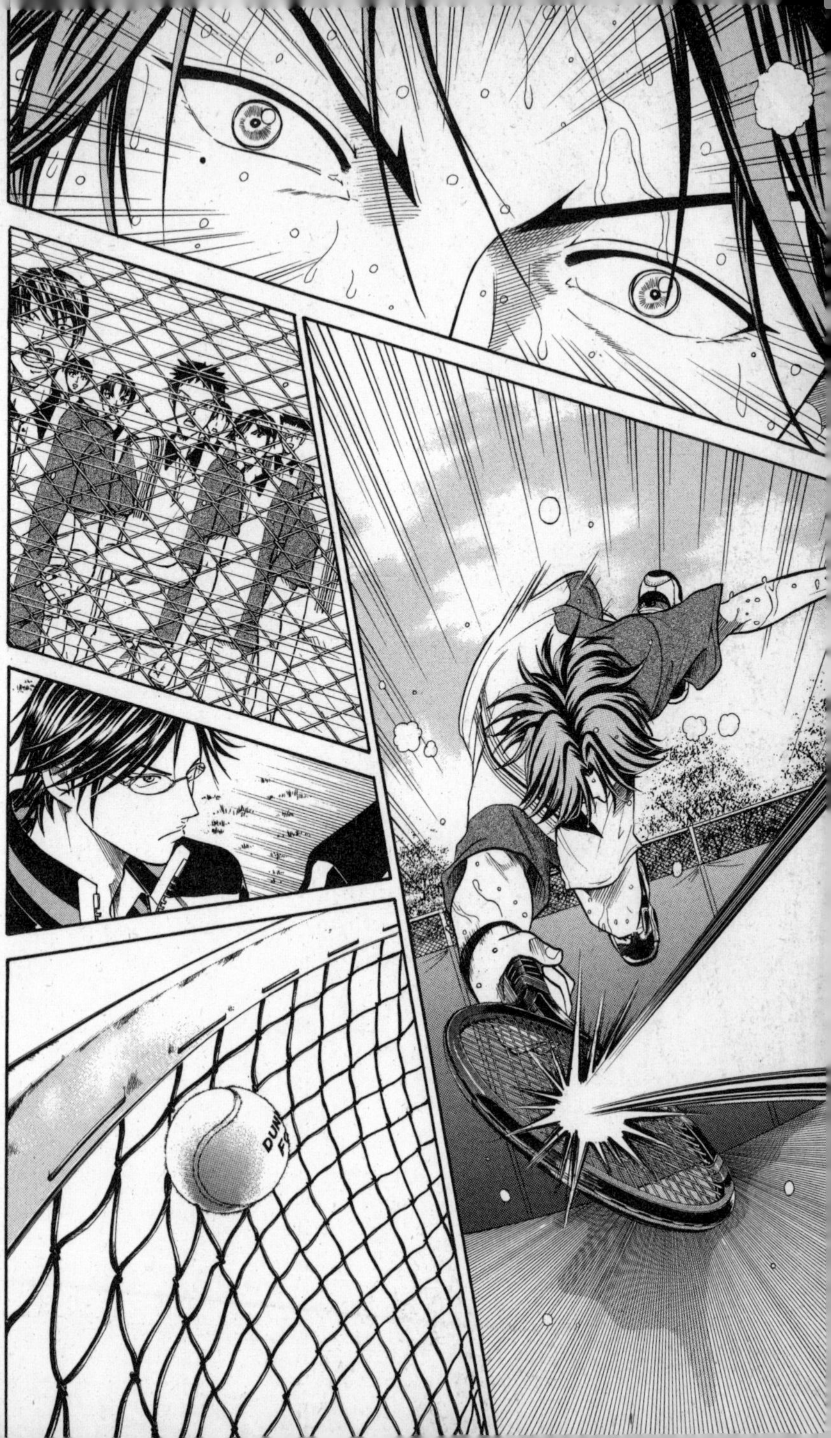

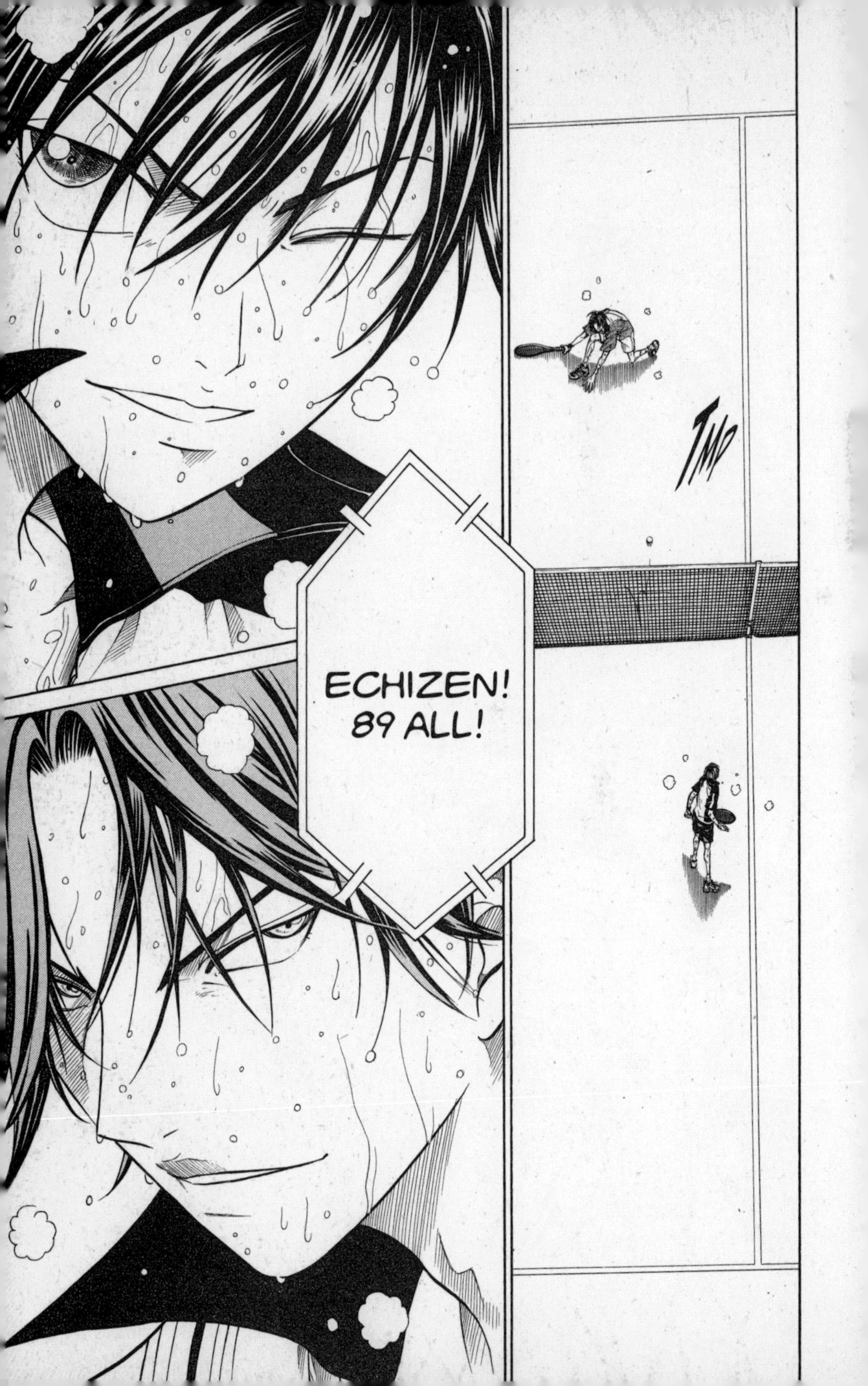
ECHIZEN! 89 ALL!
TMP

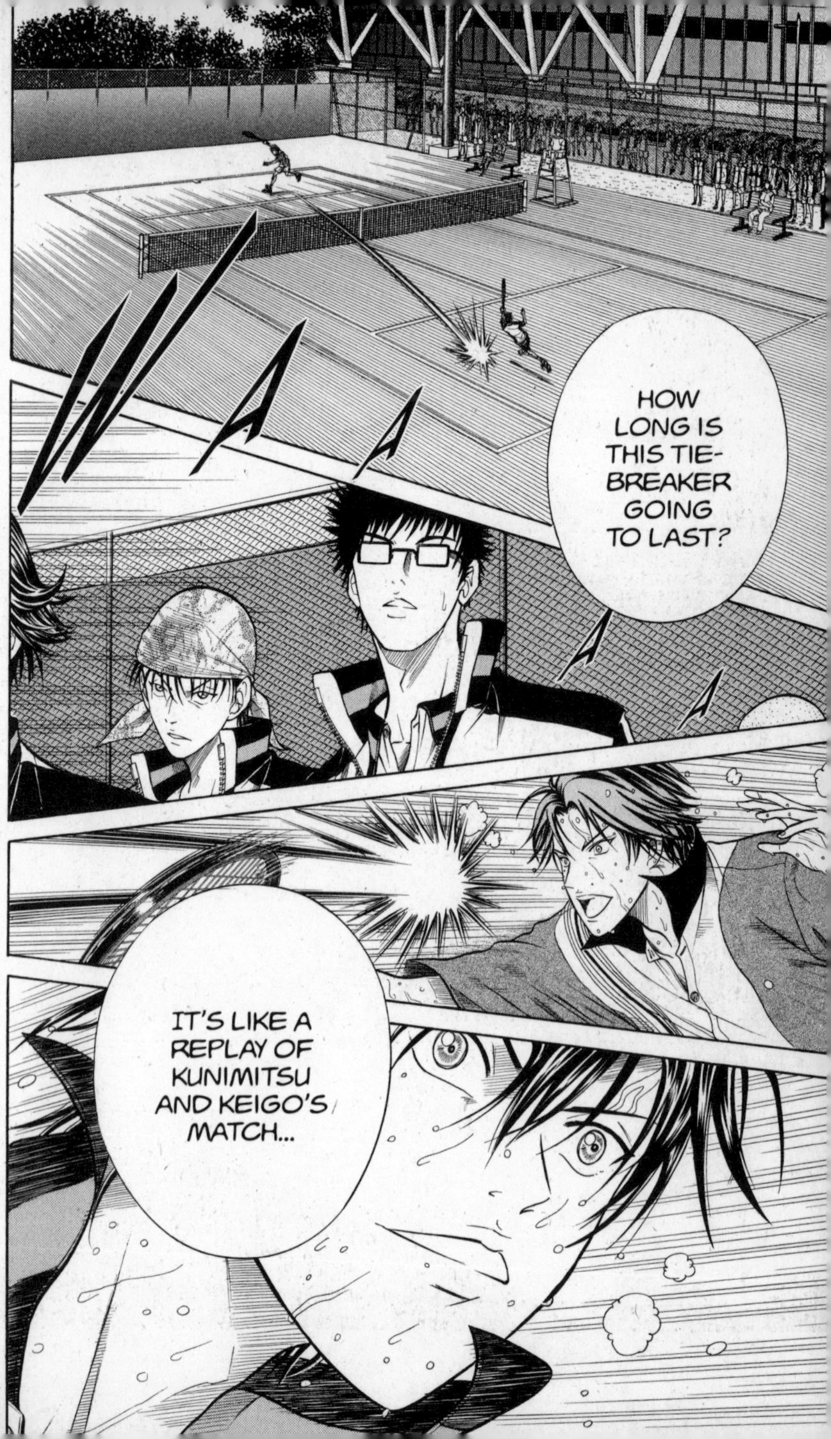
HOW LONG IS THIS TIE-BREAKER GOING TO LAST?
IT'S LIKE A REPLAY OF KUNIMITSU AND KEIGO'S MATCH...

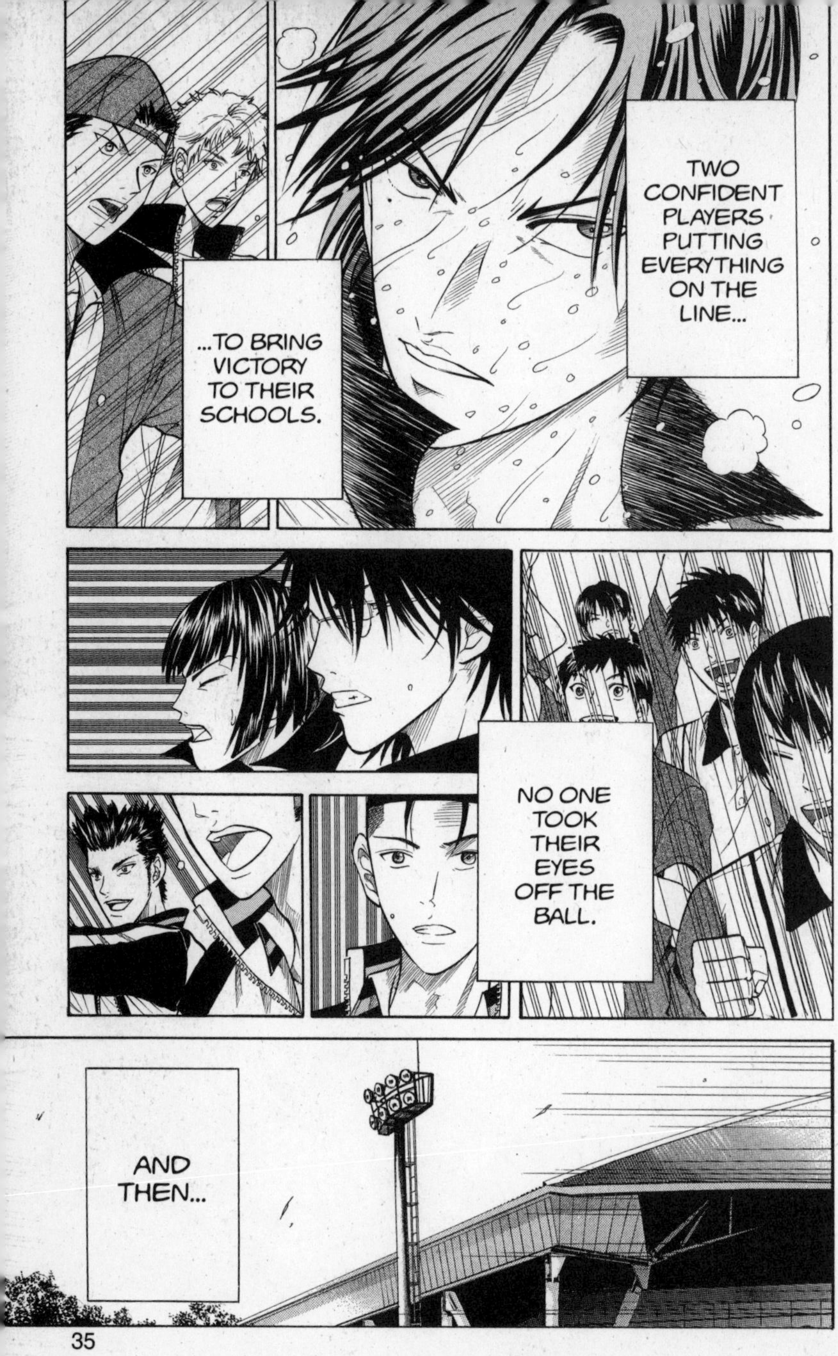
TWO CONFIDENT PLAYERS PUTTING EVERYTHING ON THE LINE...
...TO BRING VICTORY TO THEIR SCHOOLS.
NO ONE TOOK THEIR EYES OFF THE BALL.
AND THEN...

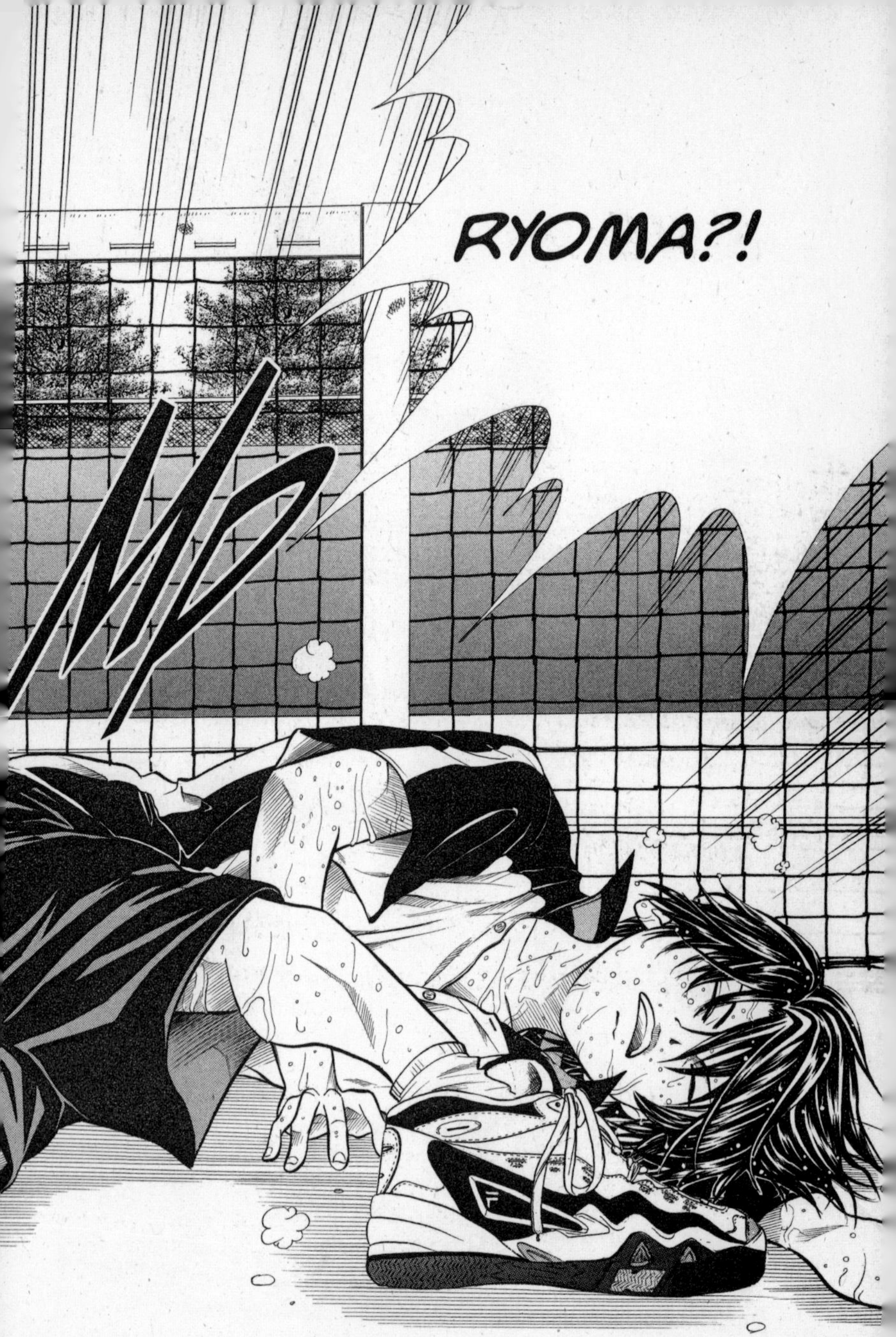
RYOMA?!
NO

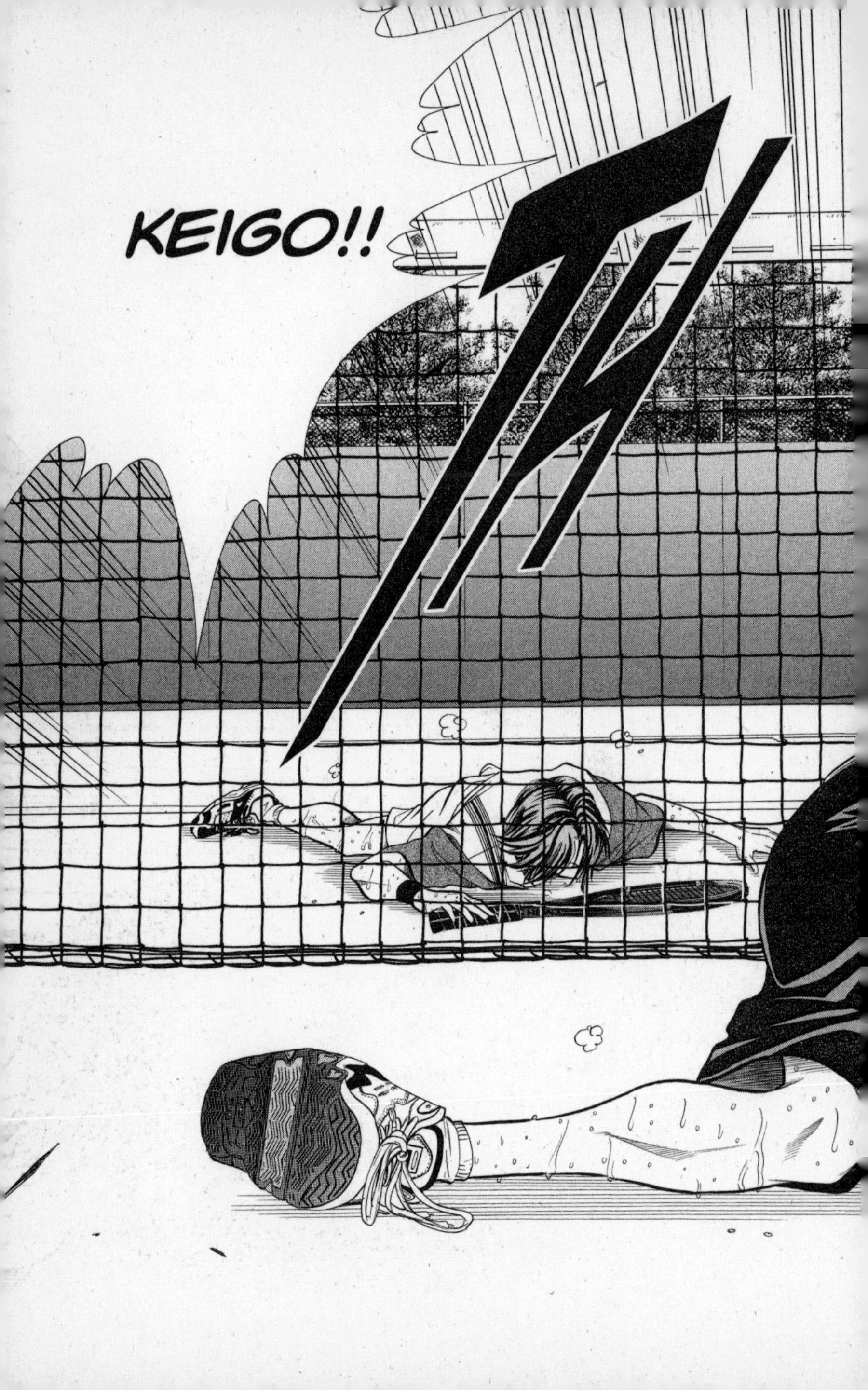
KEIGO!!

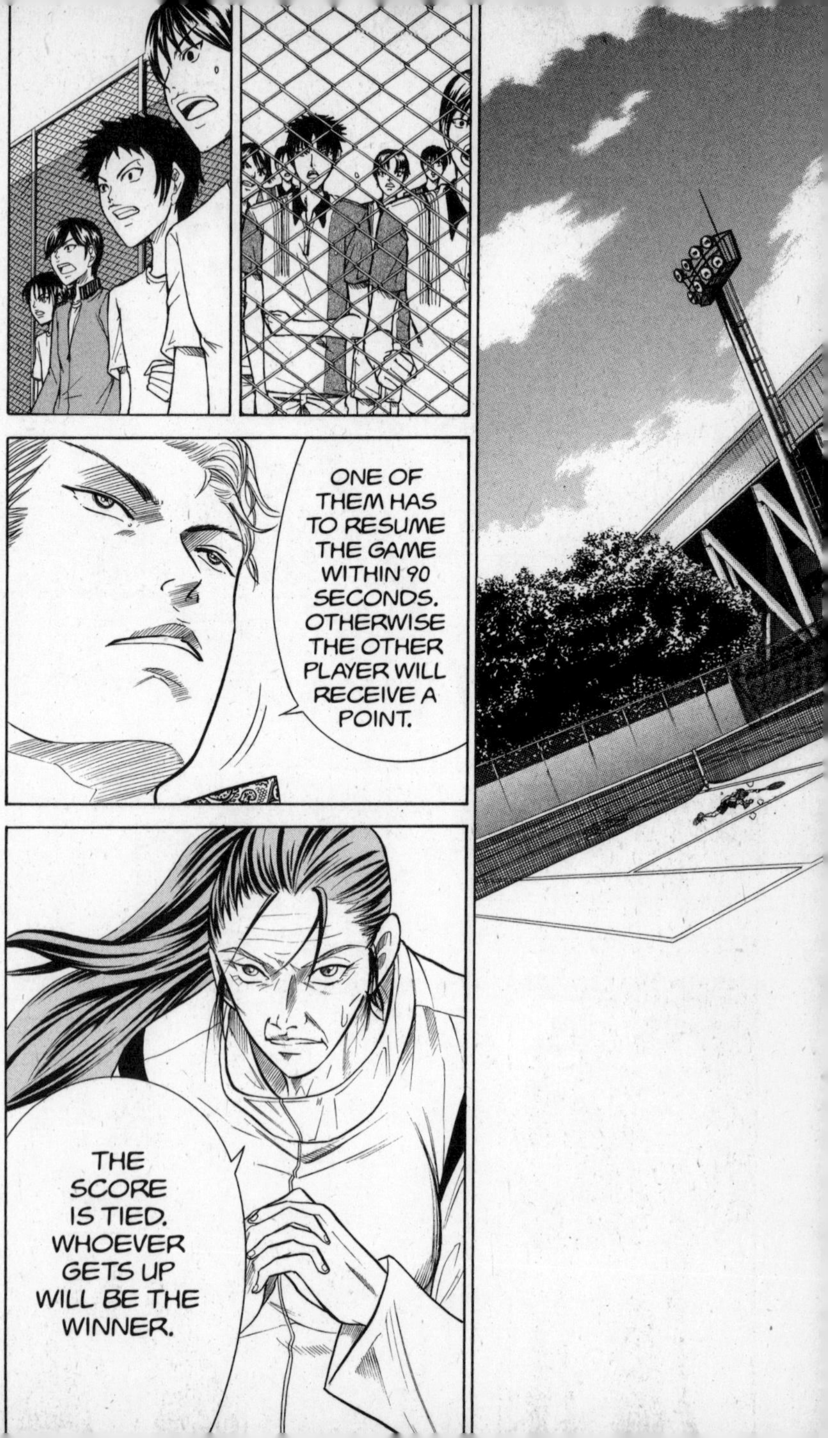
ONE OF THEM HAS TO RESUME THE GAME WITHIN 90 SECONDS. OTHERWISE THE OTHER PLAYER WILL RECEIVE A POINT.
THE SCORE IS TIED. WHOEVER GETS UP WILL BE THE WINNER.

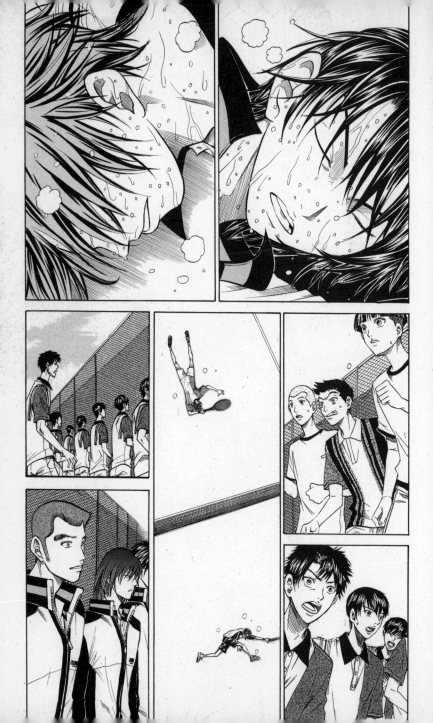

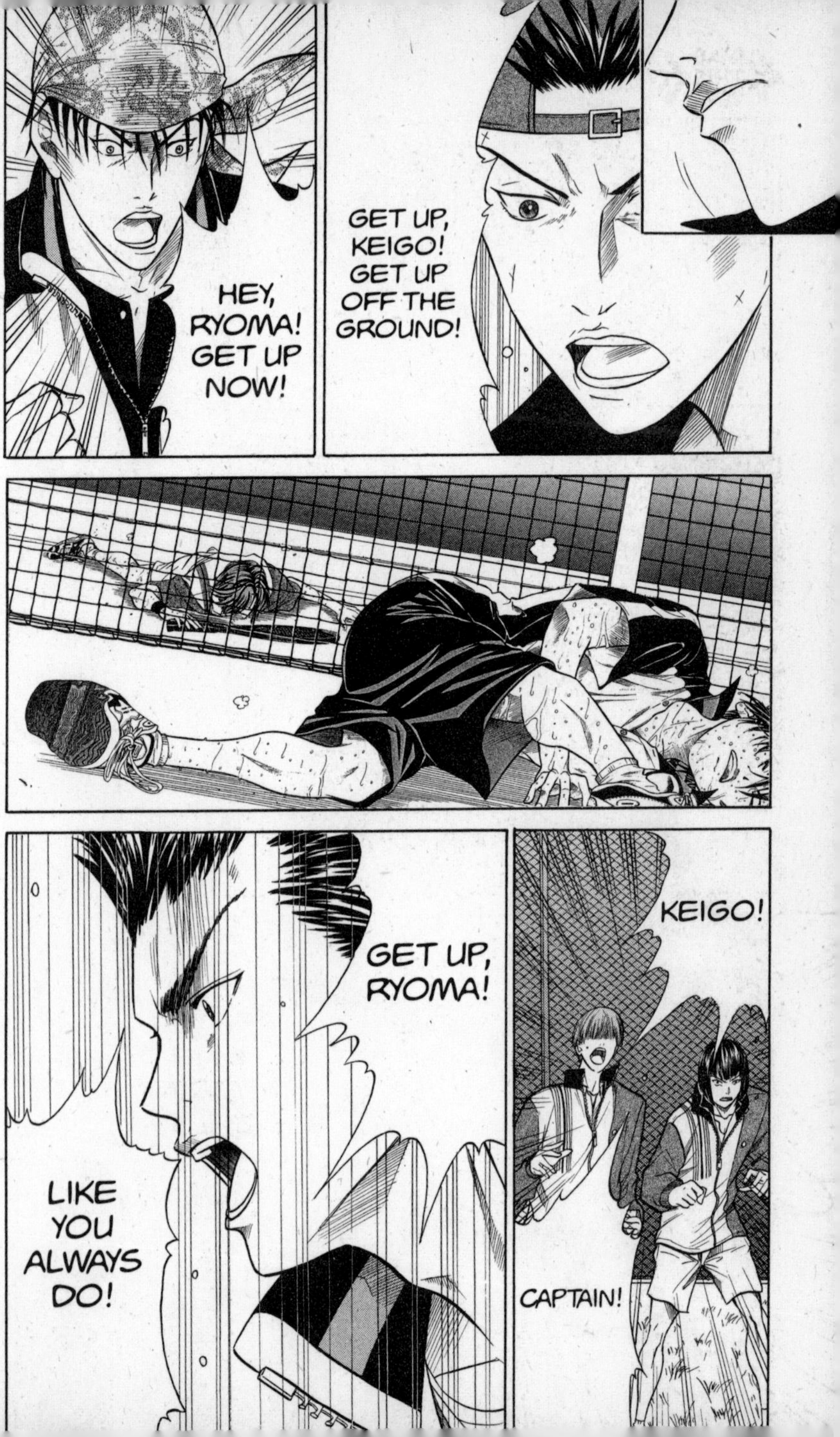
GET UP, KEIGO! GET UP OFF THE GROUND!
HEY, RYOMA! GET UP NOW!
KEIGO!
CAPTAIN!
GET UP, RYOMA!
LIKE YOU ALWAYS DO!

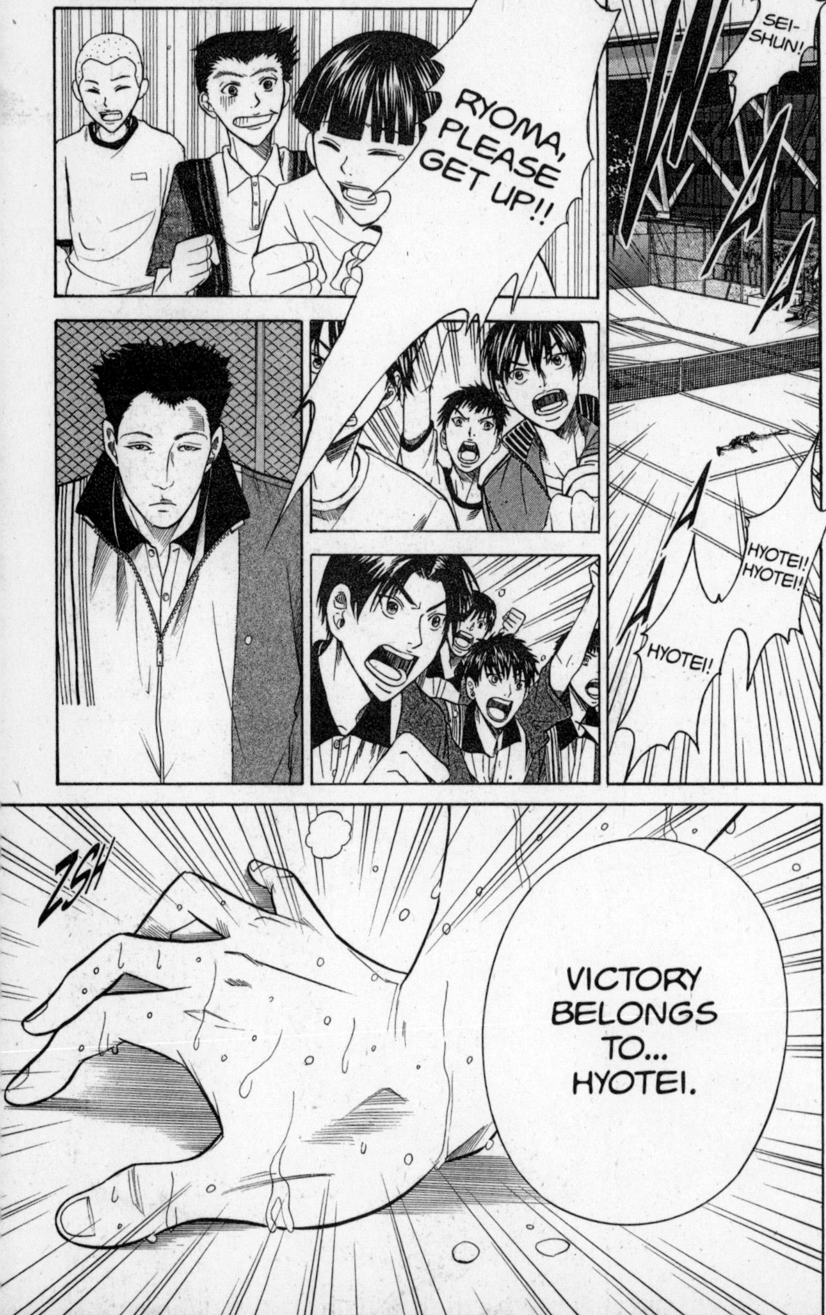
READ THIS WAY
SEI-SHUN!
RYOMA, PLEASE GET UP!!
HYOTEI! HYOTEI!
HYOTEI!
VICTORY BELONGS TO... HYOTEI.
ZSH

テニスの王子様

THE PRINCE OF TENNIS

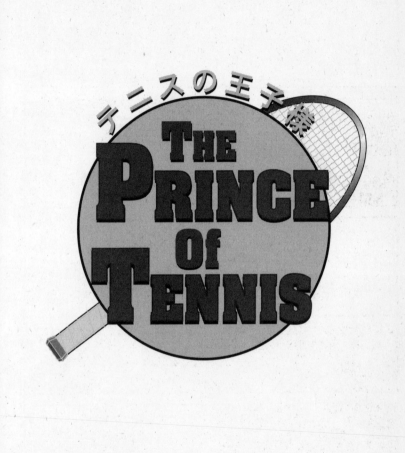

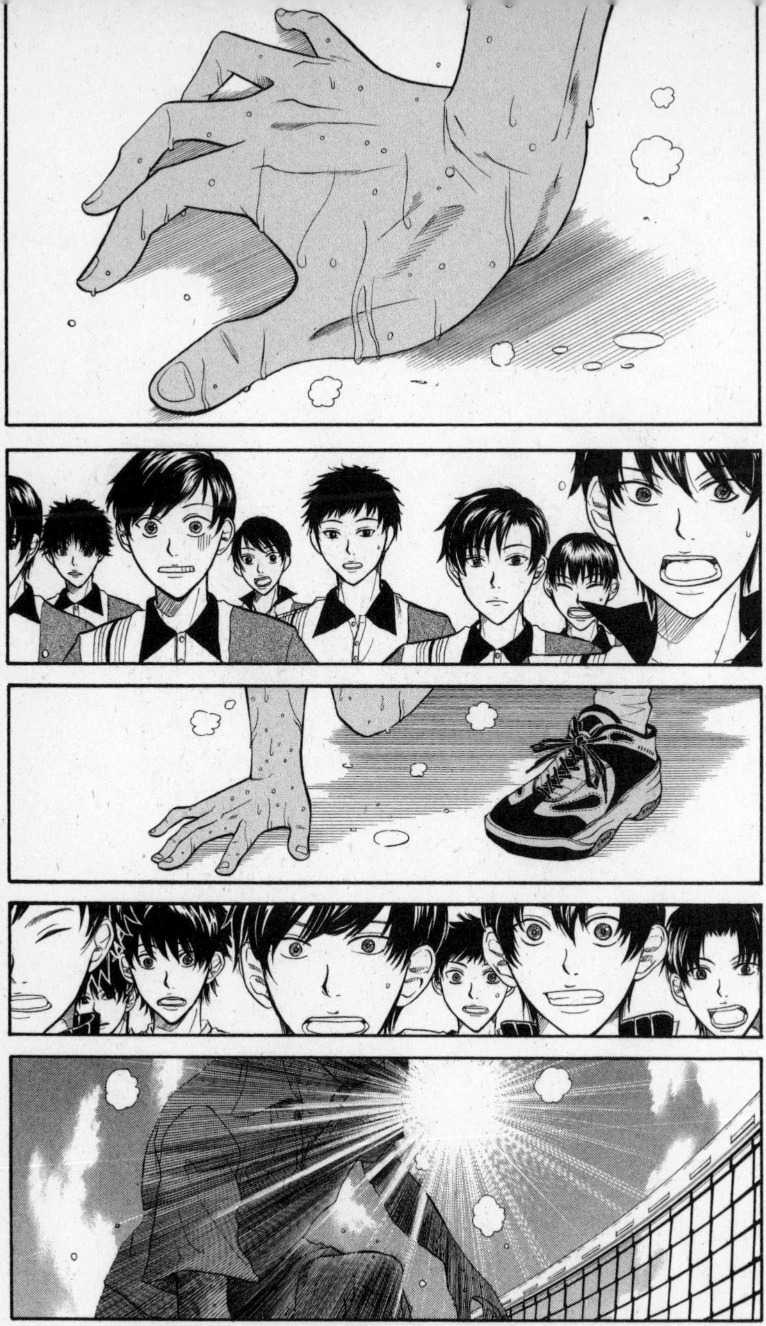

GENIUS 305: FIRST-EVER DEFEAT

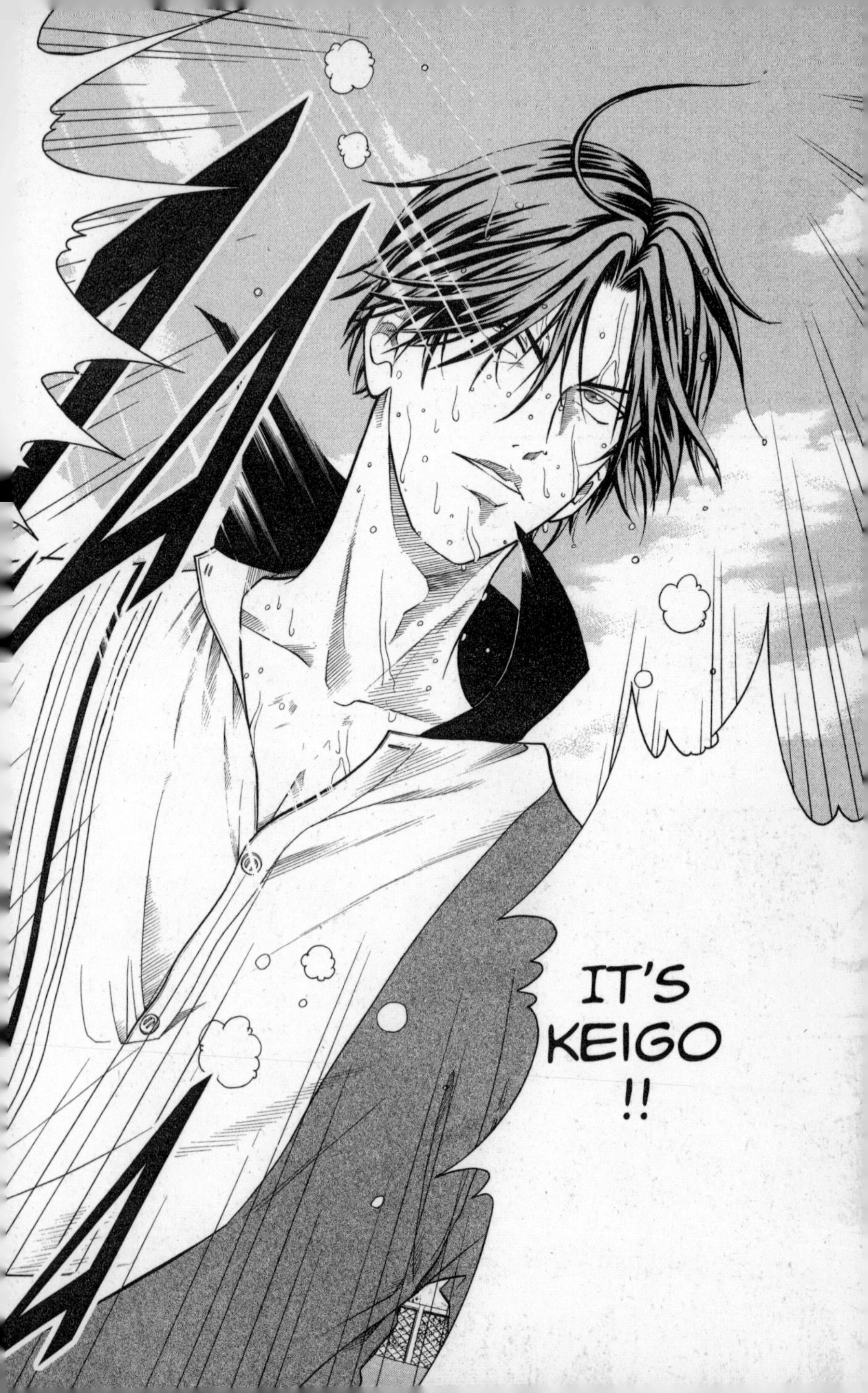
IT'S KEIGO !!

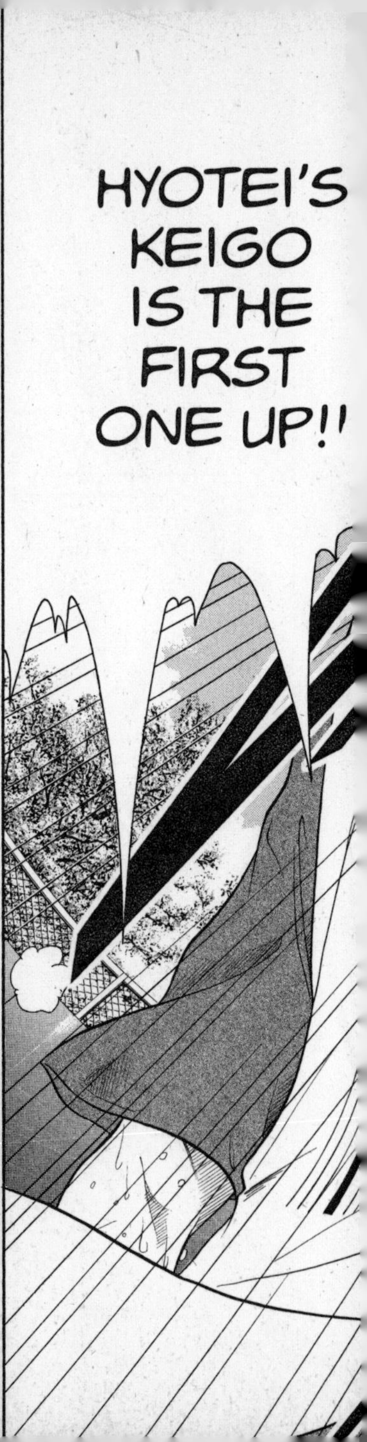
HYOTEI'S KEIGO IS THE FIRST ONE UP!!

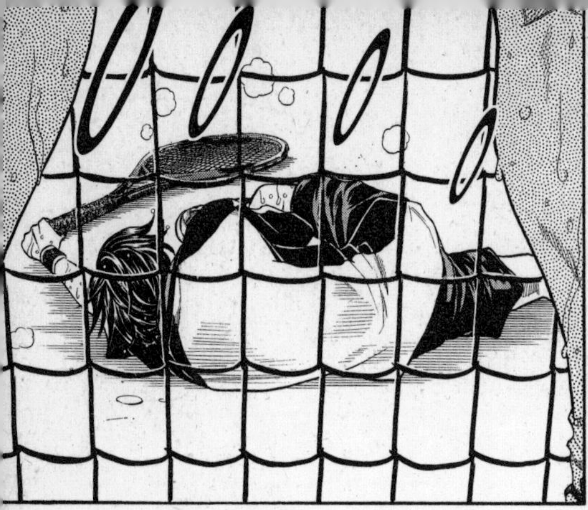

GENIUS 305:

FIRST-EVER DEFEAT

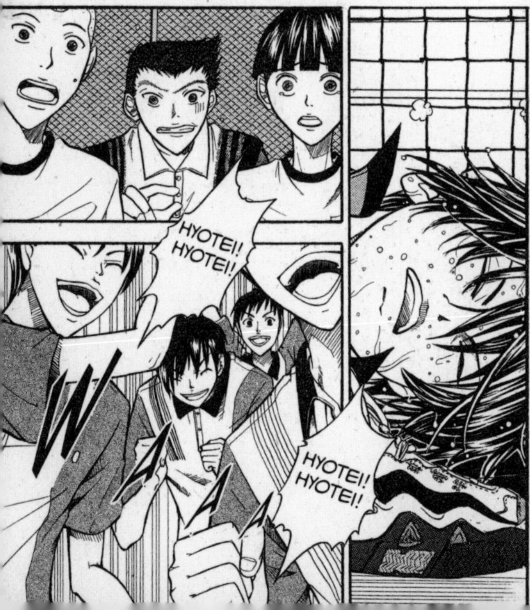
HYOTEI! HYOTEI!
HYOTEI! HYOTEI!

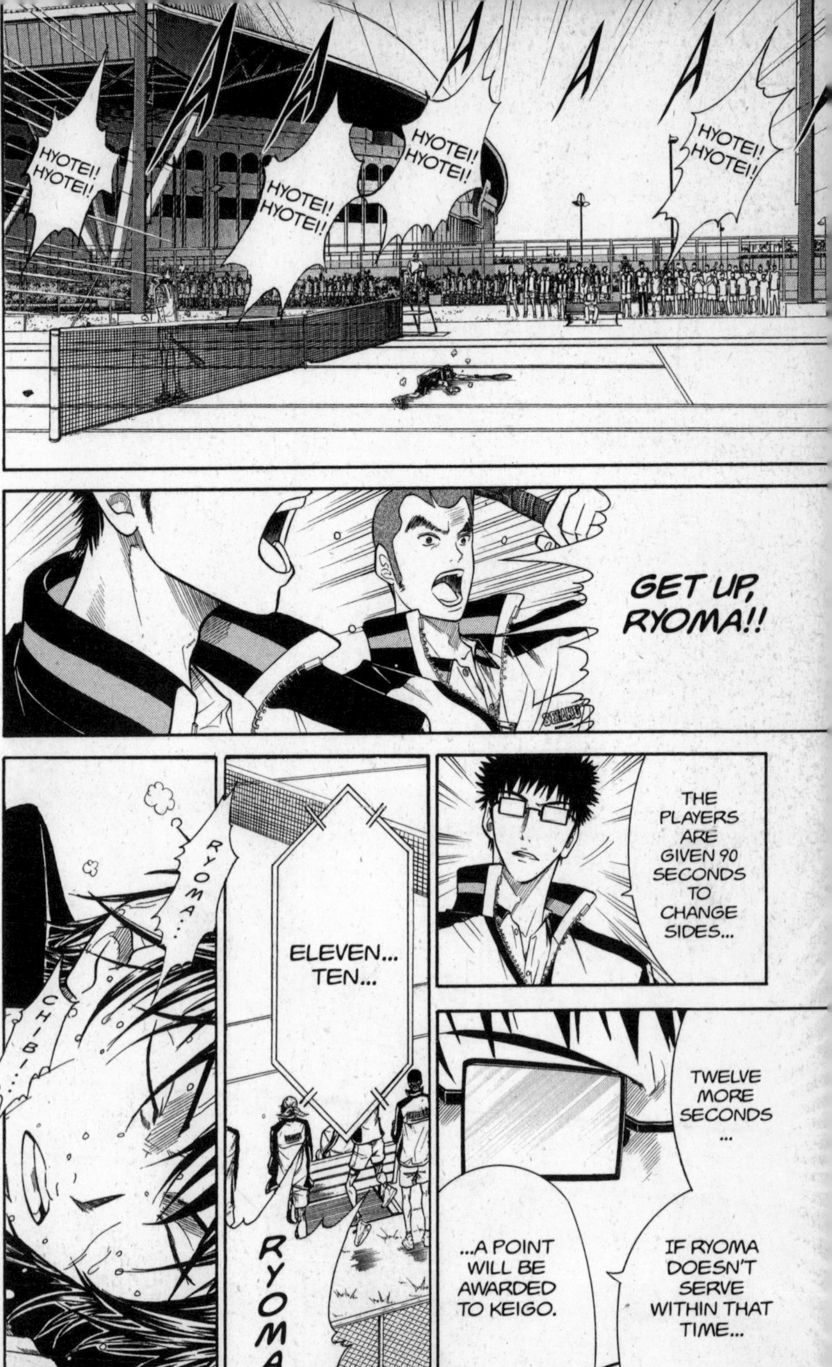
HYOTEI!! HYOTEI!!
HYOTEI!! HYOTEI!!
HYOTEI!! HYOTEI!!
HYOTEI!! HYOTEI!!
GET UP, RYOMA!!
THE PLAYERS ARE GIVEN 90 SECONDS TO CHANGE SIDES...
TWELVE MORE SECONDS...
IF RYOMA DOESN'T SERVE WITHIN THAT TIME...
...A POINT WILL BE AWARDED TO KEIGO.
ELEVEN... TEN...
RYOMA!!
RYOMA...
CHIBI...

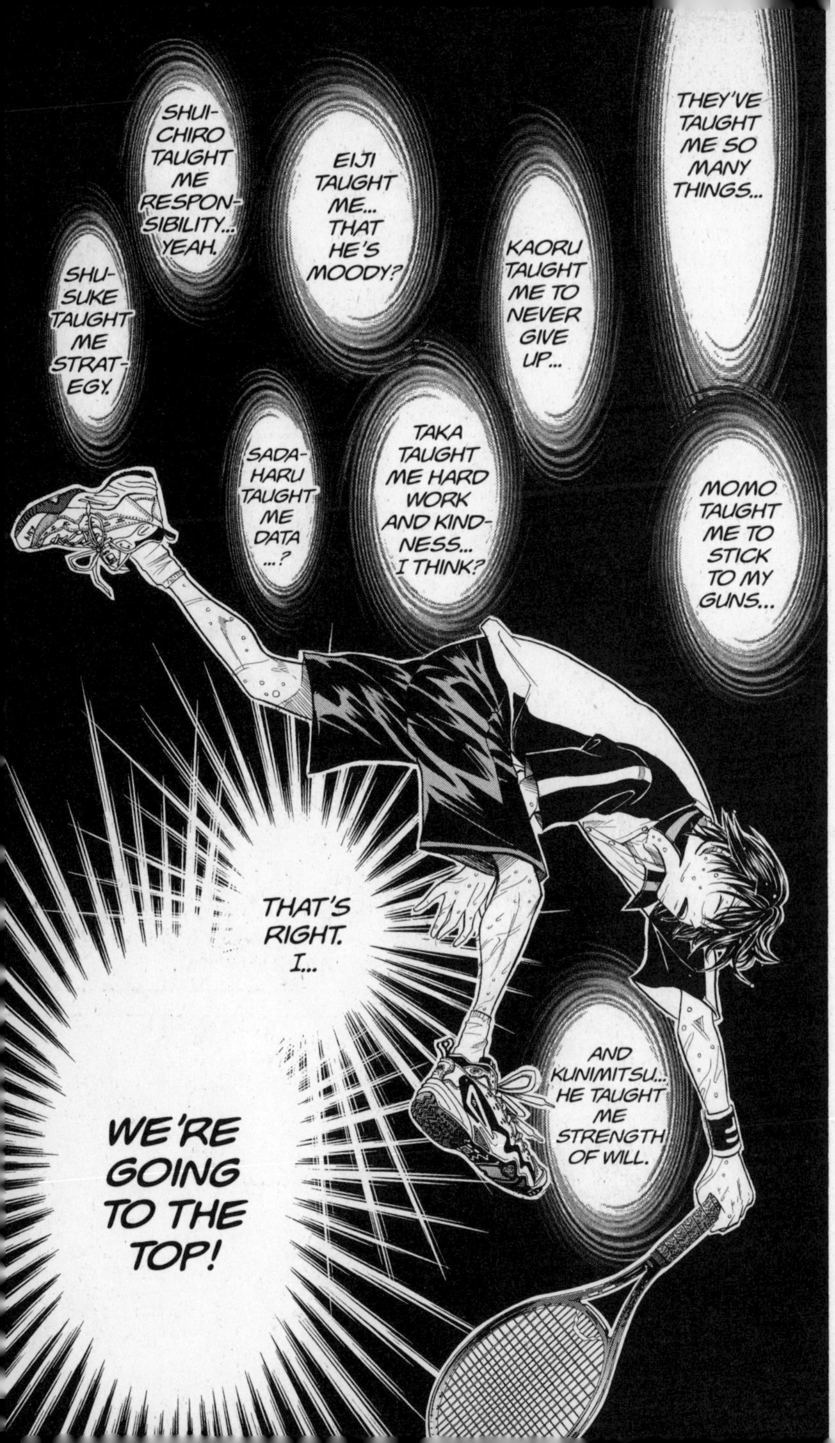
THEY'VE TAUGHT ME SO MANY THINGS...
KAORU TAUGHT ME TO NEVER GIVE UP...
MOMO TAUGHT ME TO STICK TO MY GUNS...
EIJI TAUGHT ME... THAT HE'S MOODY?
TAKA TAUGHT ME HARD WORK AND KIND-NESS... I THINK?
SHUI-CHIRO TAUGHT ME RESPON-SIBILITY... YEAH.
SADA-HARU TAUGHT ME DATA ...?
SHU-SUKE TAUGHT ME STRAT-EGY.
AND KUNIMITSU... HE TAUGHT ME STRENGTH OF WILL.
THAT'S RIGHT. I...
WE'RE GOING TO THE TOP!

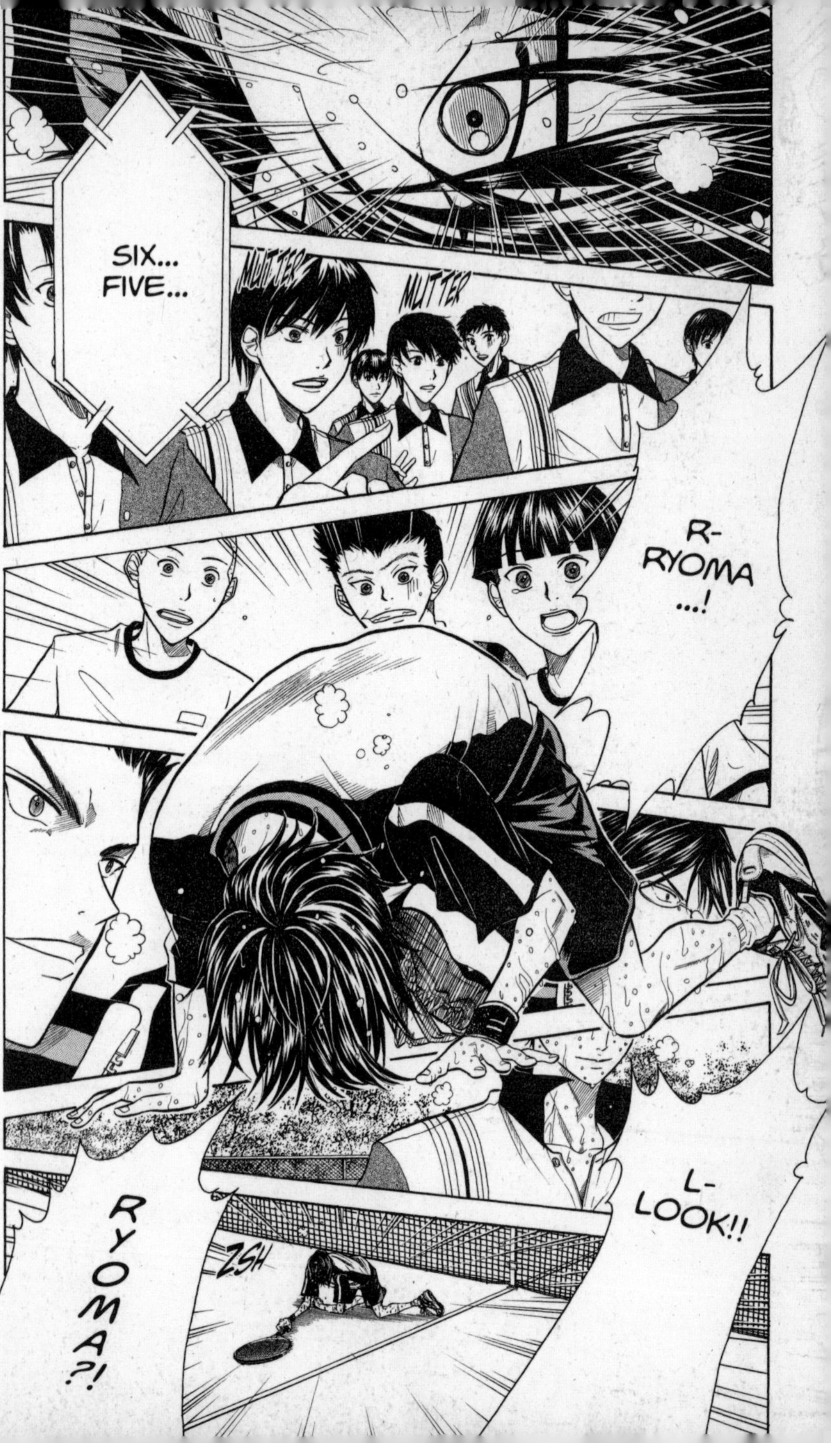
SIX... FIVE...
MUTTER
MUTTER
R-RYOMA ...!
L-LOOK!!
ZSH
RYOMA?!

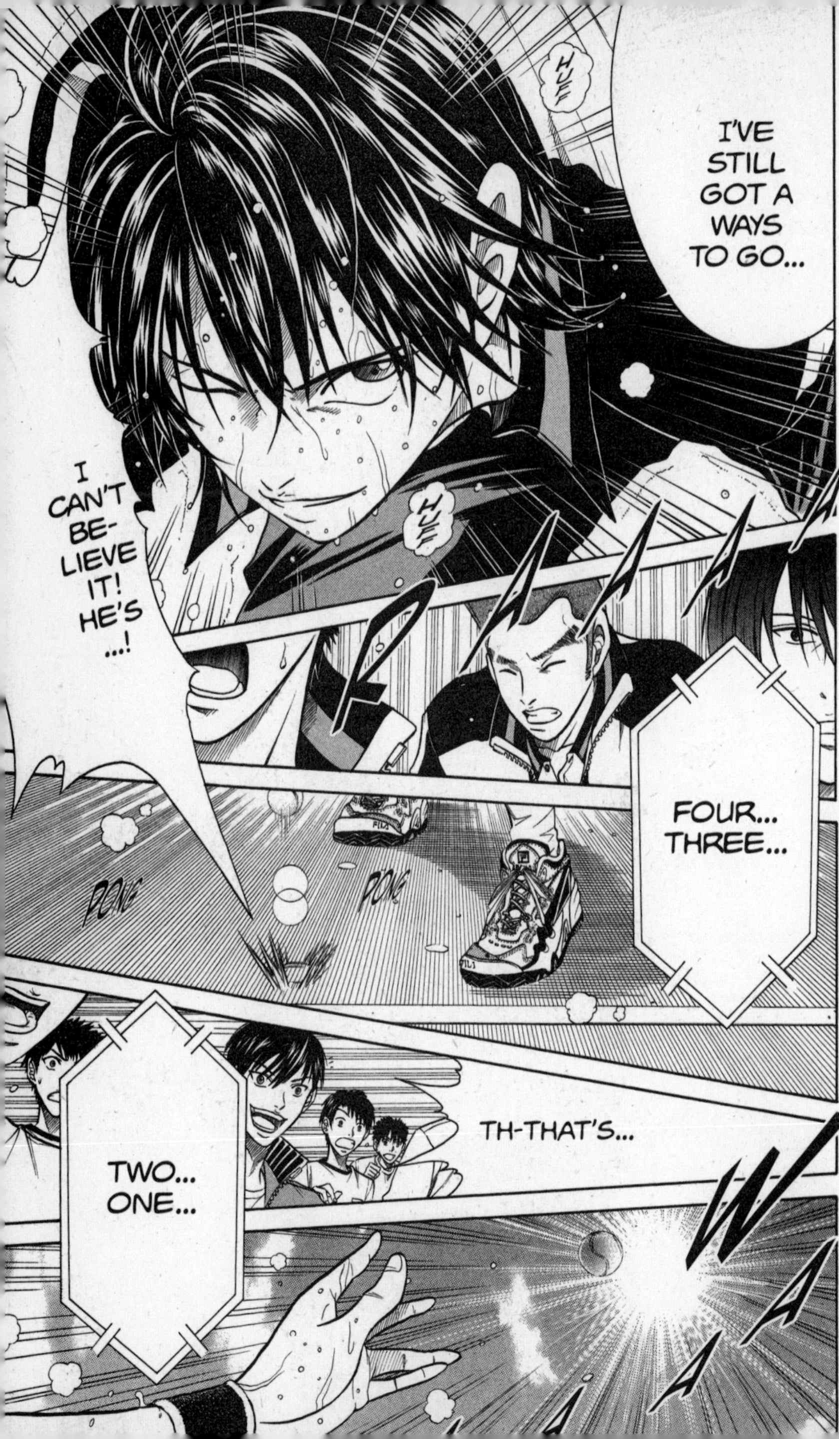
HUF
I'VE STILL GOT A WAYS TO GO...
HUF
I CAN'T BE-LIEVE IT! HE'S ...!
FOUR... THREE...
PONG
PONG
TH-THAT'S...
TWO... ONE...

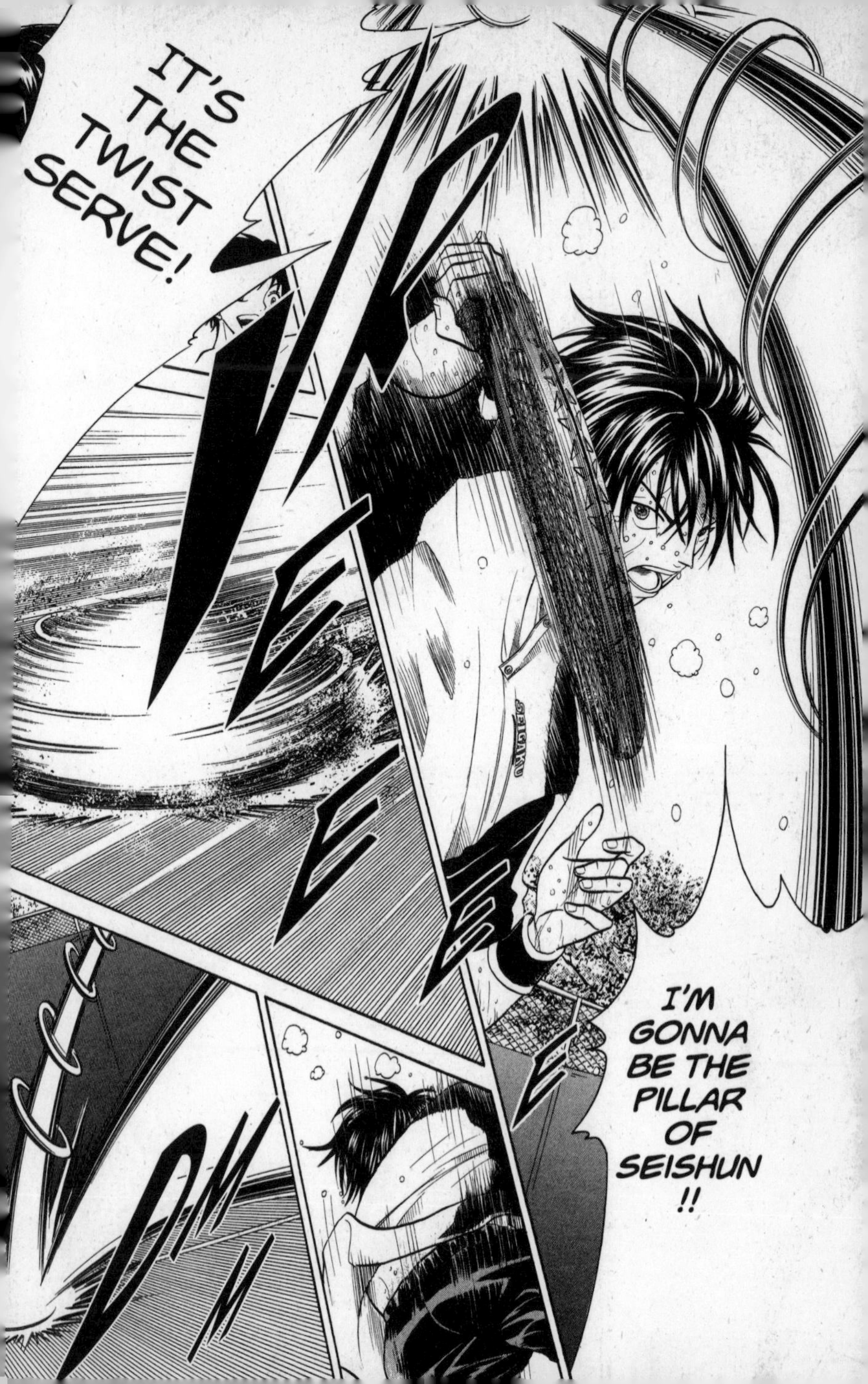

IT'S THE TWIST SERVE!
I'M GONNA BE THE PILLAR OF SEISHUN !!

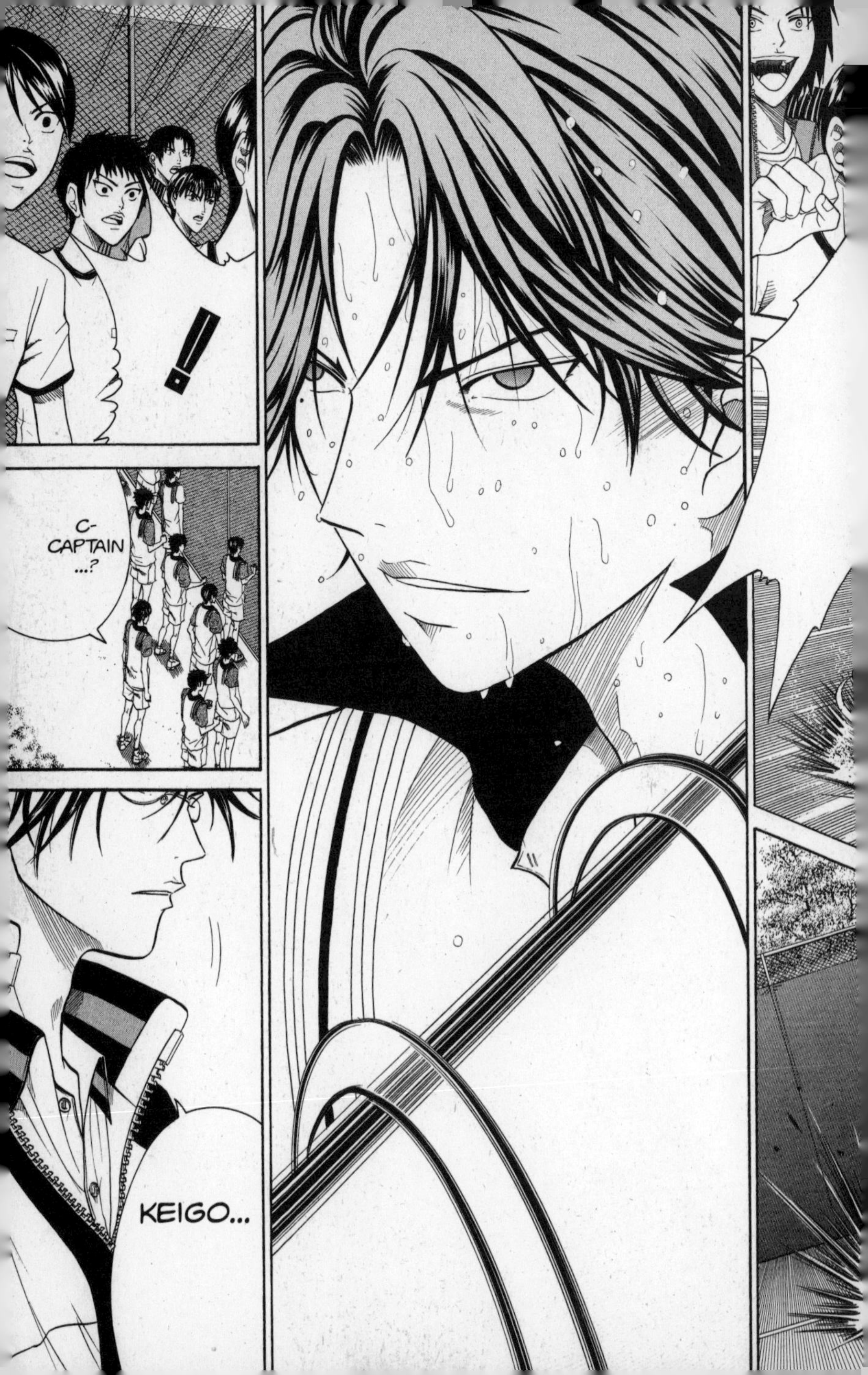
!
C-CAPTAIN ...?
KEIGO...

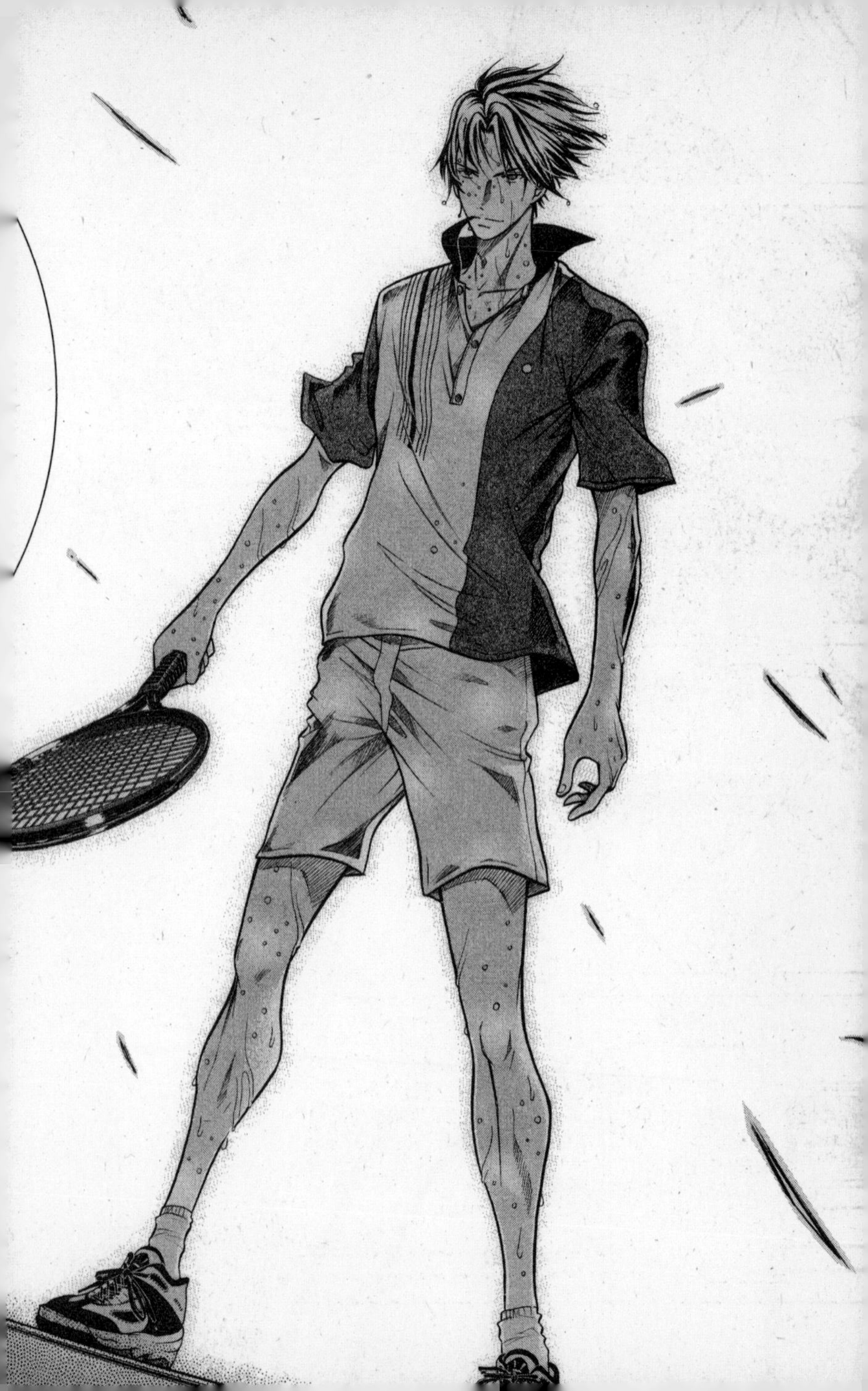

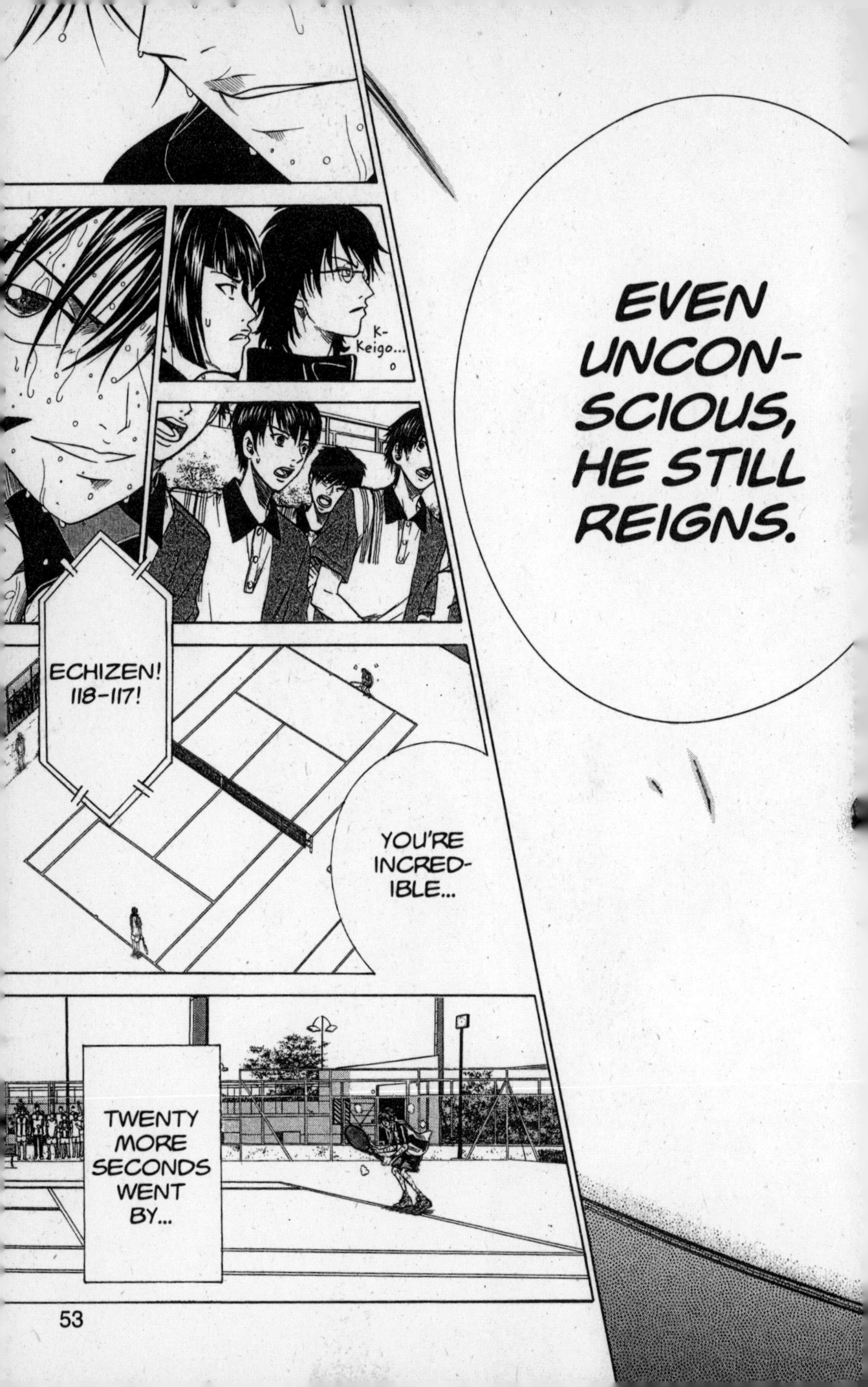
EVEN UNCONSCIOUS, HE STILL REIGNS.
K-Keigo...
ECHIZEN! 118-117!
YOU'RE INCREDIBLE...
TWENTY MORE SECONDS WENT BY...

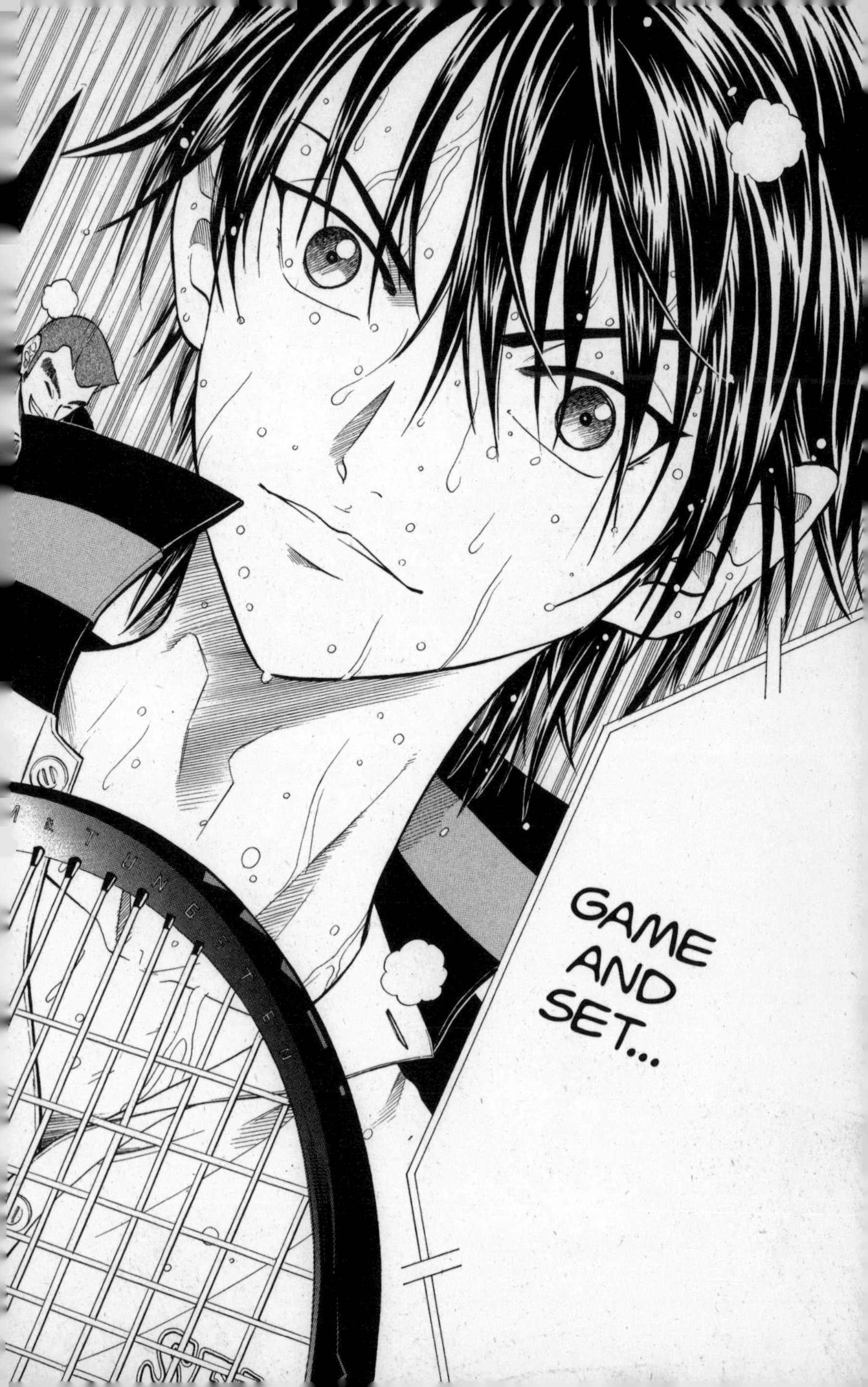
GAME AND SET...

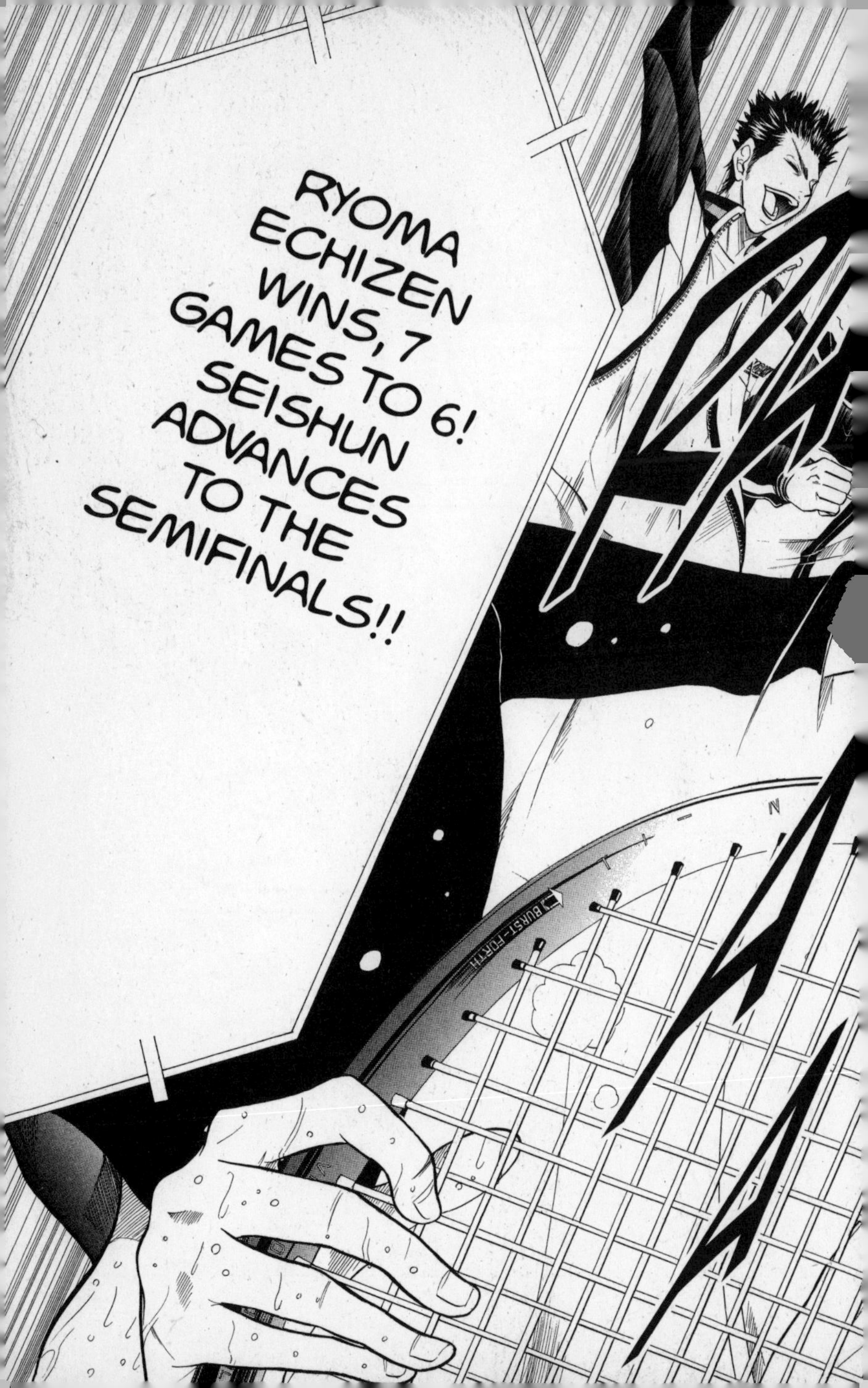
RYOMA ECHIZEN WINS, 7 GAMES TO 6! SEISHUN ADVANCES TO THE SEMIFINALS!!
BURST-FORTH

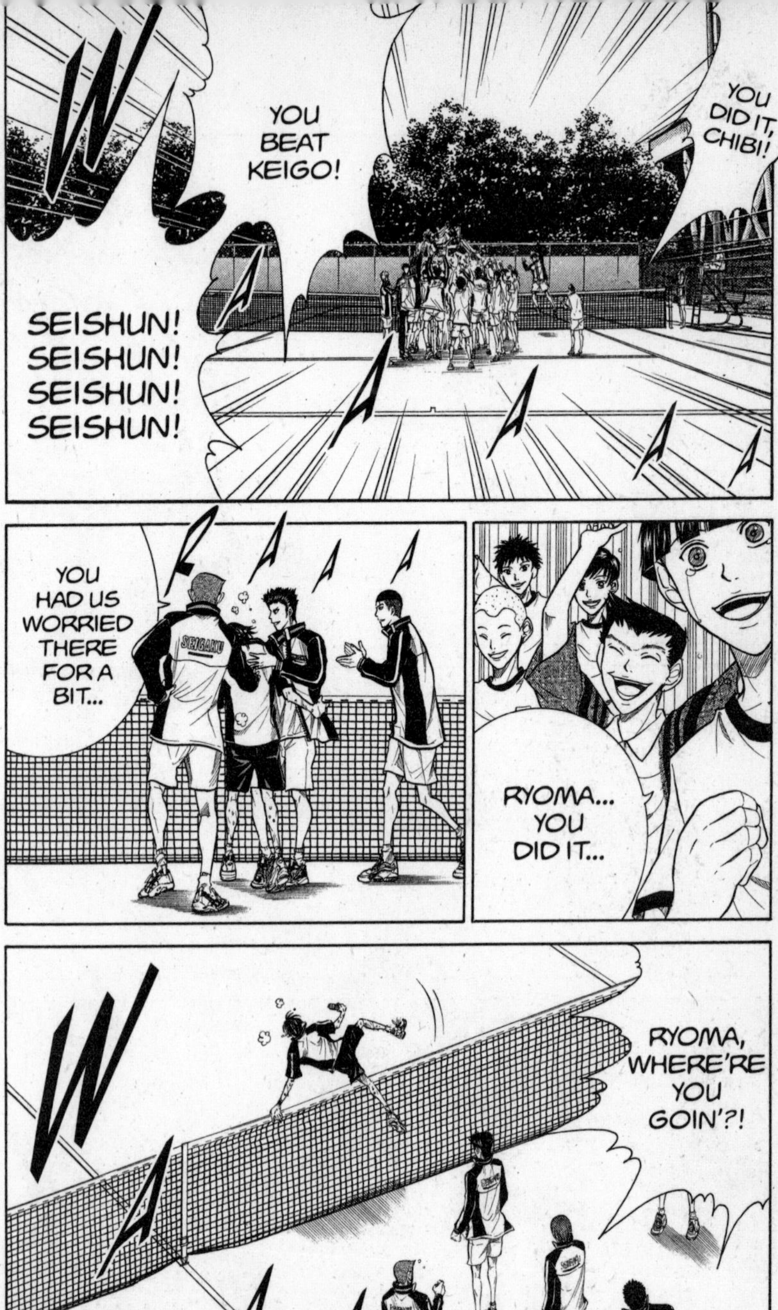
YOU DID IT, CHIBI!
YOU BEAT KEIGO!
SEISHUN! SEISHUN! SEISHUN! SEISHUN!
WAAAAAA
RAAAA
RYOMA... YOU DID IT...
YOU HAD US WORRIED THERE FOR A BIT...
RYOMA, WHERE'RE YOU GOIN'?!
WAAA

READ THIS WAY

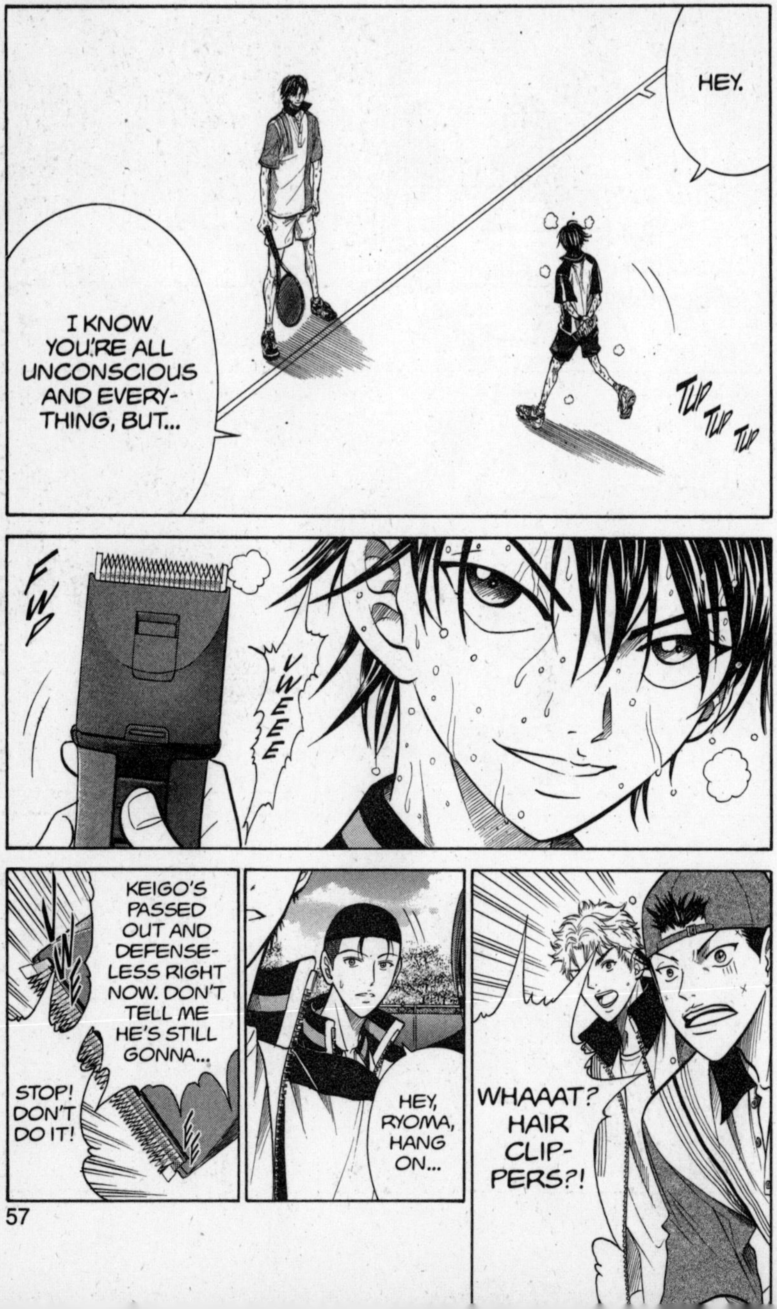
HEY.
I KNOW YOU'RE ALL UNCONSCIOUS AND EVERY-THING, BUT...
TUP TUP TUP
VWEEEE
FWD
WHAAAT? HAIR CLIP-PERS?!
HEY, RYOMA, HANG ON...
KEIGO'S PASSED OUT AND DEFENSE-LESS RIGHT NOW. DON'T TELL ME HE'S STILL GONNA...
STOP! DON'T DO IT!

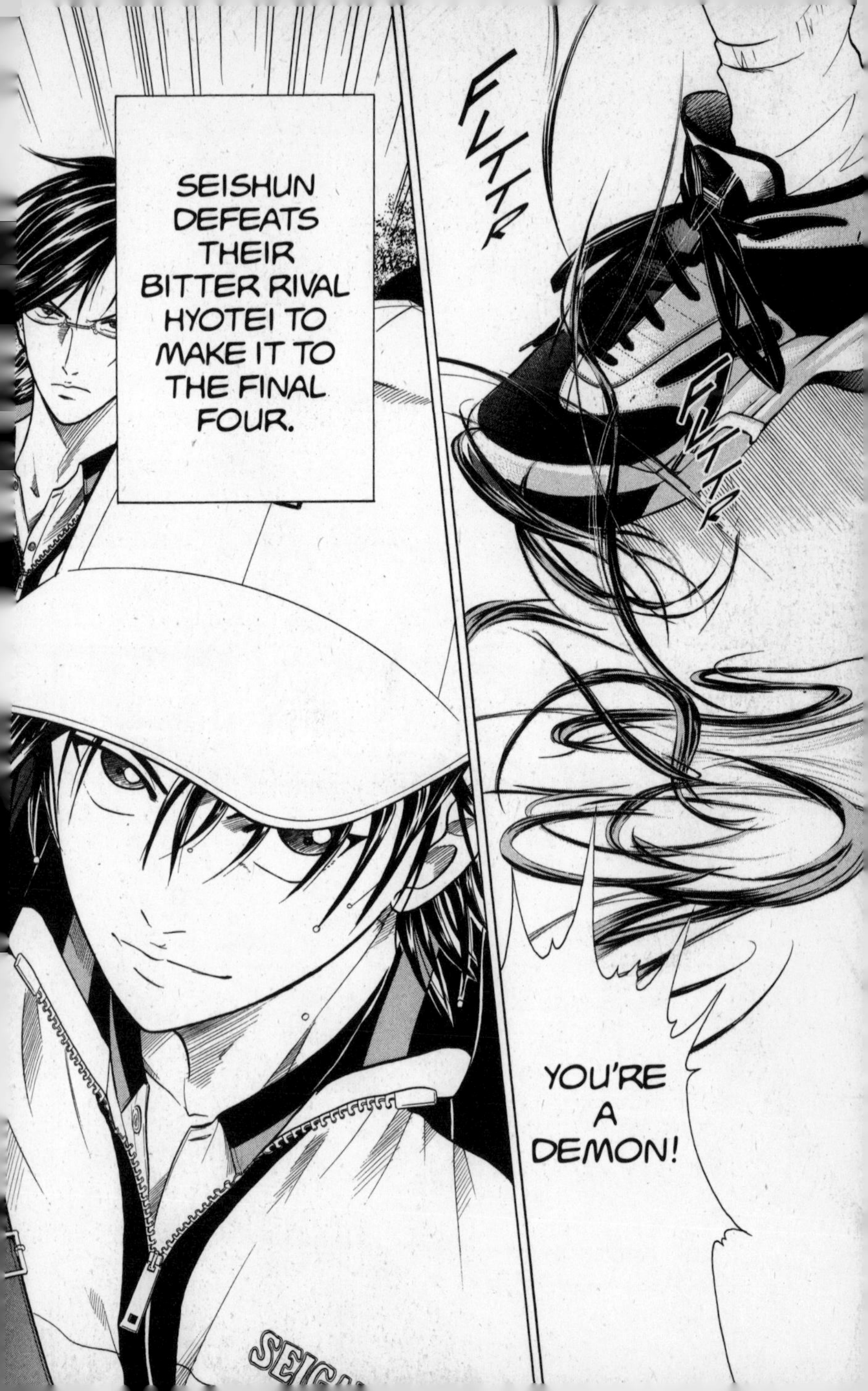
YOU'RE A DEMON!
SEISHUN DEFEATS THEIR BITTER RIVAL HYOTEI TO MAKE IT TO THE FINAL FOUR.

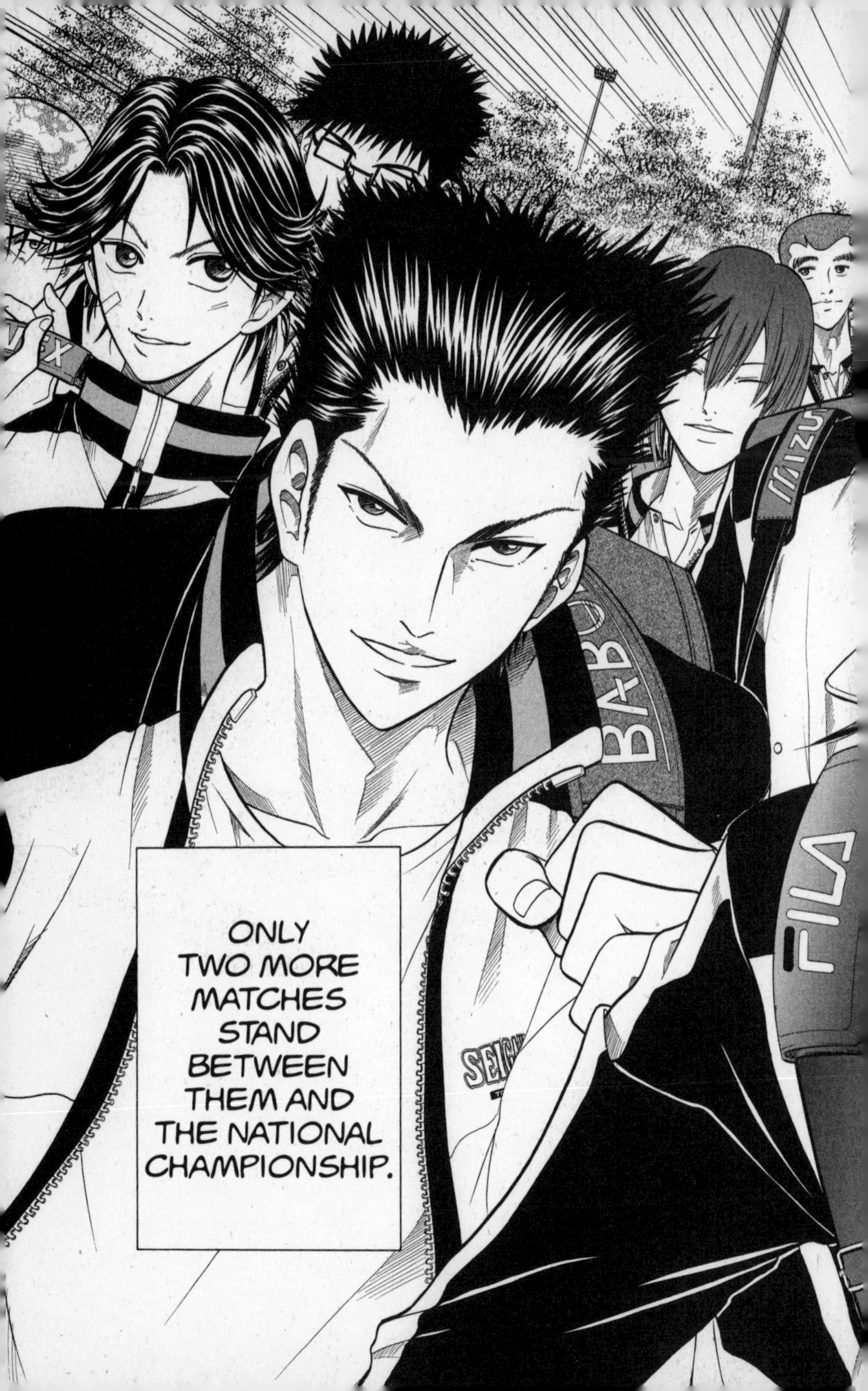
ONLY TWO MORE MATCHES STAND BETWEEN THEM AND THE NATIONAL CHAMPIONSHIP.
BABOLAT
FILA

テニスの王子様

THE PRINCE OF TENNIS

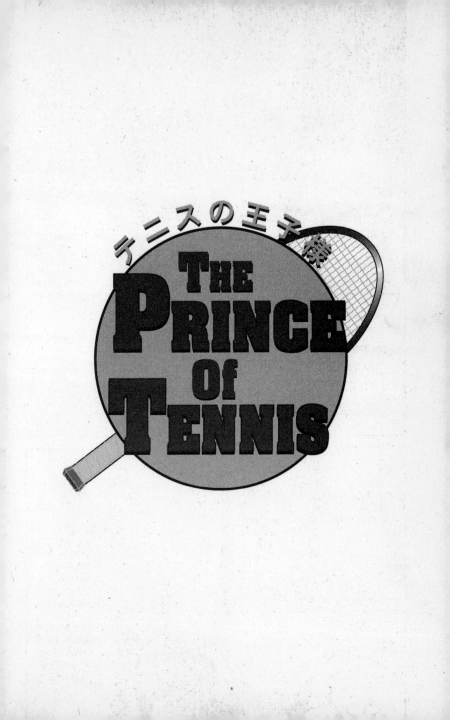

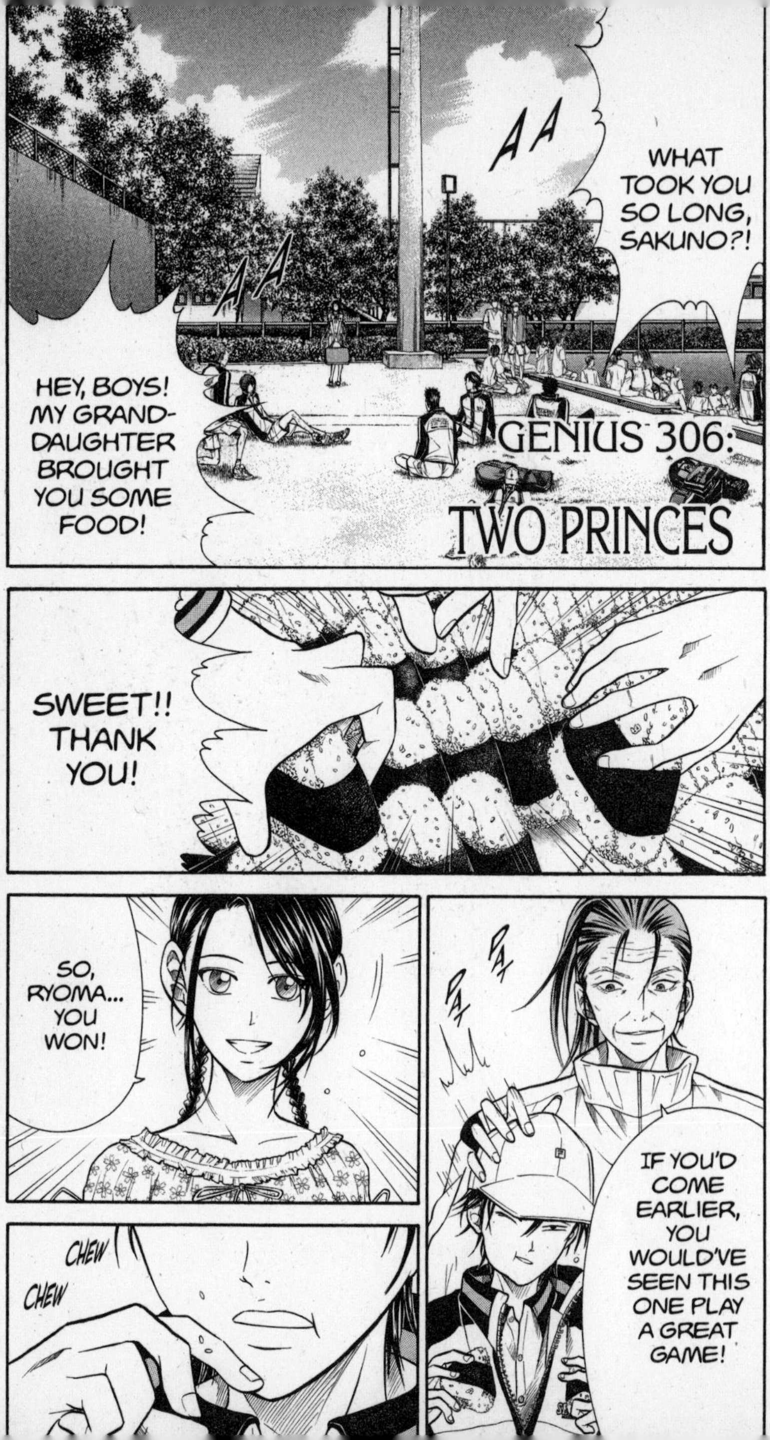
AA
WHAT TOOK YOU SO LONG, SAKUNO?!
AA
HEY, BOYS! MY GRAND-DAUGHTER BROUGHT YOU SOME FOOD!
GENIUS 306:
TWO PRINCES
SWEET!! THANK YOU!
DA
DA
IF YOU'D COME EARLIER, YOU WOULD'VE SEEN THIS ONE PLAY A GREAT GAME!
SO, RYOMA... YOU WON!
CHEW
CHEW

GENIUS 306: TWO PRINCES

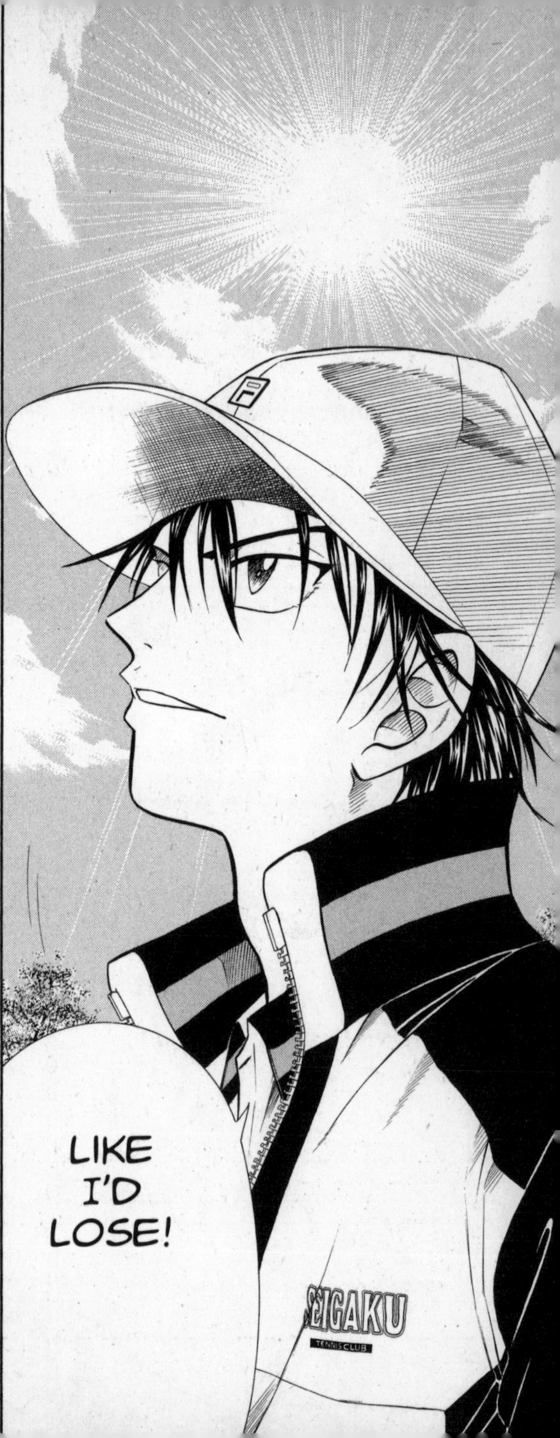
LIKE I'D LOSE!
SEIGAKU
TENNIS CLUB

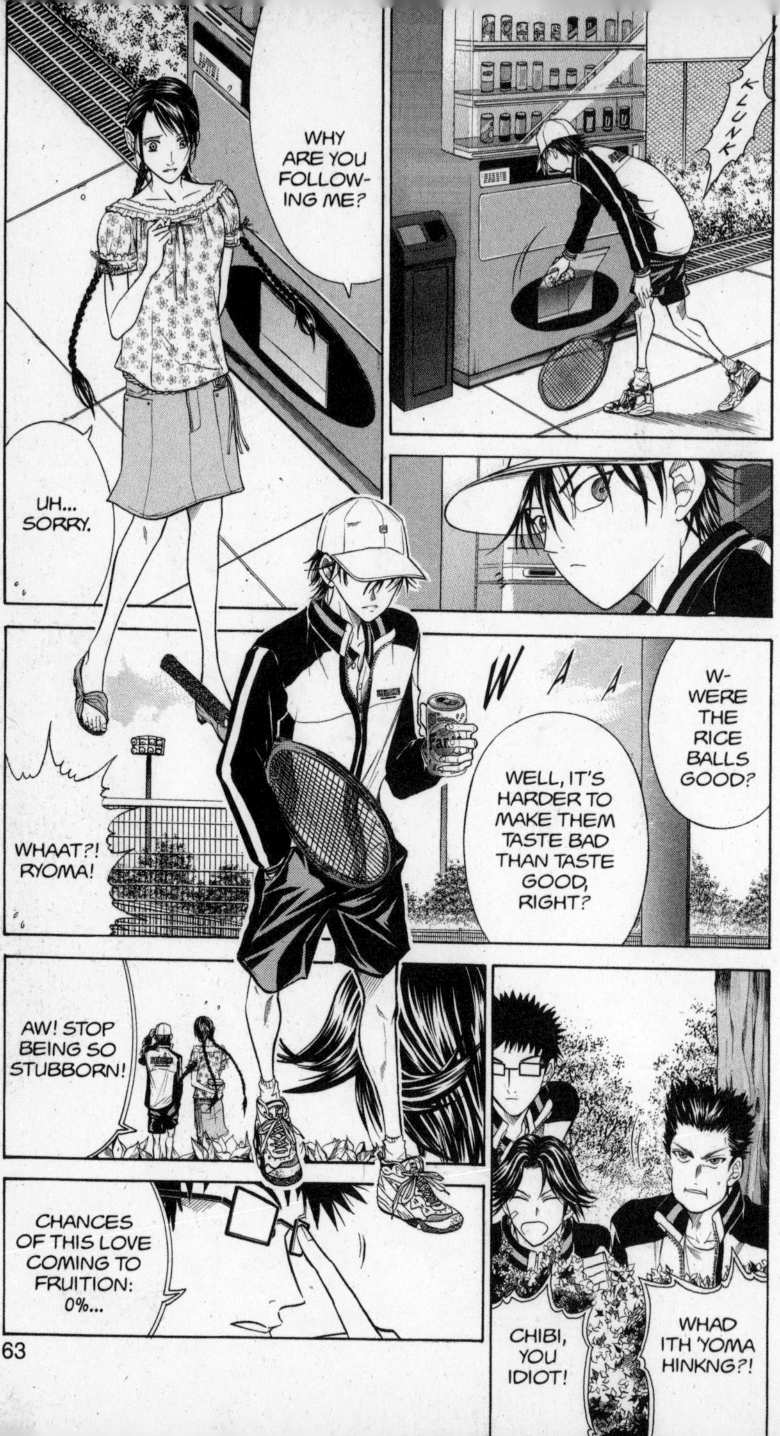
KLUNK
WHY ARE YOU FOLLOWING ME?
UH... SORRY.
W-WERE THE RICE BALLS GOOD?
WELL, IT'S HARDER TO MAKE THEM TASTE BAD THAN TASTE GOOD, RIGHT?
WAA
WHAAT?! RYOMA!
WHAD ITH 'YOMA HINKNG?!
CHIBI, YOU IDIOT!
AW! STOP BEING SO STUBBORN!
CHANCES OF THIS LOVE COMING TO FRUITION: 0%...

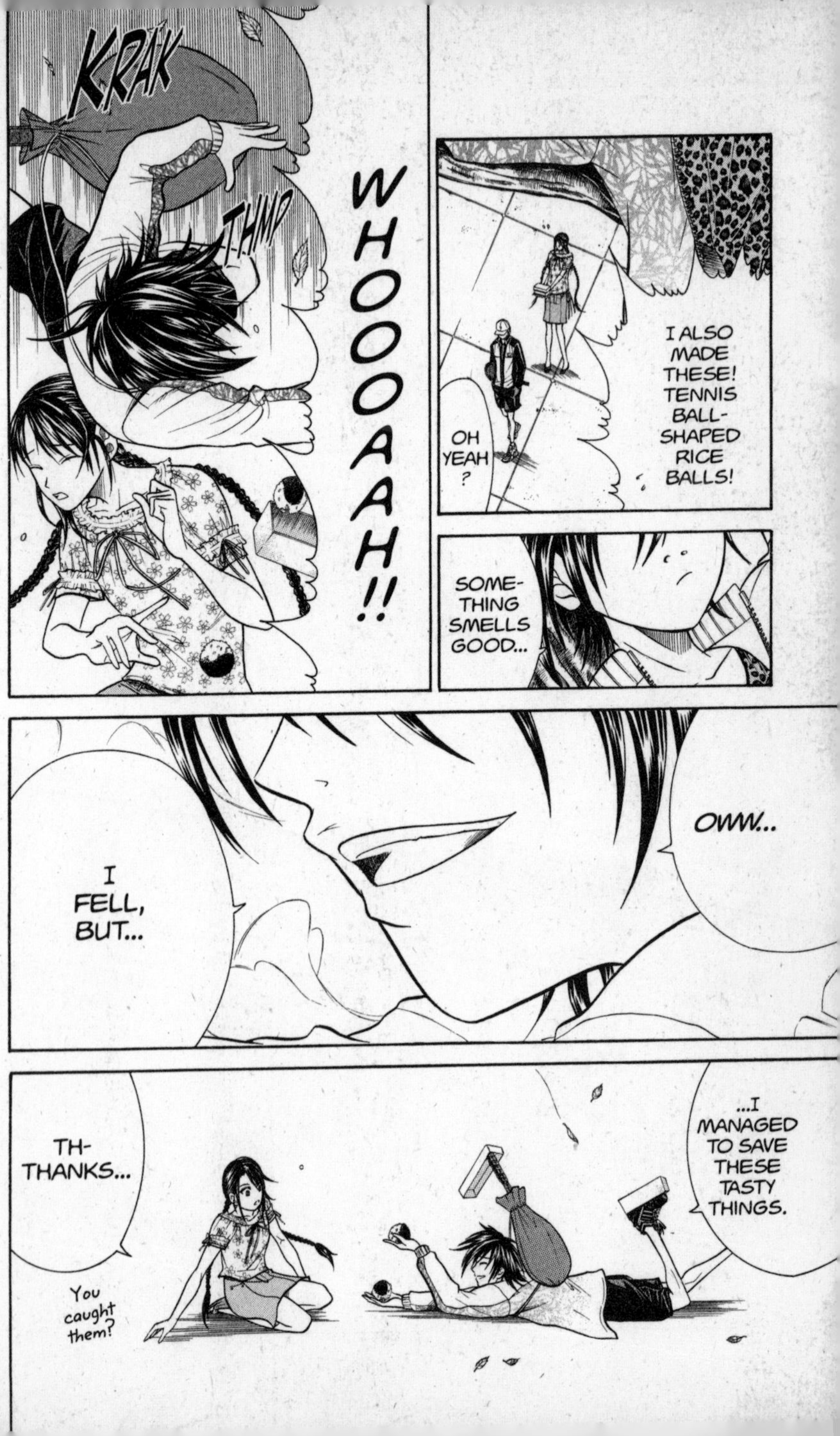
I ALSO MADE THESE! TENNIS BALL-SHAPED RICE BALLS!
OH YEAH?
SOME-THING SMELLS GOOD...
WHOOOAAAH!!
KRAK
THMP
OWW...
I FELL, BUT...
...I MANAGED TO SAVE THESE TASTY THINGS.
TH-THANKS...
You caught them?

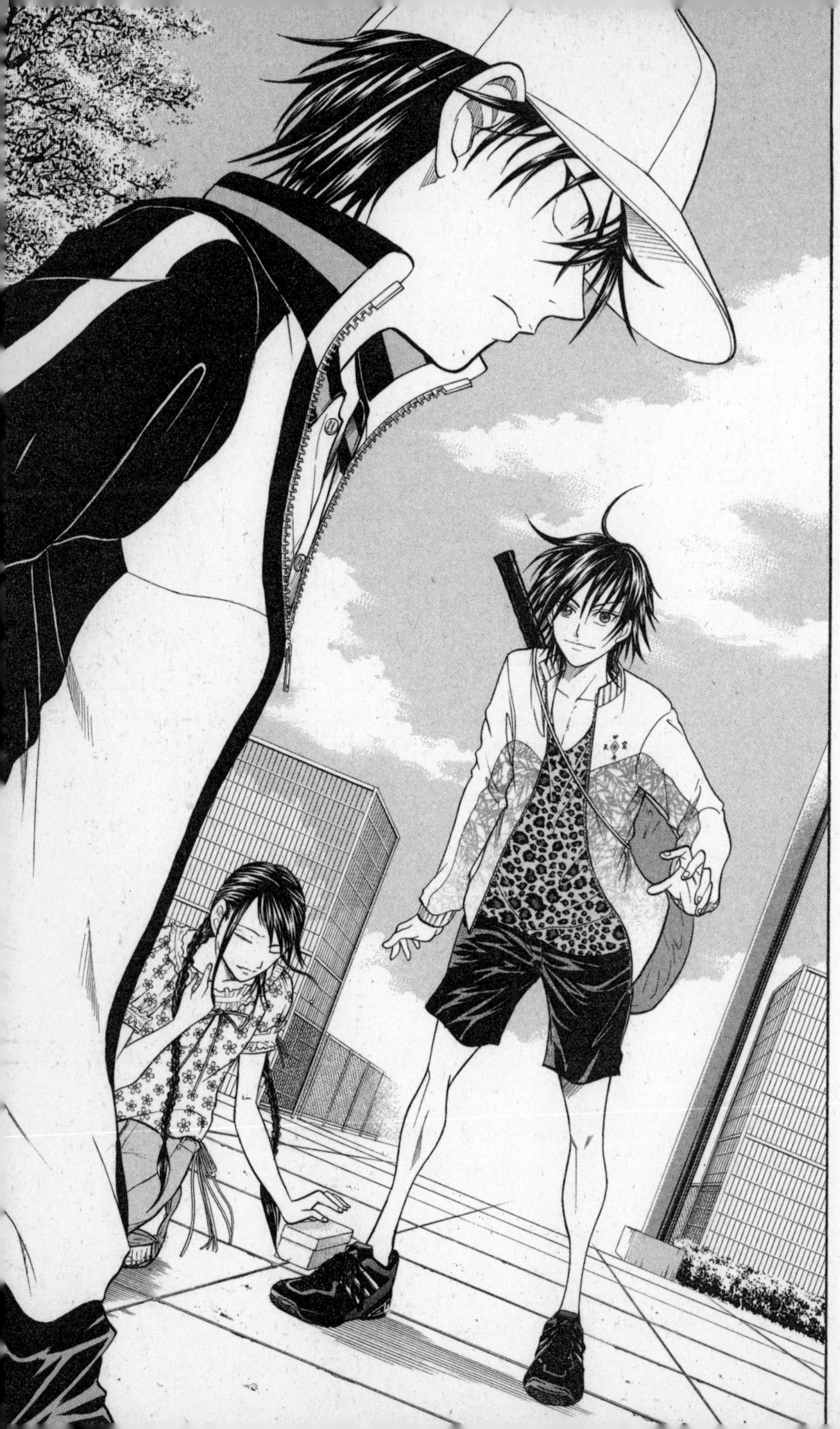

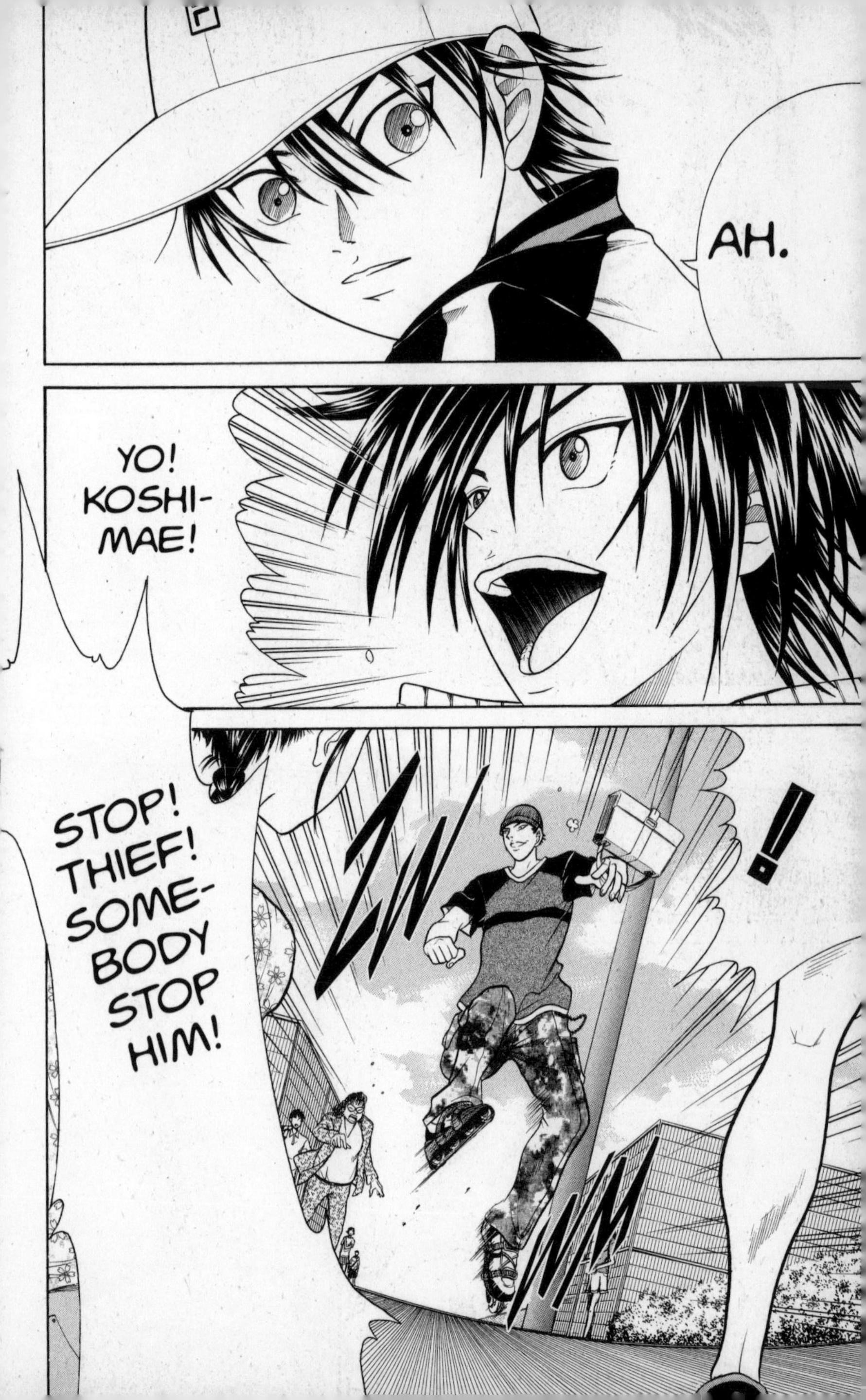
AH.
YO! KOSHI-MAE!
!
STOP! THIEF! SOME-BODY STOP HIM!

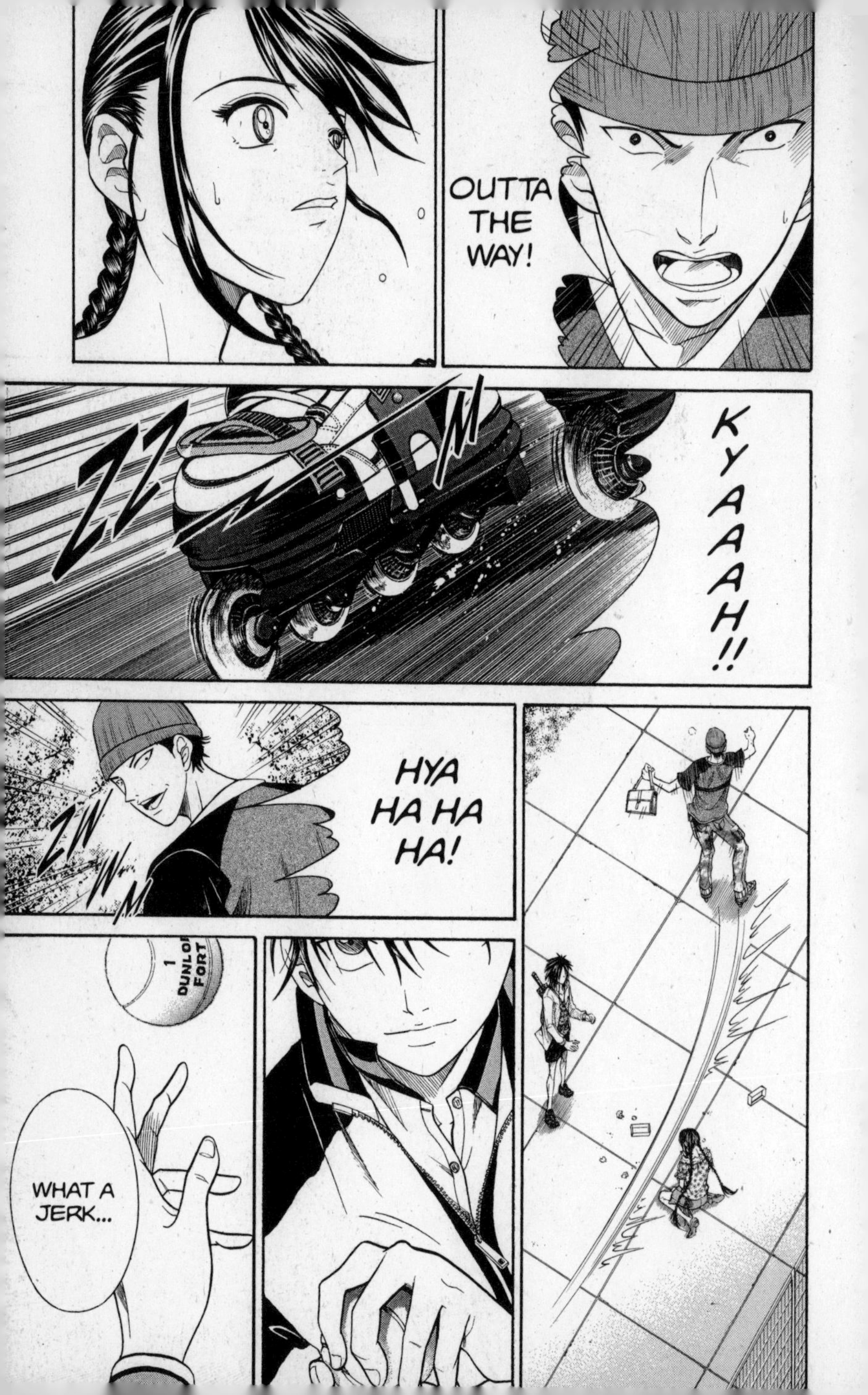
OUTTA THE WAY!
KYAAAAH!!
HYA HA HA HA!
WHAT A JERK...

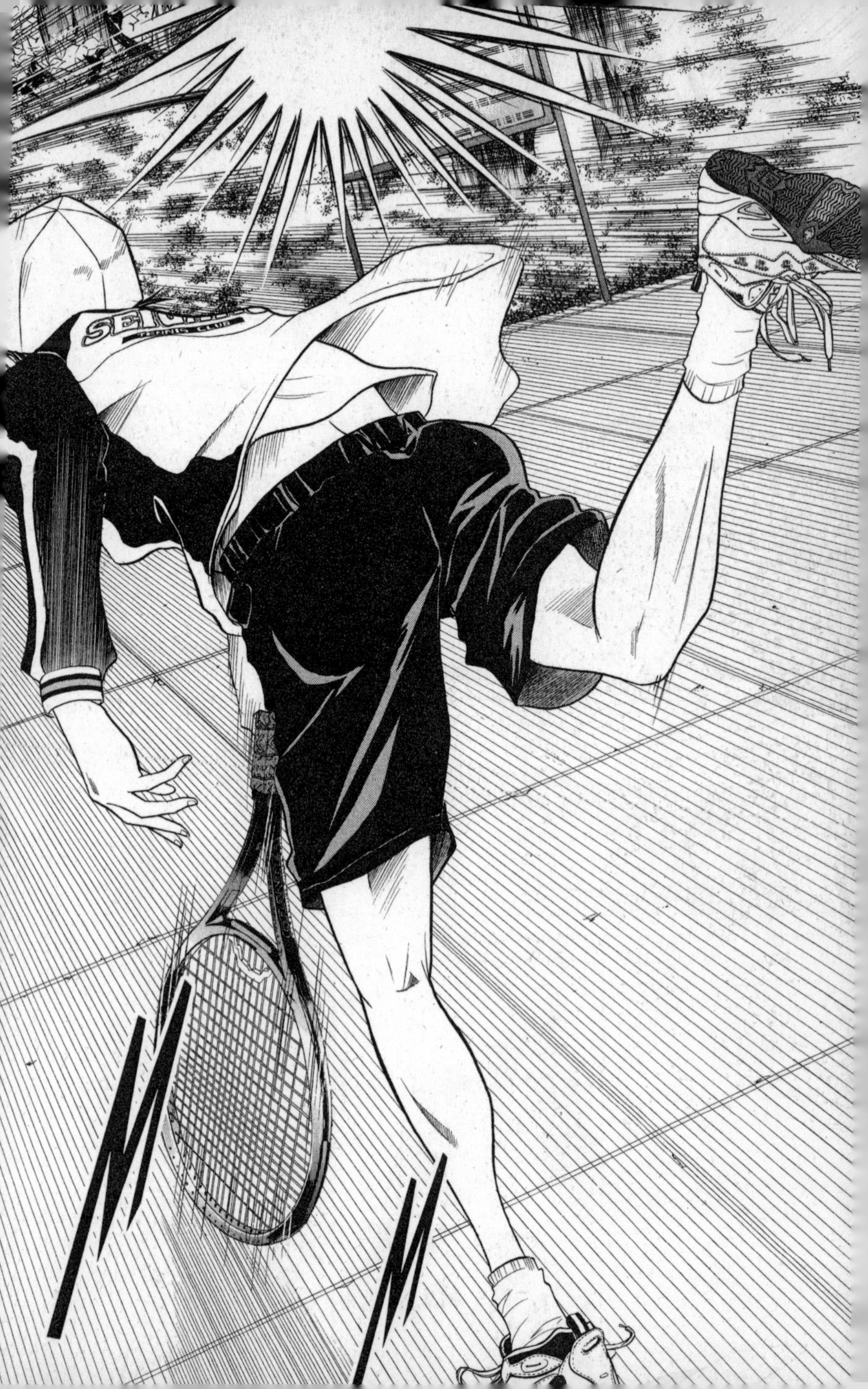
TENNIS CLUB

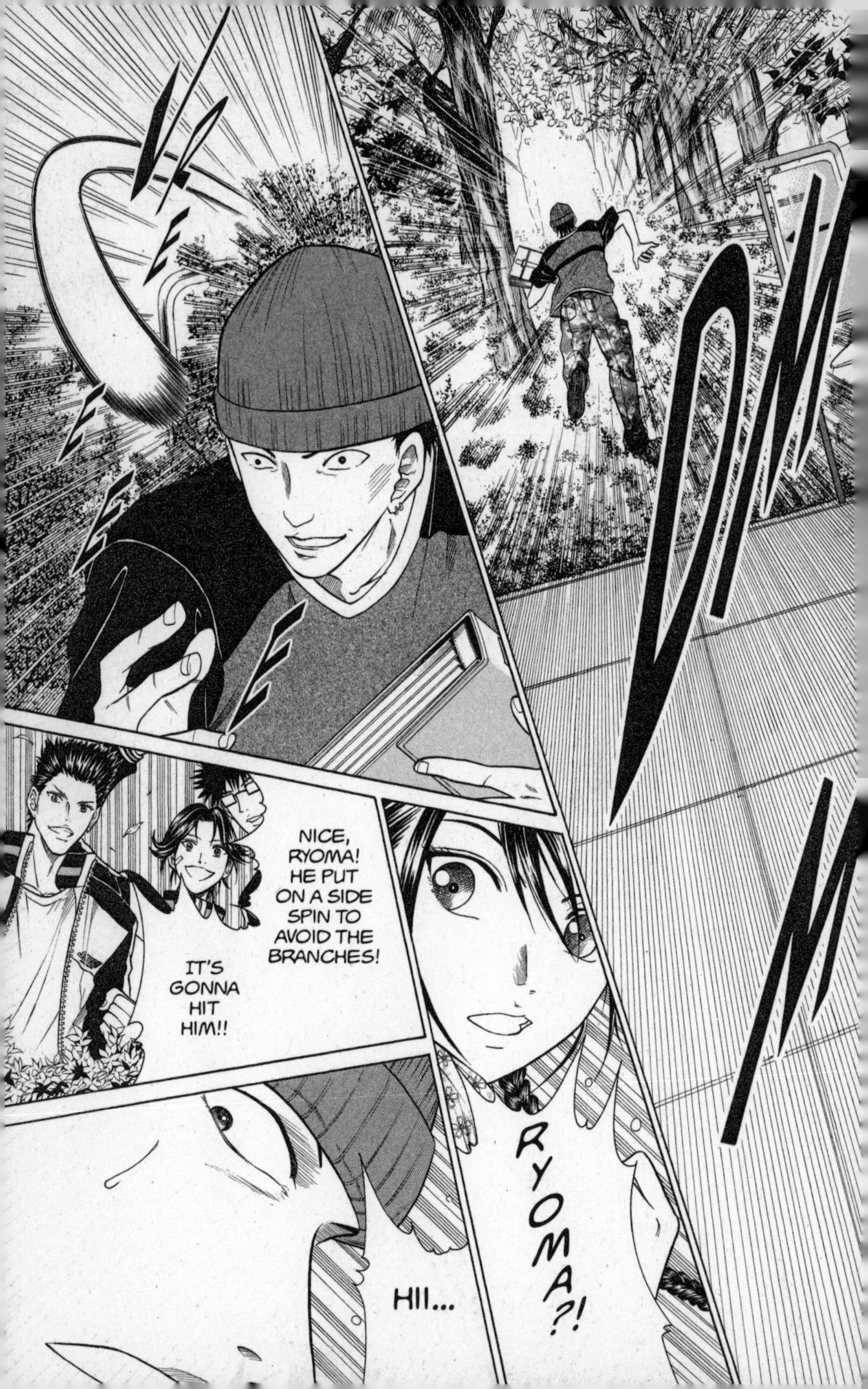
NICE, RYOMA! HE PUT ON A SIDE SPIN TO AVOID THE BRANCHES!
IT'S GONNA HIT HIM!!
RYOMA?!
HII...

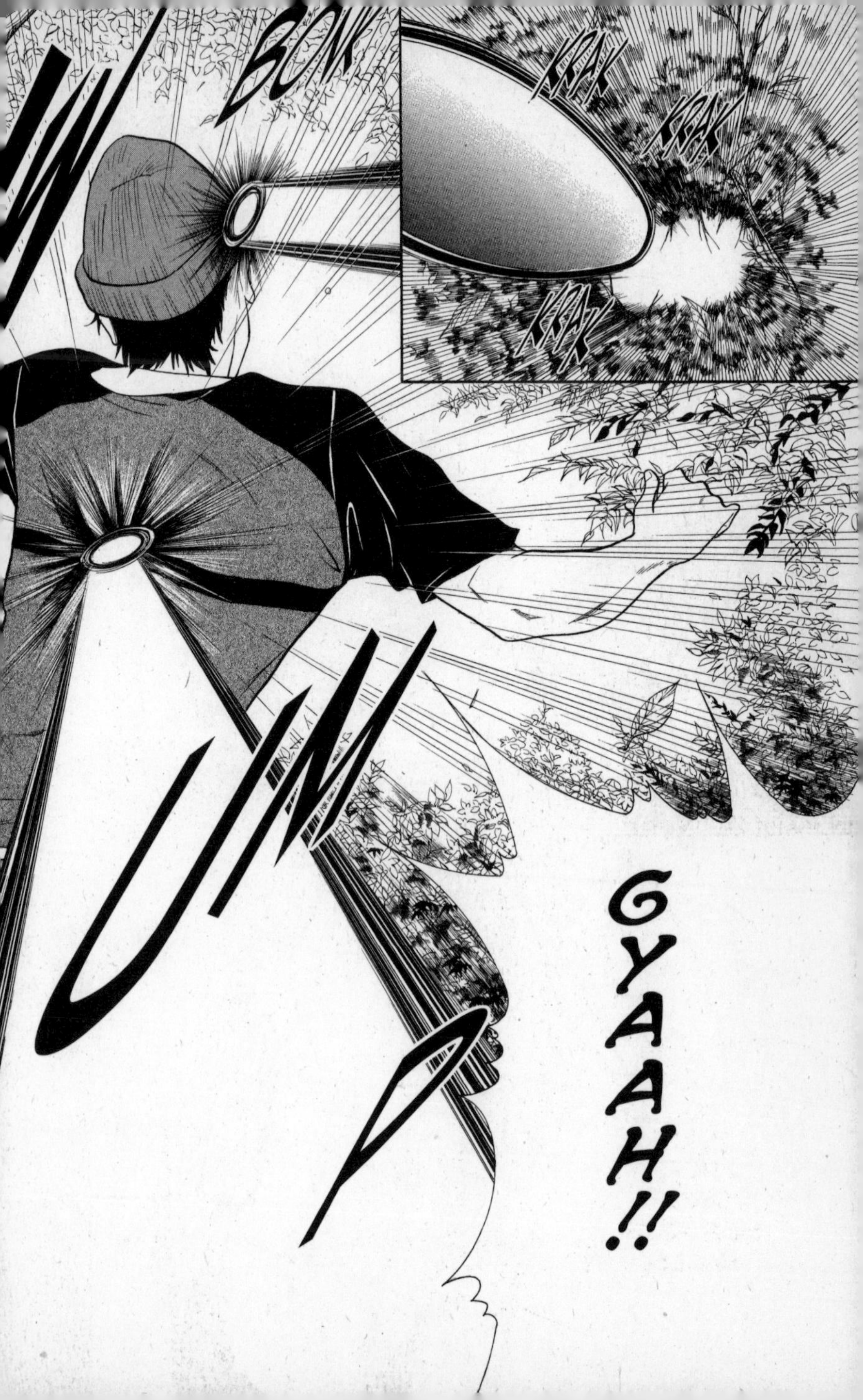
KRAK
KRAK
KRAK
BONK
GYAAH!!

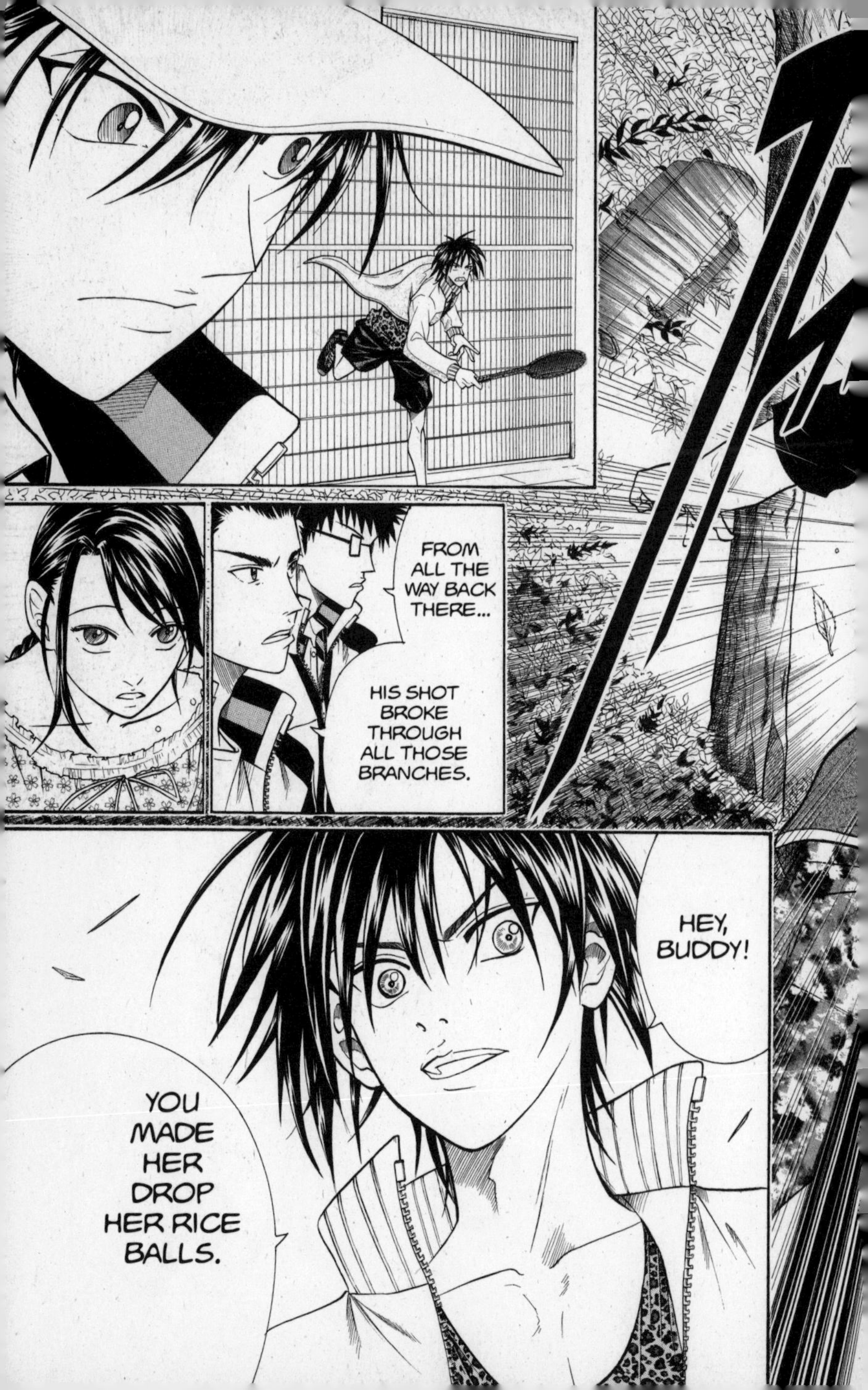
FROM ALL THE WAY BACK THERE...
HIS SHOT BROKE THROUGH ALL THOSE BRANCHES.
HEY, BUDDY!
YOU MADE HER DROP HER RICE BALLS.

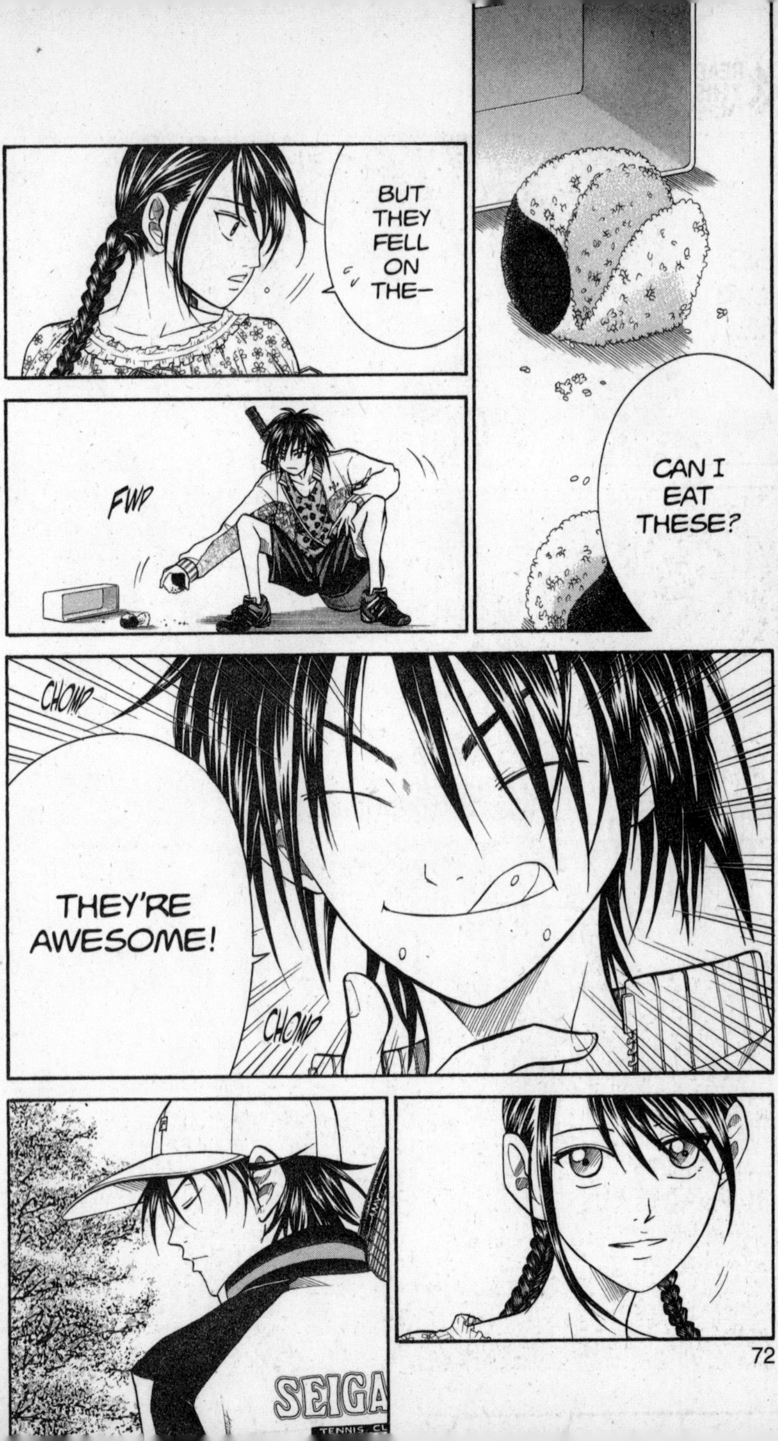
CAN I EAT THESE?
BUT THEY FELL ON THE–
FWP
CHOMP
THEY'RE AWESOME!
CHOMP
SEIGA

READ THIS WAY

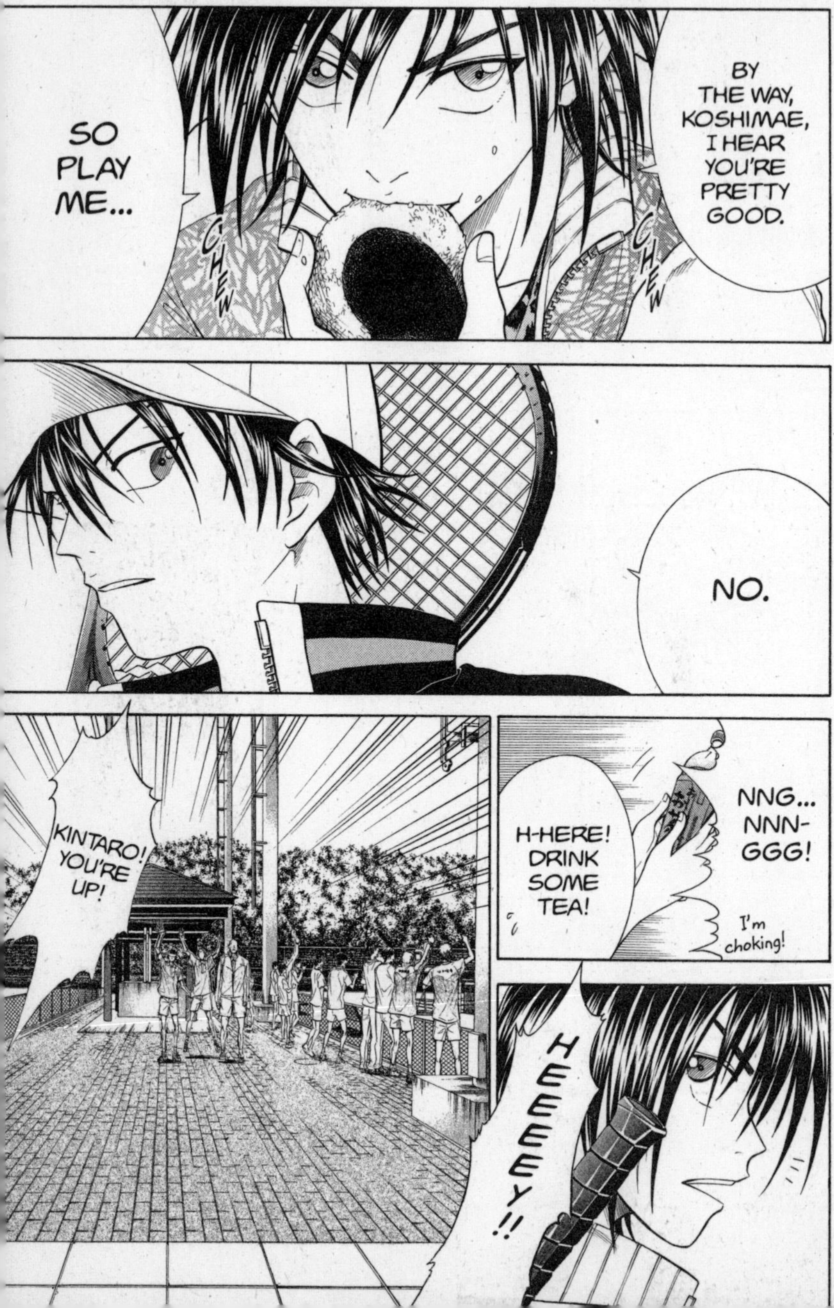
BY THE WAY, KOSHIMAE, I HEAR YOU'RE PRETTY GOOD.
CHEW
CHEW
SO PLAY ME...
NO.
NNG... NNN-GGG!
H-HERE! DRINK SOME TEA!
I'm choking!
HEEEEEY!!
KINTARO! YOU'RE UP!

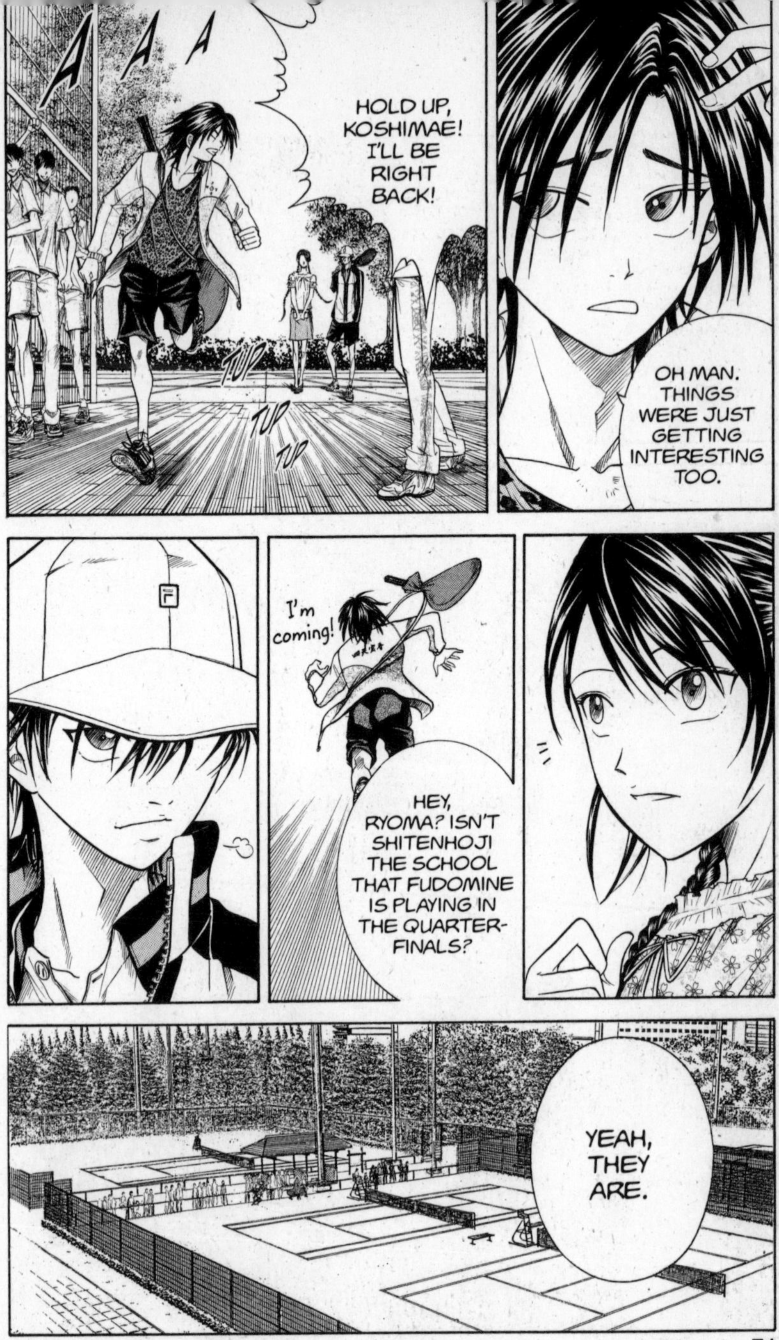
OH MAN. THINGS WERE JUST GETTING INTERESTING TOO.
A A A
HOLD UP, KOSHIMAE! I'LL BE RIGHT BACK!
TUP
TUP
TUP
I'm coming!
HEY, RYOMA? ISN'T SHITENHOJI THE SCHOOL THAT FUDOMINE IS PLAYING IN THE QUARTER-FINALS?
YEAH, THEY ARE.

READ THIS WAY

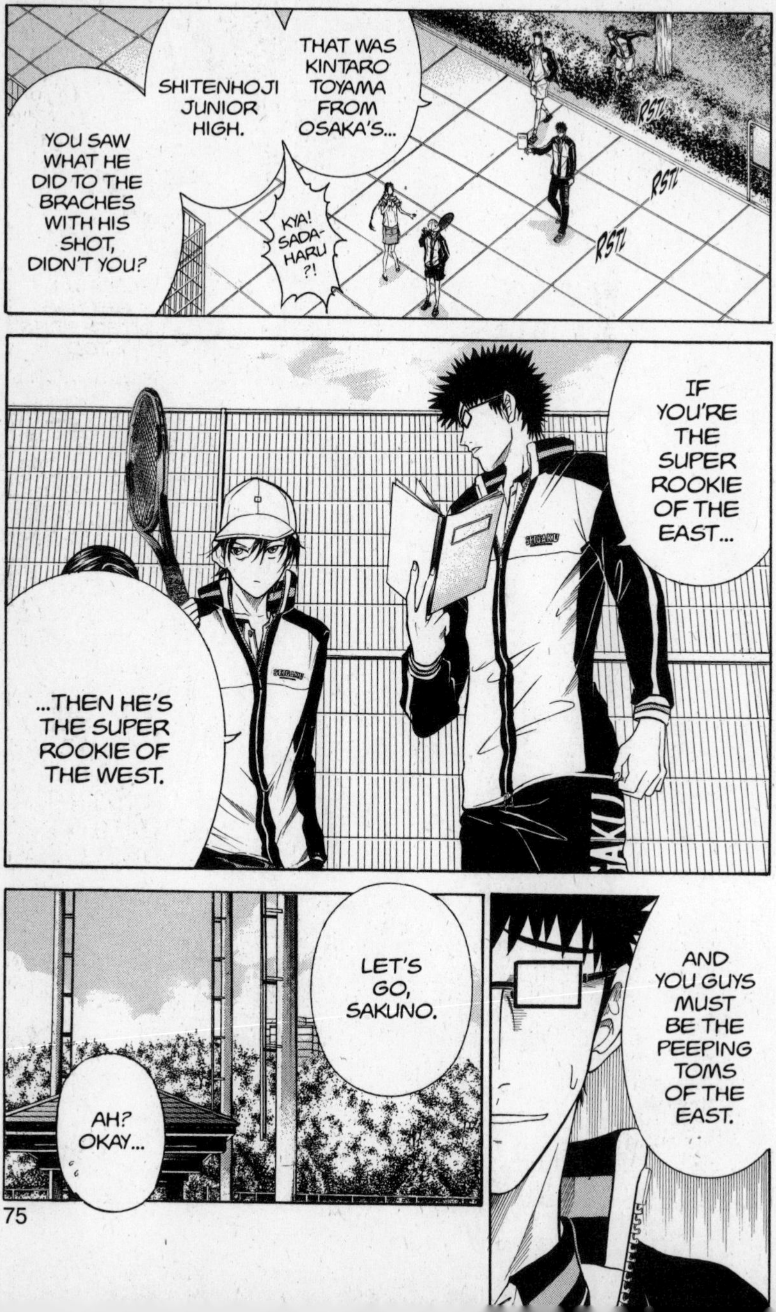
RSTL
RSTL
RSTL
THAT WAS KINTARO TOYAMA FROM OSAKA'S...
SHITENHOJI JUNIOR HIGH.
KYA! SADA-HARU?!
YOU SAW WHAT HE DID TO THE BRACHES WITH HIS SHOT, DIDN'T YOU?
IF YOU'RE THE SUPER ROOKIE OF THE EAST...
...THEN HE'S THE SUPER ROOKIE OF THE WEST.
AND YOU GUYS MUST BE THE PEEPING TOMS OF THE EAST.
LET'S GO, SAKUNO.
AH? OKAY...

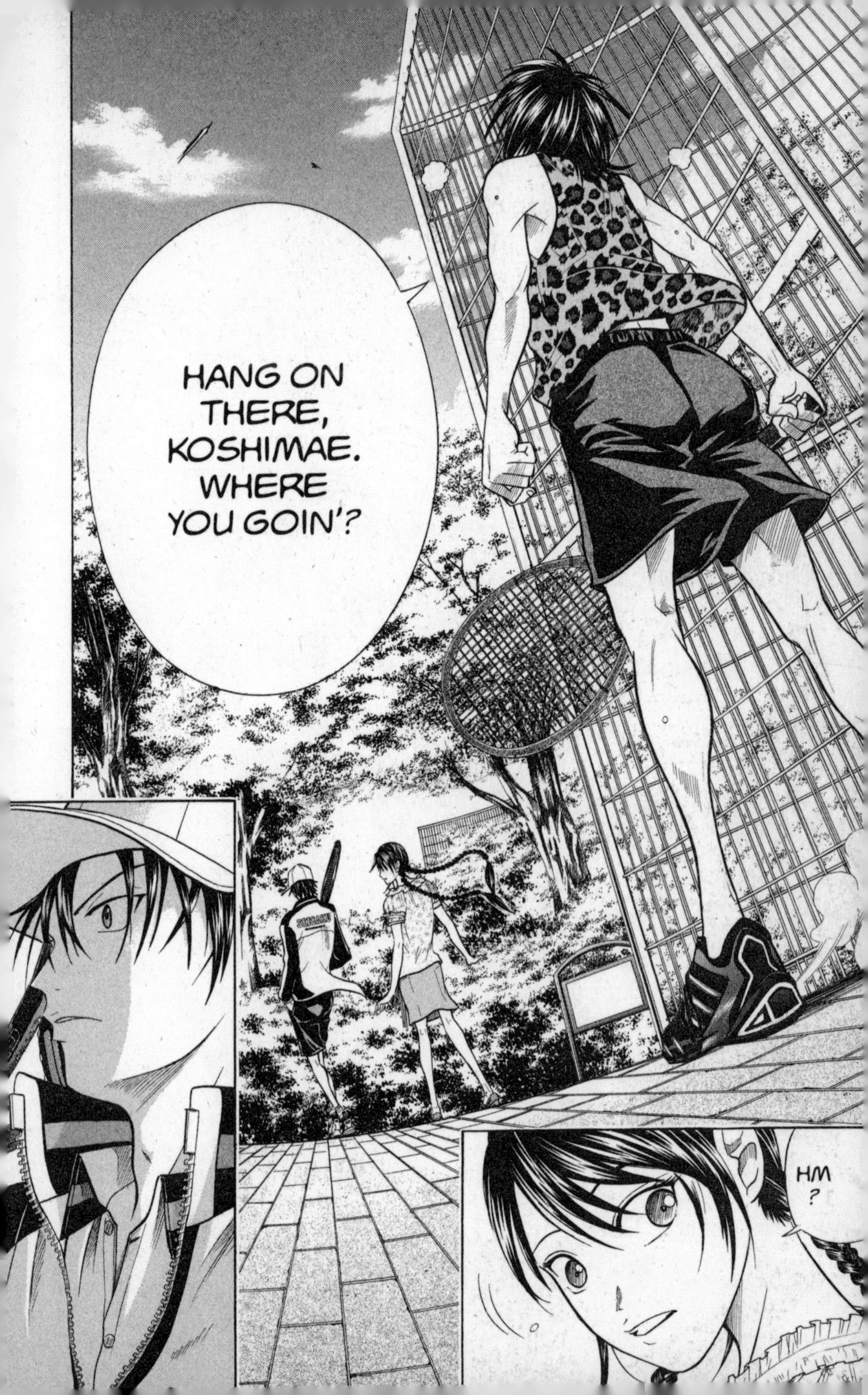
HANG ON THERE, KOSHIMAE. WHERE YOU GOIN'?
HM ?

READ THIS WAY

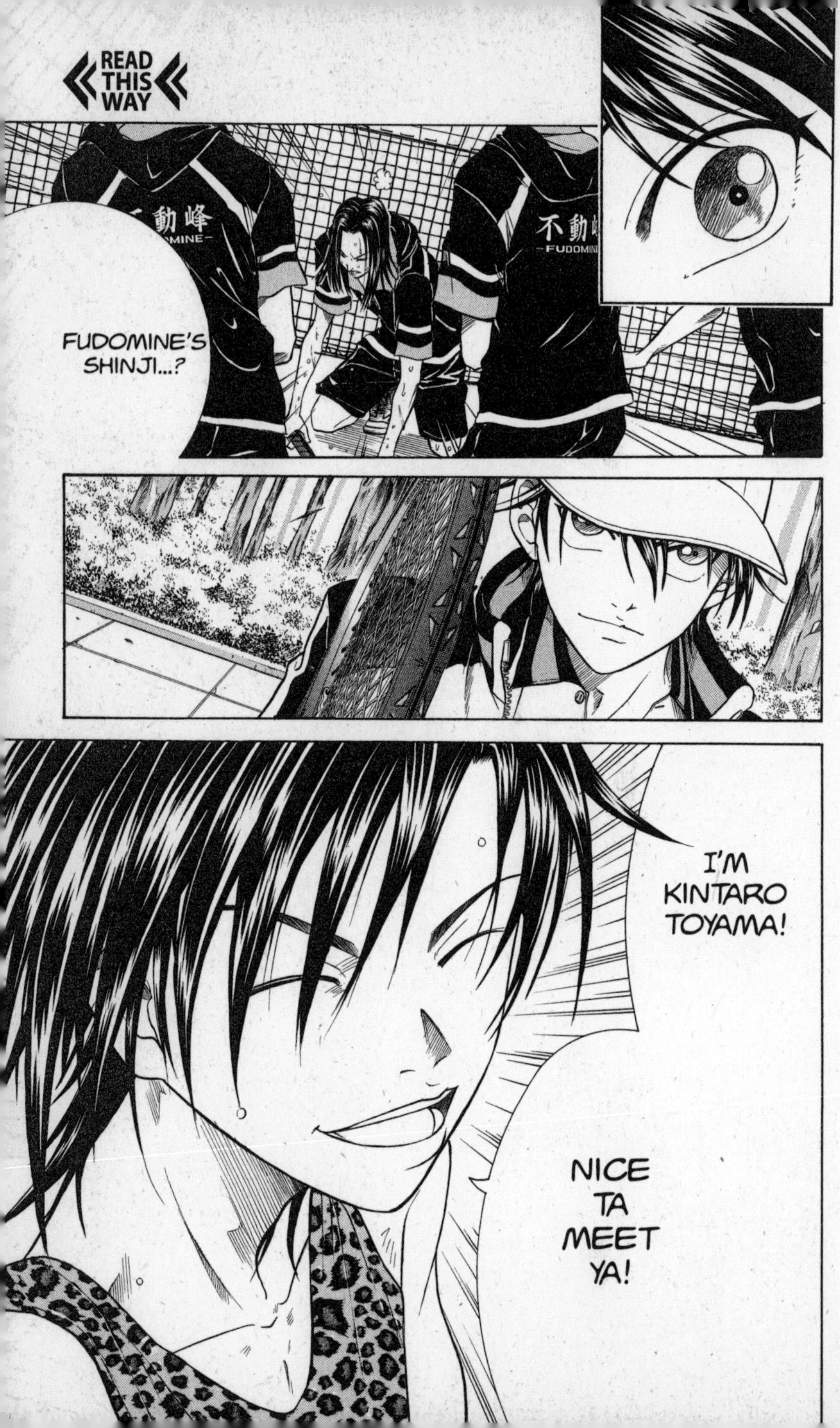
FUDOMINE'S SHINJI...?
I'M KINTARO TOYAMA!
NICE TA MEET YA!

テニスの王子様

THE PRINCE OF TENNIS

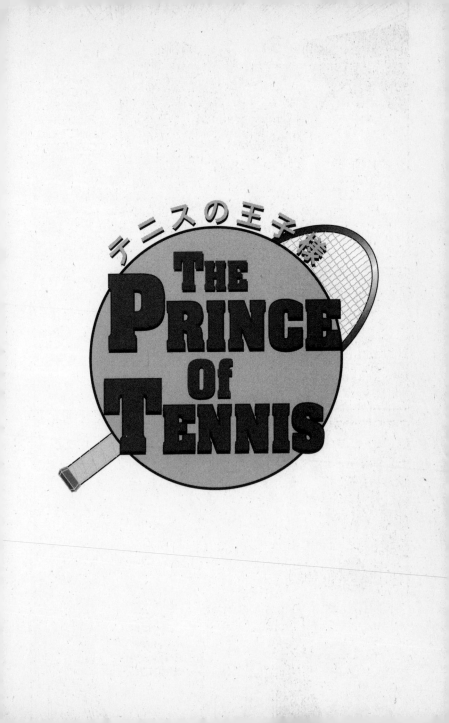

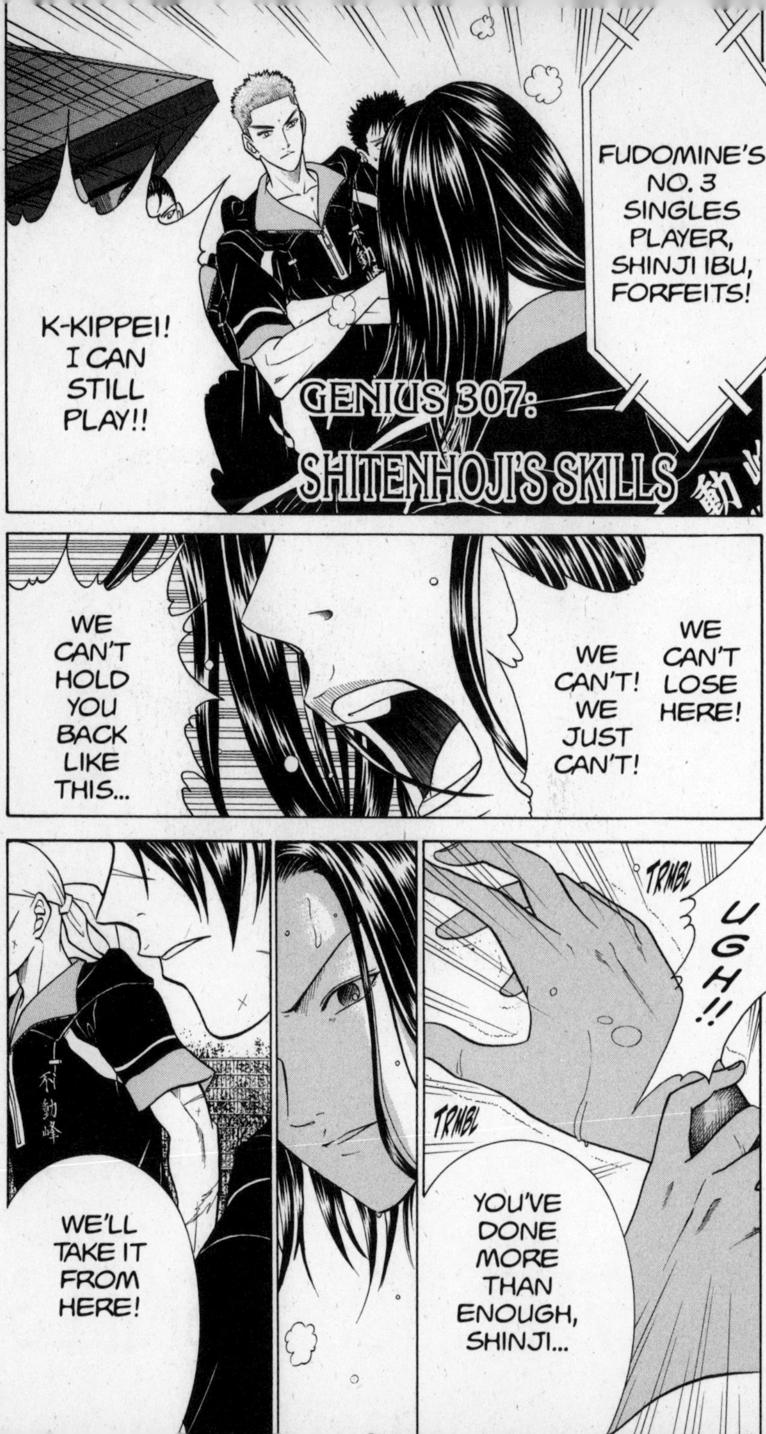
FUDOMINE'S NO. 3 SINGLES PLAYER, SHINJI IBU, FORFEITS!
GENIUS 307: SHITENHOJI'S SKILLS
K-KIPPEI! I CAN STILL PLAY!!
WE CAN'T LOSE HERE!
WE CAN'T! WE JUST CAN'T!
WE CAN'T HOLD YOU BACK LIKE THIS...
TRMBL
UGH!!
TRMBL
YOU'VE DONE MORE THAN ENOUGH, SHINJI...
WE'LL TAKE IT FROM HERE!

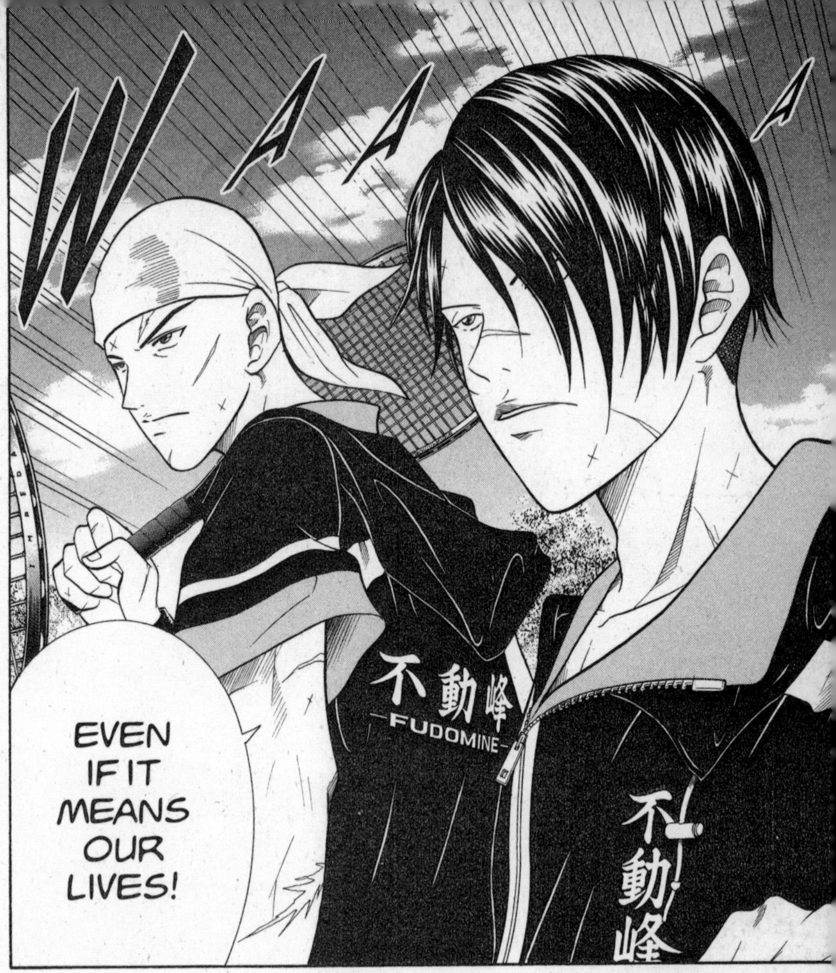
WAAAA
EVEN IF IT MEANS OUR LIVES!
不動峰
—FUDOMINE—
不動峰

GENIUS 307:

SHITENHOJI'S SKILLS

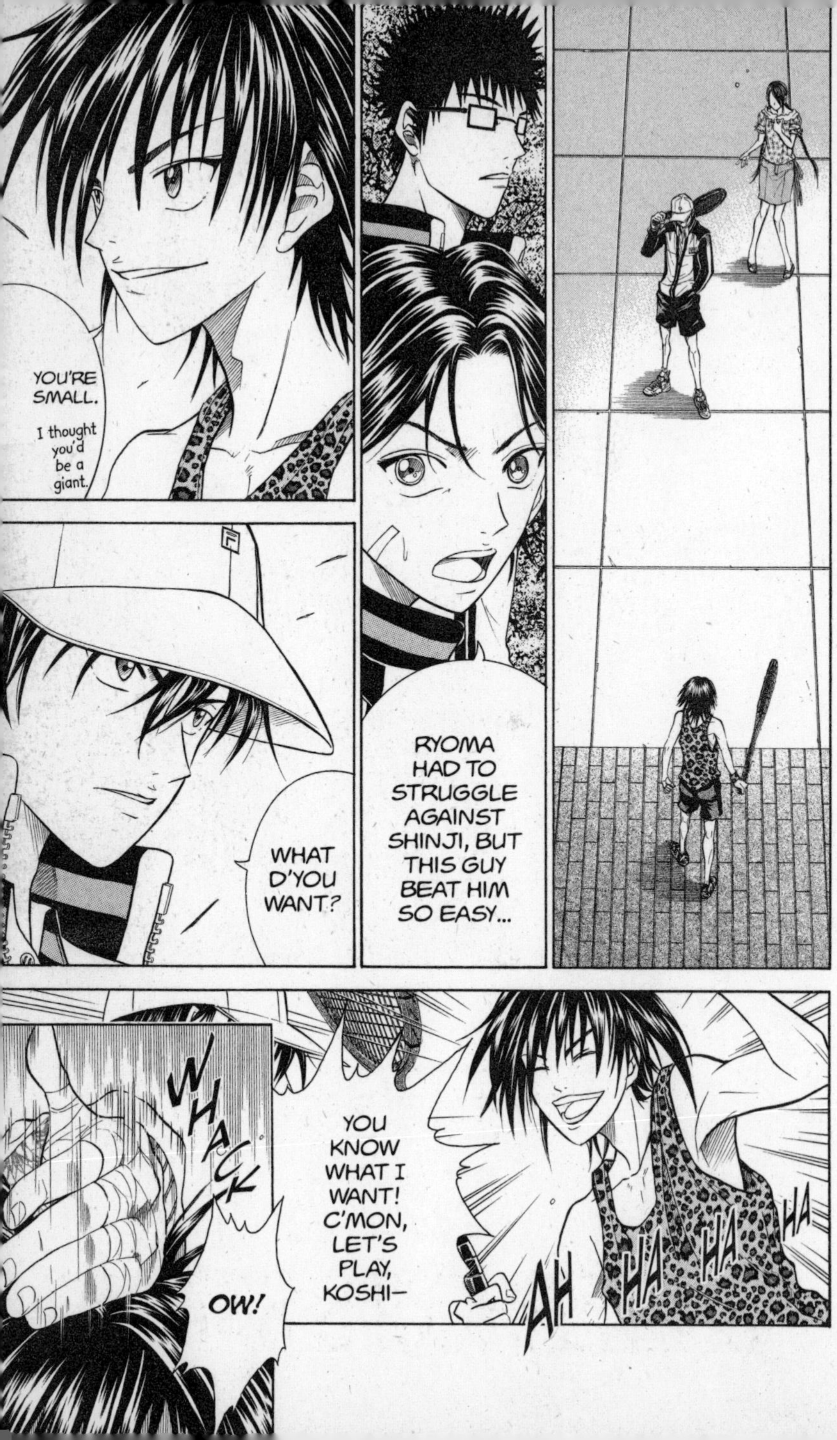
RYOMA HAD TO STRUGGLE AGAINST SHINJI, BUT THIS GUY BEAT HIM SO EASY...
YOU'RE SMALL.
I thought you'd be a giant.
WHAT D'YOU WANT?
YOU KNOW WHAT I WANT! C'MON, LET'S PLAY, KOSHI—
AH HA HA HA HA
WHACK
OW!

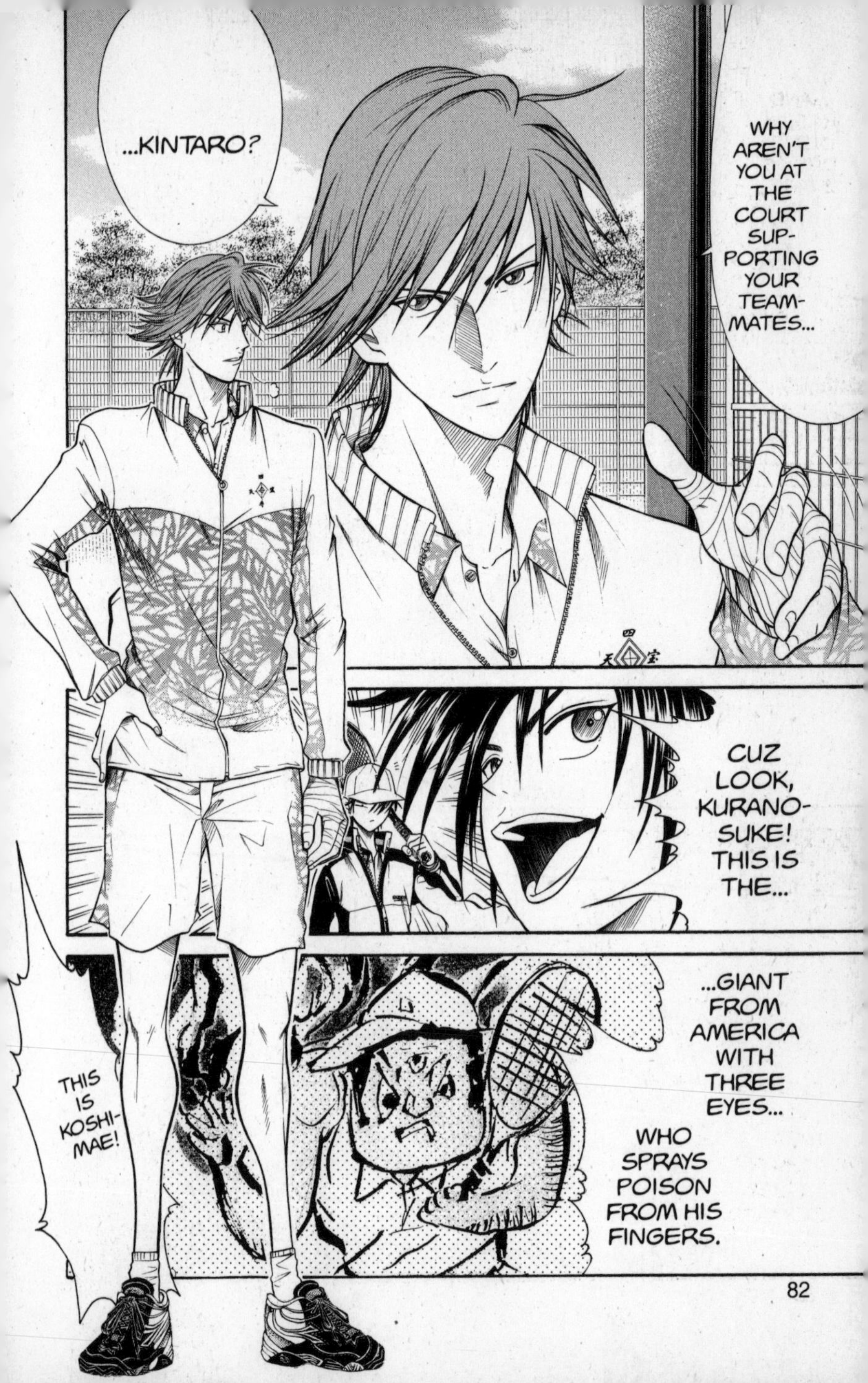
WHY AREN'T YOU AT THE COURT SUPPORTING YOUR TEAMMATES...
...KINTARO?
CUZ LOOK, KURANOSUKE! THIS IS THE...
...GIANT FROM AMERICA WITH THREE EYES...
WHO SPRAYS POISON FROM HIS FINGERS.
THIS IS KOSHIMAE!

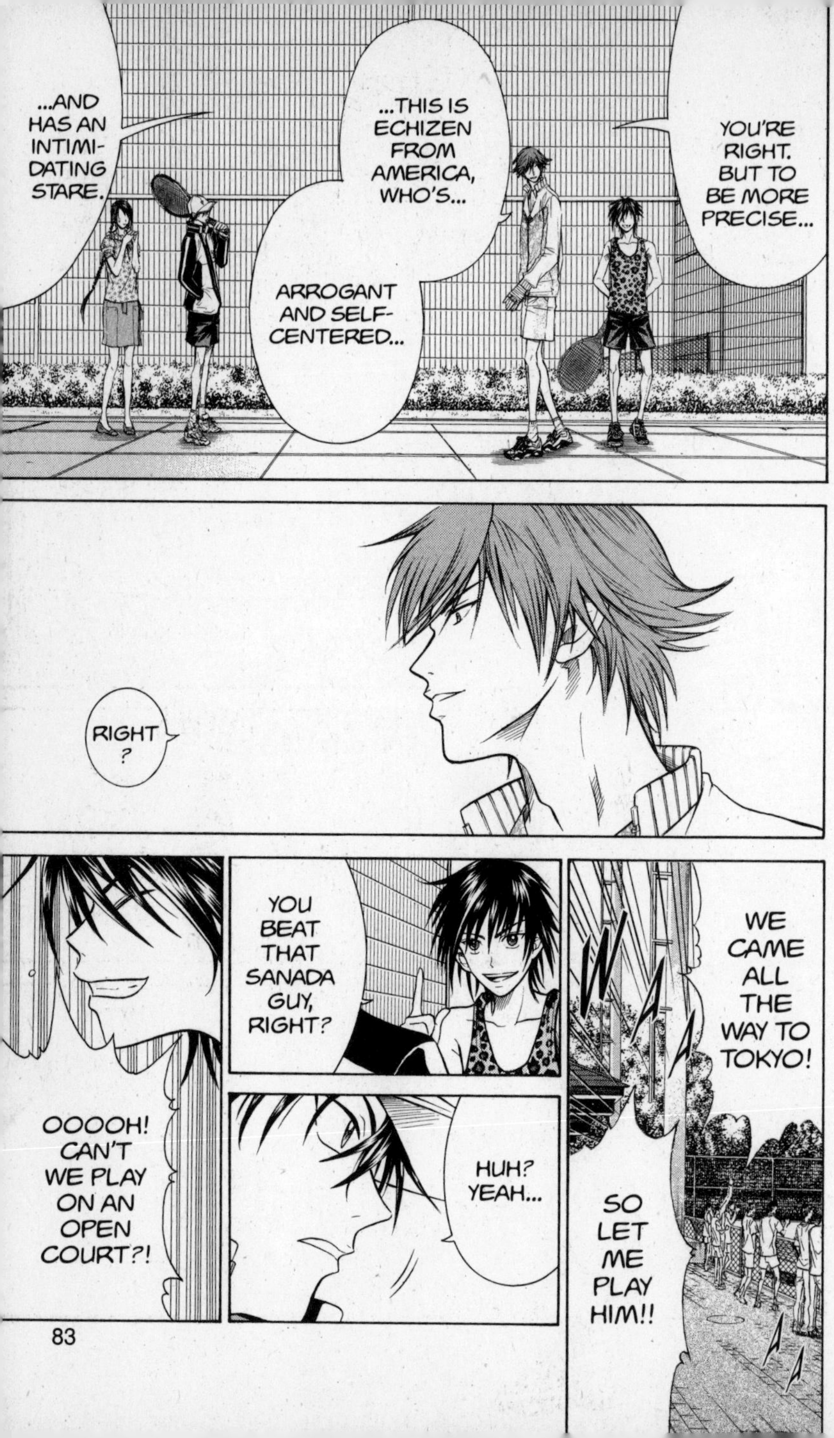
YOU'RE RIGHT. BUT TO BE MORE PRECISE...
...THIS IS ECHIZEN FROM AMERICA, WHO'S...
ARROGANT AND SELF-CENTERED...
...AND HAS AN INTIMIDATING STARE.
RIGHT?
WE CAME ALL THE WAY TO TOKYO!
SO LET ME PLAY HIM!!
YOU BEAT THAT SANADA GUY, RIGHT?
HUH? YEAH...
OOOOH! CAN'T WE PLAY ON AN OPEN COURT?!

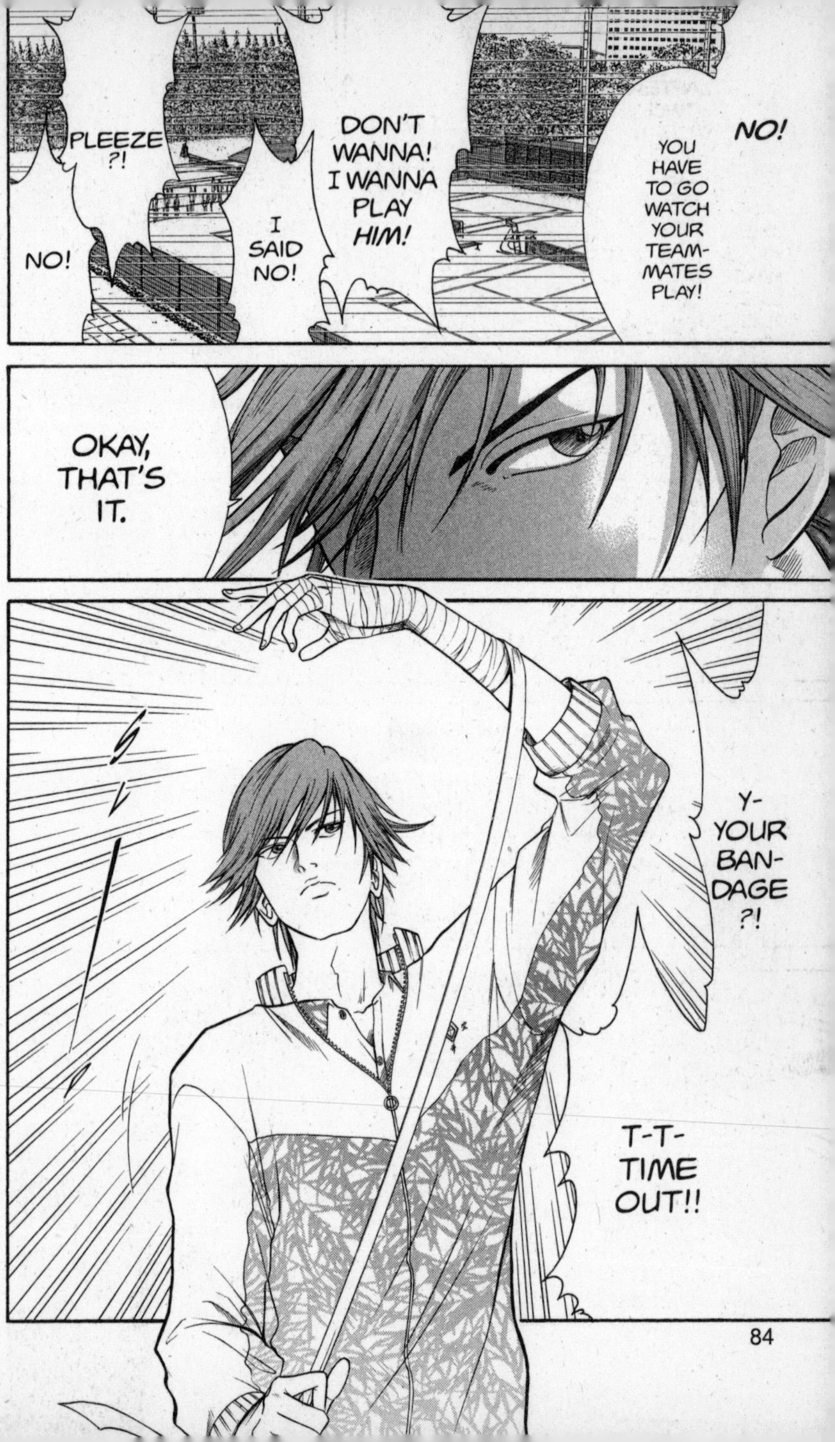
NO!
YOU HAVE TO GO WATCH YOUR TEAM-MATES PLAY!
DON'T WANNA! I WANNA PLAY *HIM!*
I SAID NO!
PLEEZE ?!
NO!
OKAY, THAT'S IT.
Y-YOUR BAN-DAGE ?!
T-T-TIME OUT!!

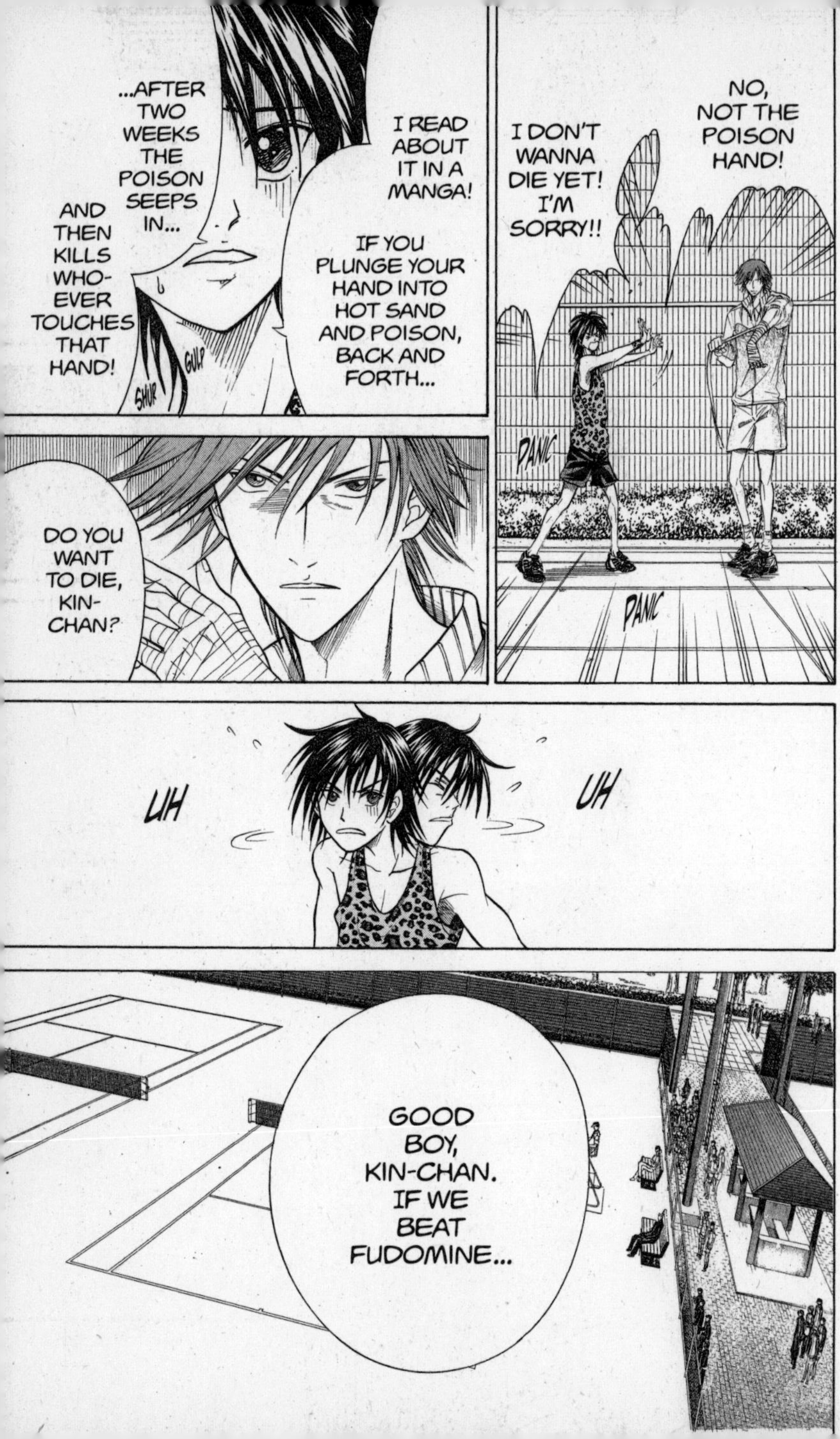
NO, NOT THE POISON HAND!
I DON'T WANNA DIE YET! I'M SORRY!!
PANIC
PANIC
I READ ABOUT IT IN A MANGA!
IF YOU PLUNGE YOUR HAND INTO HOT SAND AND POISON, BACK AND FORTH...
...AFTER TWO WEEKS THE POISON SEEPS IN...
AND THEN KILLS WHO-EVER TOUCHES THAT HAND!
GULP
SHUP
DO YOU WANT TO DIE, KIN-CHAN?
UH
UH
GOOD BOY, KIN-CHAN. IF WE BEAT FUDOMINE...

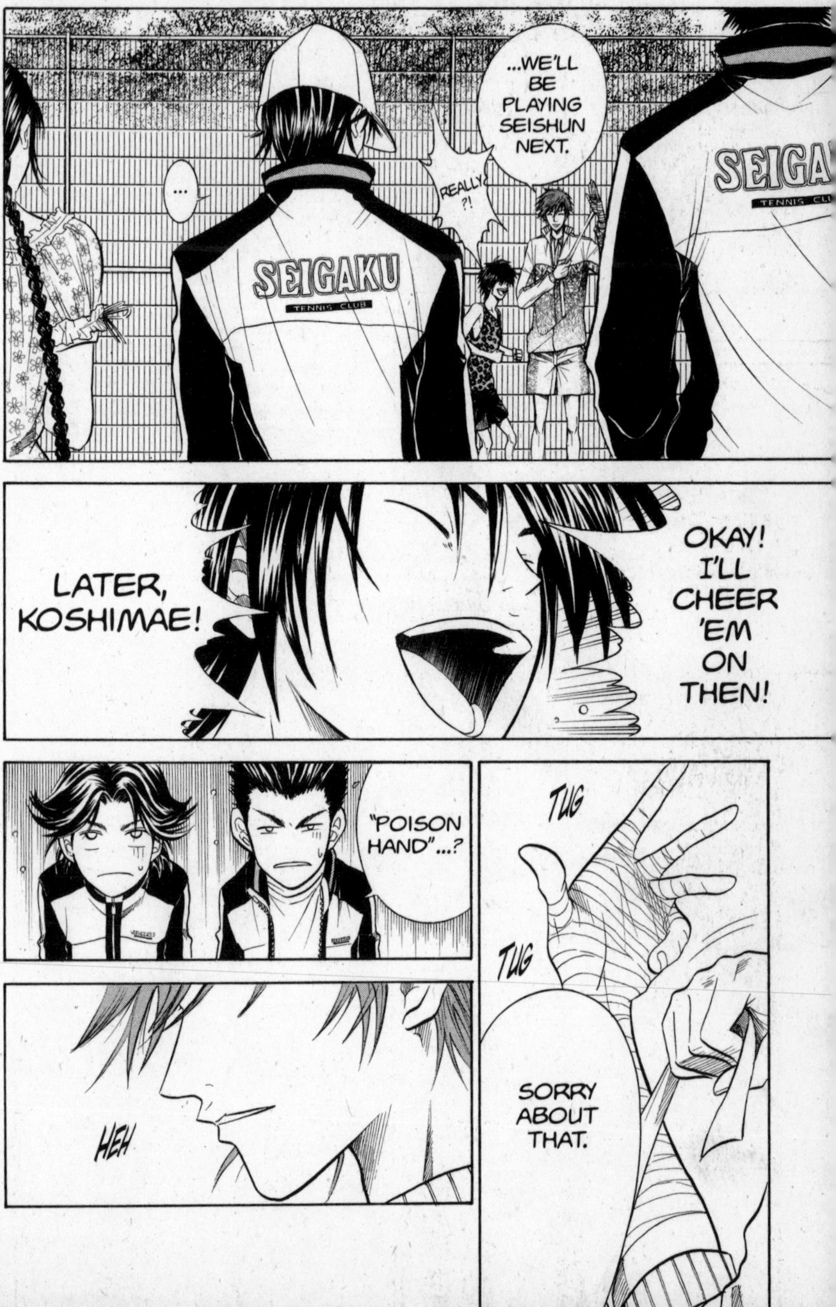
...WE'LL BE PLAYING SEISHUN NEXT.
REALLY?!
...
OKAY! I'LL CHEER 'EM ON THEN!
LATER, KOSHIMAE!
TUG
TUG
SORRY ABOUT THAT.
"POISON HAND"...?
HEH

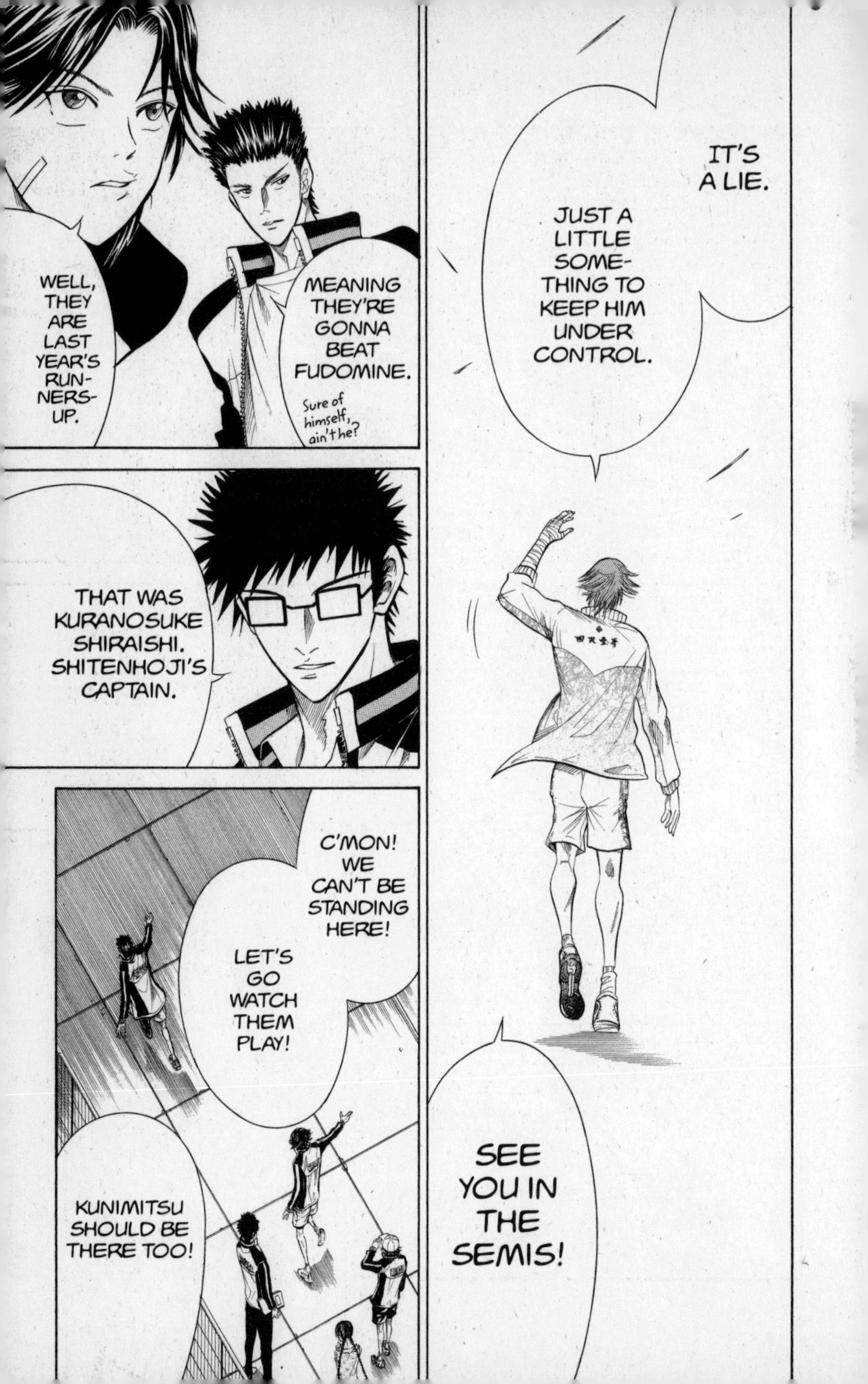
IT'S A LIE.
JUST A LITTLE SOMETHING TO KEEP HIM UNDER CONTROL.
SEE YOU IN THE SEMIS!
MEANING THEY'RE GONNA BEAT FUDOMINE.
Sure of himself, ain't he?
WELL, THEY ARE LAST YEAR'S RUNNERS-UP.
THAT WAS KURANOSUKE SHIRAISHI. SHITENHOJI'S CAPTAIN.
C'MON! WE CAN'T BE STANDING HERE!
LET'S GO WATCH THEM PLAY!
KUNIMITSU SHOULD BE THERE TOO!

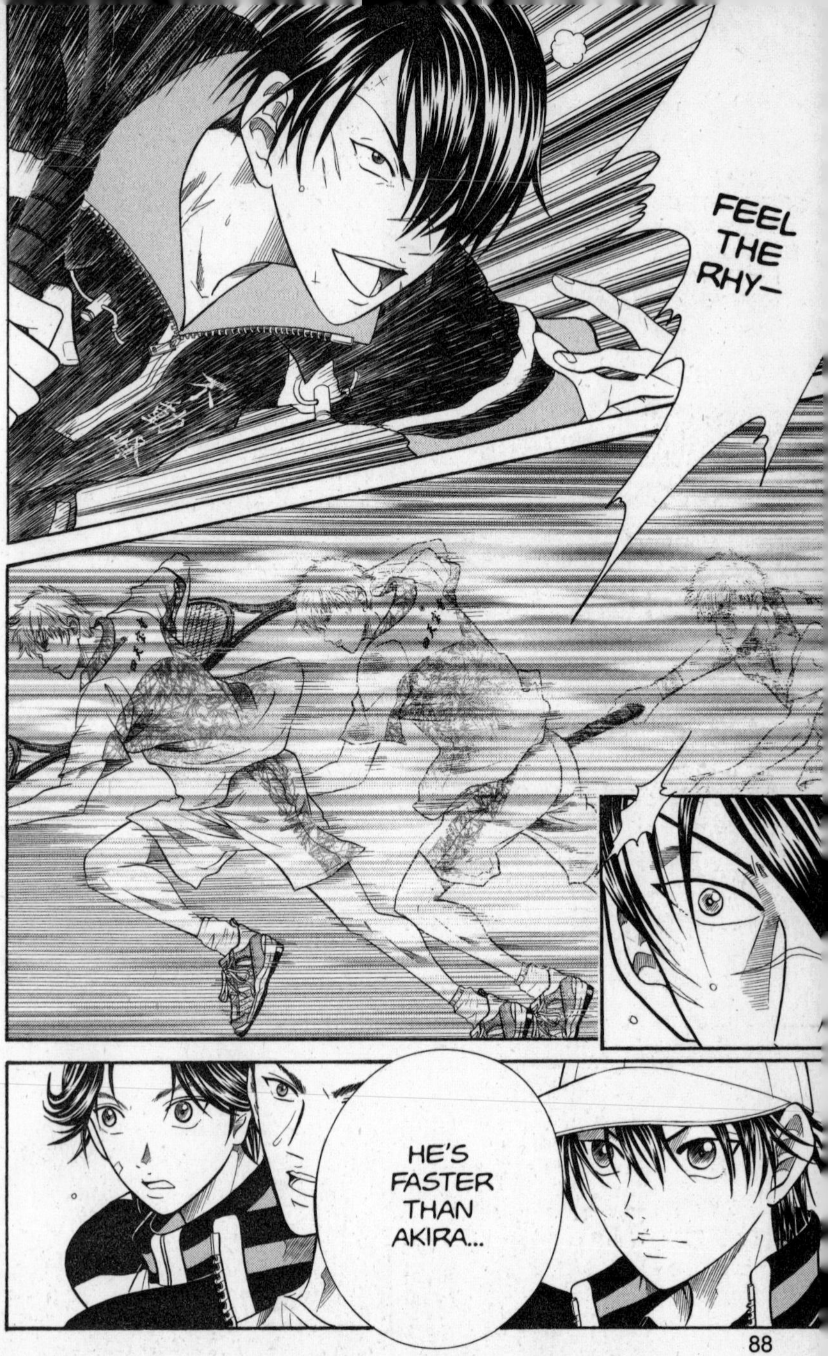
FEEL THE RHY–
HE'S FASTER THAN AKIRA...

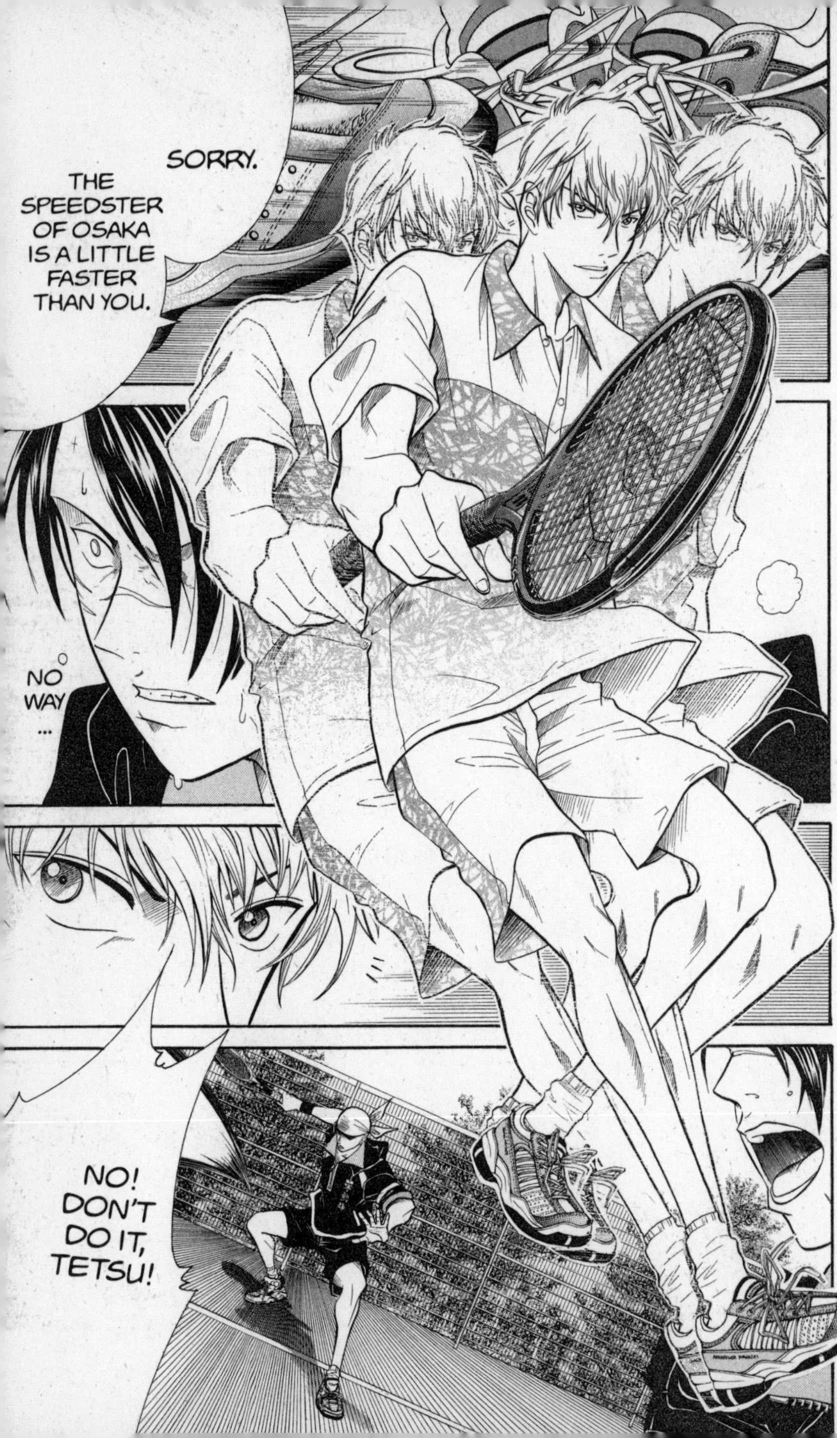
SORRY.
THE SPEEDSTER OF OSAKA IS A LITTLE FASTER THAN YOU.
NO WAY ...
NO! DON'T DO IT, TETSU!

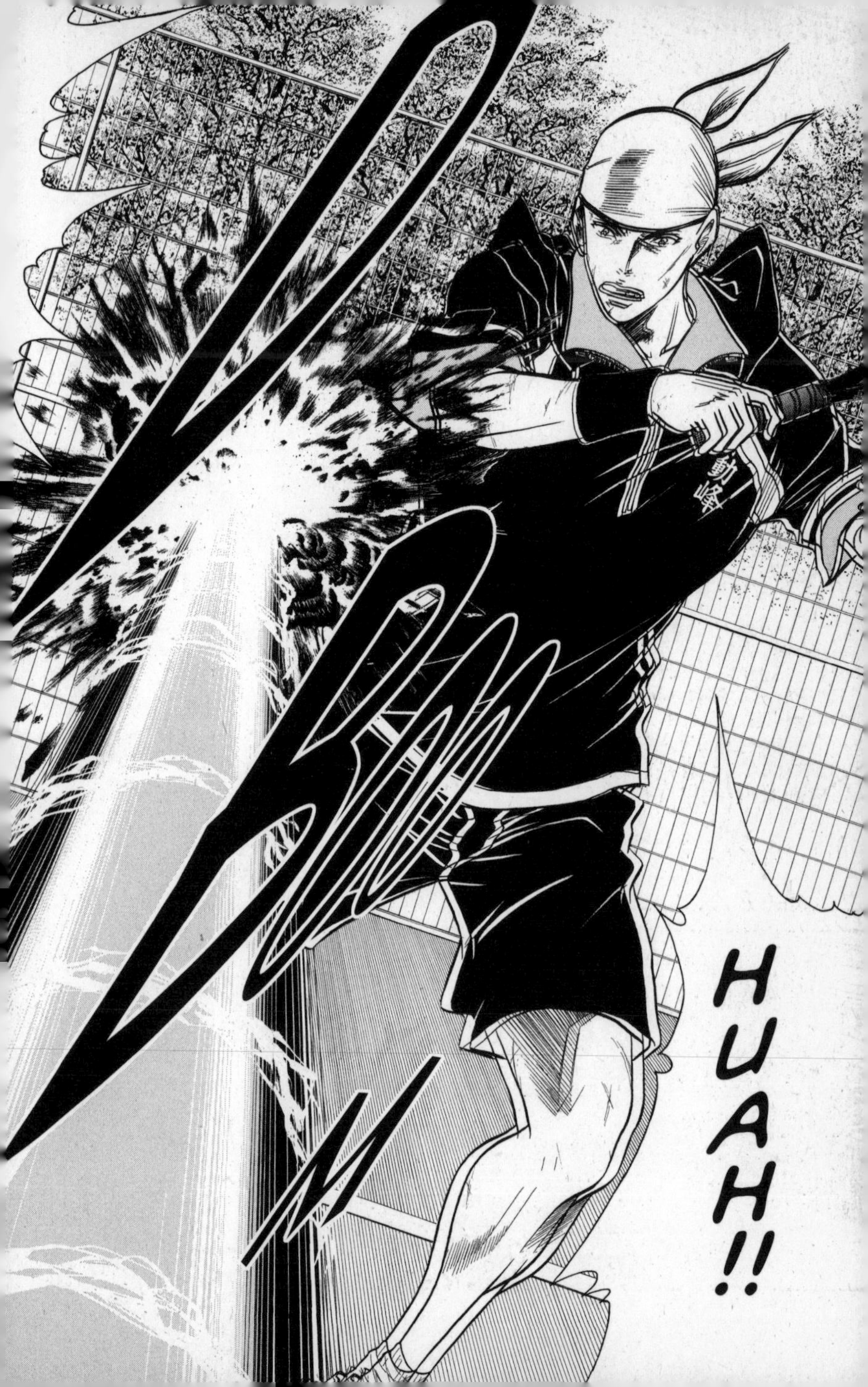
動峰
HUAH!!

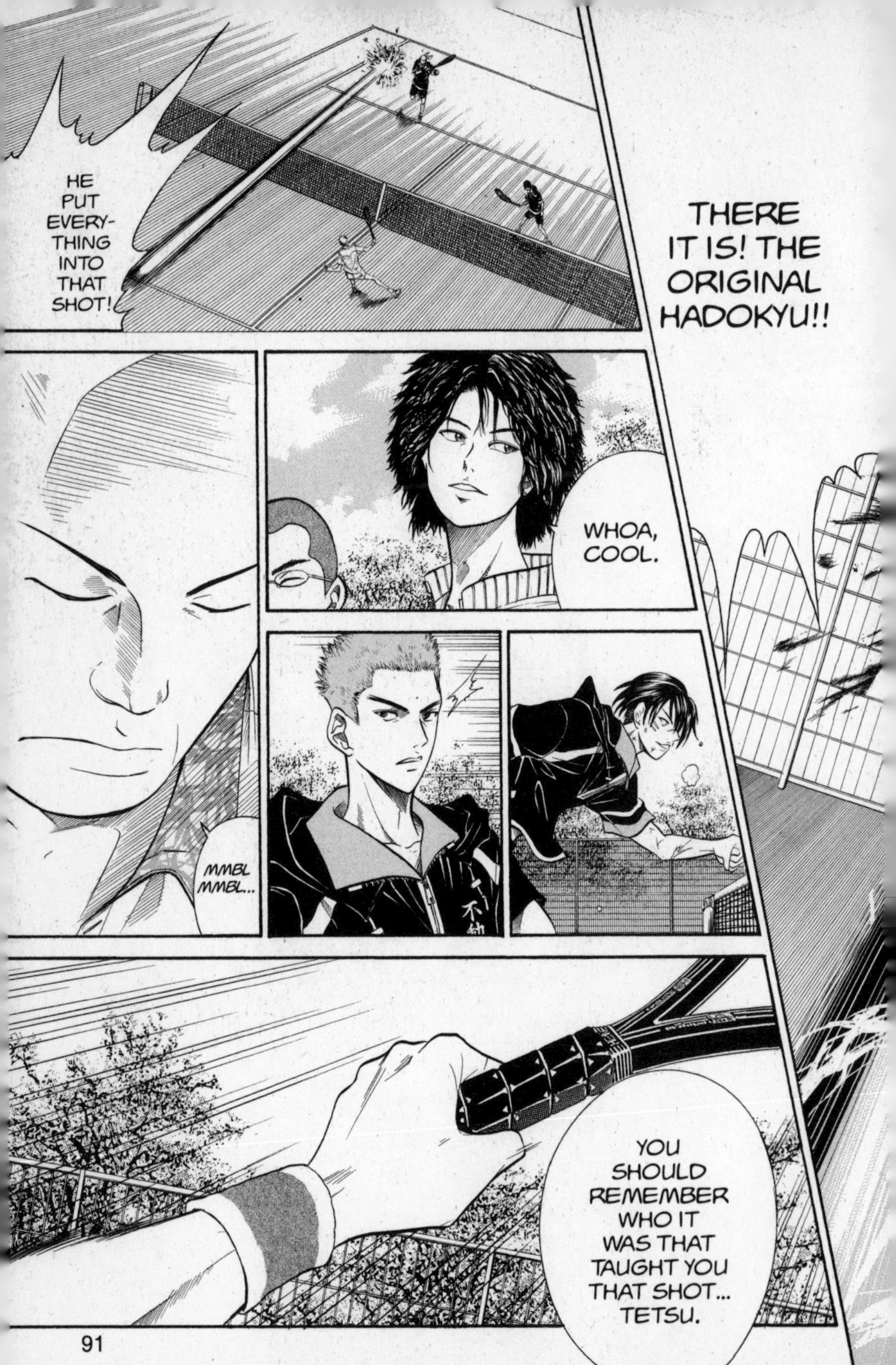
THERE IT IS! THE ORIGINAL HADOKYU!!
HE PUT EVERY-THING INTO THAT SHOT!
WHOA, COOL.
MMBL MMBL...
YOU SHOULD REMEMBER WHO IT WAS THAT TAUGHT YOU THAT SHOT... TETSU.

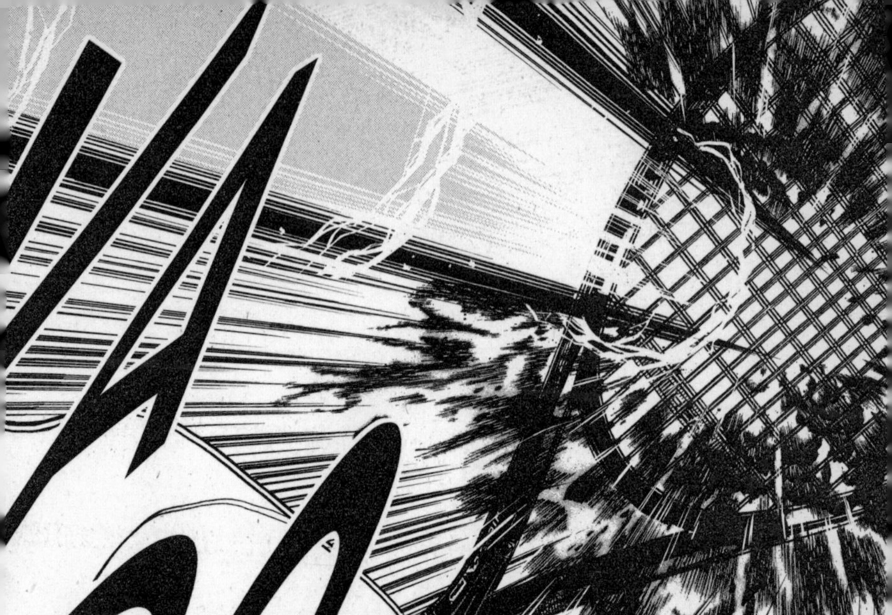

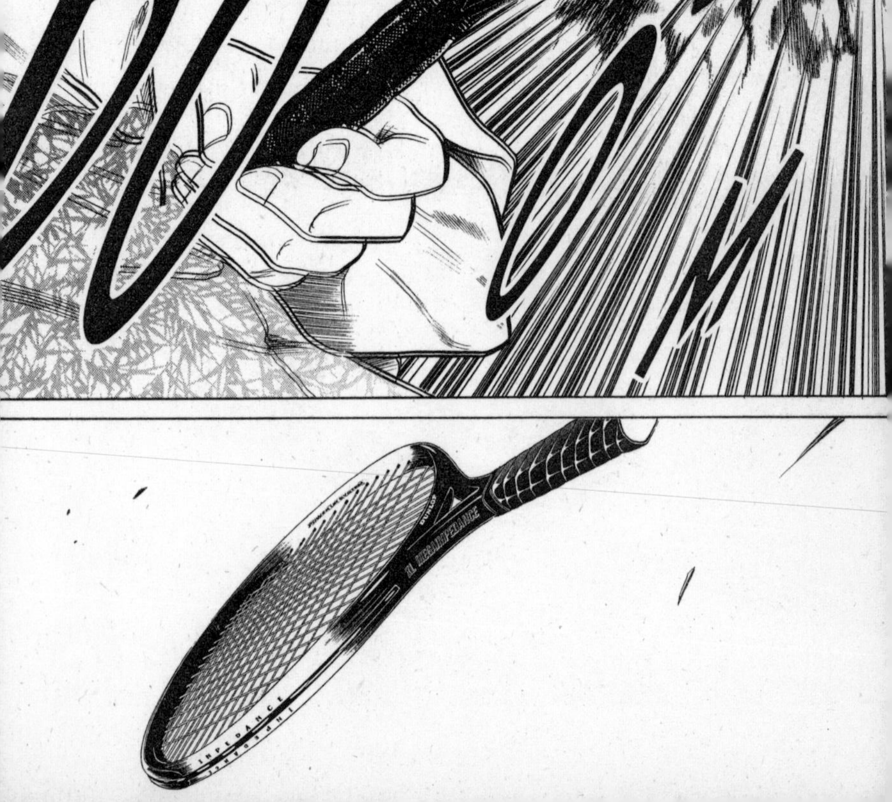

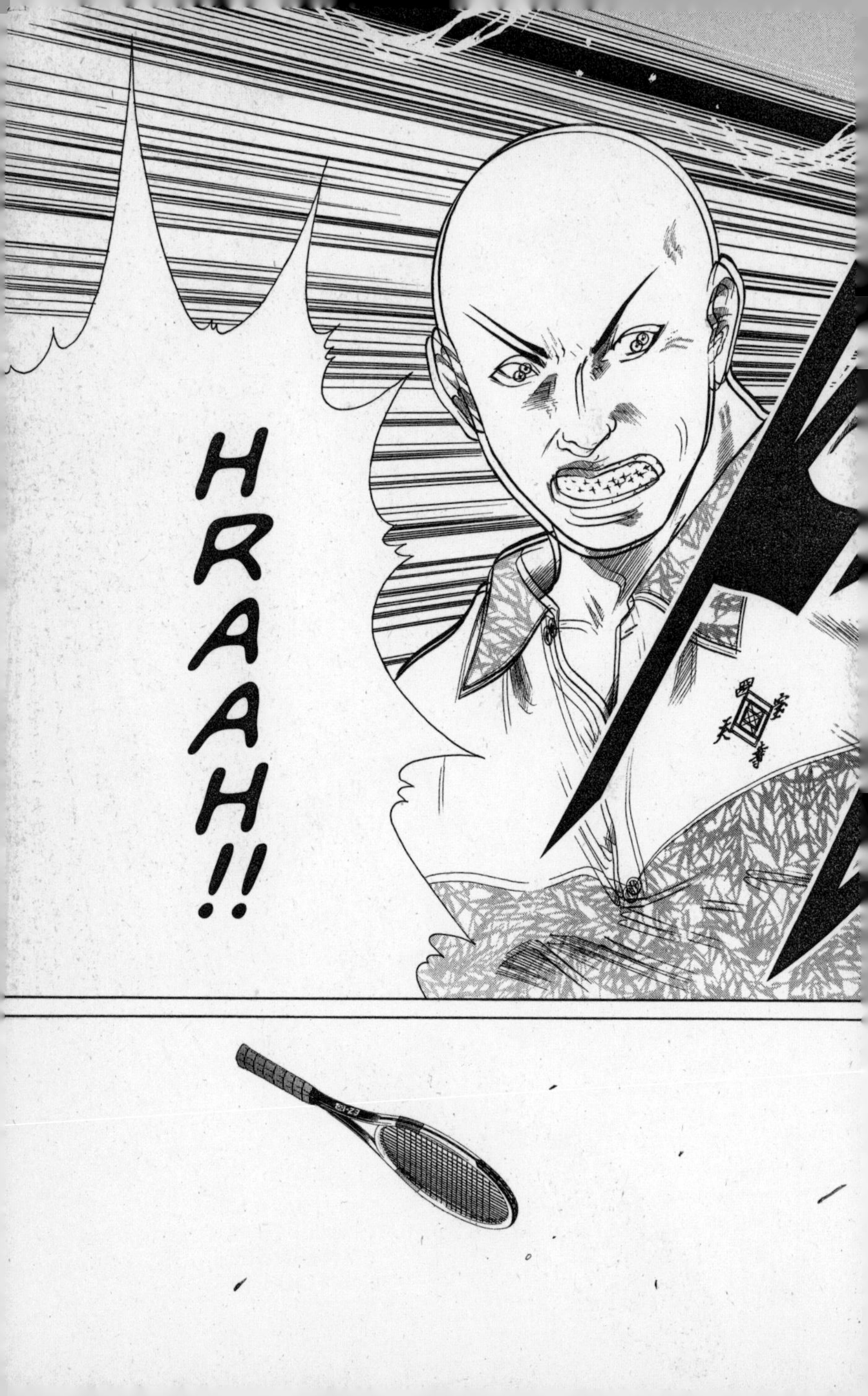
HRAAH!!

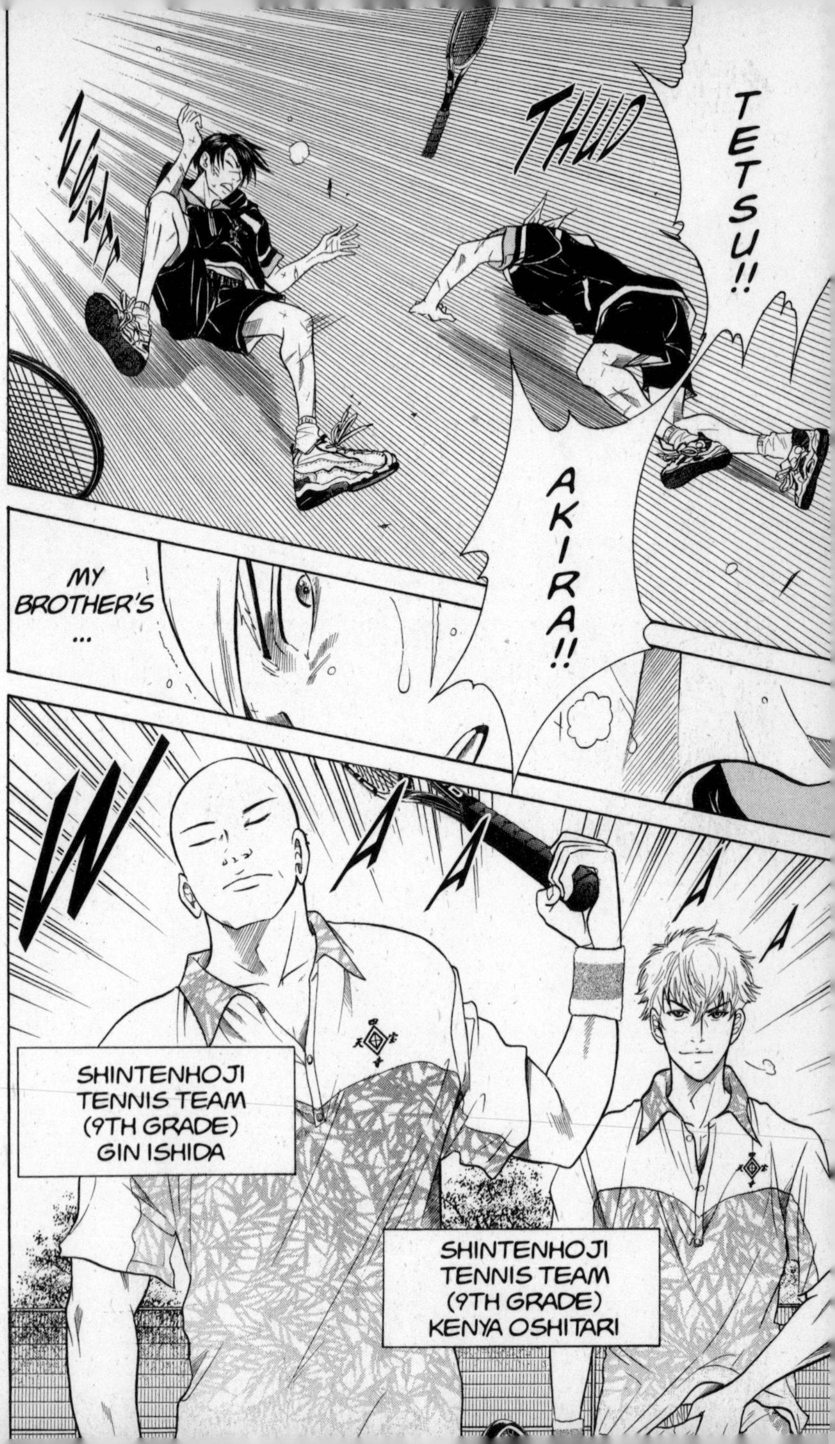
TETSU!!
THUD
AKIRA!!
MY BROTHER'S ...
SHINTENHOJI TENNIS TEAM (9TH GRADE) KENYA OSHITARI
SHINTENHOJI TENNIS TEAM (9TH GRADE) GIN ISHIDA

READ THIS WAY

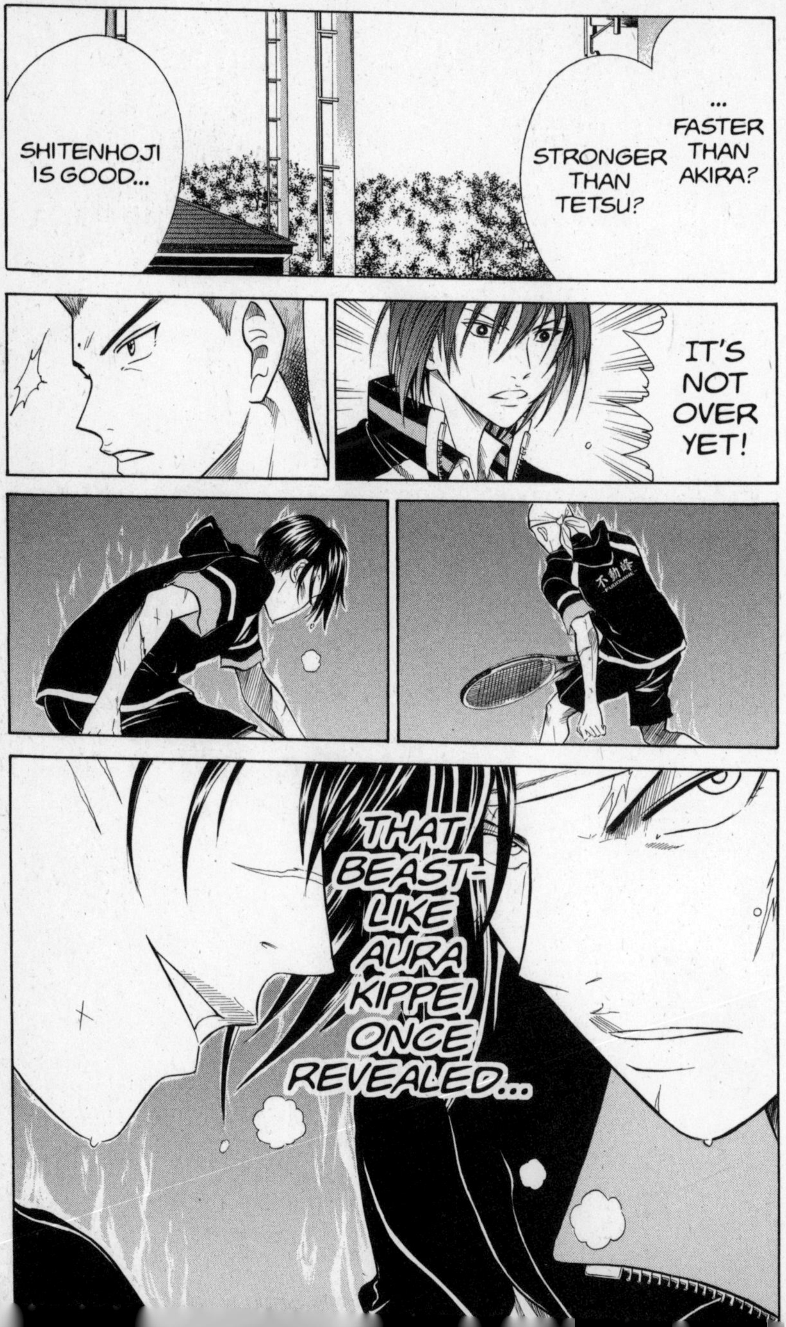
... FASTER THAN AKIRA?
STRONGER THAN TETSU?
SHITENHOJI IS GOOD...
IT'S NOT OVER YET!
THAT BEAST-LIKE AURA KIPPEI ONCE REVEALED...

テニスの王子様

THE PRINCE OF TENNIS

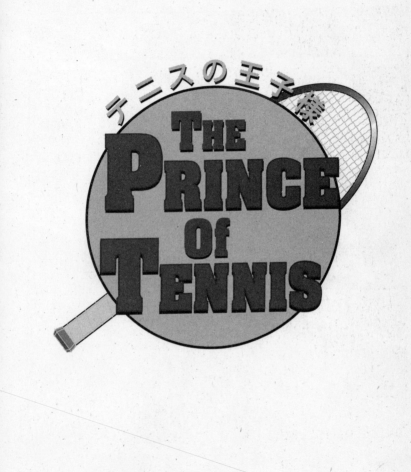

5TH GAME NO. 1 SINGLES	4TH GAME NO. 1 DOUBLES		3RD GAME NO. 2 SINGLES	2ND GAME NO. 2 DOUBLES		1ST GAME NO. 3 SINGLES
MASAYA SAKURAI (8TH GRADE) BLOOD TYPE O	KYOSUKE UCHIMURA (8TH GRADE) BLOOD TYPE B	TATSUNORI MORI (8TH GRADE) BLOOD TYPE A	KIPPEI TACHIBANA (9TH GRADE) BLOOD TYPE O	AKIRA KAMIO (8TH GRADE) BLOOD TYPE O	TETSU ISHIDA (8TH GRADE) BLOOD TYPE O	SHINJI IBU (8TH GRADE) BLOOD TYPE AB

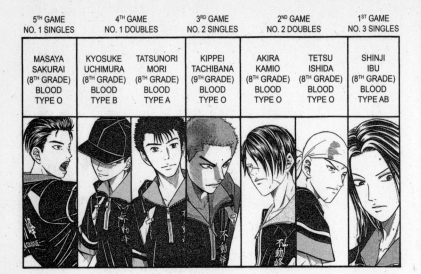

GENIUS 308:

TO GET ONE STEP CLOSER

KURANO-SUKE SHIRAISHI (9TH GRADE) BLOOD TYPE B	YUJI HITOJI (9TH GRADE) BLOOD TYPE B	KOHARU KONJIKI (9TH GRADE) BLOOD TYPE B	SENRI CHITOSE (9TH GRADE) BLOOD TYPE A	KENYA OSHITARI (9TH GRADE) BLOOD TYPE B	GIN ISHIDA (9TH GRADE) BLOOD TYPE O	KINTARO TOYAMA (7TH GRADE) BLOOD TYPE B

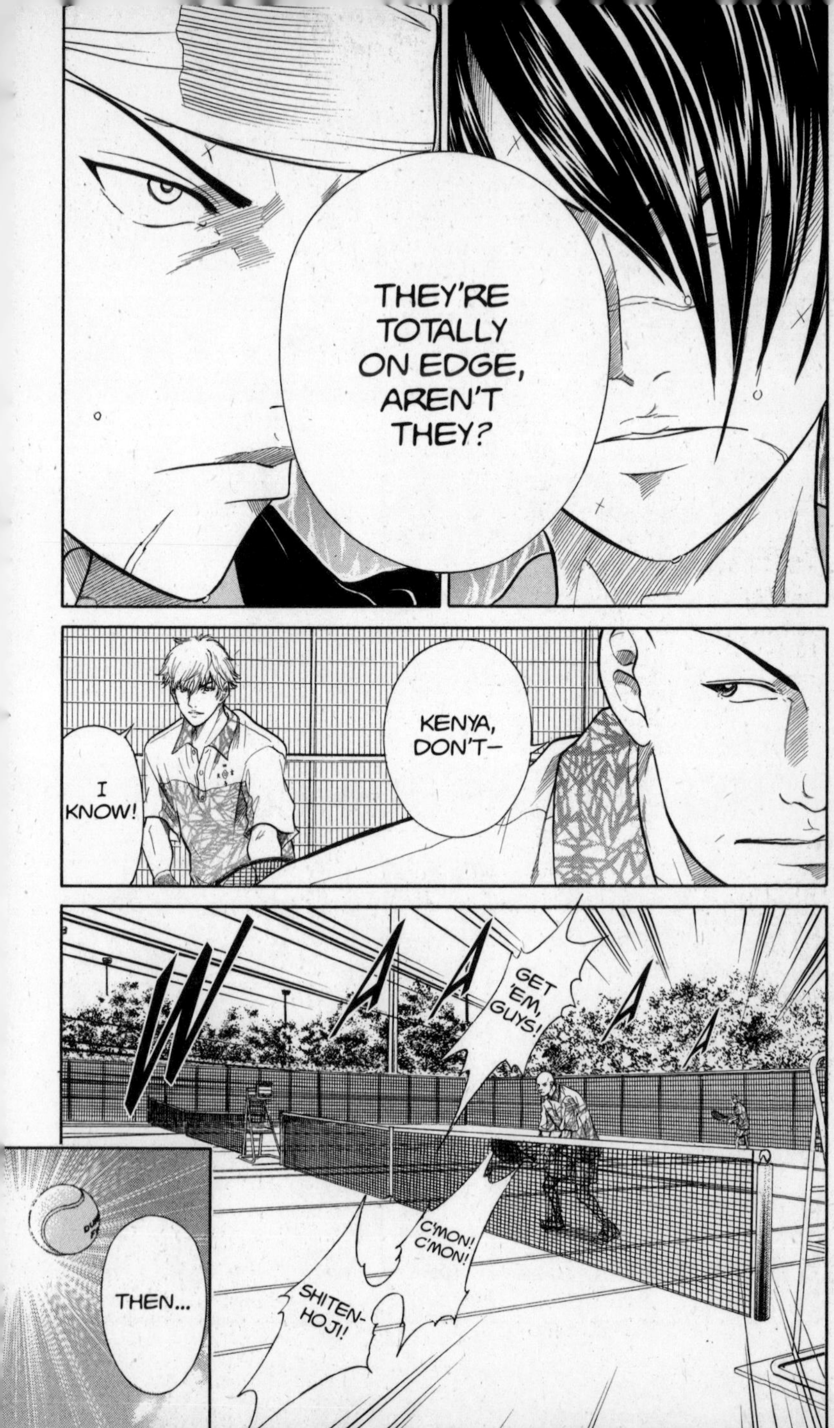
THEY'RE TOTALLY ON EDGE, AREN'T THEY?
KENYA, DON'T—
I KNOW!
GET 'EM, GUYS!
C'MON! C'MON!
SHITEN-HOJI!
THEN...

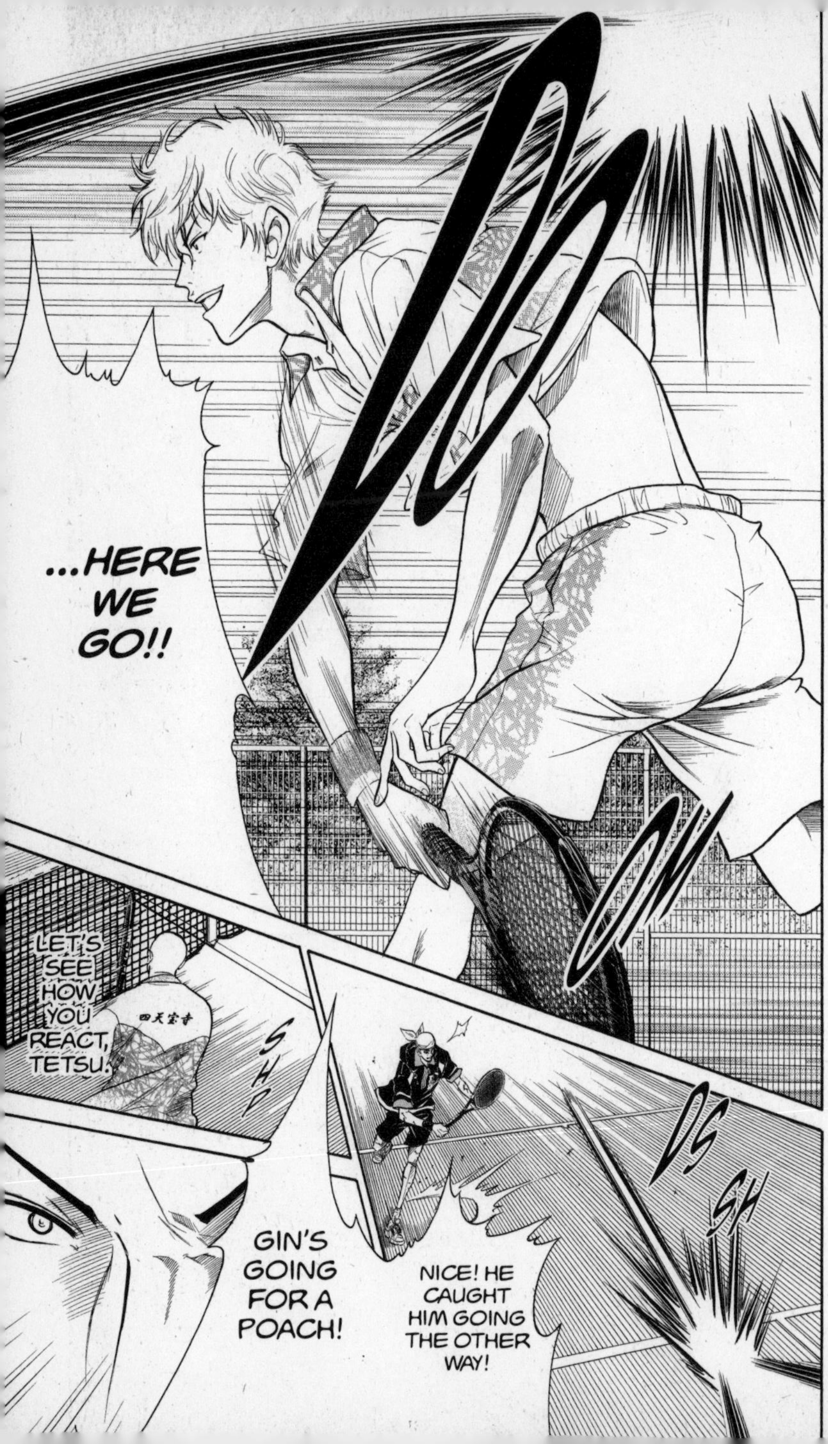
...HERE WE GO!!
LET'S SEE HOW YOU REACT, TETSU.
四天宝寺
NICE! HE CAUGHT HIM GOING THE OTHER WAY!
GIN'S GOING FOR A POACH!

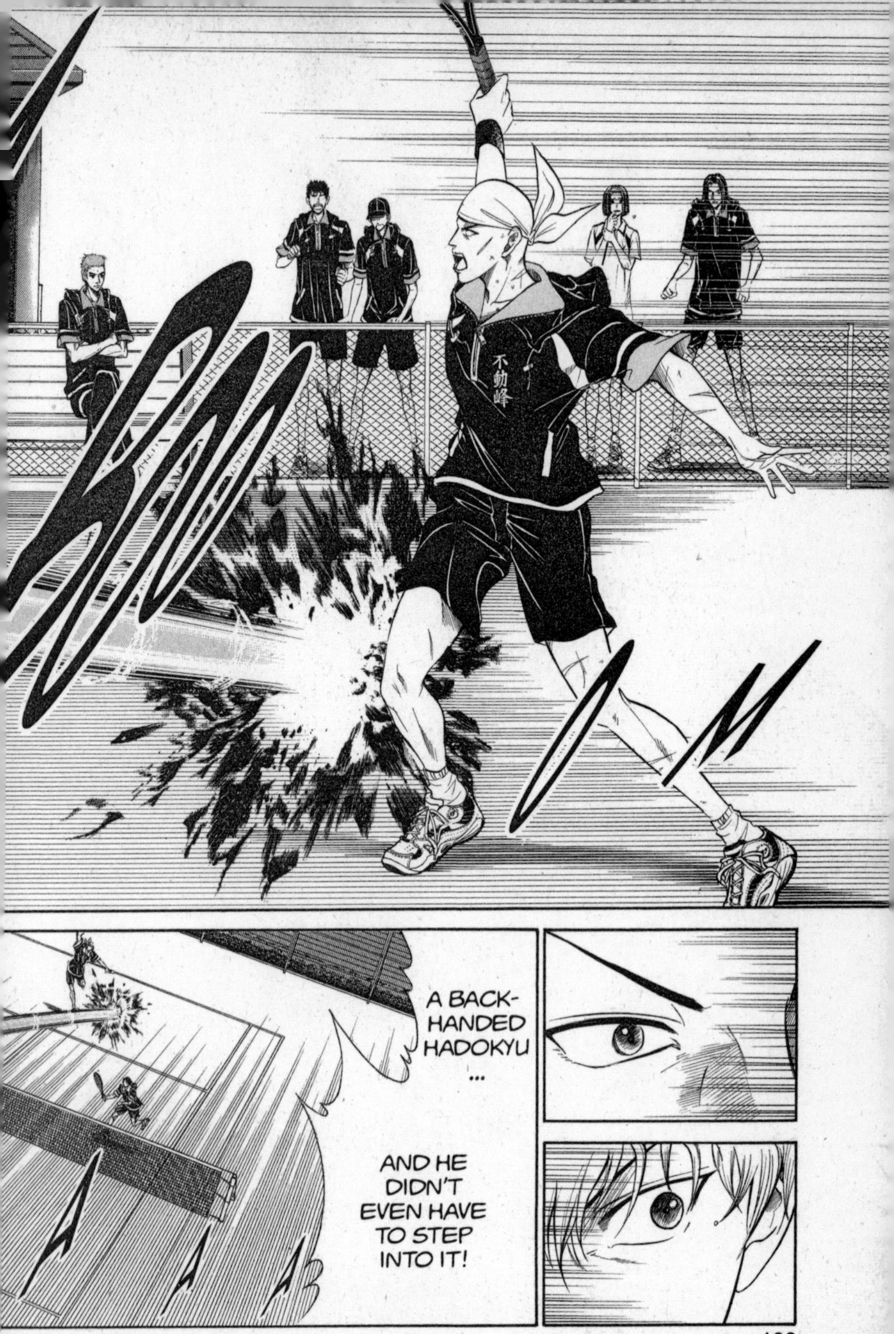
不動峰
A BACK-HANDED HADOKYU ...
AND HE DIDN'T EVEN HAVE TO STEP INTO IT!

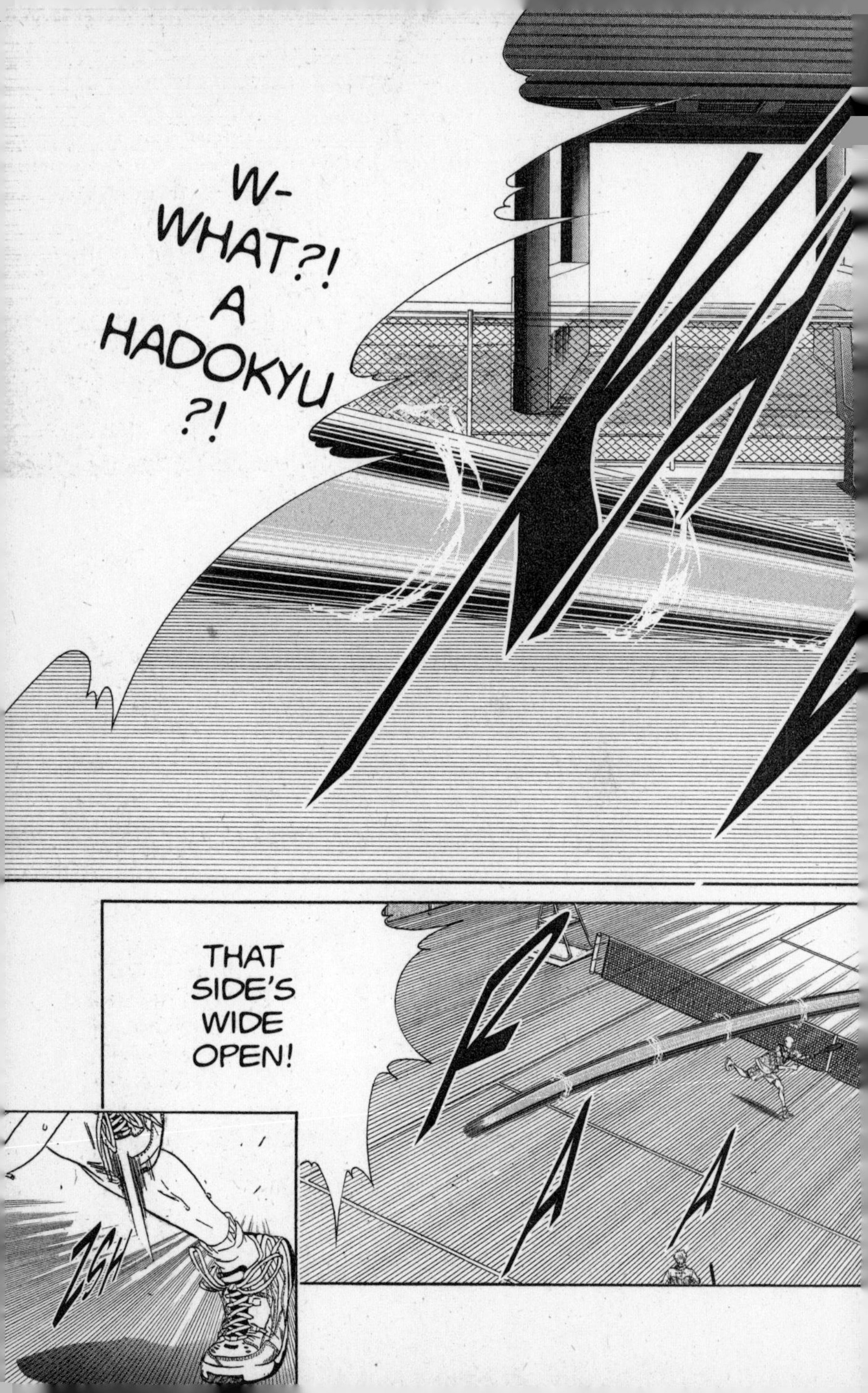
W-WHAT?! A HADOKYU?!
THAT SIDE'S WIDE OPEN!
ZSH

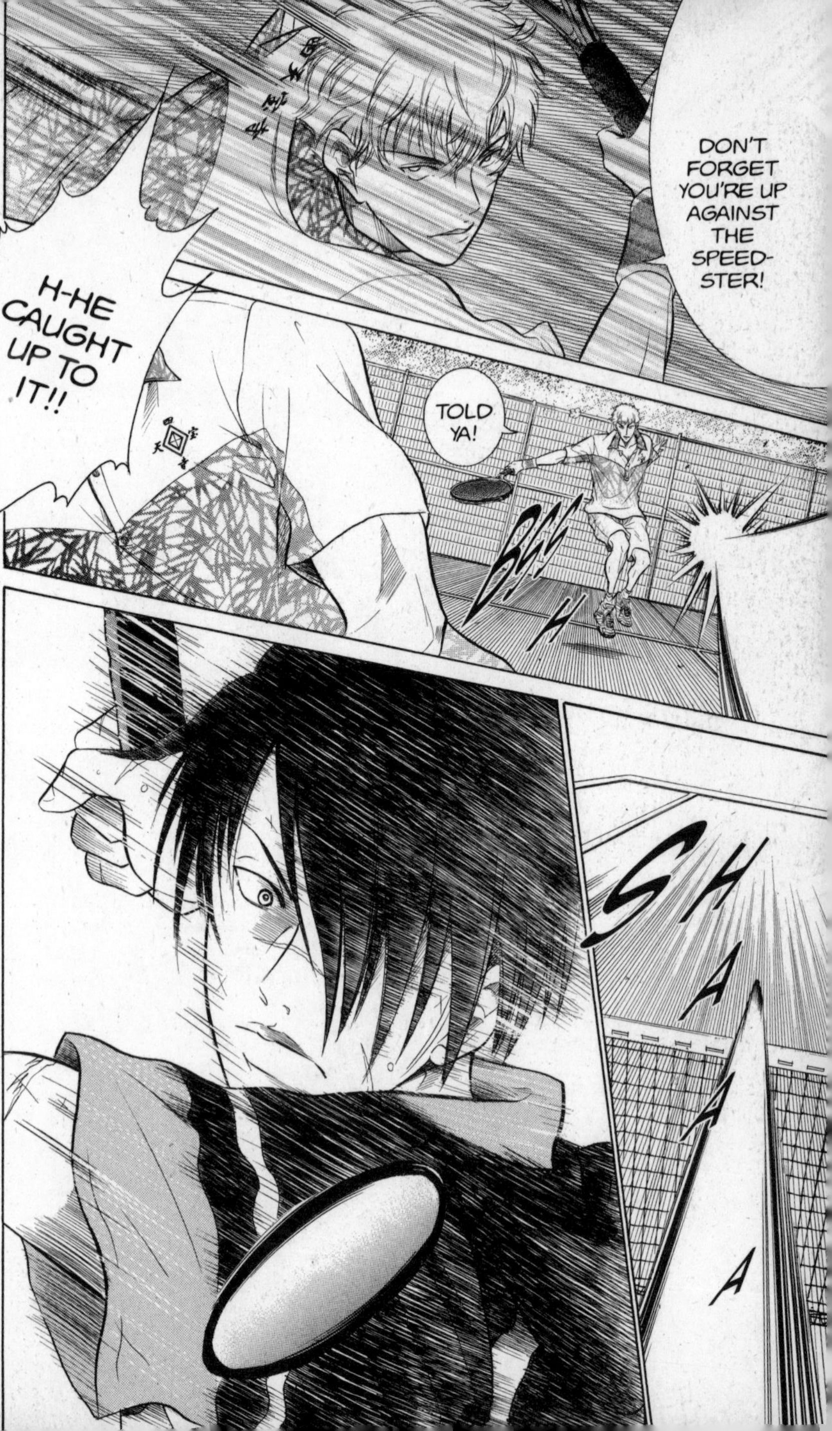
DON'T FORGET YOU'RE UP AGAINST THE SPEEDSTER!
H-HE CAUGHT UP TO IT!!
TOLD YA!
SHAAAA

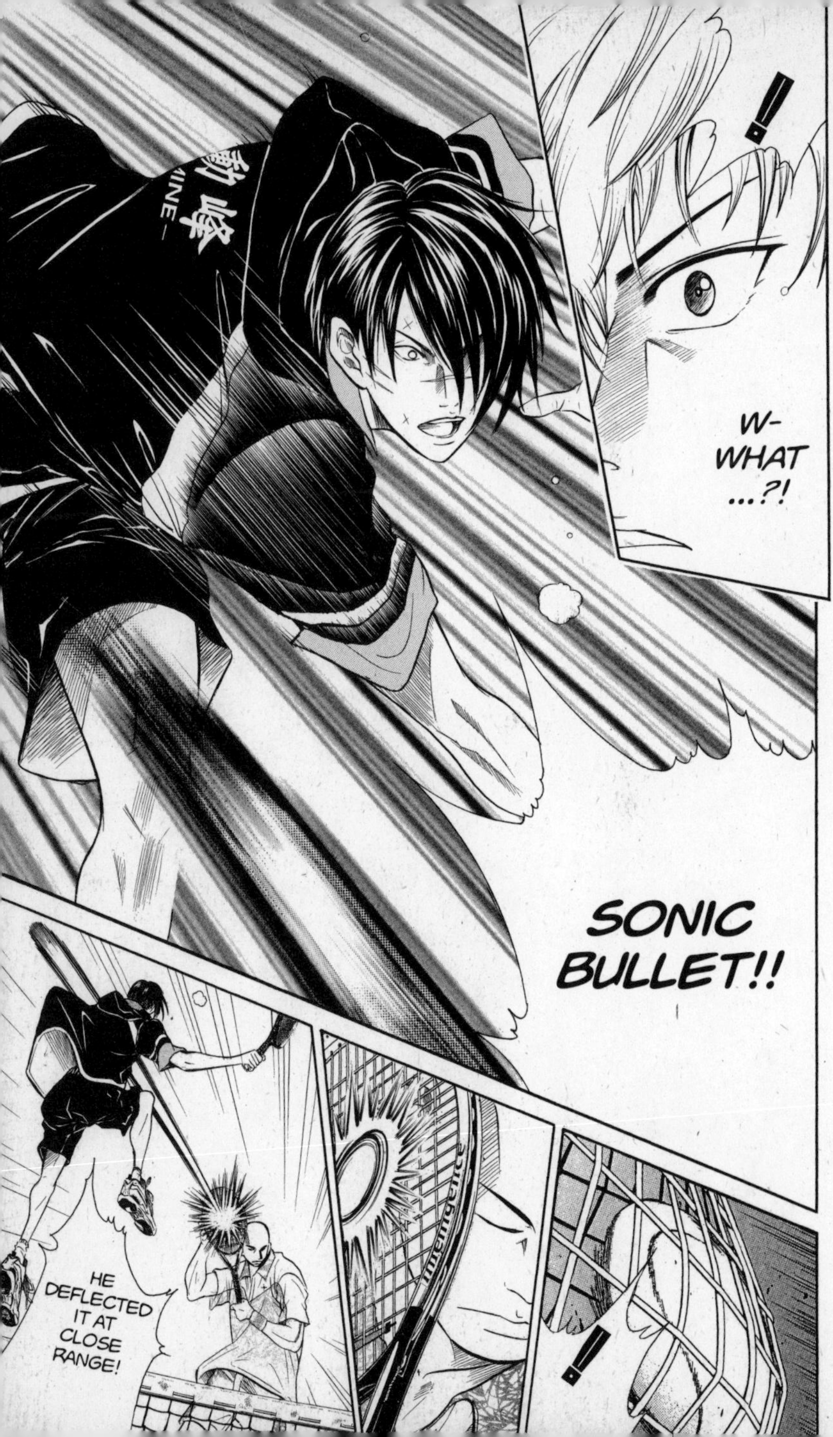
!
W-WHAT ...?!
SONIC BULLET!!
!
HE DEFLECTED IT AT CLOSE RANGE!

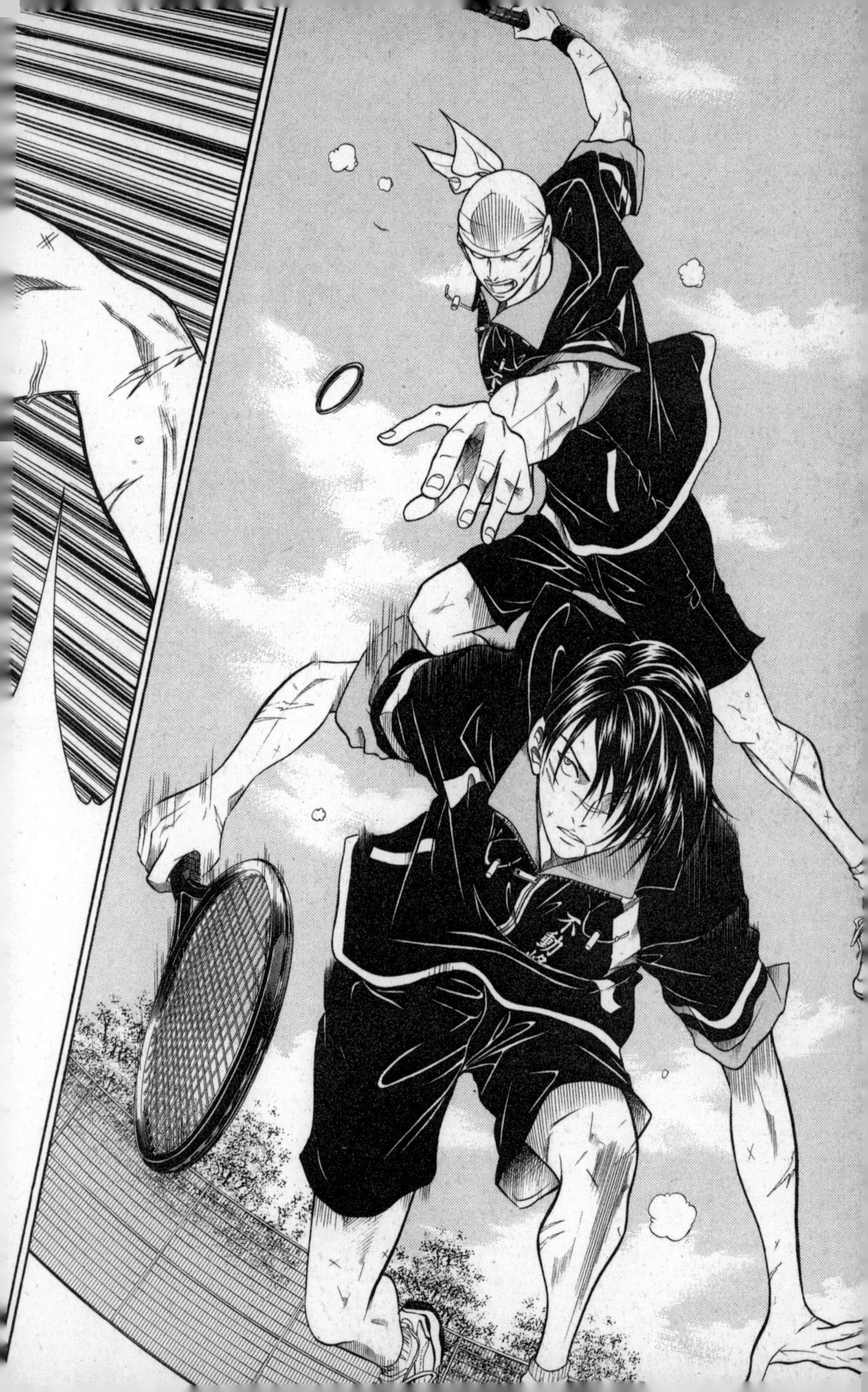

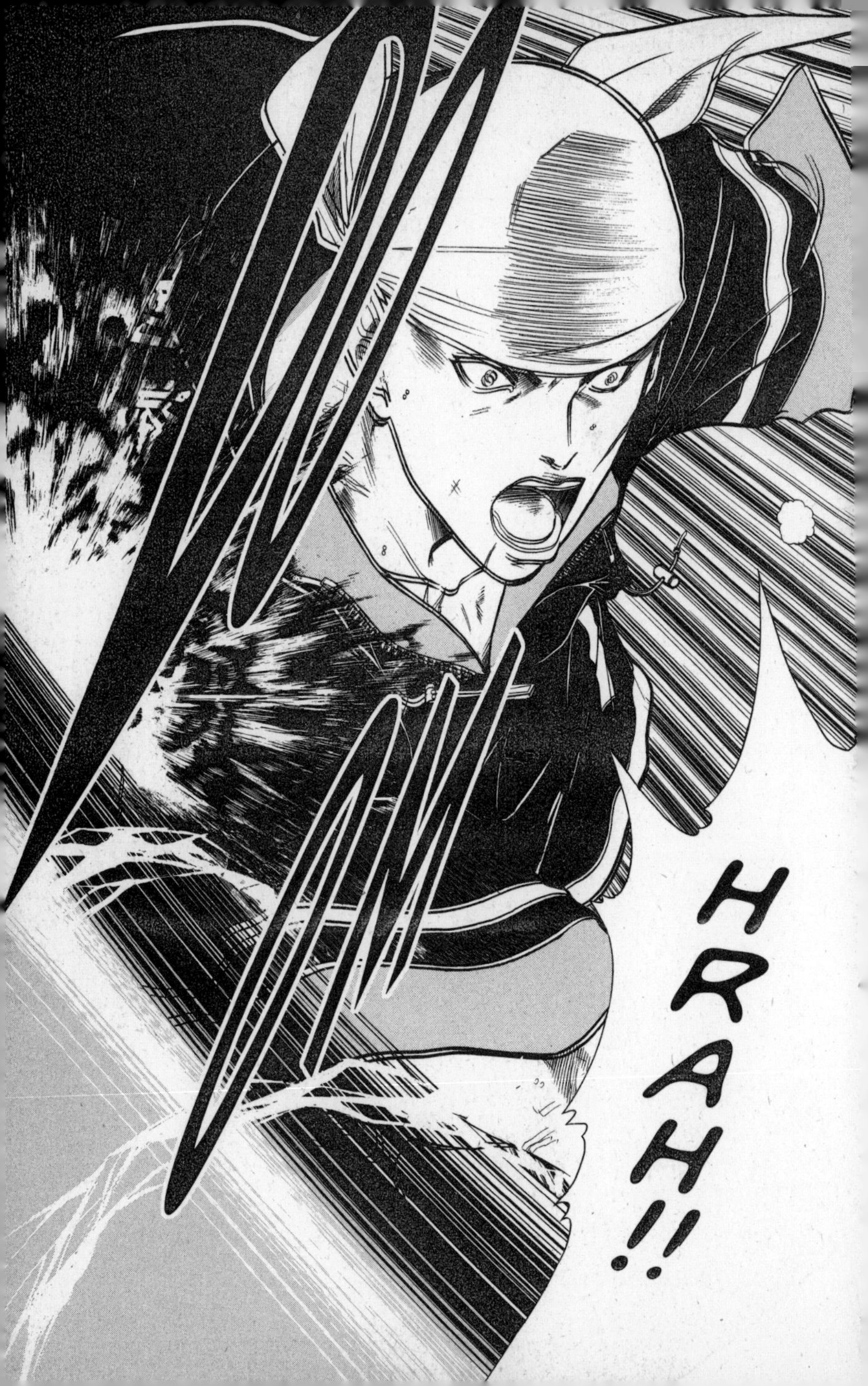
HRAH!!

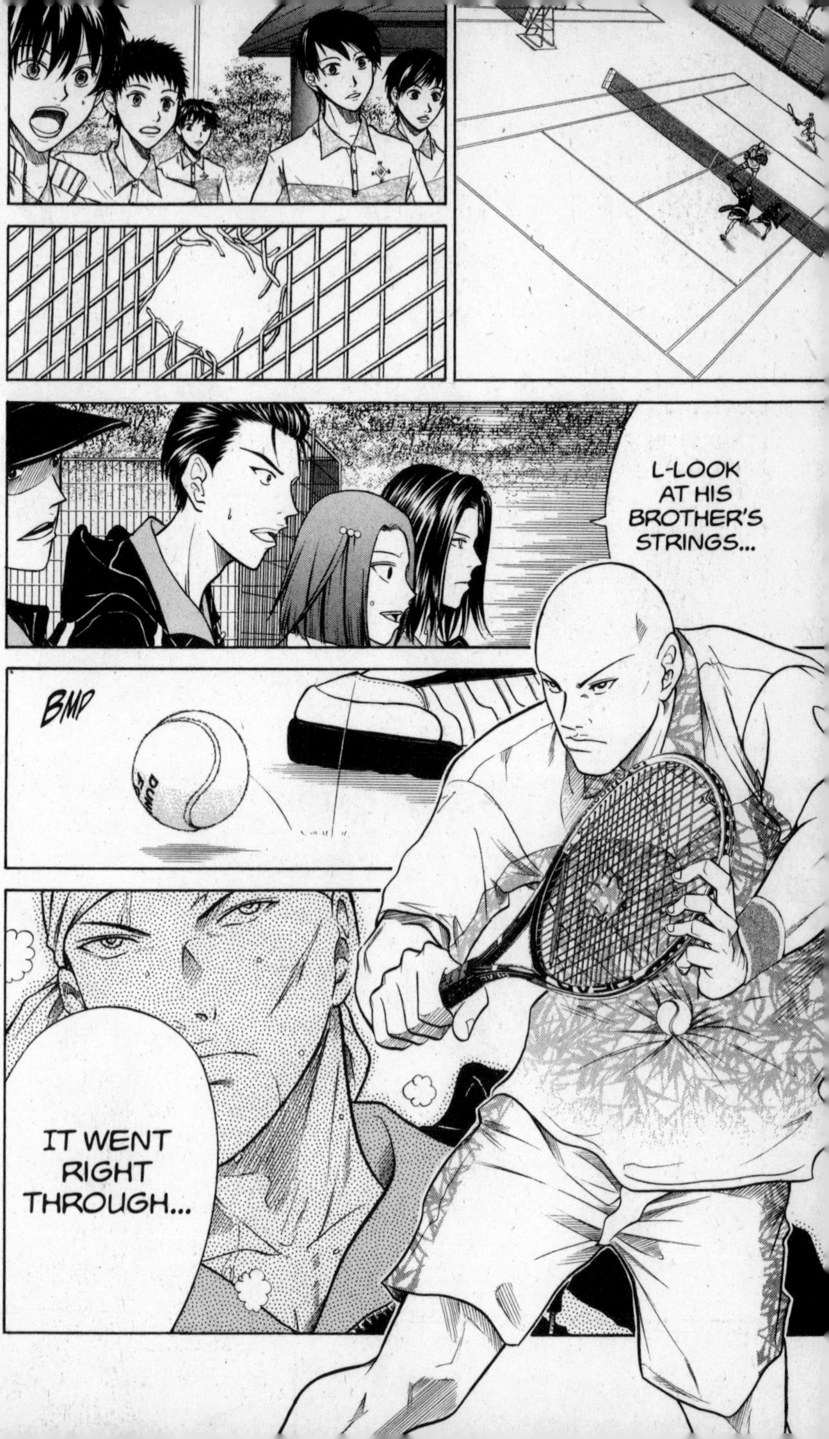
L-LOOK AT HIS BROTHER'S STRINGS...
BMP
IT WENT RIGHT THROUGH...

READ THIS WAY

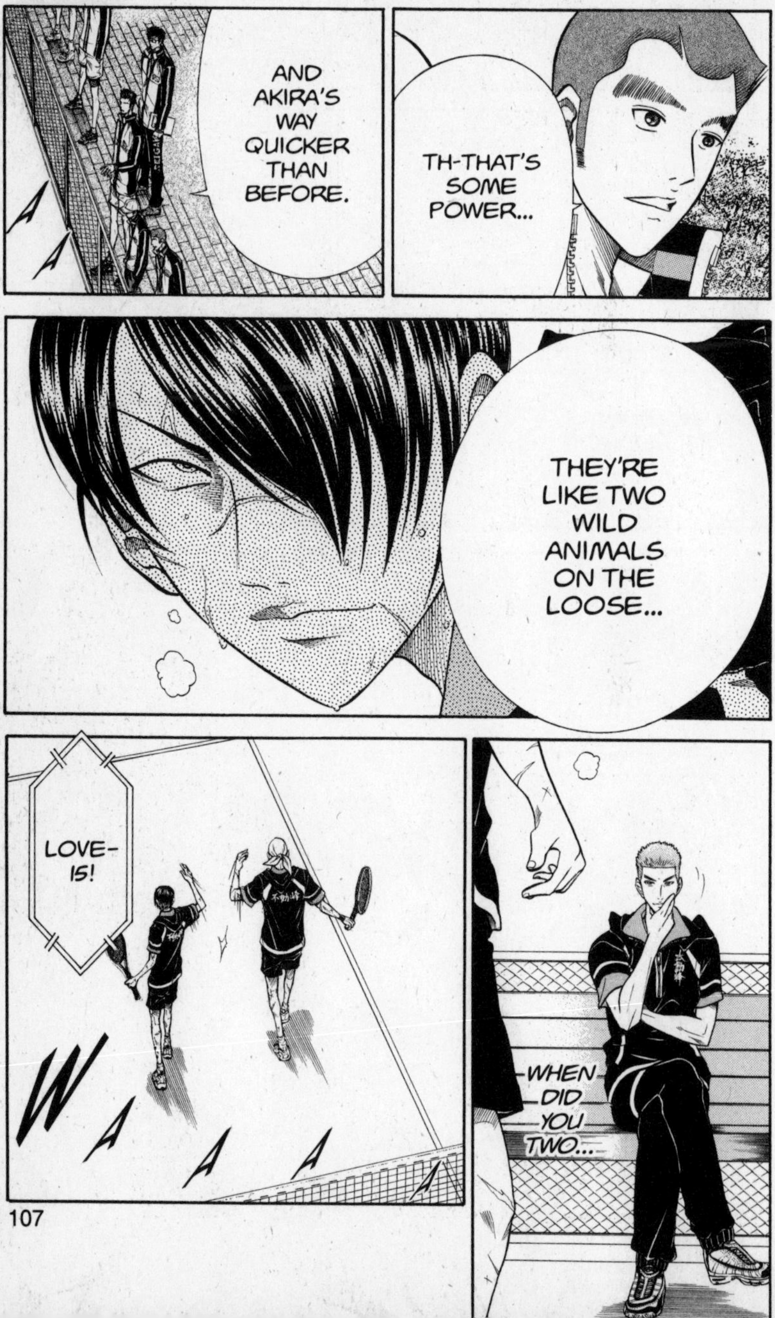
TH-THAT'S SOME POWER...
AND AKIRA'S WAY QUICKER THAN BEFORE.
AA
THEY'RE LIKE TWO WILD ANIMALS ON THE LOOSE...
WHEN DID YOU TWO...
LOVE-15!
WAAAA

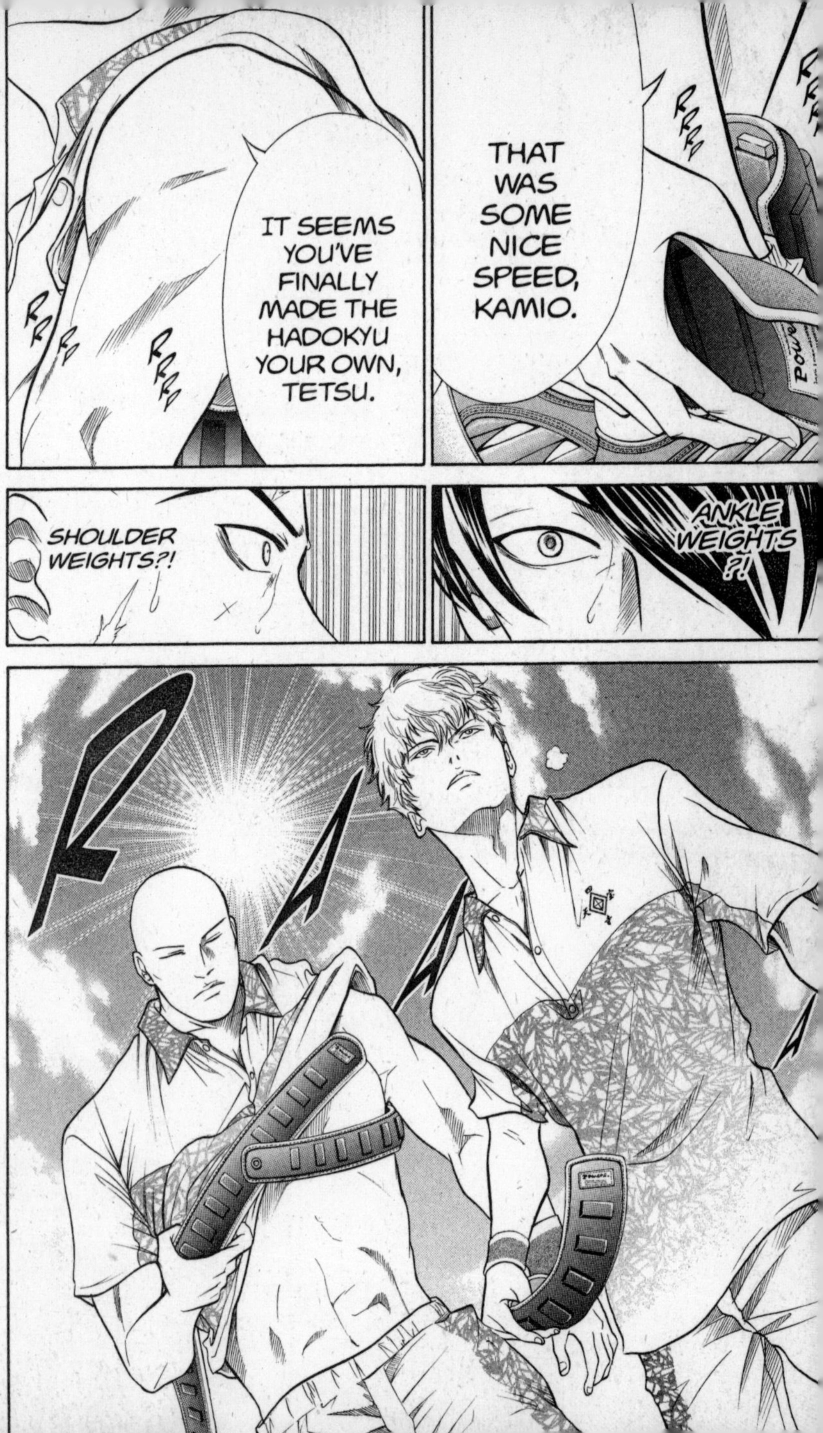
THAT WAS SOME NICE SPEED, KAMIO.
IT SEEMS YOU'VE FINALLY MADE THE HADOKYU YOUR OWN, TETSU.
ANKLE WEIGHTS?!
SHOULDER WEIGHTS?!

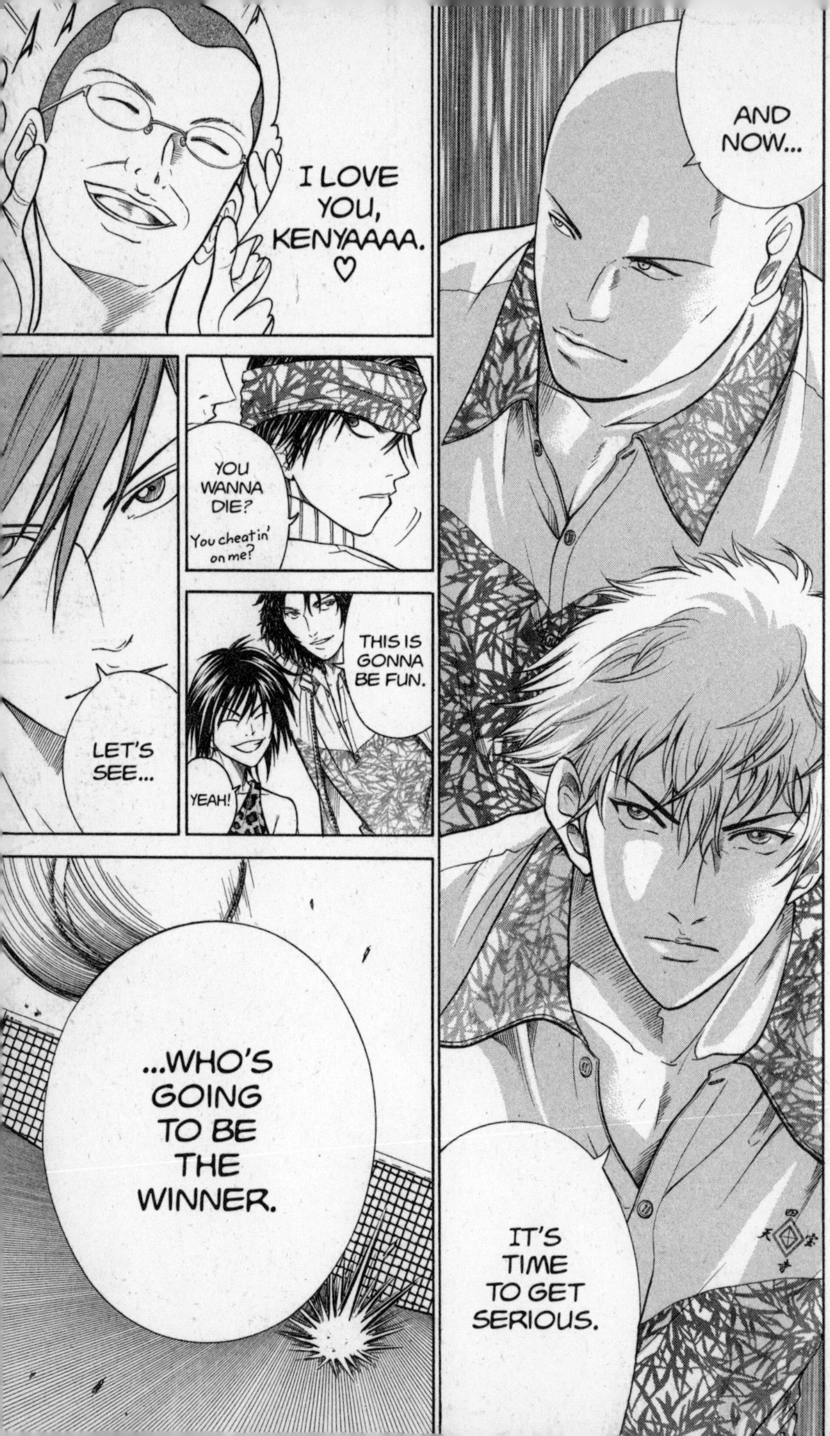
AND NOW...
IT'S TIME TO GET SERIOUS.
I LOVE YOU, KENYAAAA. ♡
YOU WANNA DIE?
You cheatin' on me?
THIS IS GONNA BE FUN.
YEAH!
LET'S SEE...
...WHO'S GOING TO BE THE WINNER.

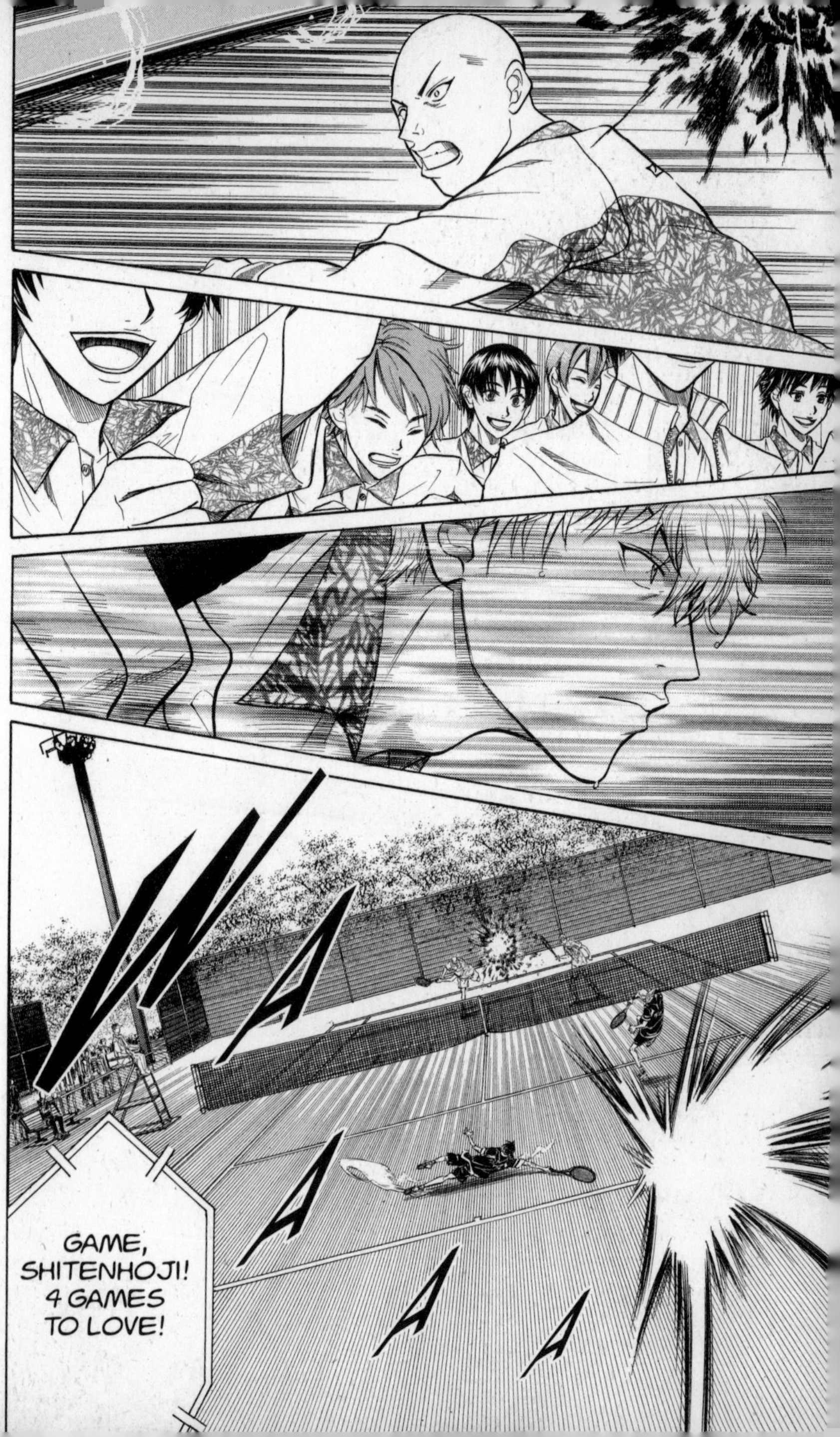
WAAAAA
GAME, SHITENHOJI! 4 GAMES TO LOVE!

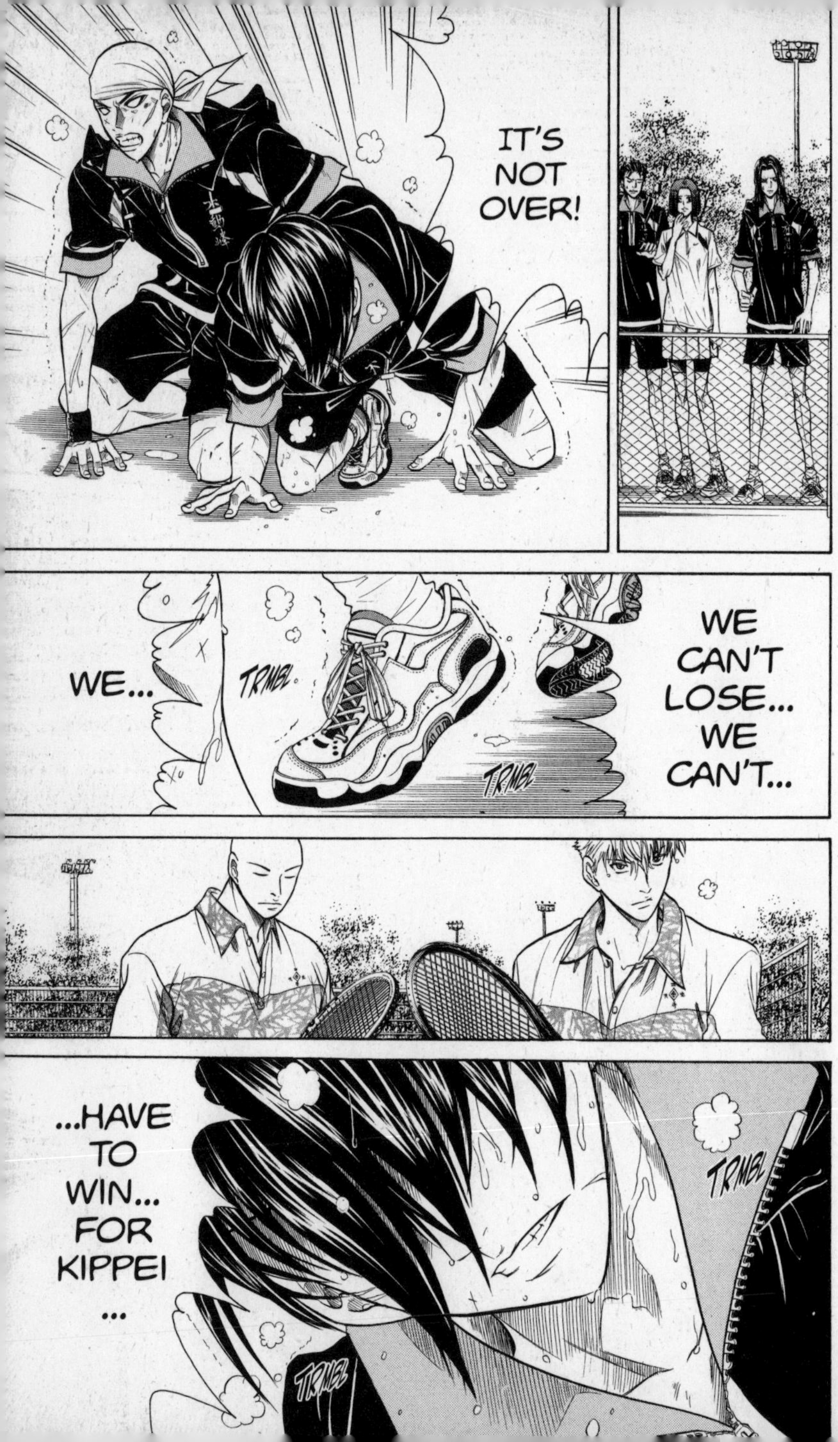
IT'S NOT OVER!
WE CAN'T LOSE... WE CAN'T...
TRMBL
TRMBL
WE...
...HAVE TO WIN... FOR KIPPEI ...
TRMBL
TRMBL

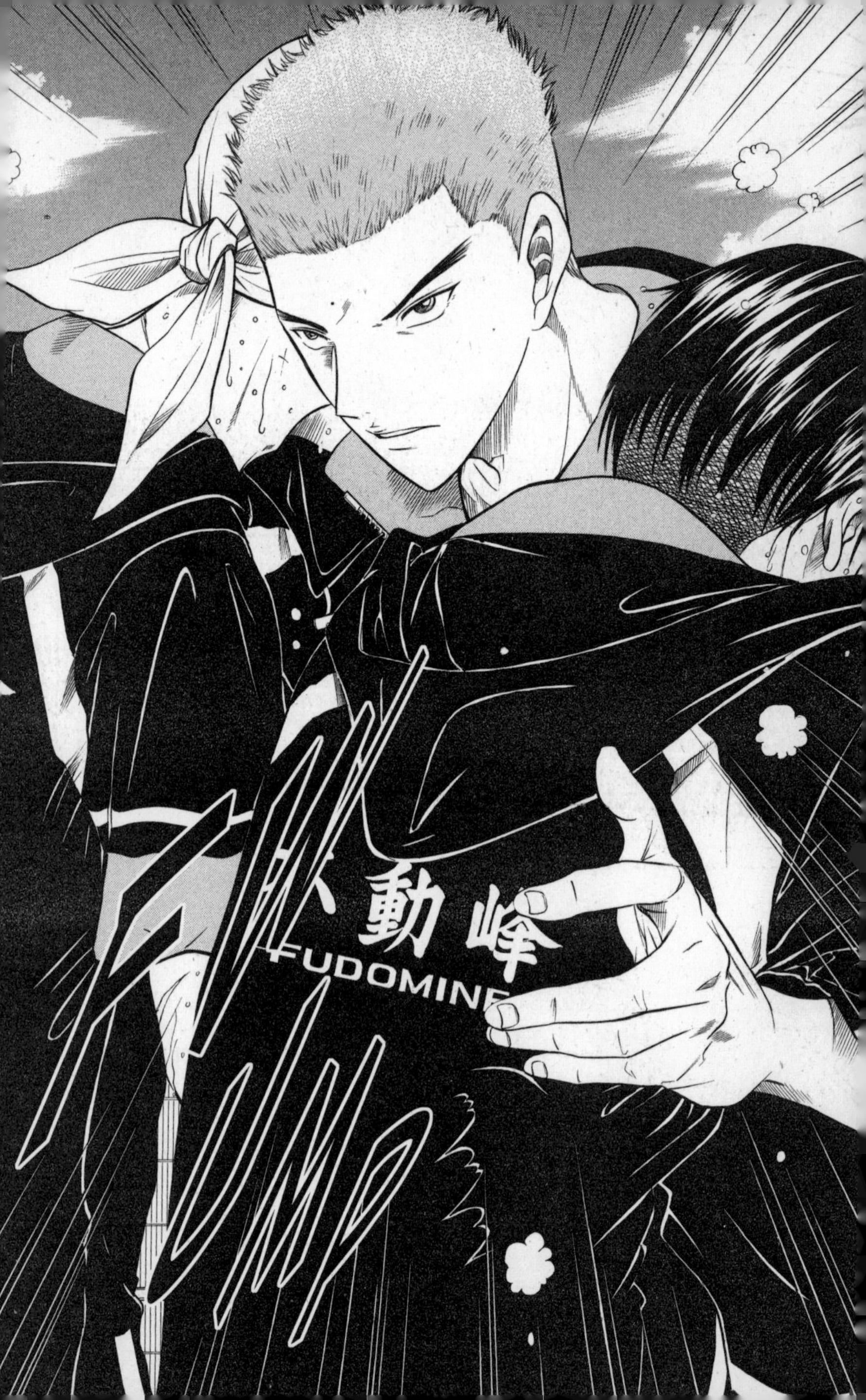
不動峰
FUDOMINE

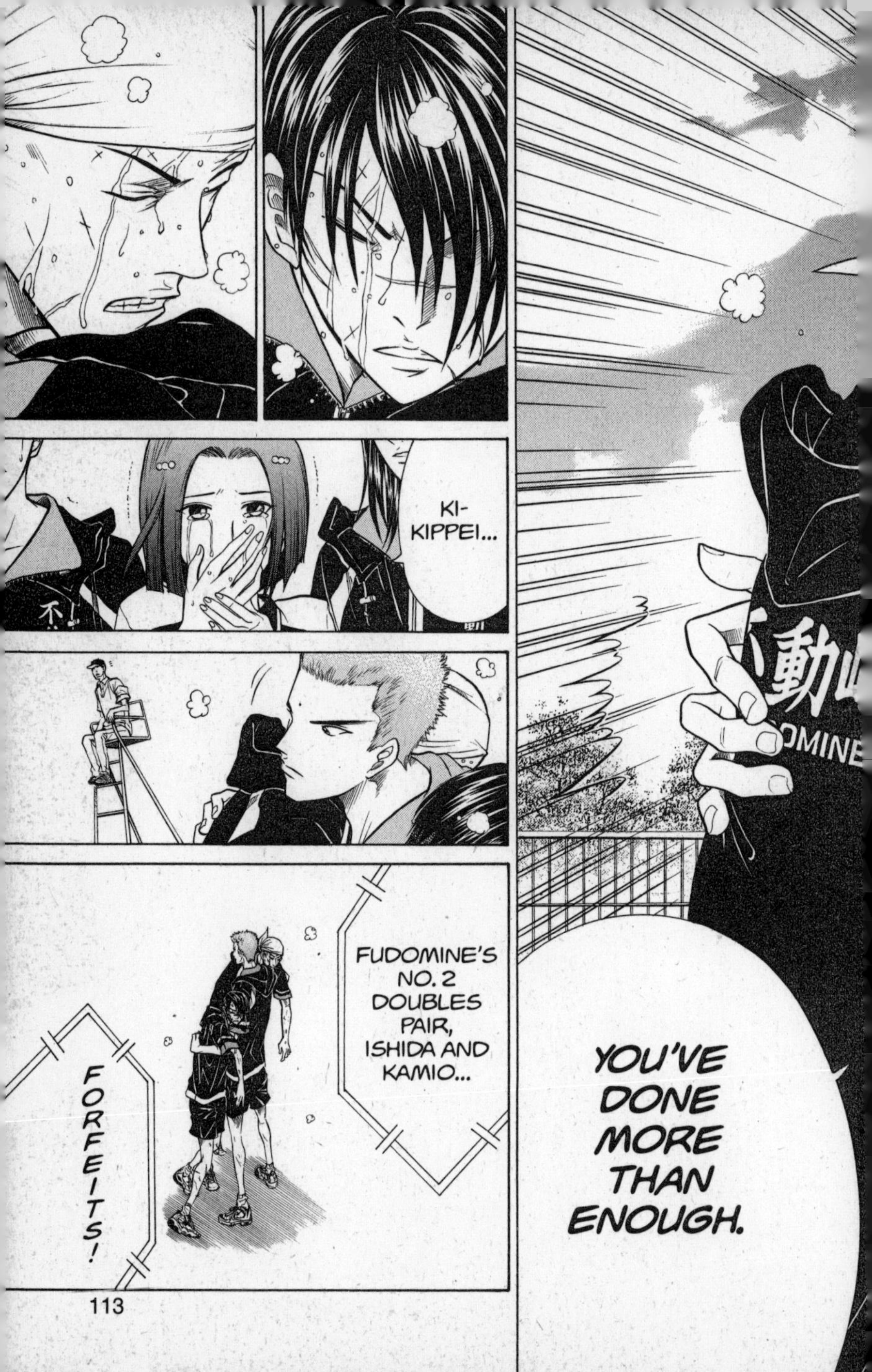
YOU'VE DONE MORE THAN ENOUGH.
KI-KIPPEI...
FUDOMINE'S NO. 2 DOUBLES PAIR, ISHIDA AND KAMIO...
FORFEITS!

テニスの王子様

THE PRINCE OF TENNIS

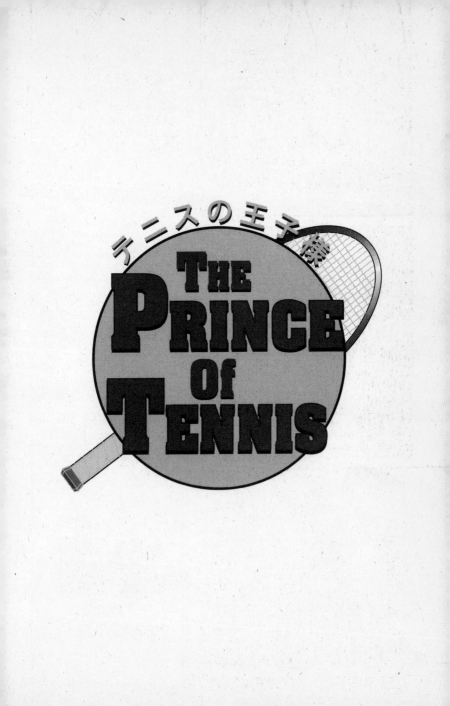

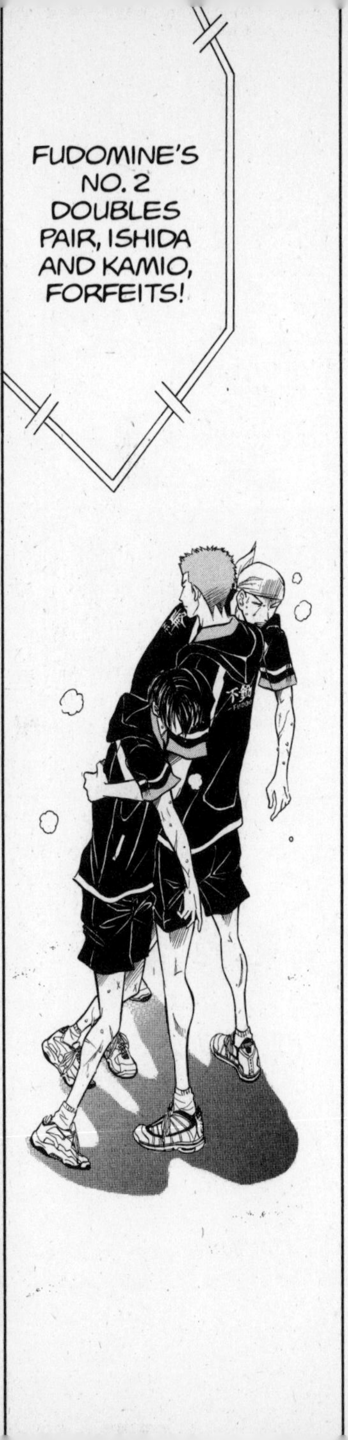
FUDOMINE'S NO. 2 DOUBLES PAIR, ISHIDA AND KAMIO, FORFEITS!

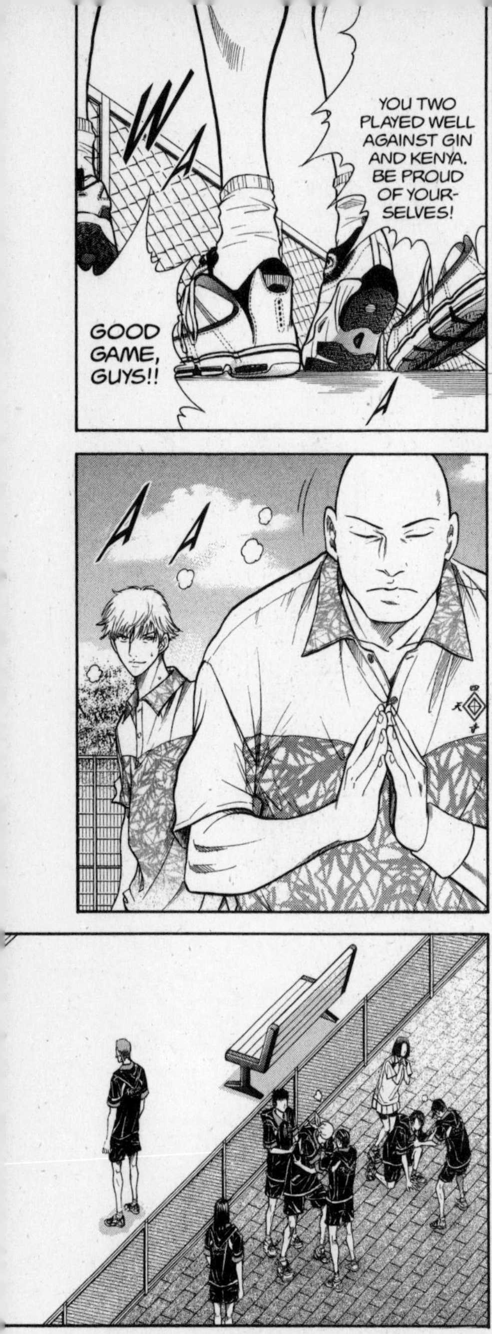
YOU TWO PLAYED WELL AGAINST GIN AND KENYA. BE PROUD OF YOUR-SELVES!
GOOD GAME, GUYS!!
WA
A
A
A
A

GENIUS 309: ATONEMENT

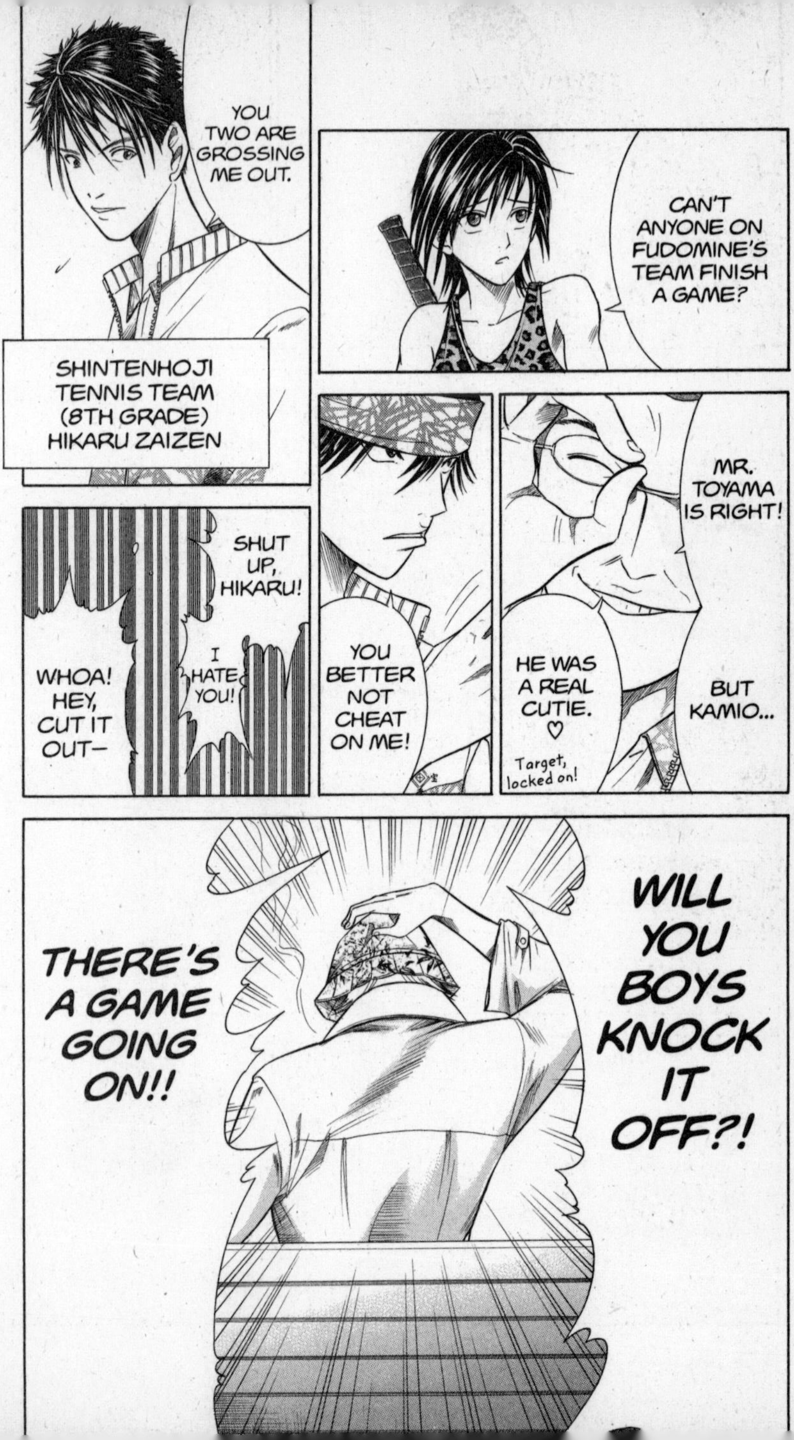
CAN'T ANYONE ON FUDOMINE'S TEAM FINISH A GAME?
YOU TWO ARE GROSSING ME OUT.
SHINTENHOJI TENNIS TEAM (8TH GRADE) HIKARU ZAIZEN
MR. TOYAMA IS RIGHT!
BUT KAMIO...
HE WAS A REAL CUTIE. ♡
Target, locked on!
YOU BETTER NOT CHEAT ON ME!
SHUT UP, HIKARU!
I HATE YOU!
WHOA! HEY, CUT IT OUT—
WILL YOU BOYS KNOCK IT OFF?!
THERE'S A GAME GOING ON!!

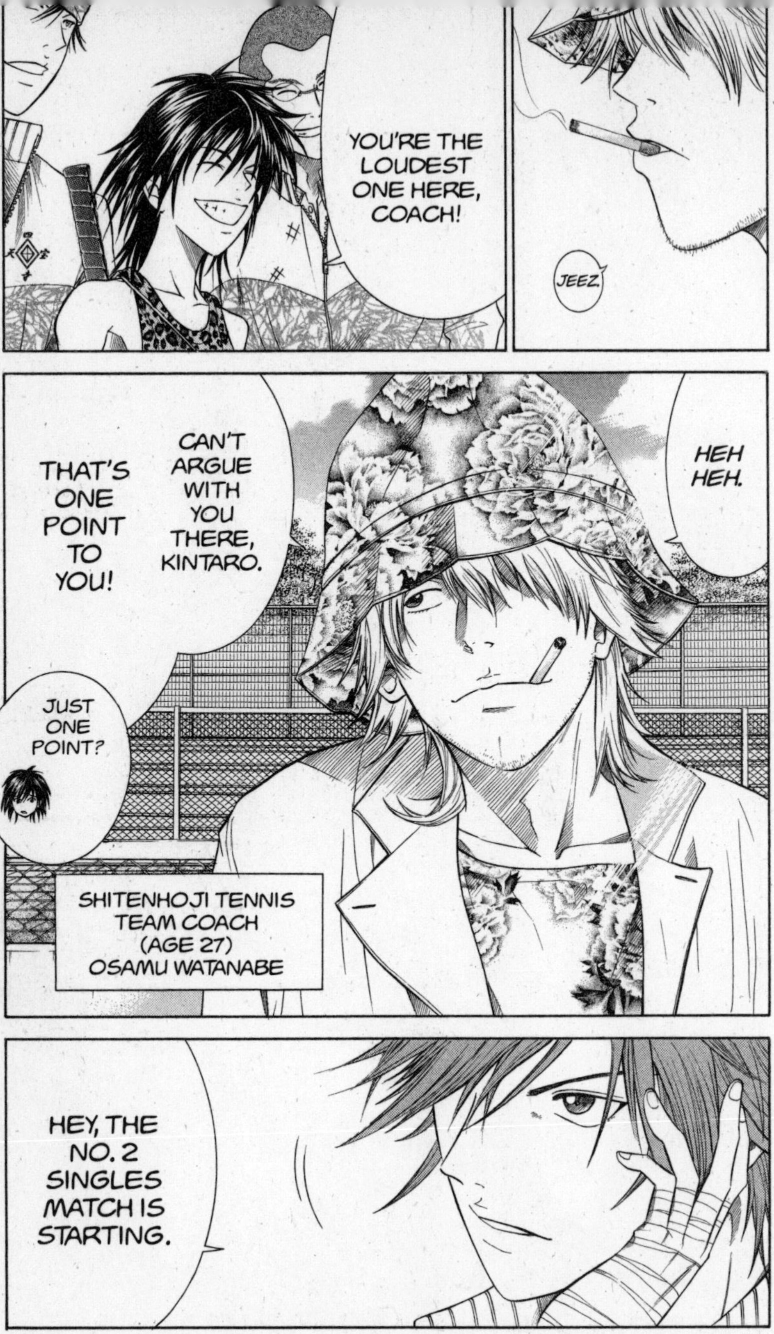
JEEZ.
YOU'RE THE LOUDEST ONE HERE, COACH!
HEH HEH.
CAN'T ARGUE WITH YOU THERE, KINTARO.
THAT'S ONE POINT TO YOU!
JUST ONE POINT?
SHITENHOJI TENNIS TEAM COACH (AGE 27) OSAMU WATANABE
HEY, THE NO. 2 SINGLES MATCH IS STARTING.

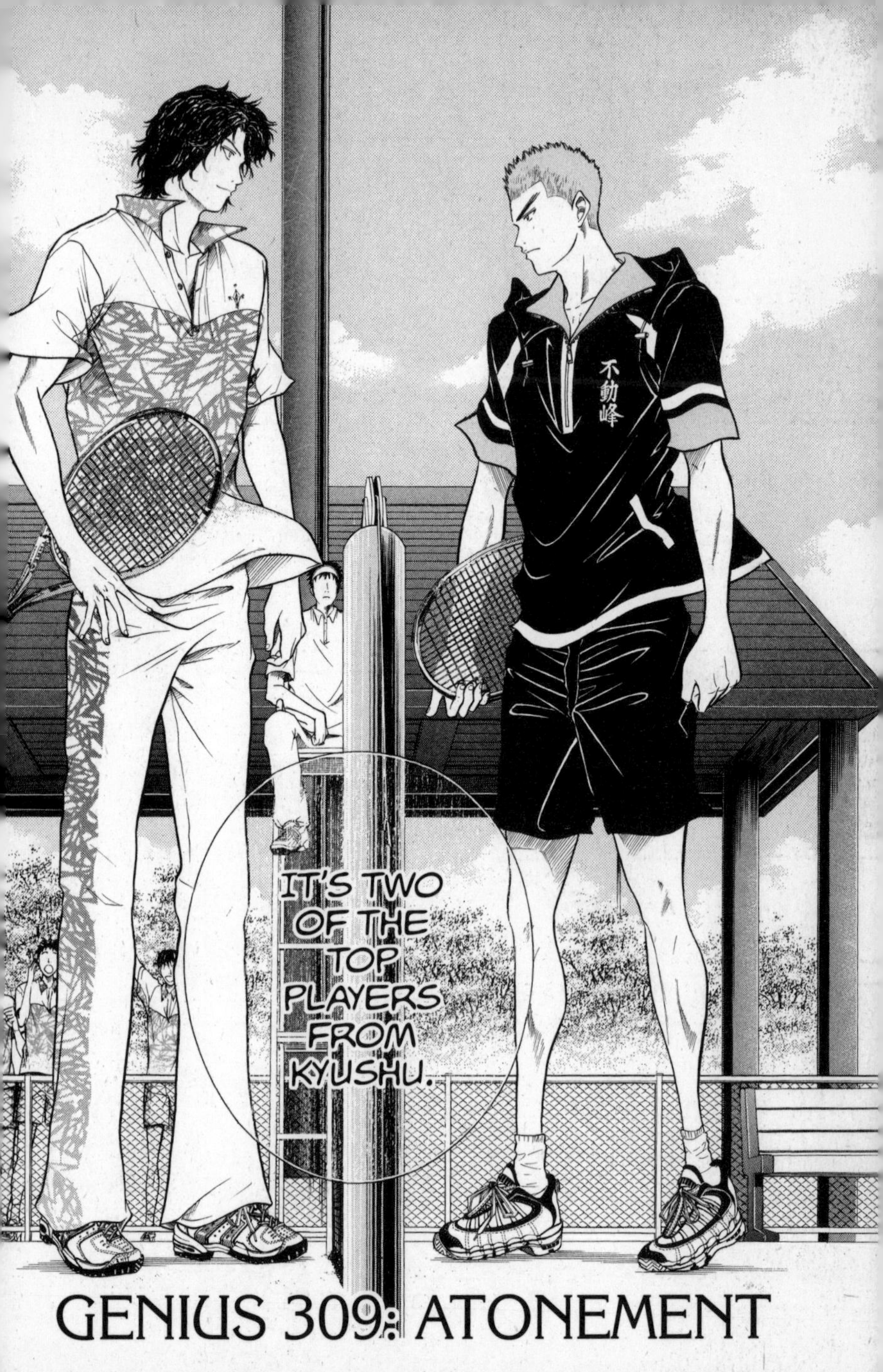
不動峰
IT'S TWO OF THE TOP PLAYERS FROM KYUSHU.

GENIUS 309: ATONEMENT

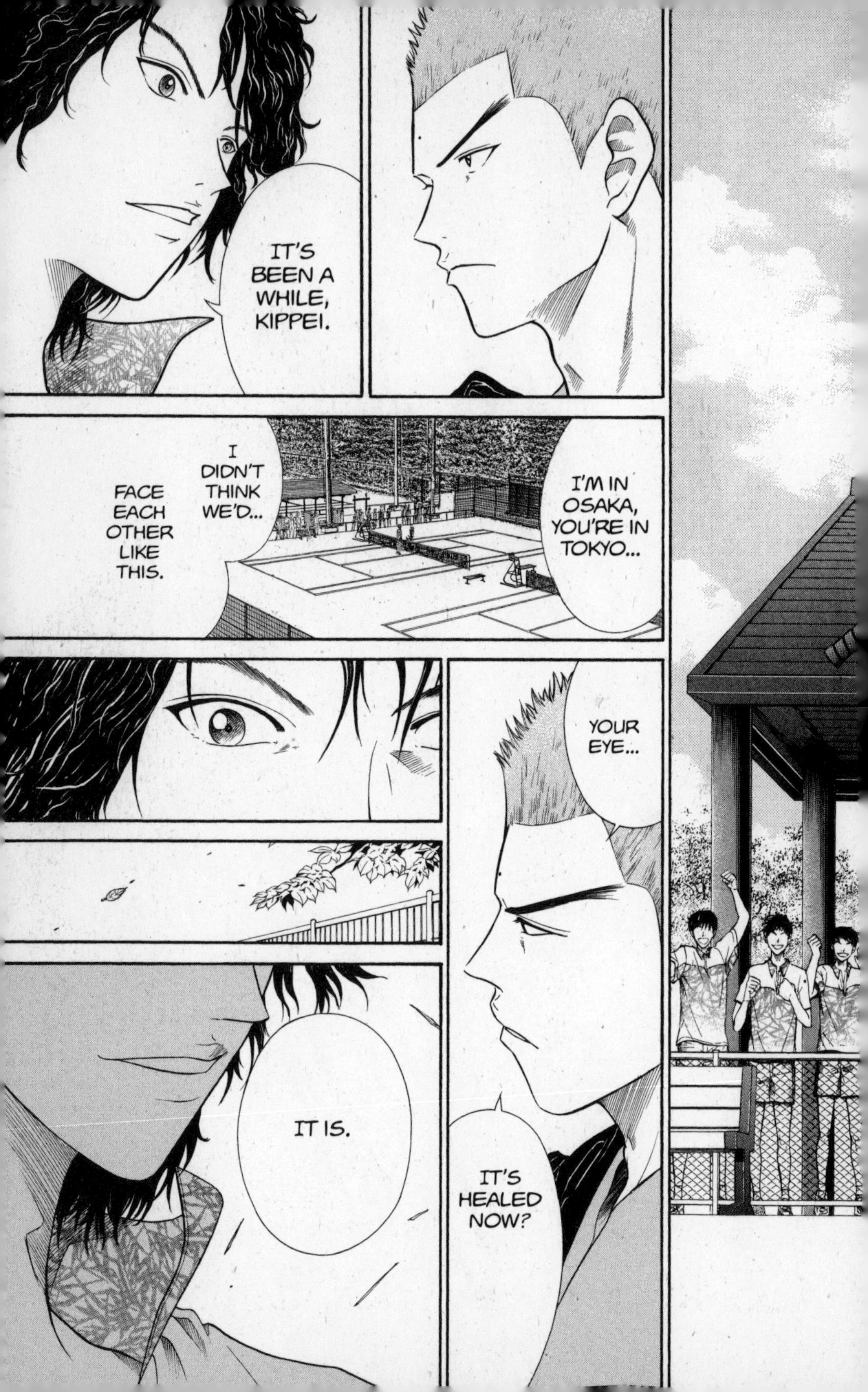
IT'S BEEN A WHILE, KIPPEI.
I'M IN OSAKA, YOU'RE IN TOKYO...
I DIDN'T THINK WE'D...
FACE EACH OTHER LIKE THIS.
YOUR EYE...
IT'S HEALED NOW?
IT IS.

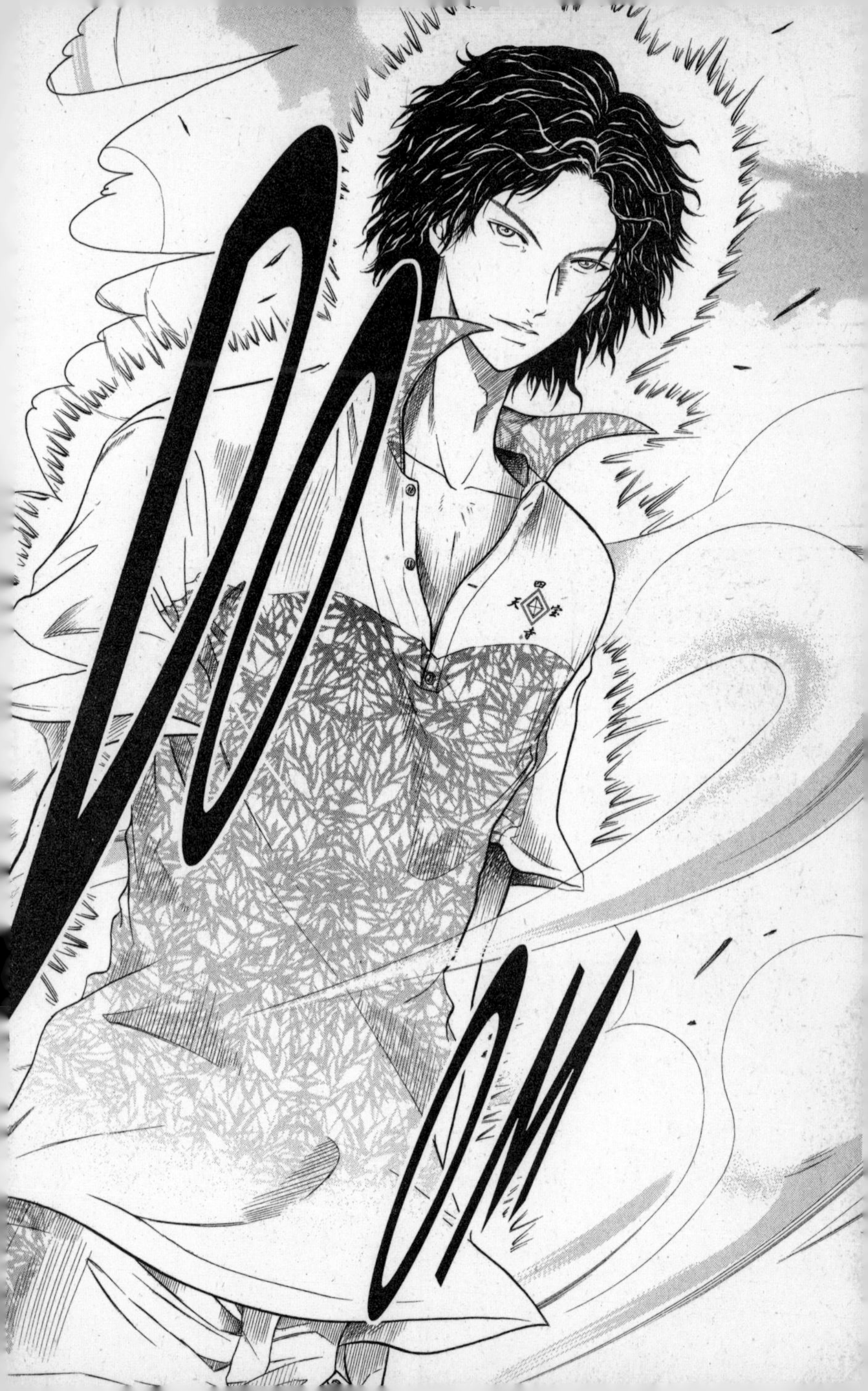
四天宝寺

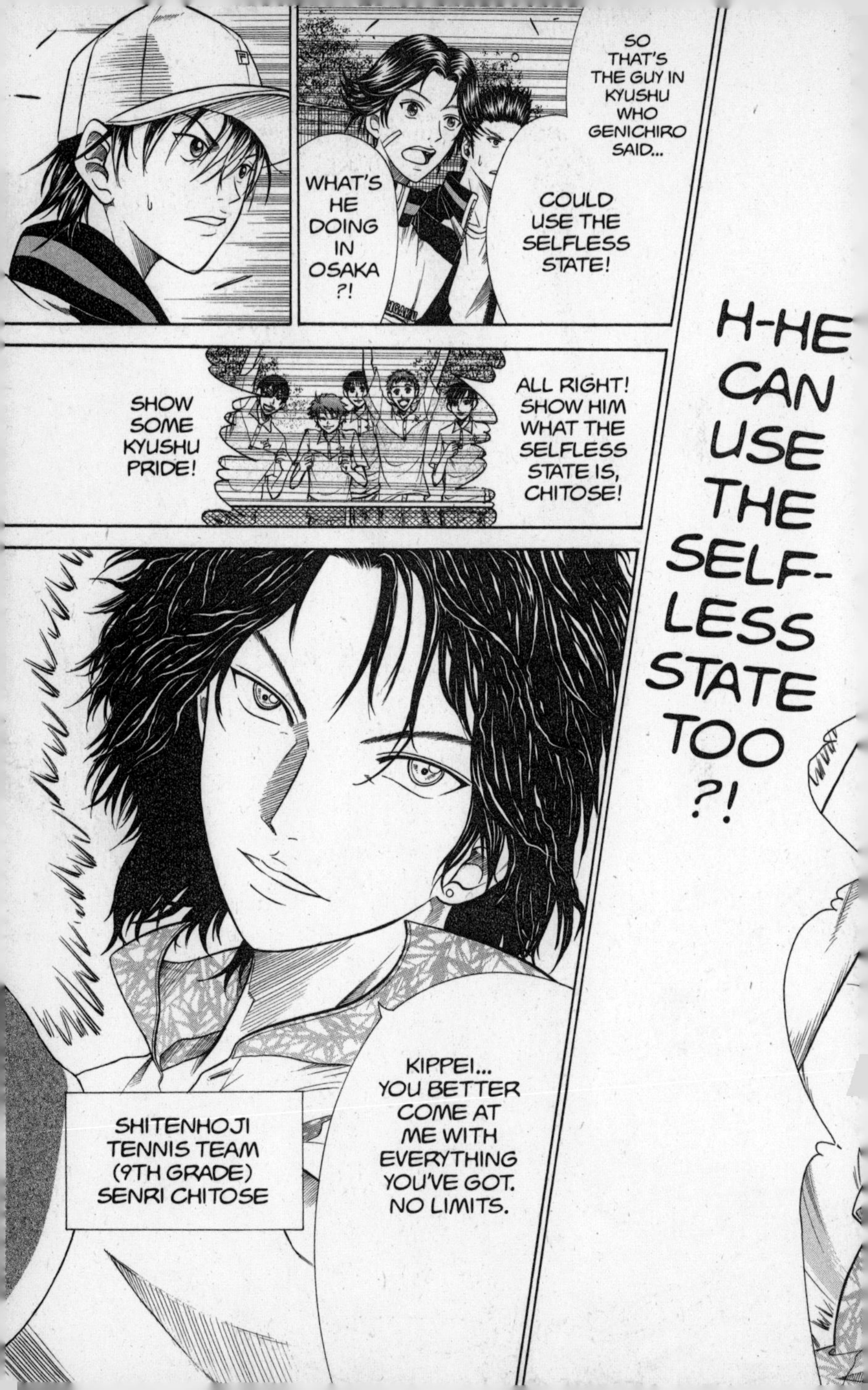

H-HE CAN USE THE SELF-LESS STATE TOO ?!
SO THAT'S THE GUY IN KYUSHU WHO GENICHIRO SAID...
COULD USE THE SELFLESS STATE!
WHAT'S HE DOING IN OSAKA ?!
ALL RIGHT! SHOW HIM WHAT THE SELFLESS STATE IS, CHITOSE!
SHOW SOME KYUSHU PRIDE!
KIPPEI... YOU BETTER COME AT ME WITH EVERYTHING YOU'VE GOT. NO LIMITS.
SHITENHOJI TENNIS TEAM (9TH GRADE) SENRI CHITOSE

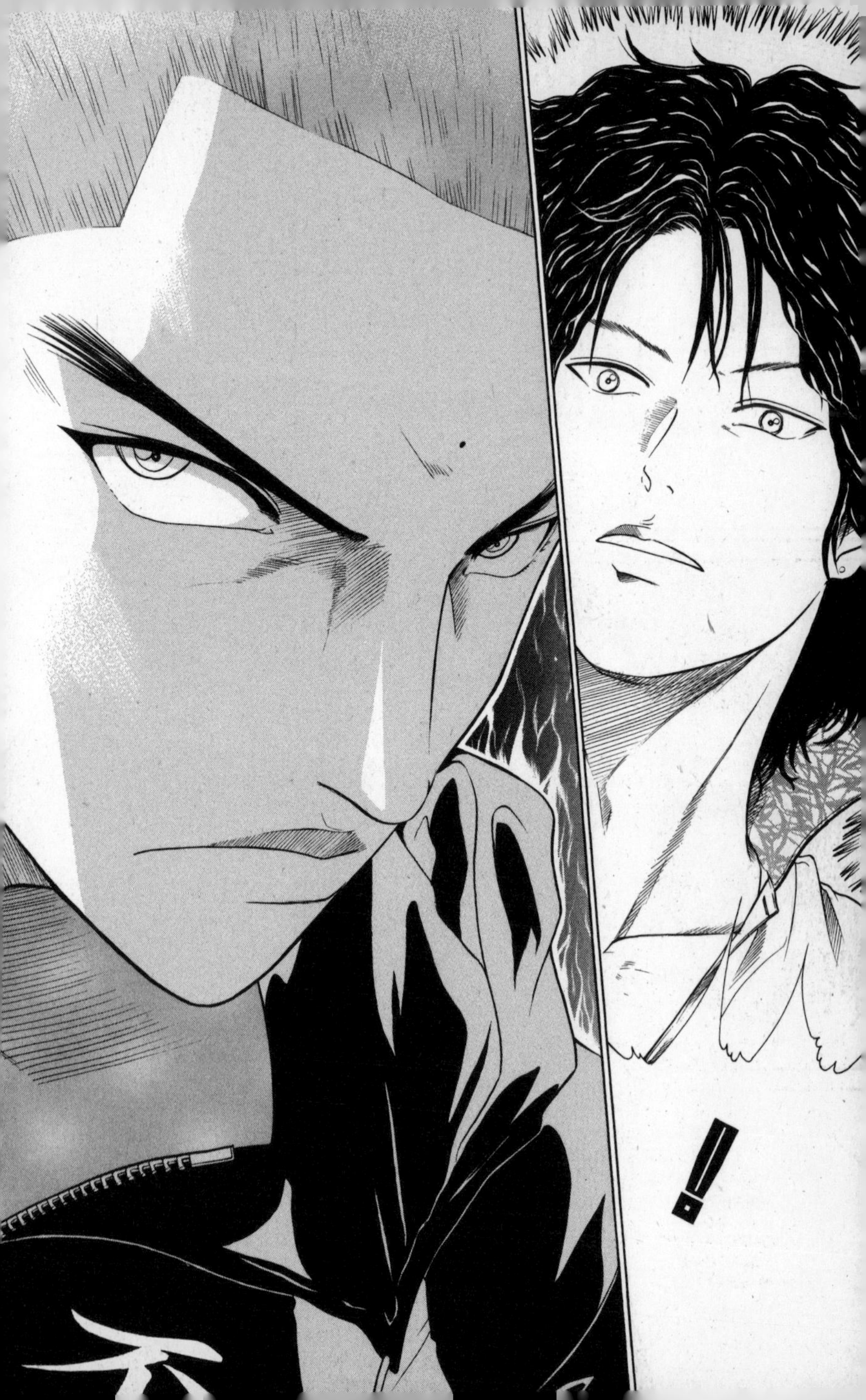
!

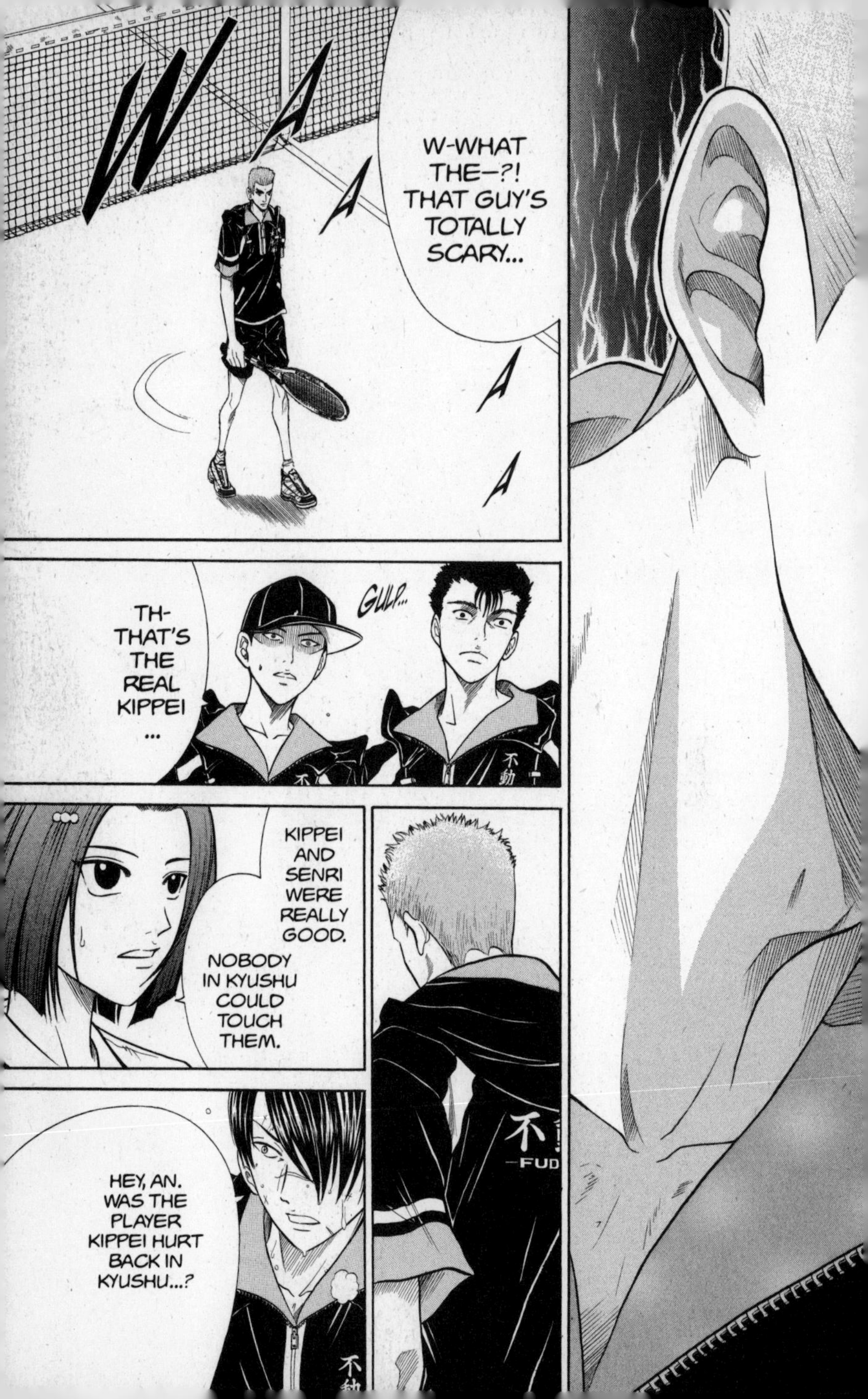
W-WHAT THE--?! THAT GUY'S TOTALLY SCARY...
WAAAAA
GULP...
TH- THAT'S THE REAL KIPPEI ...
KIPPEI AND SENRI WERE REALLY GOOD.
NOBODY IN KYUSHU COULD TOUCH THEM.
HEY, AN. WAS THE PLAYER KIPPEI HURT BACK IN KYUSHU...?

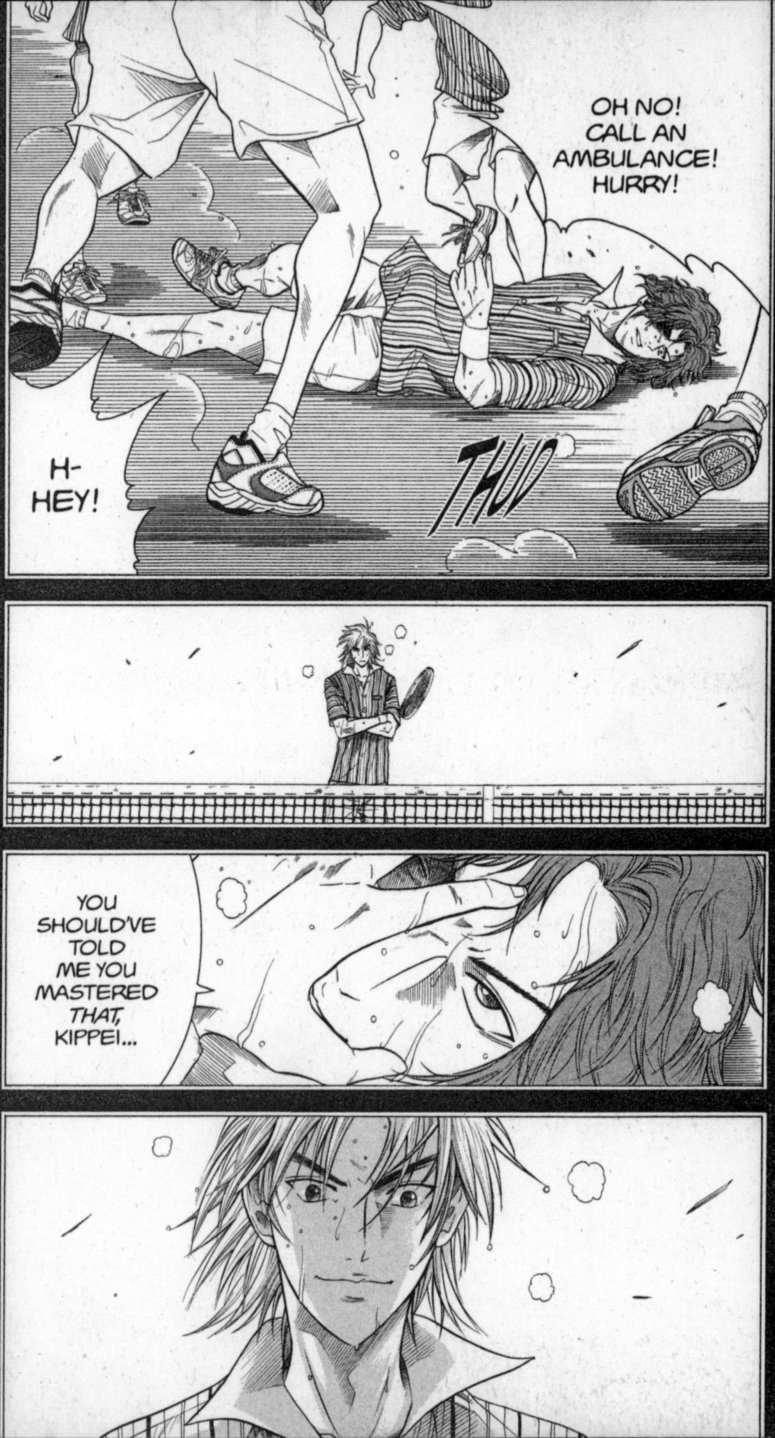
OH NO! CALL AN AMBULANCE! HURRY!
THUD
H- HEY!
YOU SHOULD'VE TOLD ME YOU MASTERED THAT, KIPPEI...

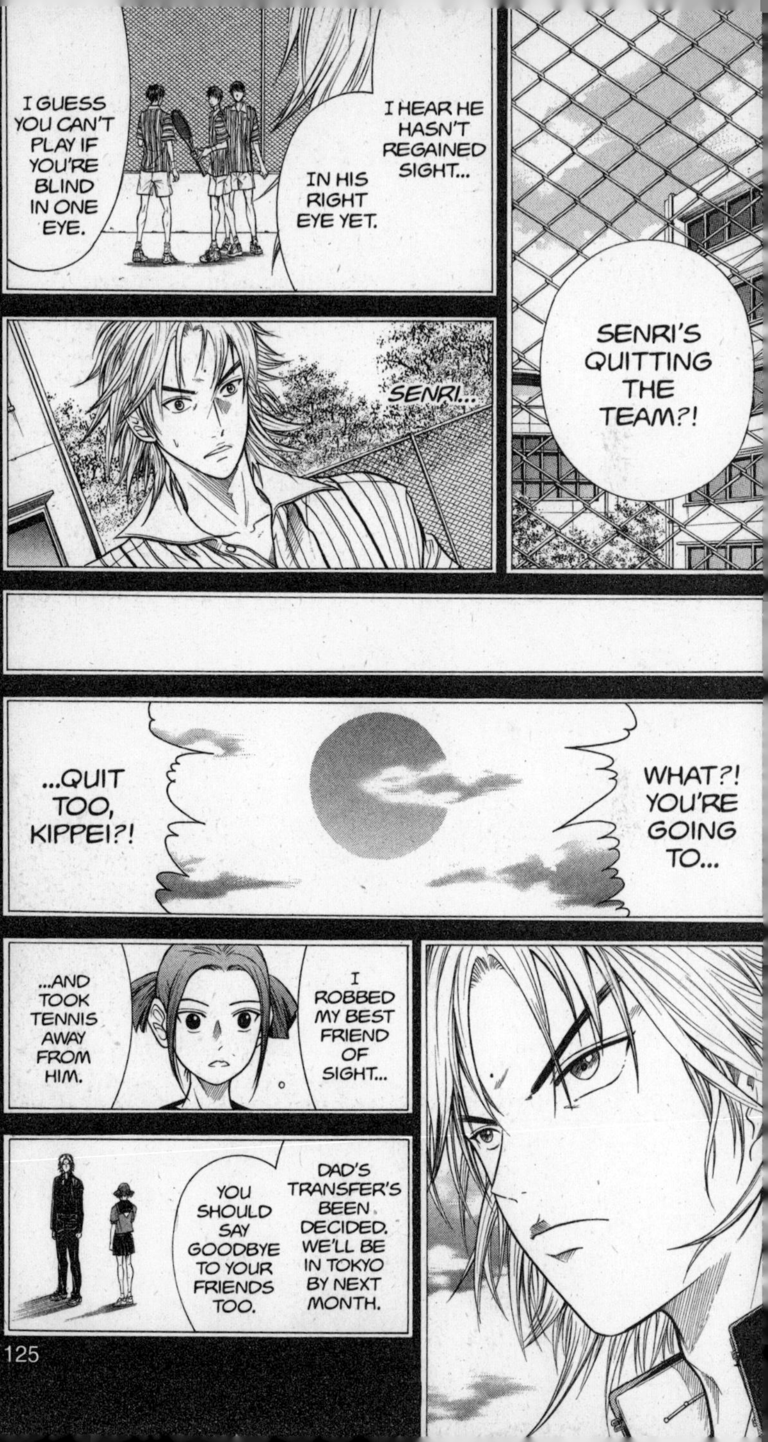
SENRI'S QUITTING THE TEAM?!
I HEAR HE HASN'T REGAINED SIGHT...
IN HIS RIGHT EYE YET.
I GUESS YOU CAN'T PLAY IF YOU'RE BLIND IN ONE EYE.
SENRI...
WHAT?! YOU'RE GOING TO...
...QUIT TOO, KIPPEI?!
I ROBBED MY BEST FRIEND OF SIGHT...
...AND TOOK TENNIS AWAY FROM HIM.
DAD'S TRANSFER'S BEEN DECIDED. WE'LL BE IN TOKYO BY NEXT MONTH.
YOU SHOULD SAY GOODBYE TO YOUR FRIENDS TOO.

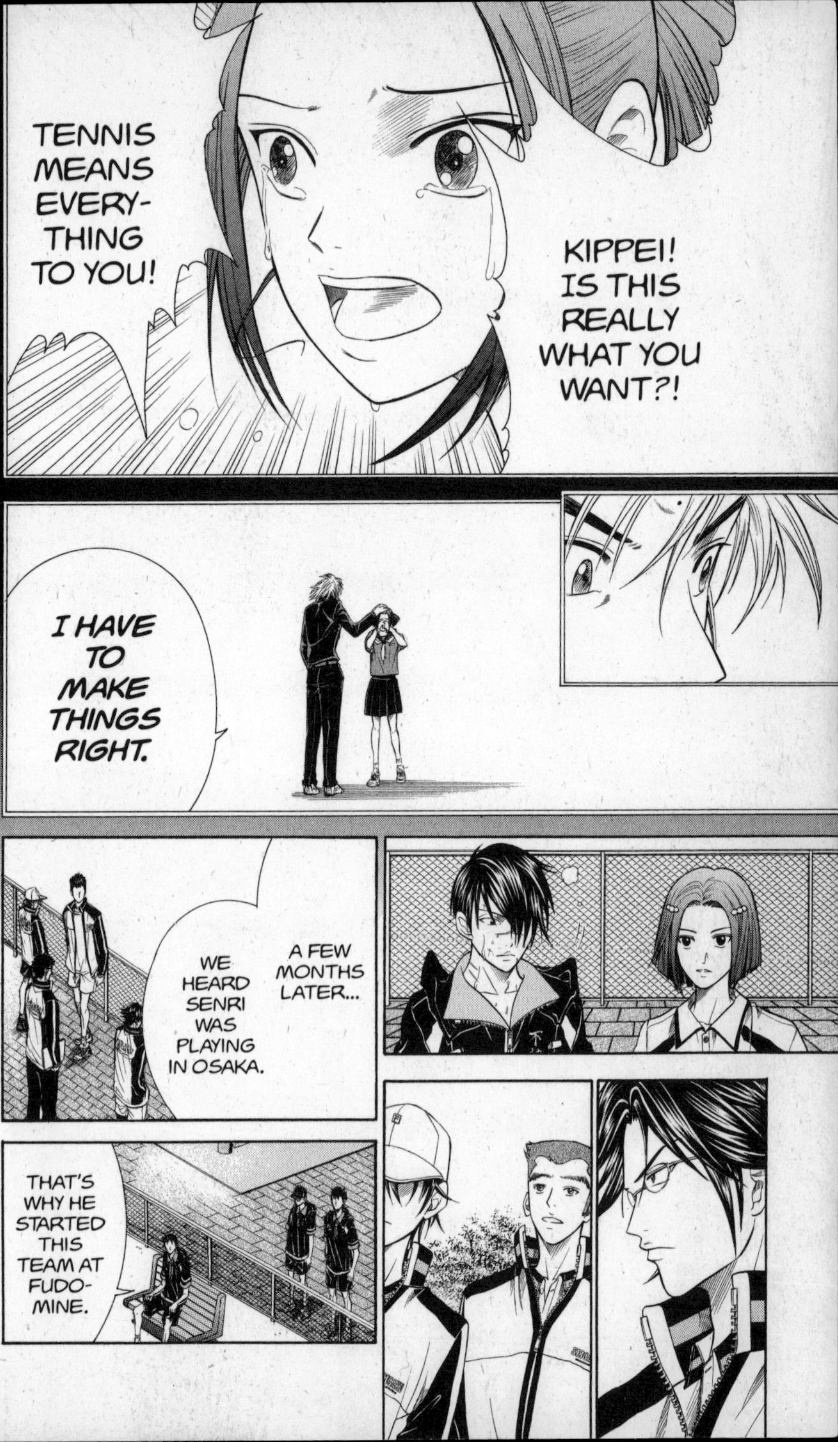
KIPPEI! IS THIS REALLY WHAT YOU WANT?!
TENNIS MEANS EVERY-THING TO YOU!
I HAVE TO MAKE THINGS RIGHT.
A FEW MONTHS LATER...
WE HEARD SENRI WAS PLAYING IN OSAKA.
THAT'S WHY HE STARTED THIS TEAM AT FUDO-MINE.

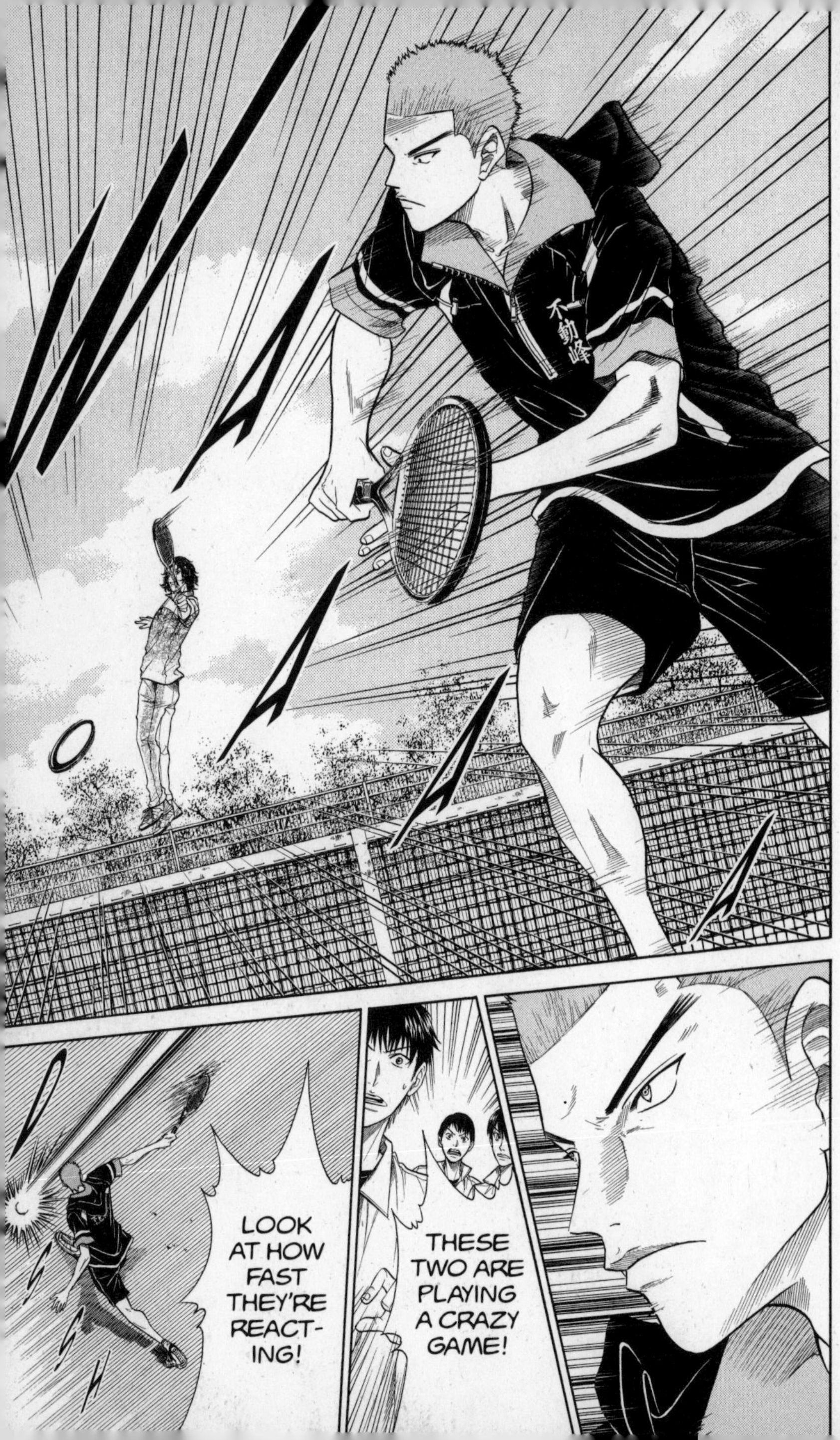
不動峰
THESE TWO ARE PLAYING A CRAZY GAME!
LOOK AT HOW FAST THEY'RE REACT-ING!

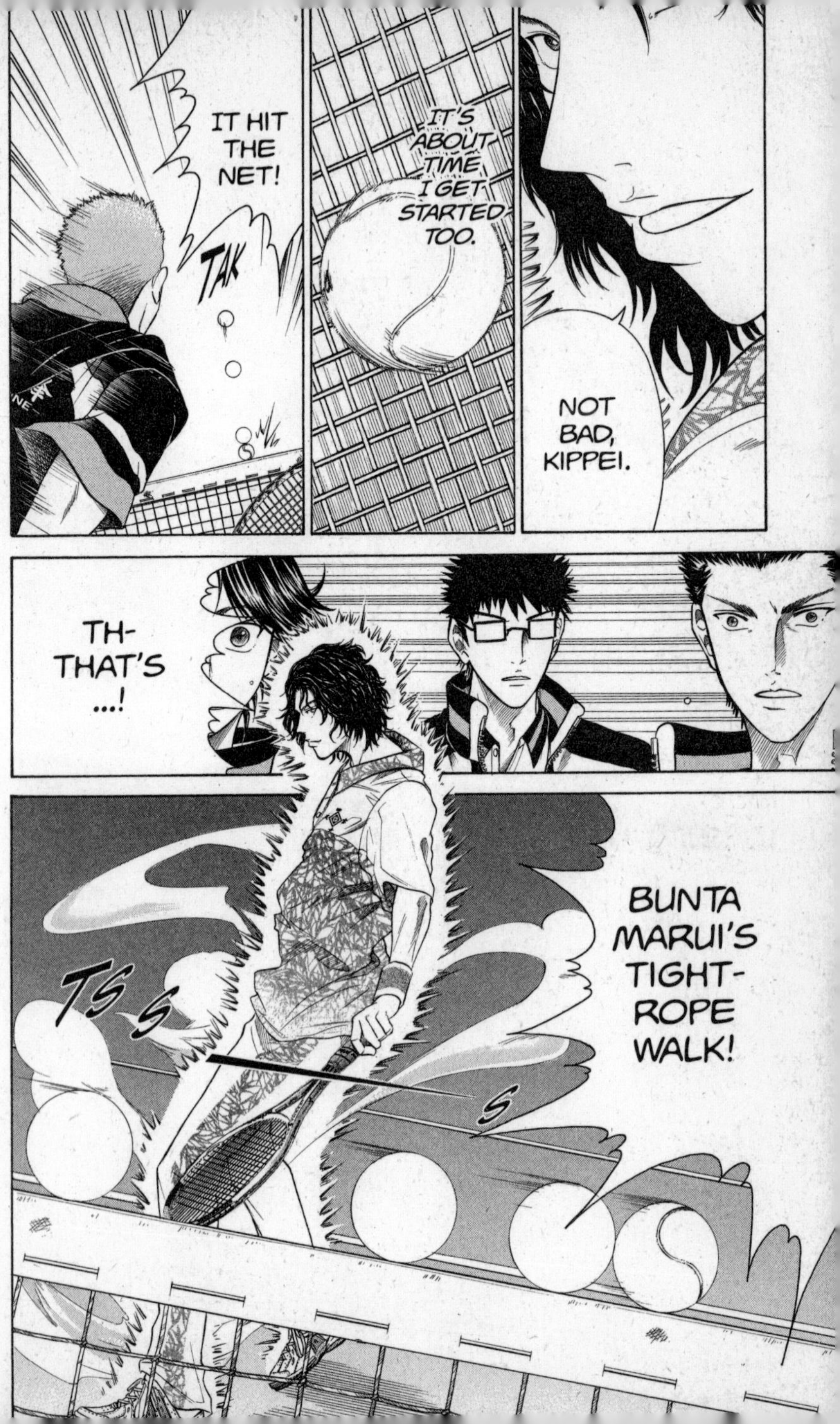
NOT BAD, KIPPEI.
IT'S ABOUT TIME I GET STARTED TOO.
IT HIT THE NET!
TAK
TH- THAT'S ...!
BUNTA MARUI'S TIGHT-ROPE WALK!
TSS
S

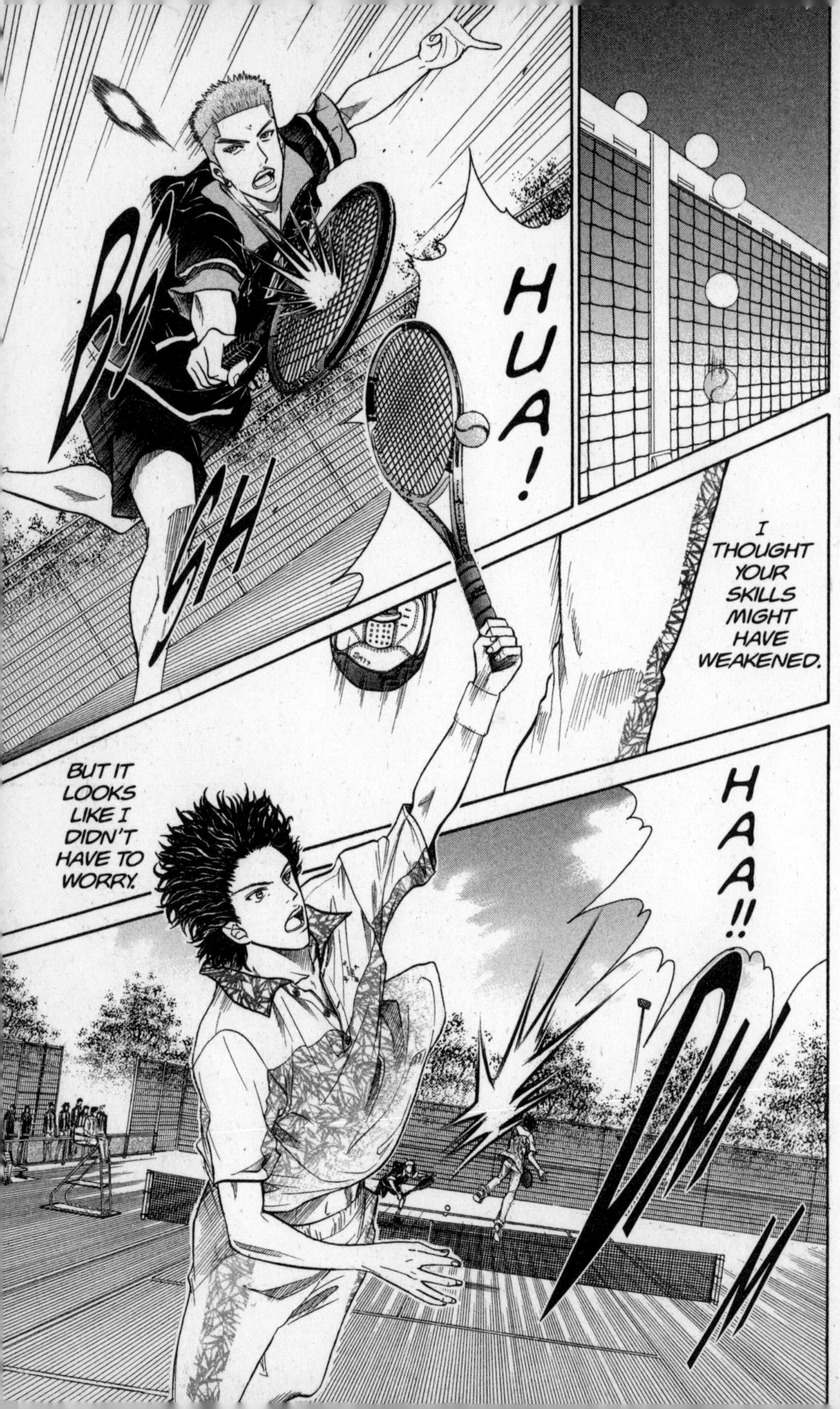
HUA!
I THOUGHT YOUR SKILLS MIGHT HAVE WEAKENED.
HAAA!!
BUT IT LOOKS LIKE I DIDN'T HAVE TO WORRY.

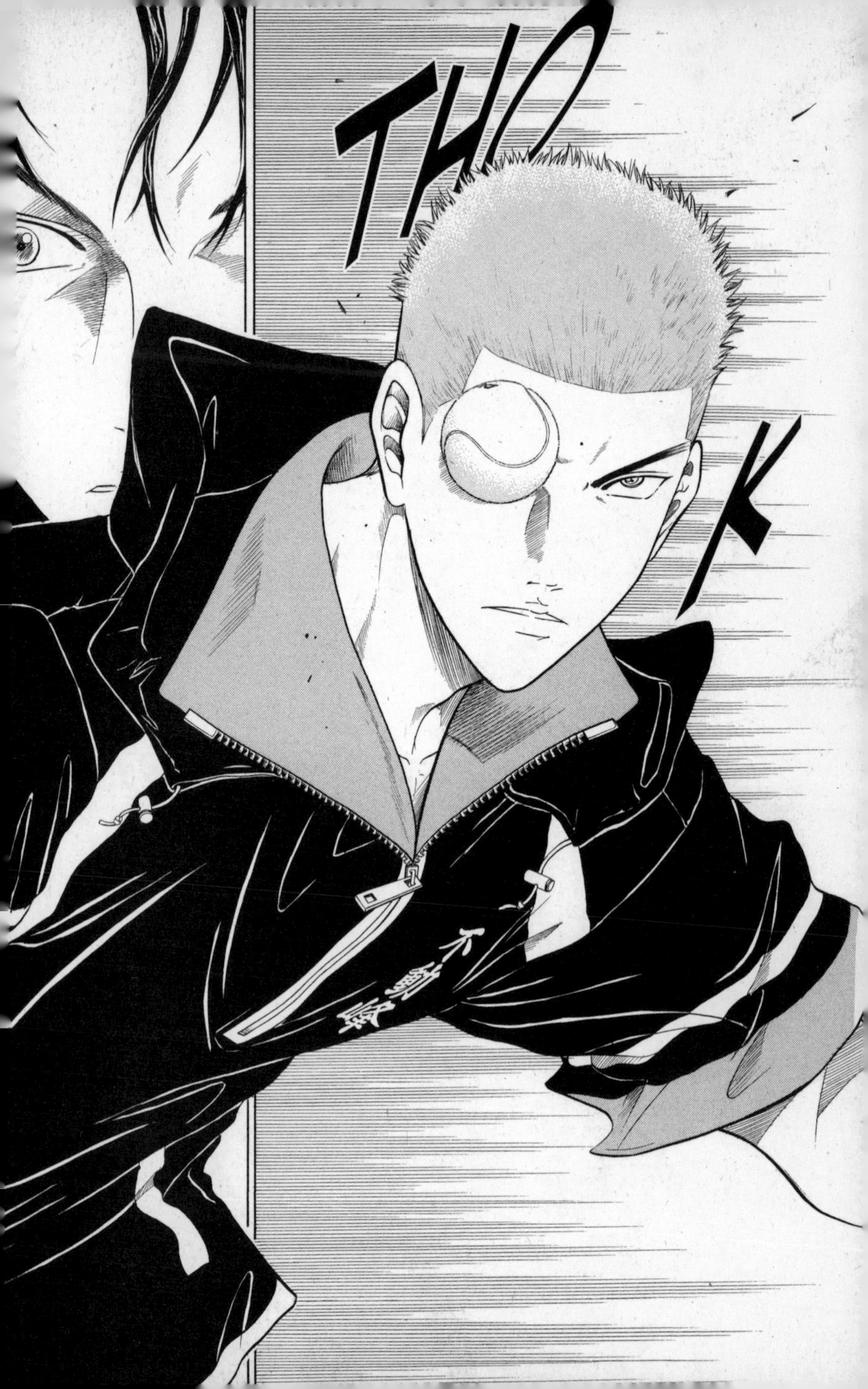
THOK
不動峰

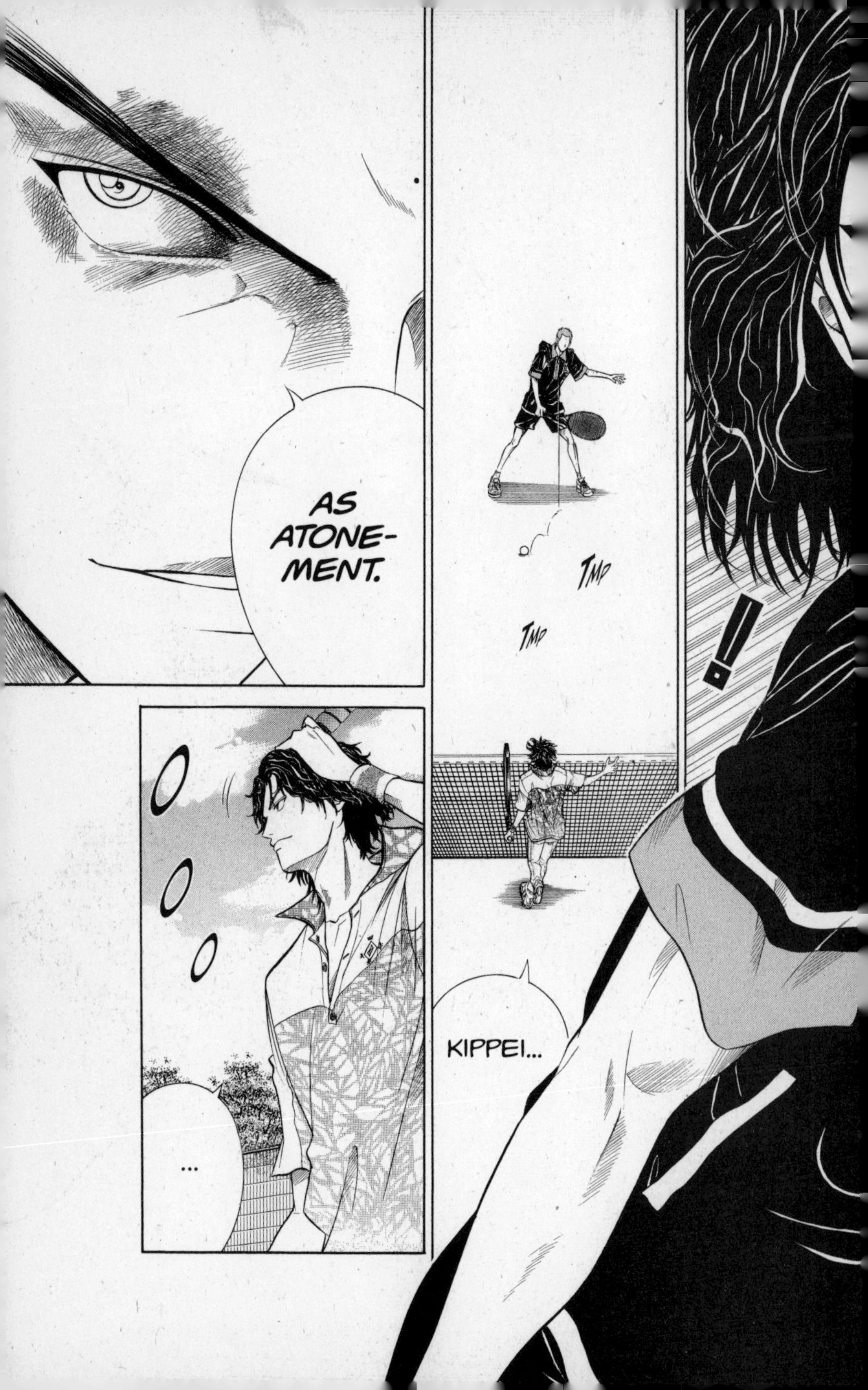
!
TMP
TMP
KIPPEI...
AS ATONEMENT.
...

テニスの王子様

THE PRINCE OF TENNIS

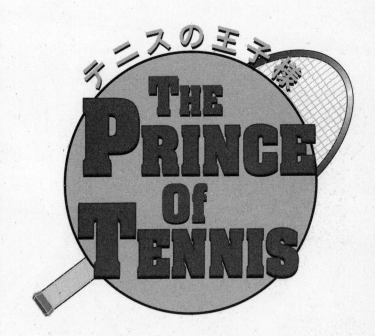

GENIUS 310:

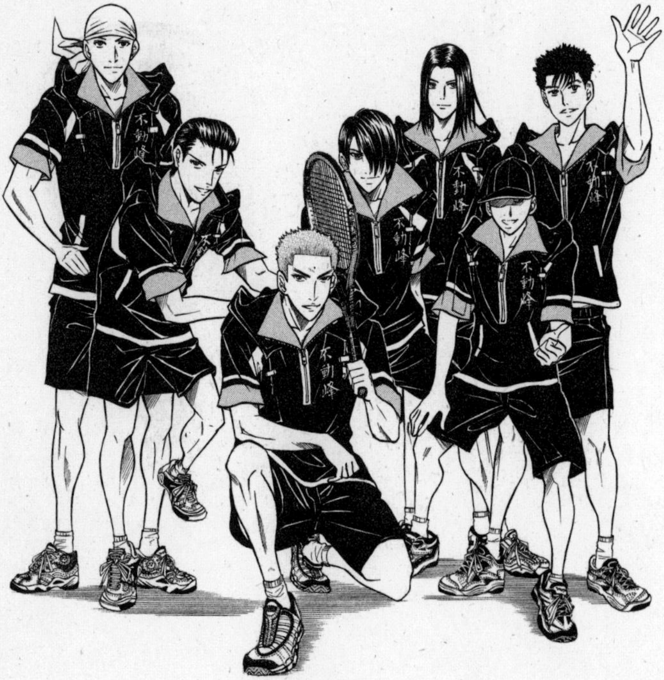
不動峰

WILD LION

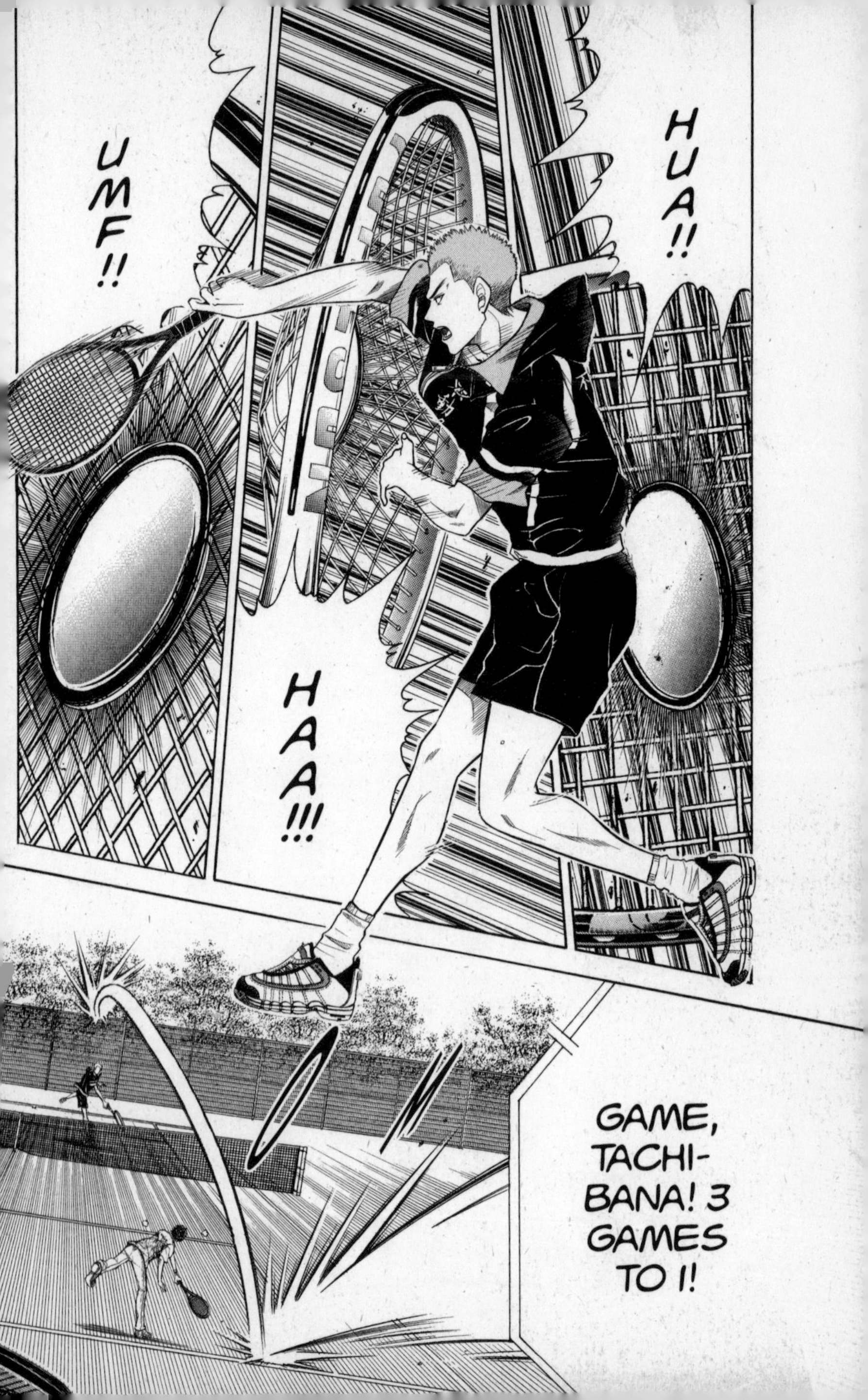
HUA!!
UMF!!
HAAA!!!
GAME, TACHI-BANA! 3 GAMES TO 1!

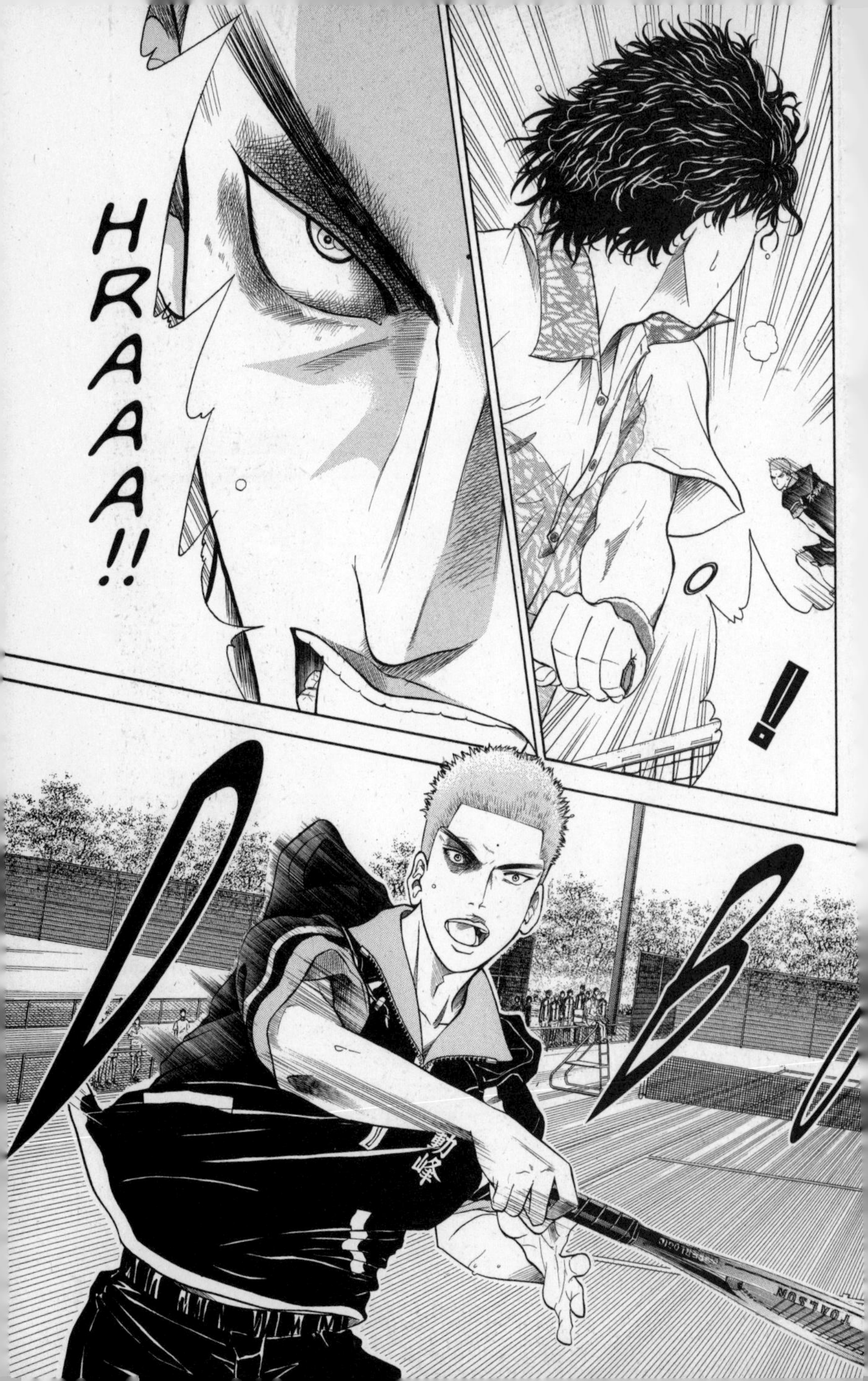
!
HRAAAA!!

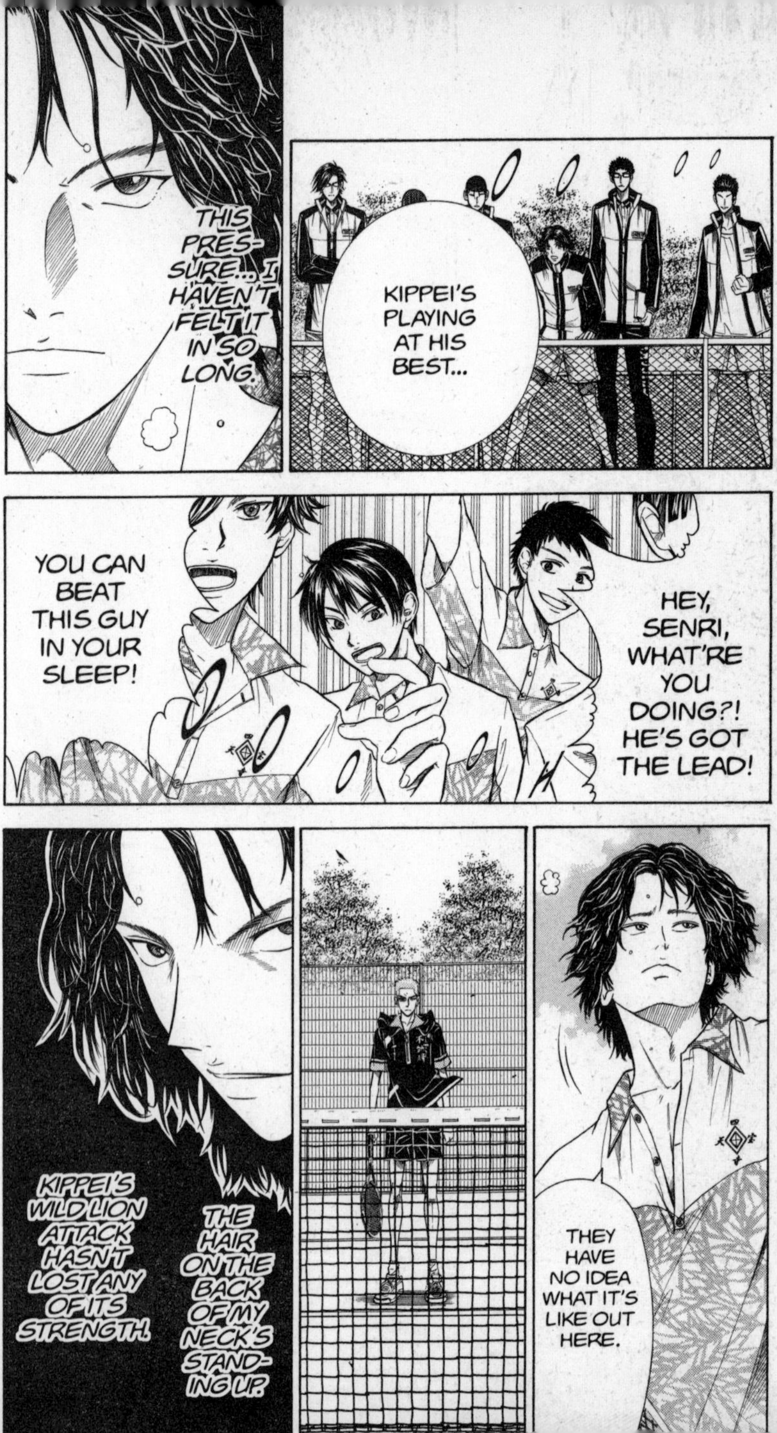
KIPPEI'S PLAYING AT HIS BEST...
THIS PRES-SURE... I HAVEN'T FELT IT IN SO LONG.
HEY, SENRI, WHAT'RE YOU DOING?! HE'S GOT THE LEAD!
YOU CAN BEAT THIS GUY IN YOUR SLEEP!
THEY HAVE NO IDEA WHAT IT'S LIKE OUT HERE.
THE HAIR ON THE BACK OF MY NECK'S STAND-ING UP.
KIPPEI'S WILD LION ATTACK HASN'T LOST ANY OF ITS STRENGTH.

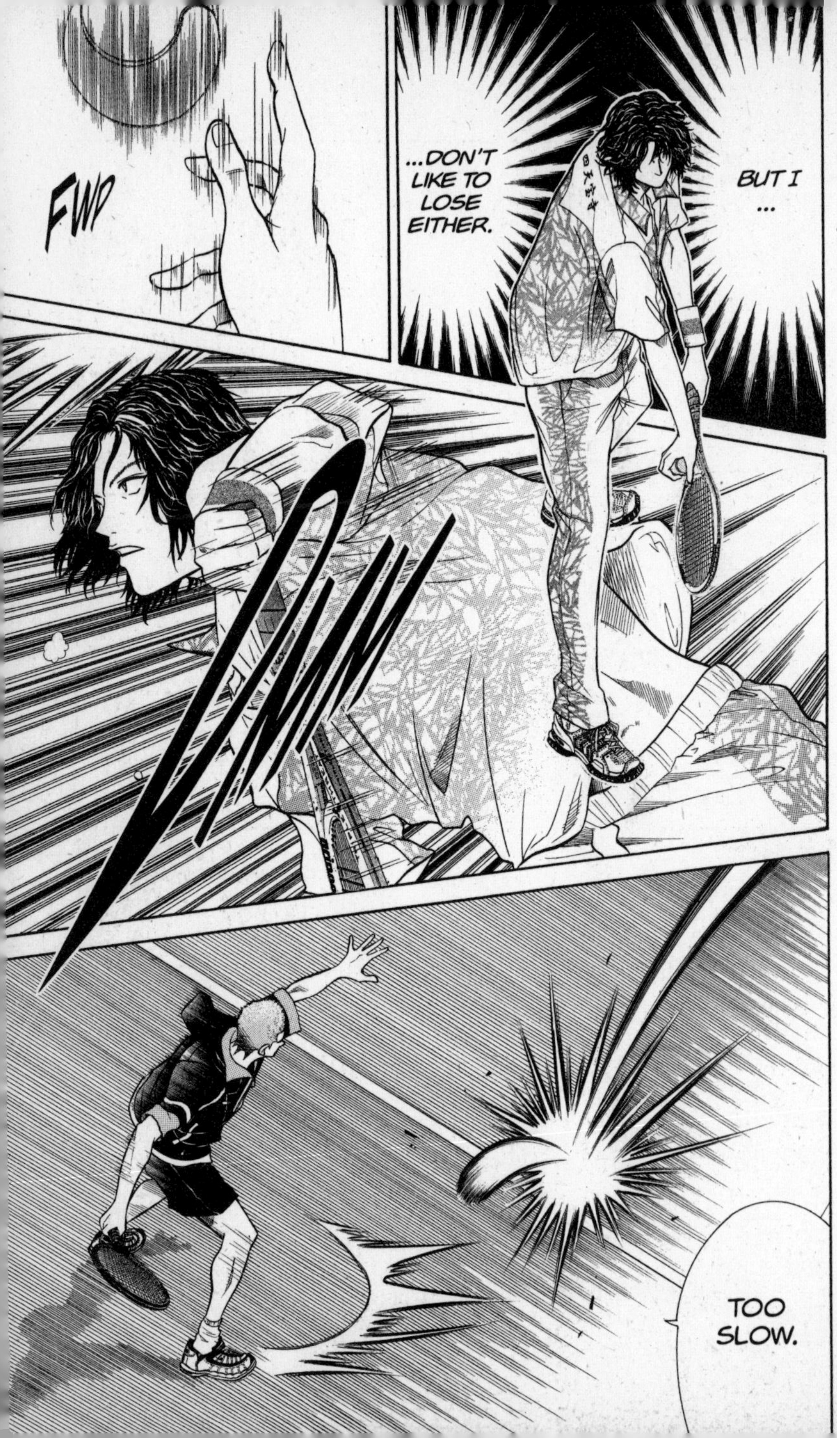
BUT I ...
...DON'T LIKE TO LOSE EITHER.
FWP
TOO SLOW.

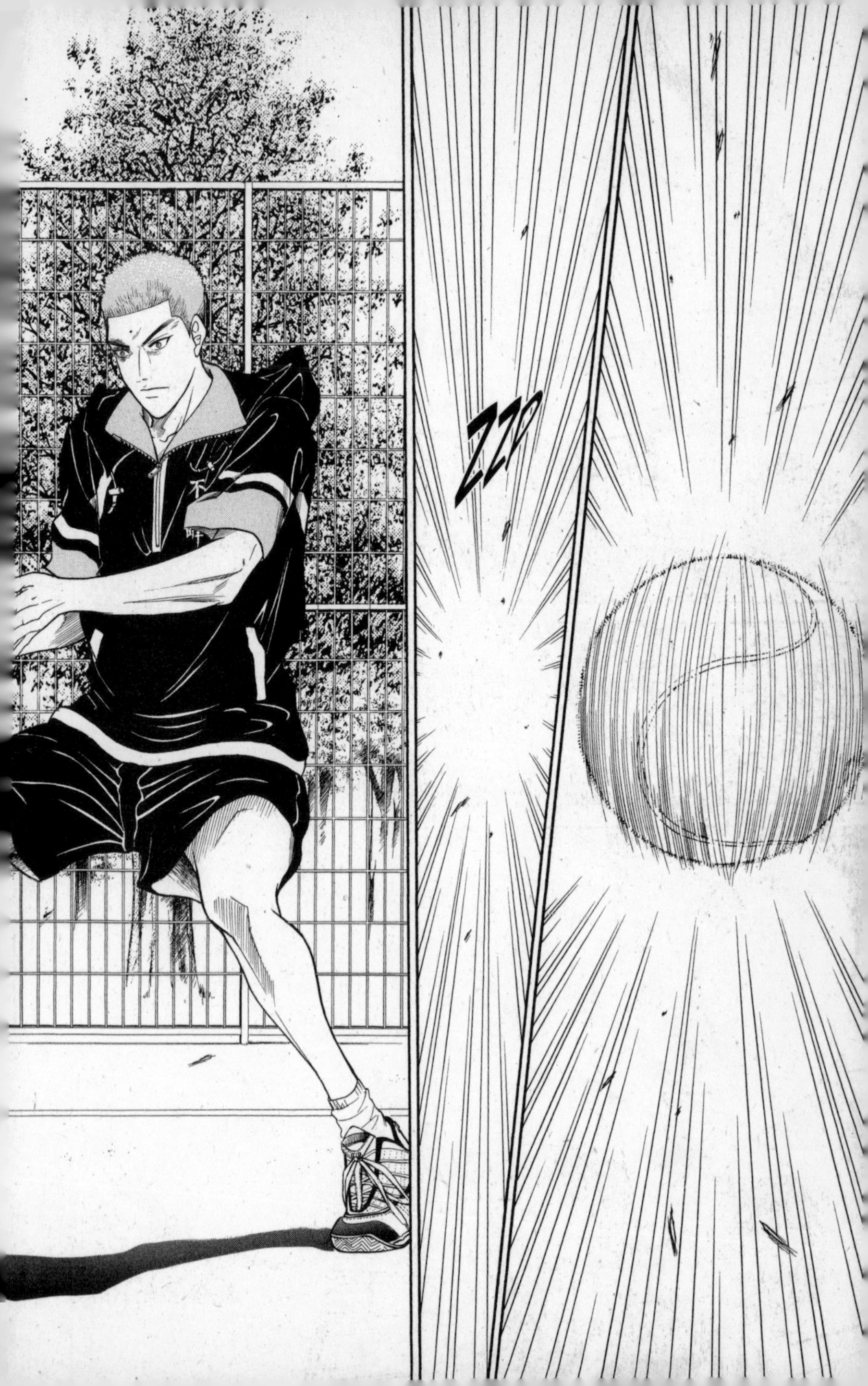
ZZP

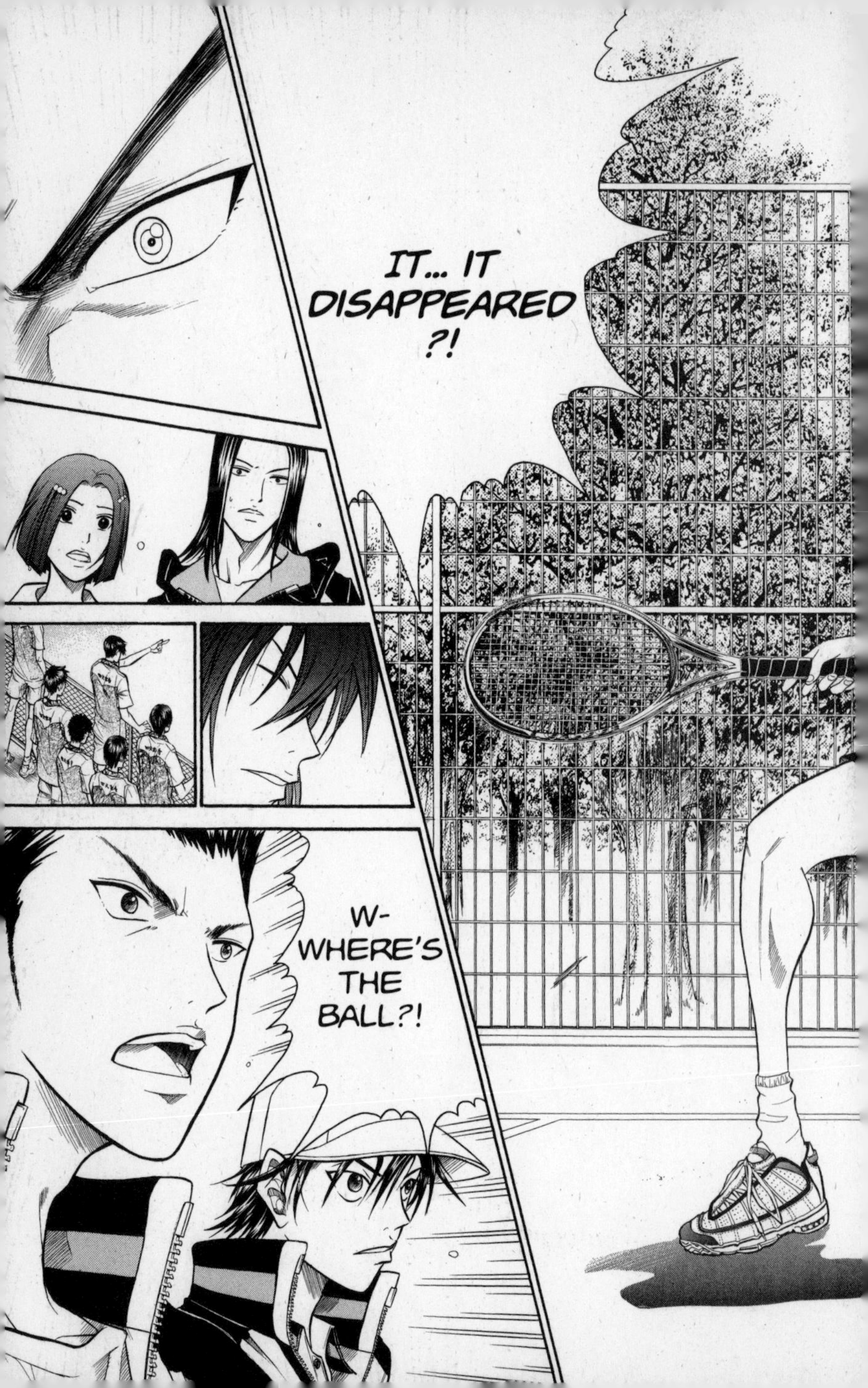
IT... IT DISAPPEARED?!
W-WHERE'S THE BALL?!

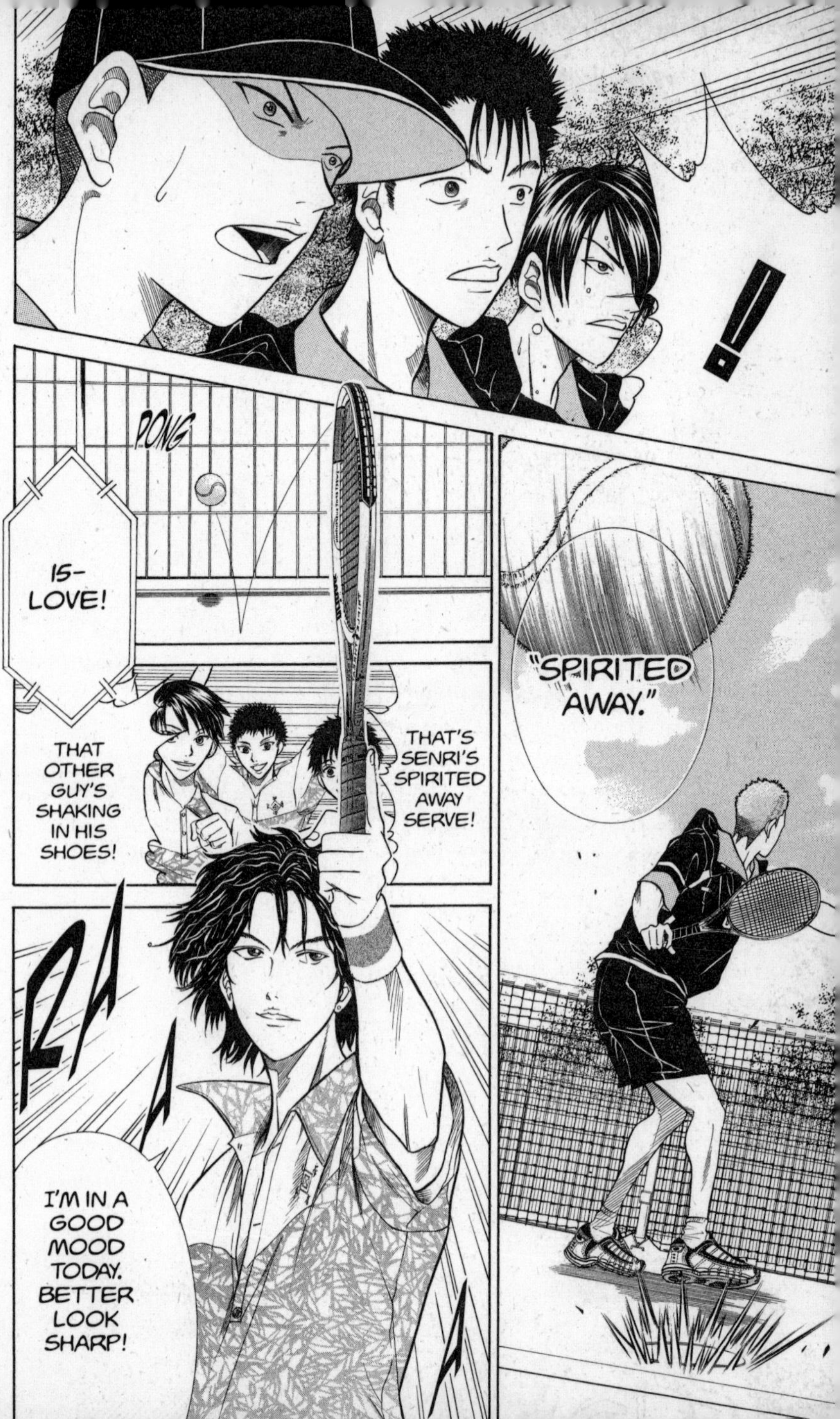
!
"SPIRITED AWAY."
PONG
15-LOVE!
THAT'S SENRI'S SPIRITED AWAY SERVE!
THAT OTHER GUY'S SHAKING IN HIS SHOES!
I'M IN A GOOD MOOD TODAY. BETTER LOOK SHARP!

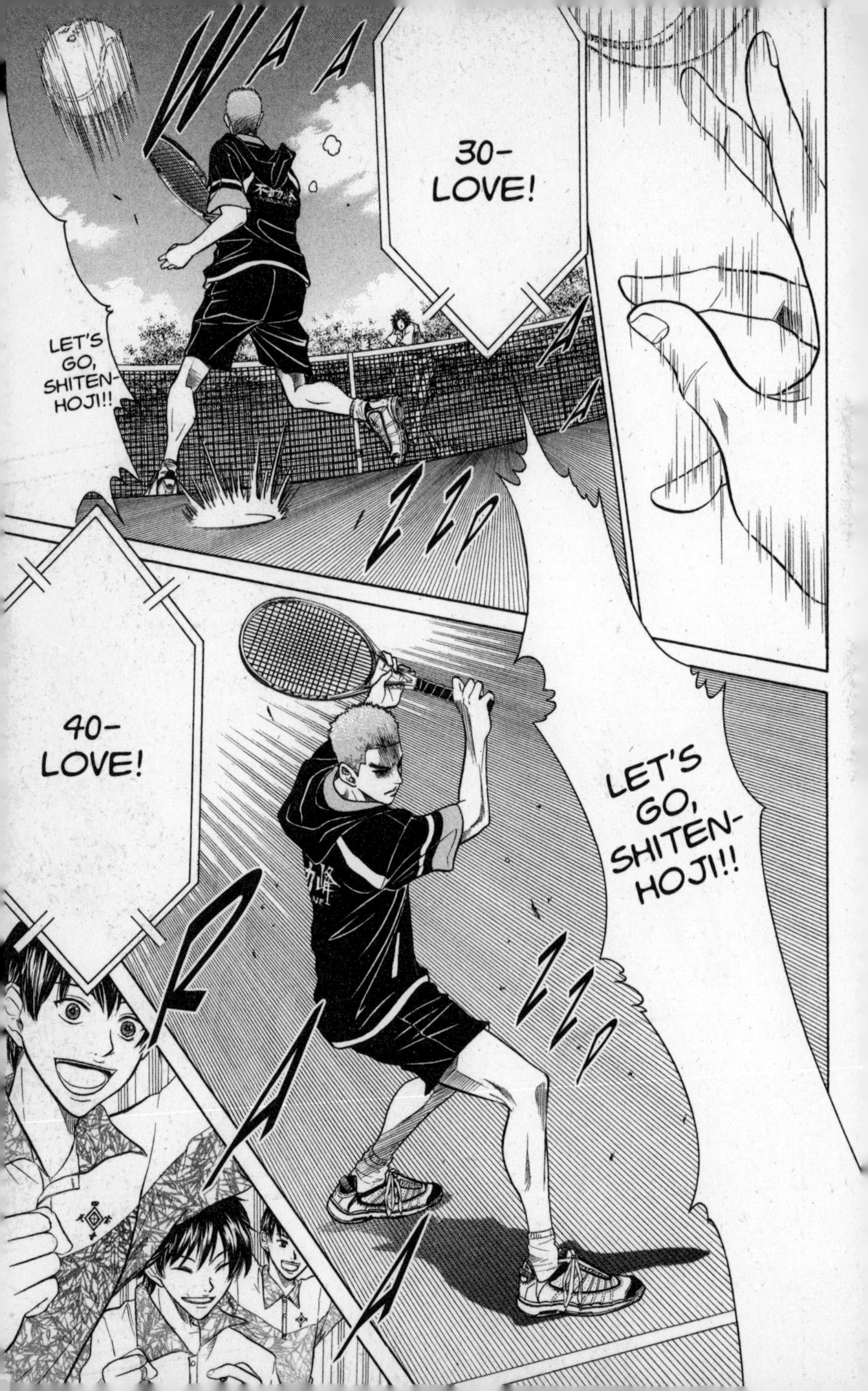
30-
LOVE!
LET'S GO, SHITEN-HOJI!!
LET'S GO, SHITEN-HOJI!!
40-
LOVE!

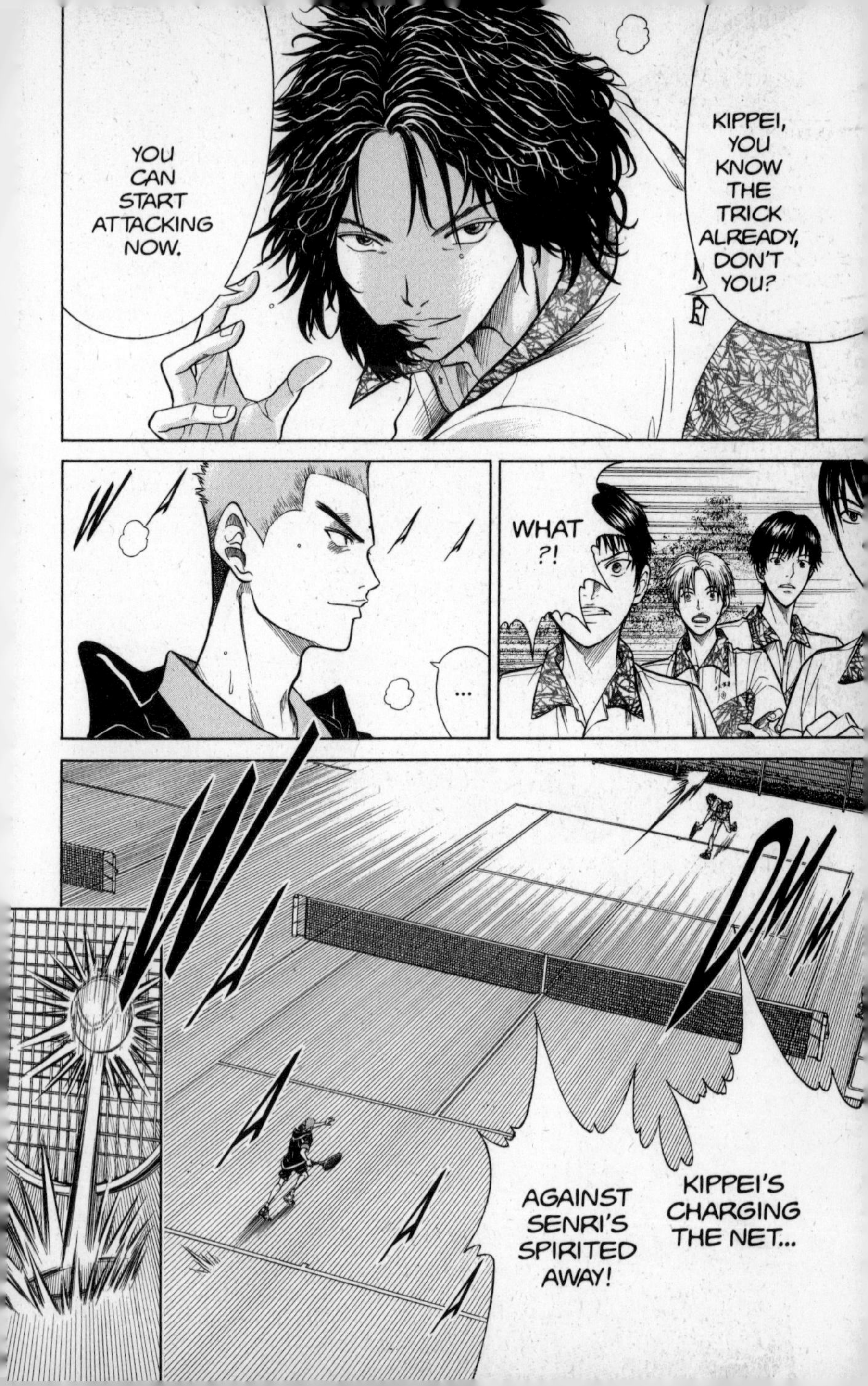
KIPPEI, YOU KNOW THE TRICK ALREADY, DON'T YOU?
YOU CAN START ATTACKING NOW.
WHAT ?!
...
KIPPEI'S CHARGING THE NET...
AGAINST SENRI'S SPIRITED AWAY!

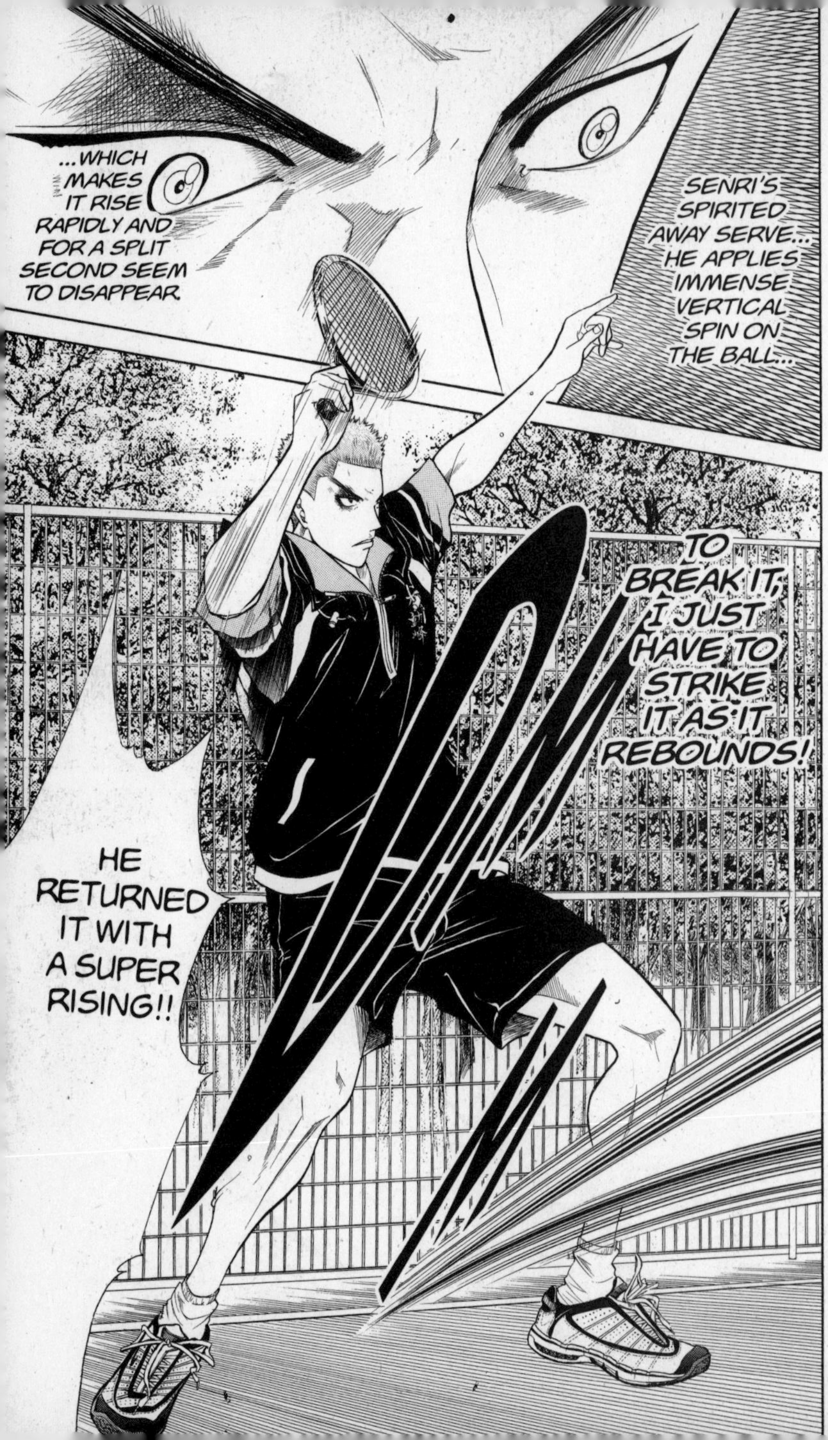
SENRI'S SPIRITED AWAY SERVE... HE APPLIES IMMENSE VERTICAL SPIN ON THE BALL...
...WHICH MAKES IT RISE RAPIDLY AND FOR A SPLIT SECOND SEEM TO DISAPPEAR.
TO BREAK IT, I JUST HAVE TO STRIKE IT AS IT REBOUNDS!
HE RETURNED IT WITH A SUPER RISING!!

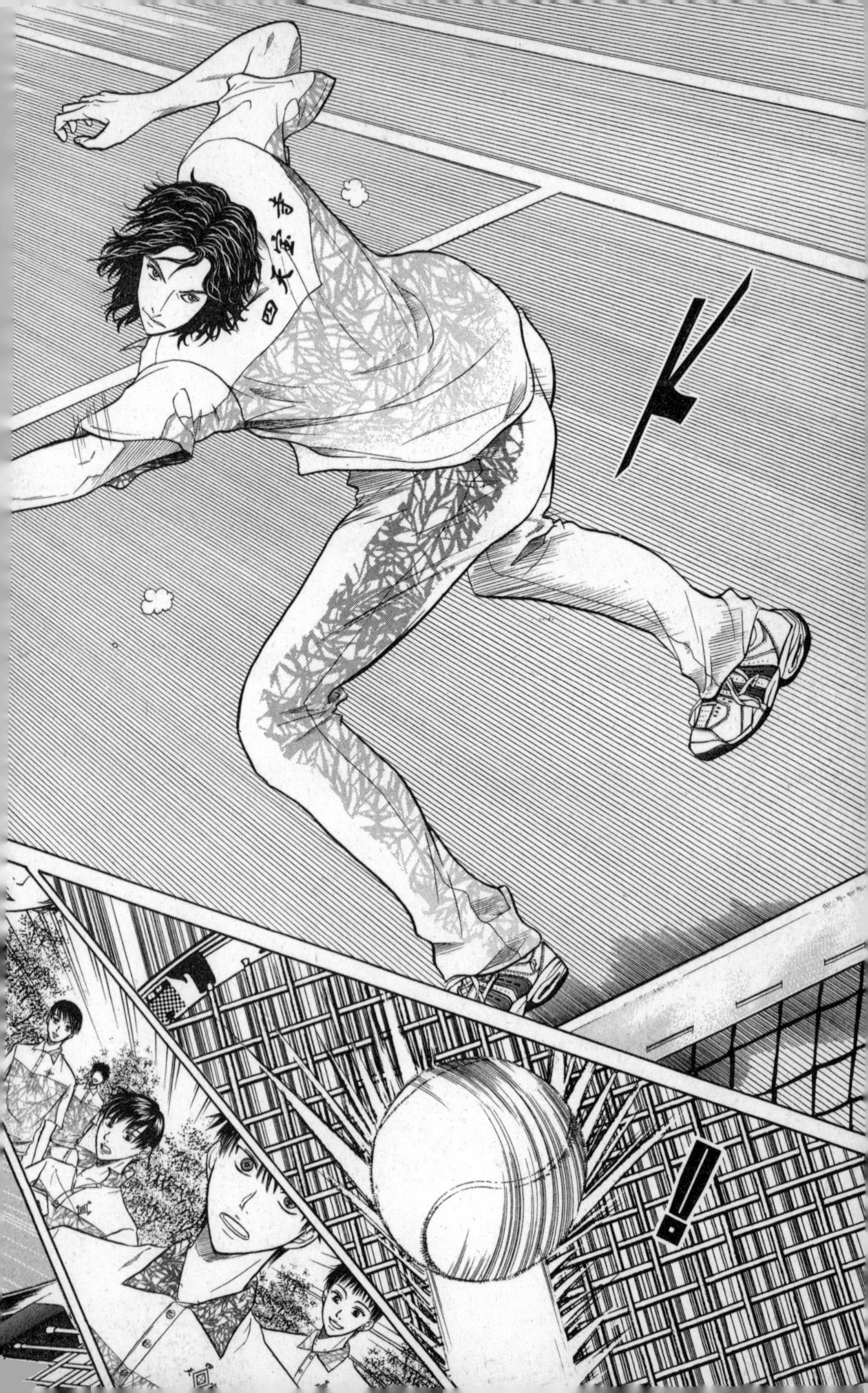
!

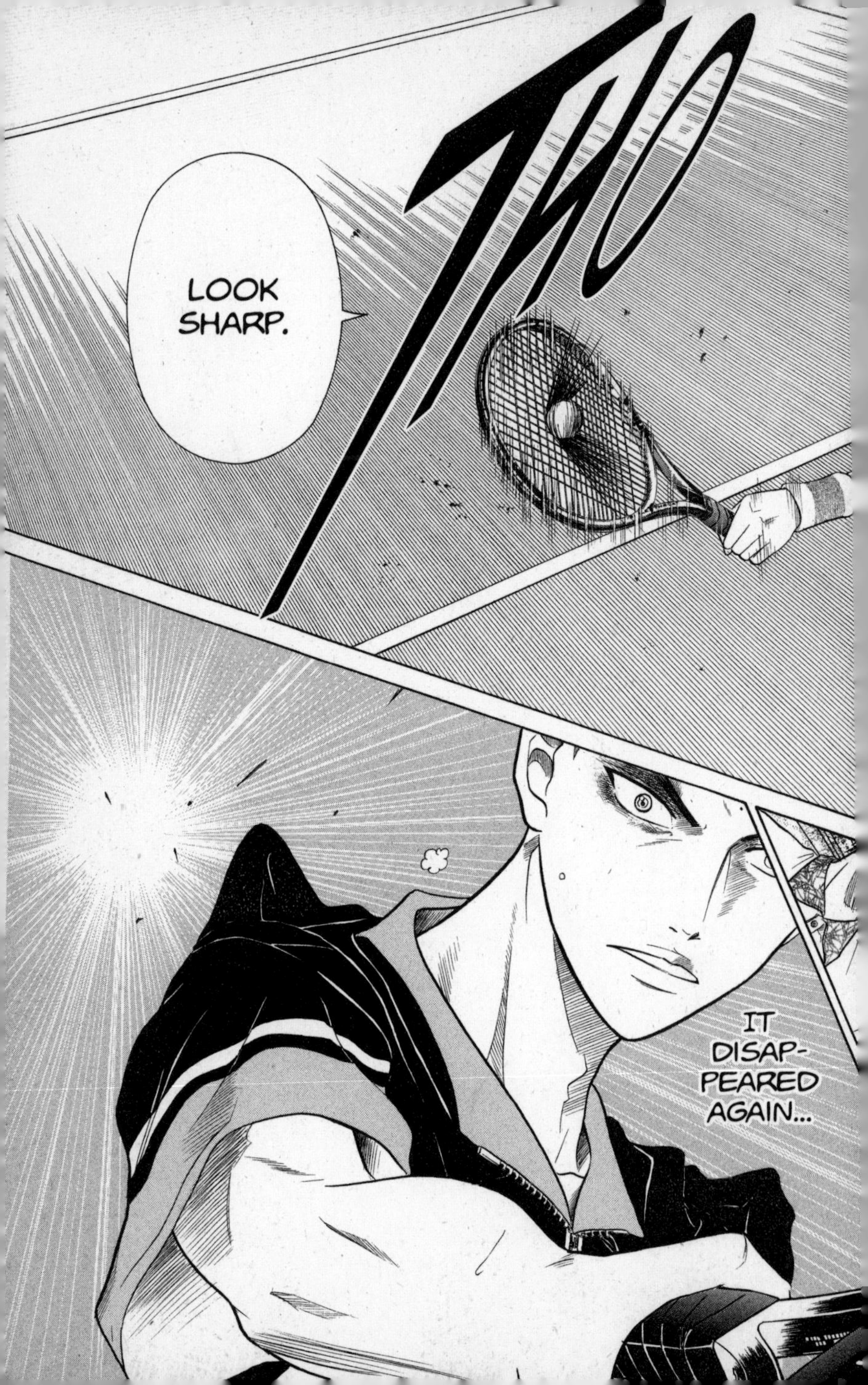
LOOK SHARP.
IT DISAP-PEARED AGAIN...

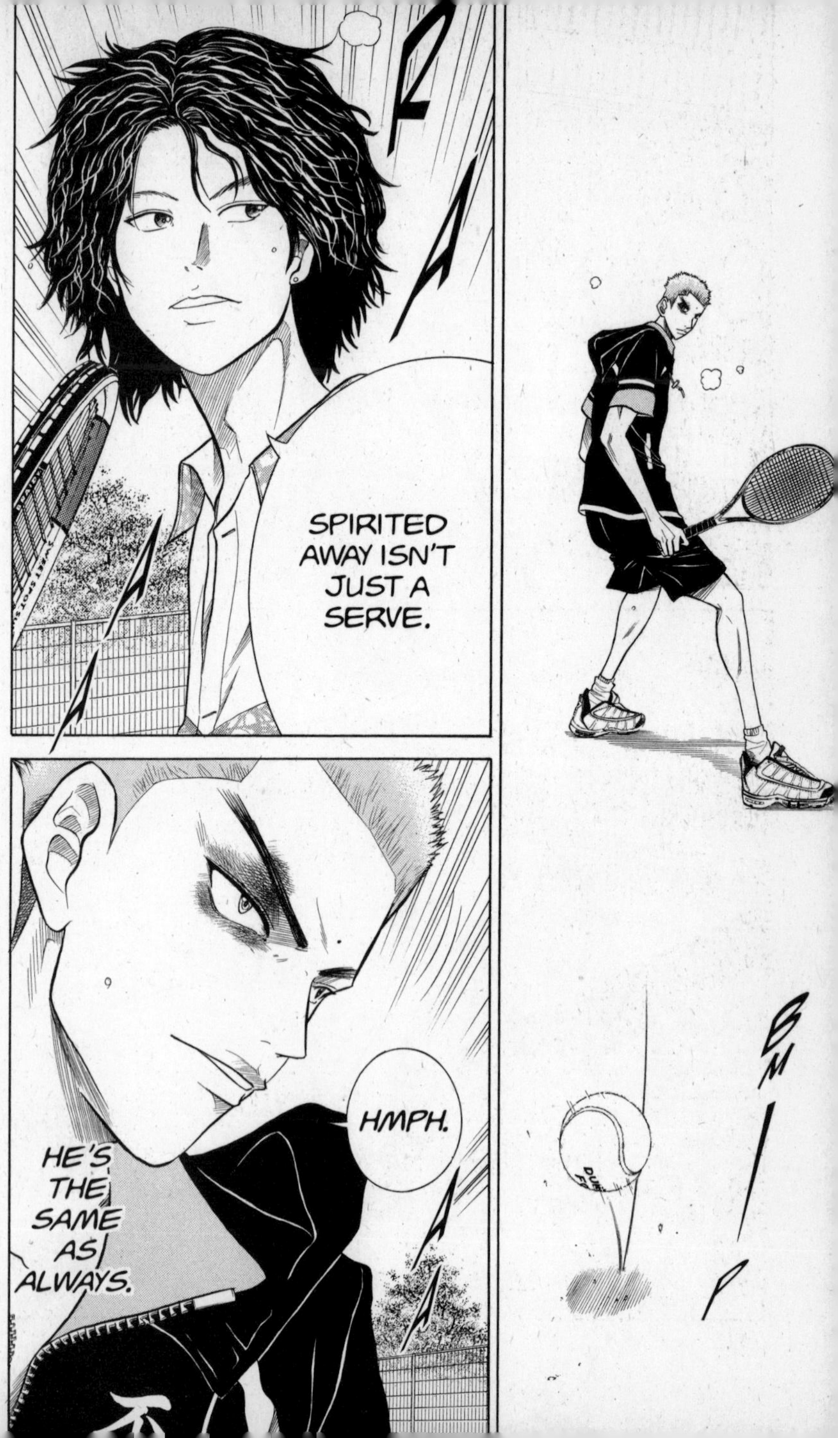
BMP
SPIRITED AWAY ISN'T JUST A SERVE.
HMPH.
HE'S THE SAME AS ALWAYS.

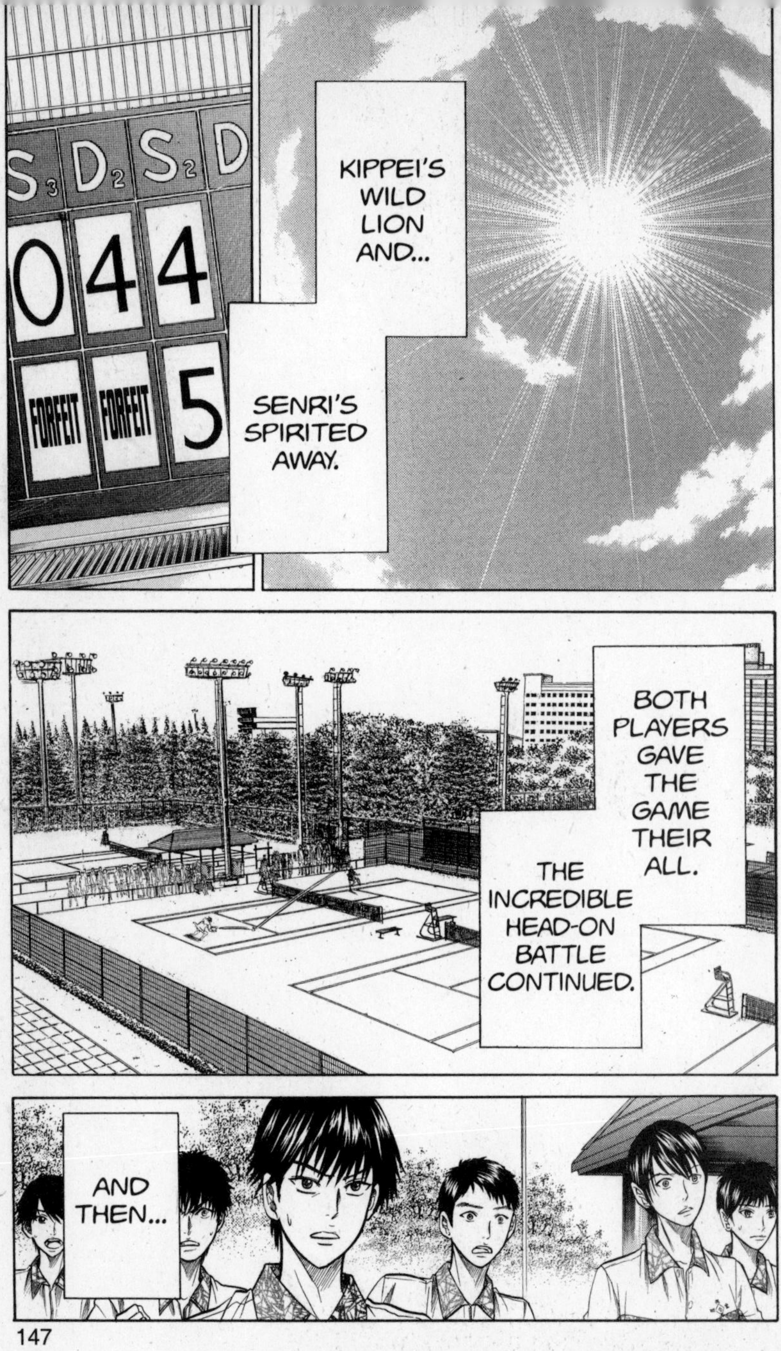
KIPPEI'S WILD LION AND...
SENRI'S SPIRITED AWAY.
S3 D2 S2 D
0 4 4
FORFEIT FORFEIT 5
BOTH PLAYERS GAVE THE GAME THEIR ALL.
THE INCREDIBLE HEAD-ON BATTLE CONTINUED.
AND THEN...

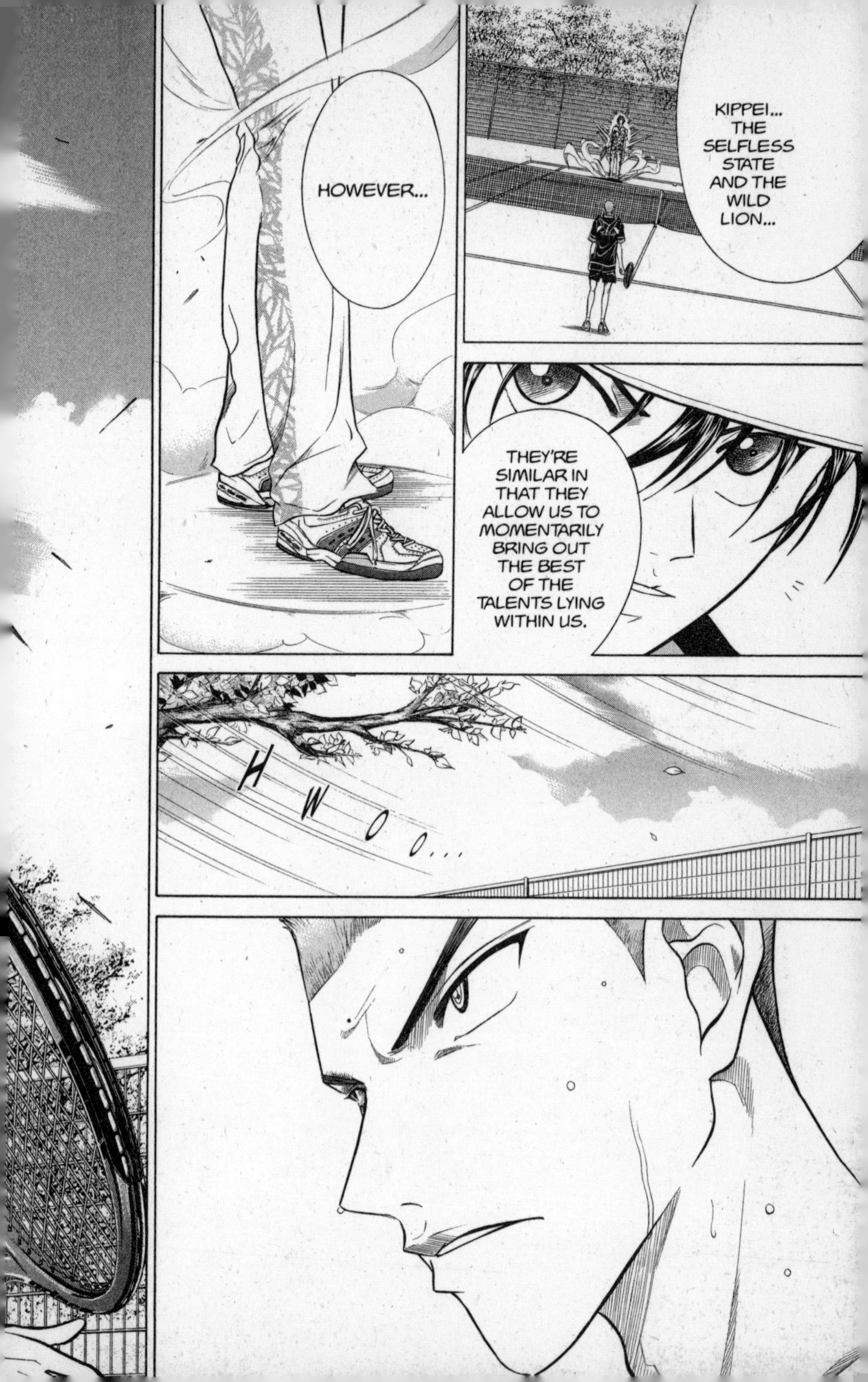
KIPPEI... THE SELFLESS STATE AND THE WILD LION...
THEY'RE SIMILAR IN THAT THEY ALLOW US TO MOMENTARILY BRING OUT THE BEST OF THE TALENTS LYING WITHIN US.
HOWEVER...
HWOO...

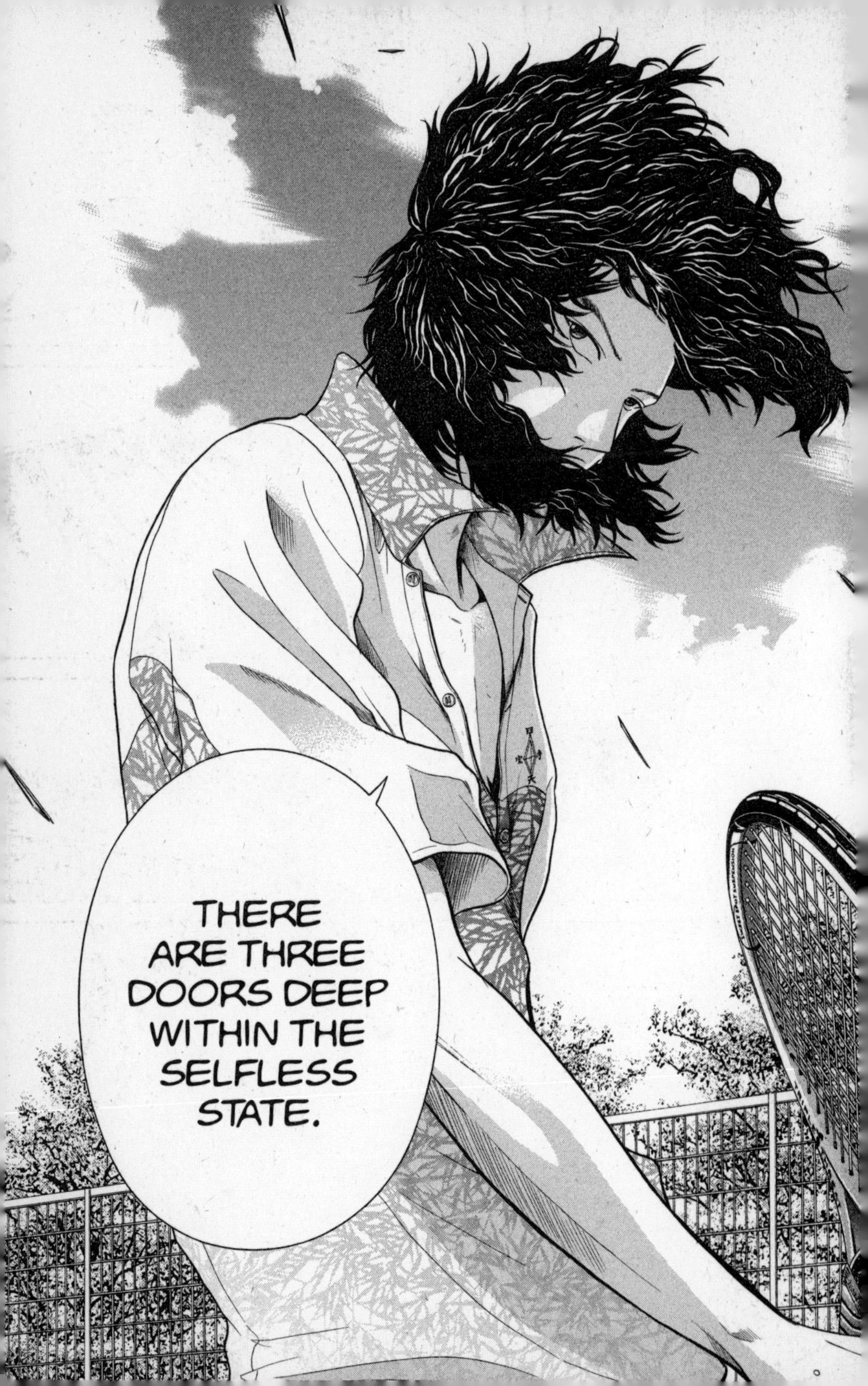
THERE ARE THREE DOORS DEEP WITHIN THE SELFLESS STATE.

テニスの王子様

THE PRINCE OF TENNIS

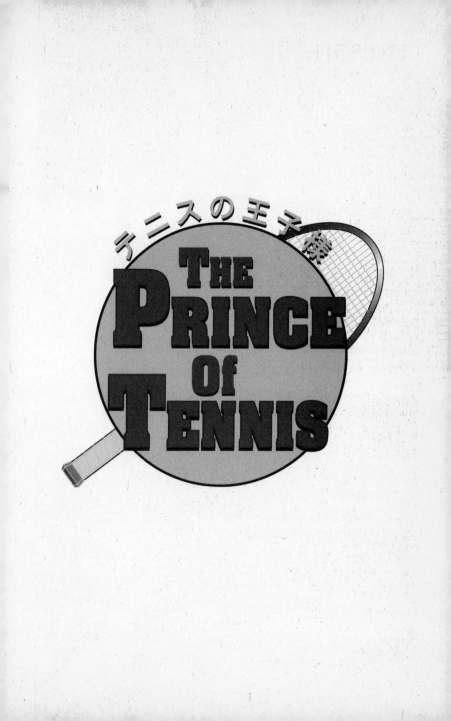

GENIUS 311: THE DEPTHS OF SELFLESSNESS

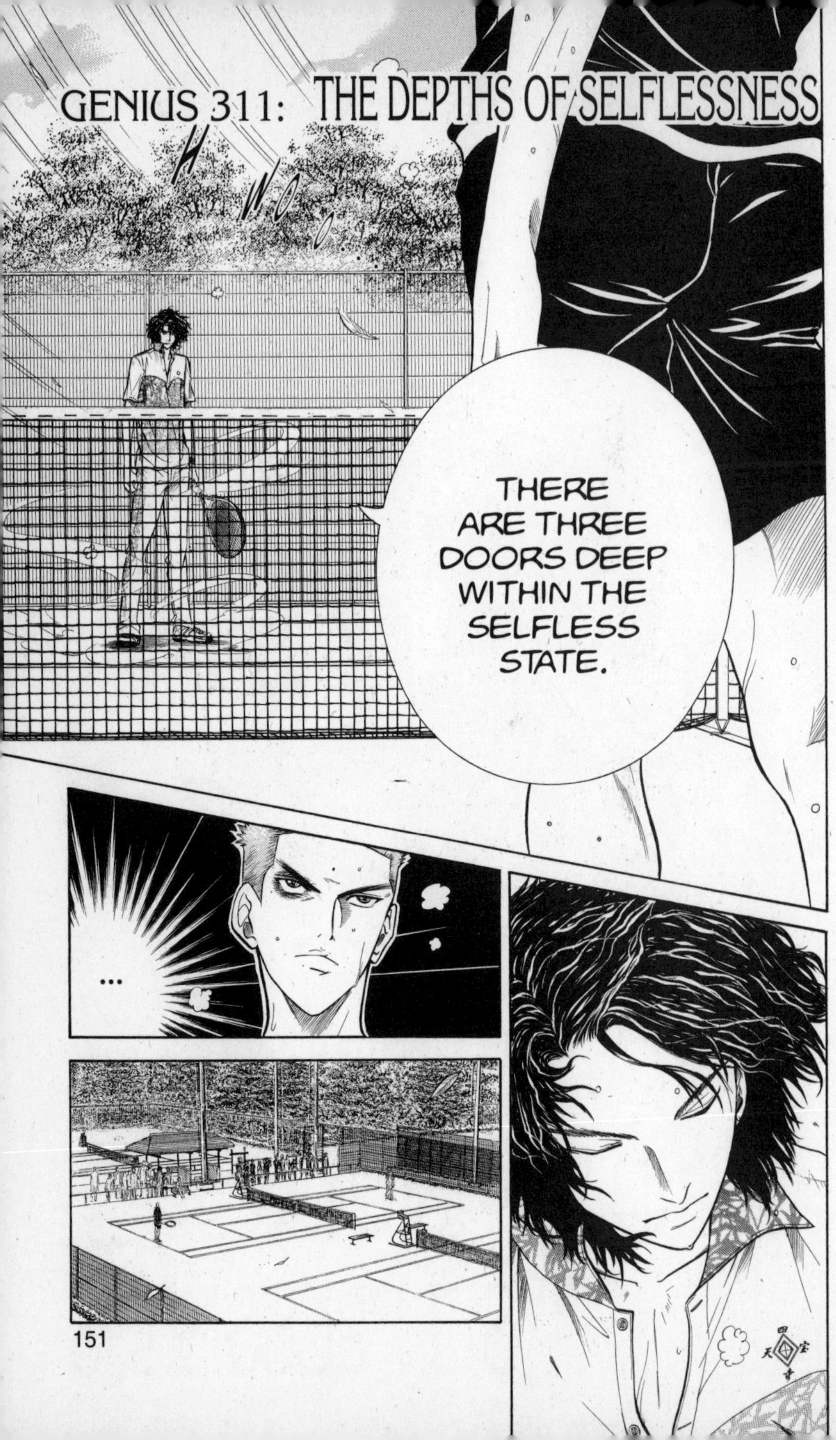
THERE ARE THREE DOORS DEEP WITHIN THE SELFLESS STATE.
...

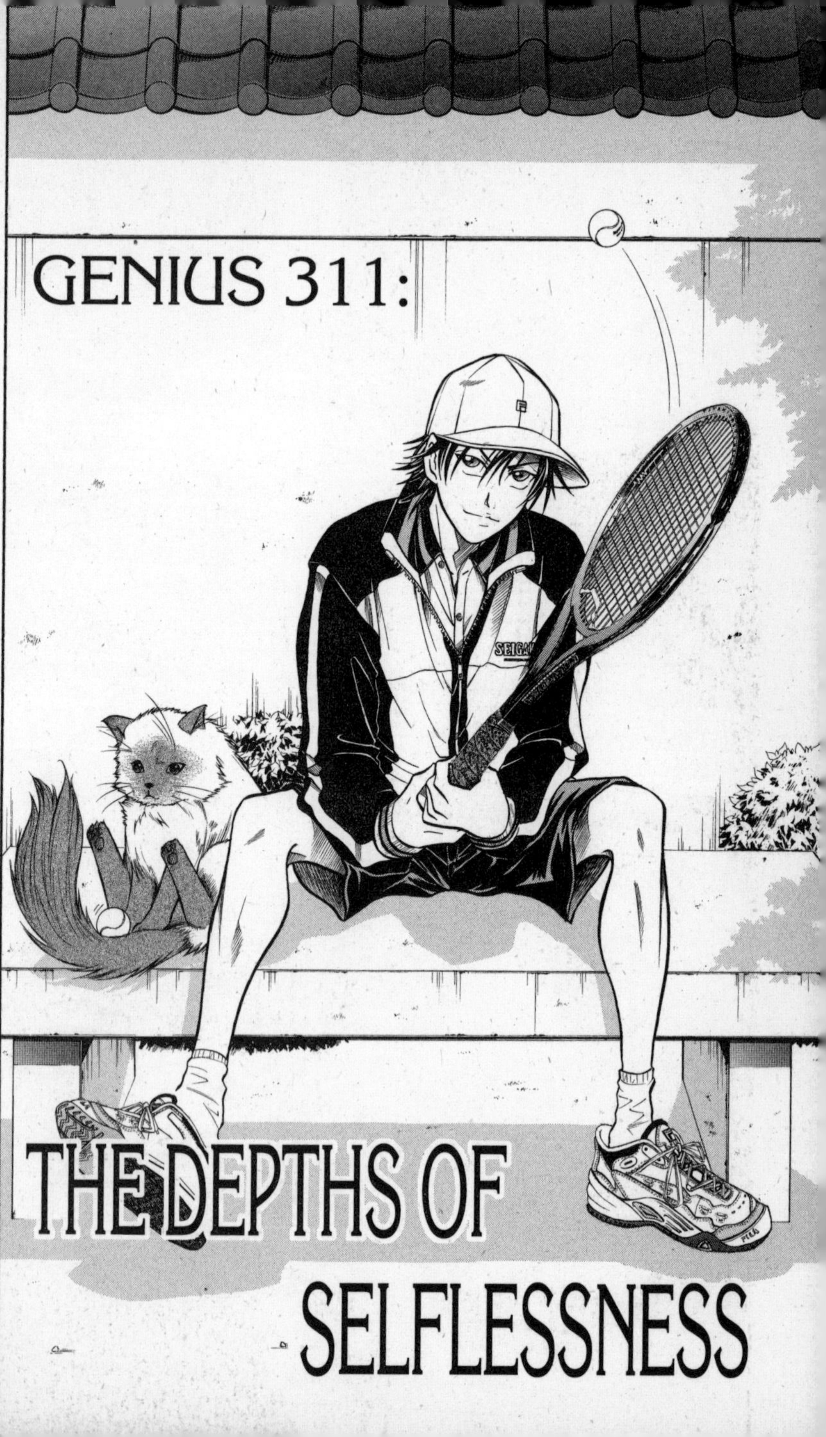
GENIUS 311:
THE DEPTHS OF SELFLESSNESS

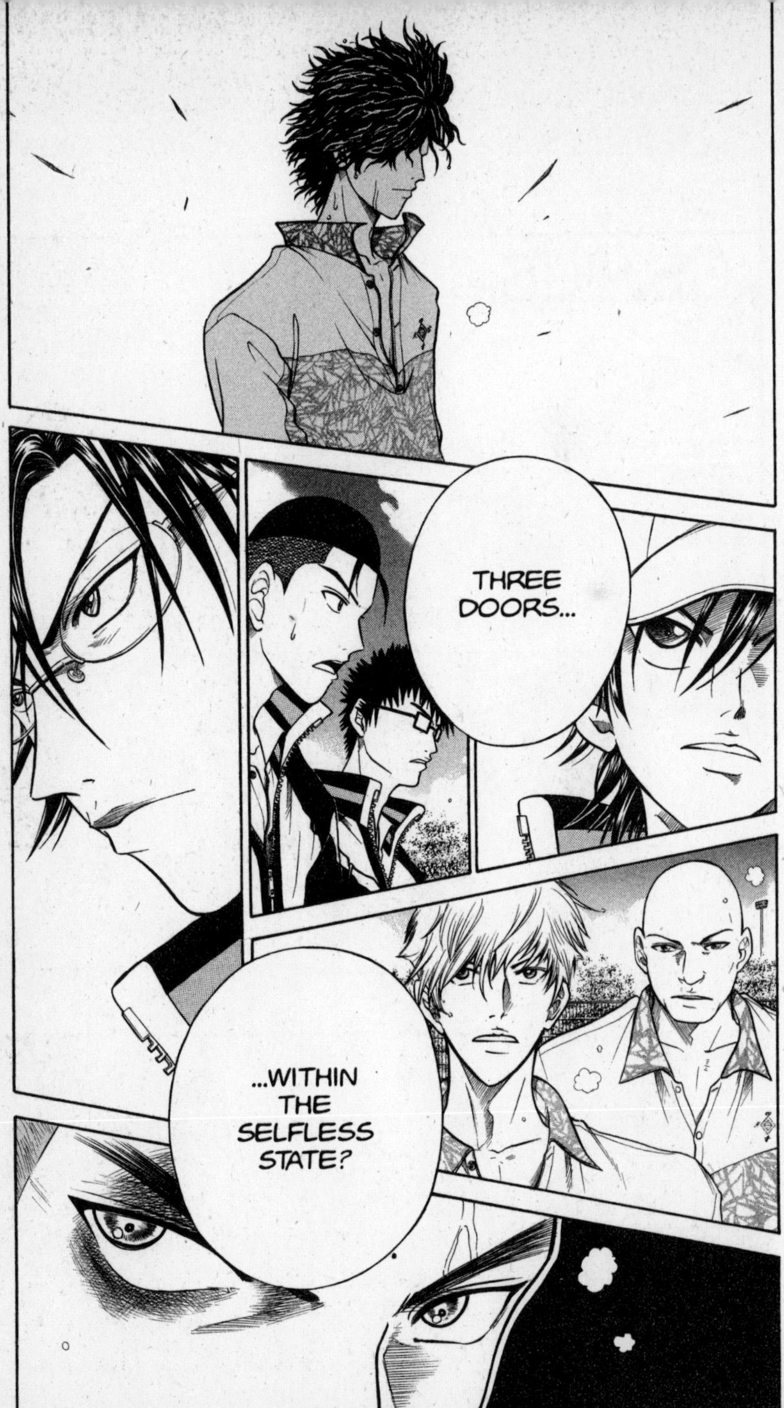
THREE DOORS...
...WITHIN THE SELFLESS STATE?

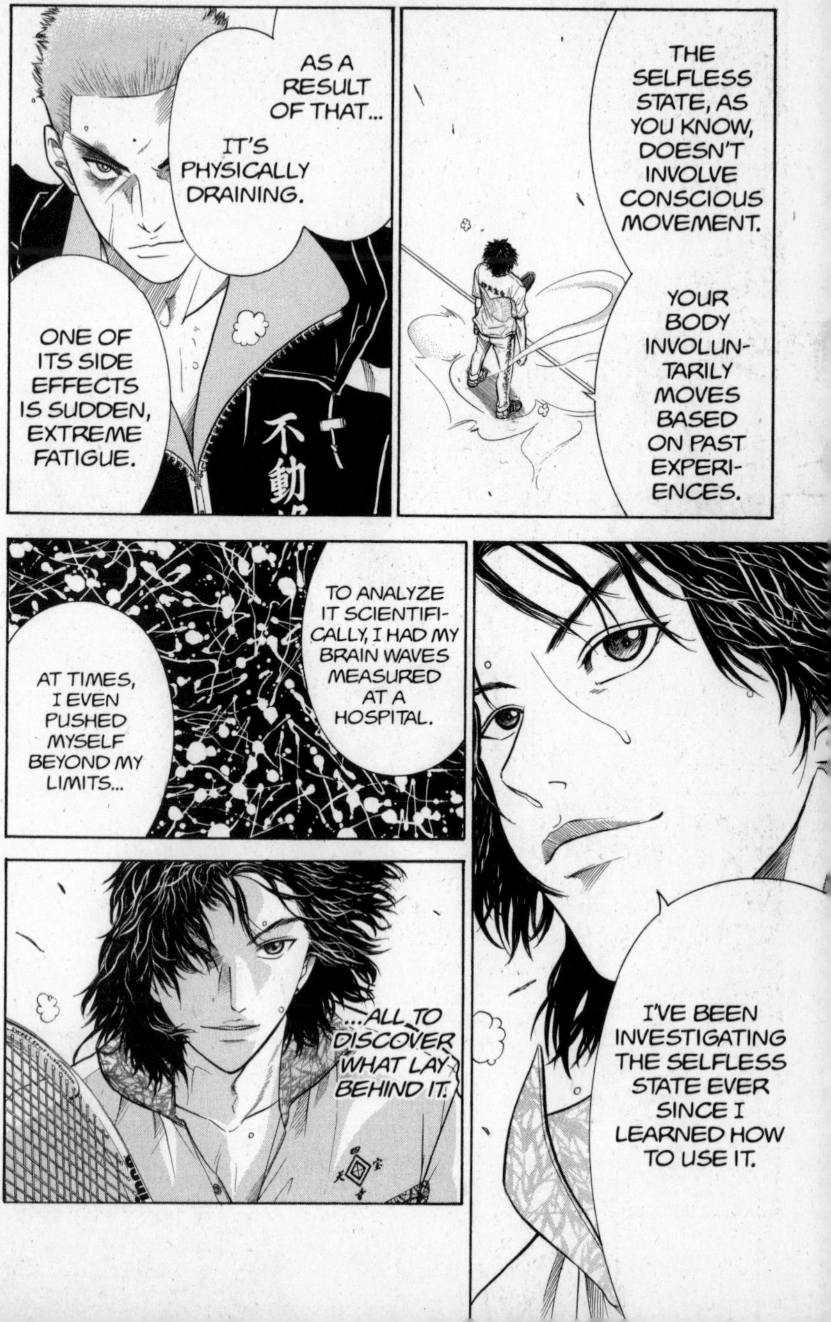

THE SELFLESS STATE, AS YOU KNOW, DOESN'T INVOLVE CONSCIOUS MOVEMENT.
YOUR BODY INVOLUN-TARILY MOVES BASED ON PAST EXPERI-ENCES.
AS A RESULT OF THAT...
IT'S PHYSICALLY DRAINING.
ONE OF ITS SIDE EFFECTS IS SUDDEN, EXTREME FATIGUE.
不動
I'VE BEEN INVESTIGATING THE SELFLESS STATE EVER SINCE I LEARNED HOW TO USE IT.
TO ANALYZE IT SCIENTIFI-CALLY, I HAD MY BRAIN WAVES MEASURED AT A HOSPITAL.
AT TIMES, I EVEN PUSHED MYSELF BEYOND MY LIMITS...
...ALL TO DISCOVER WHAT LAY BEHIND IT.

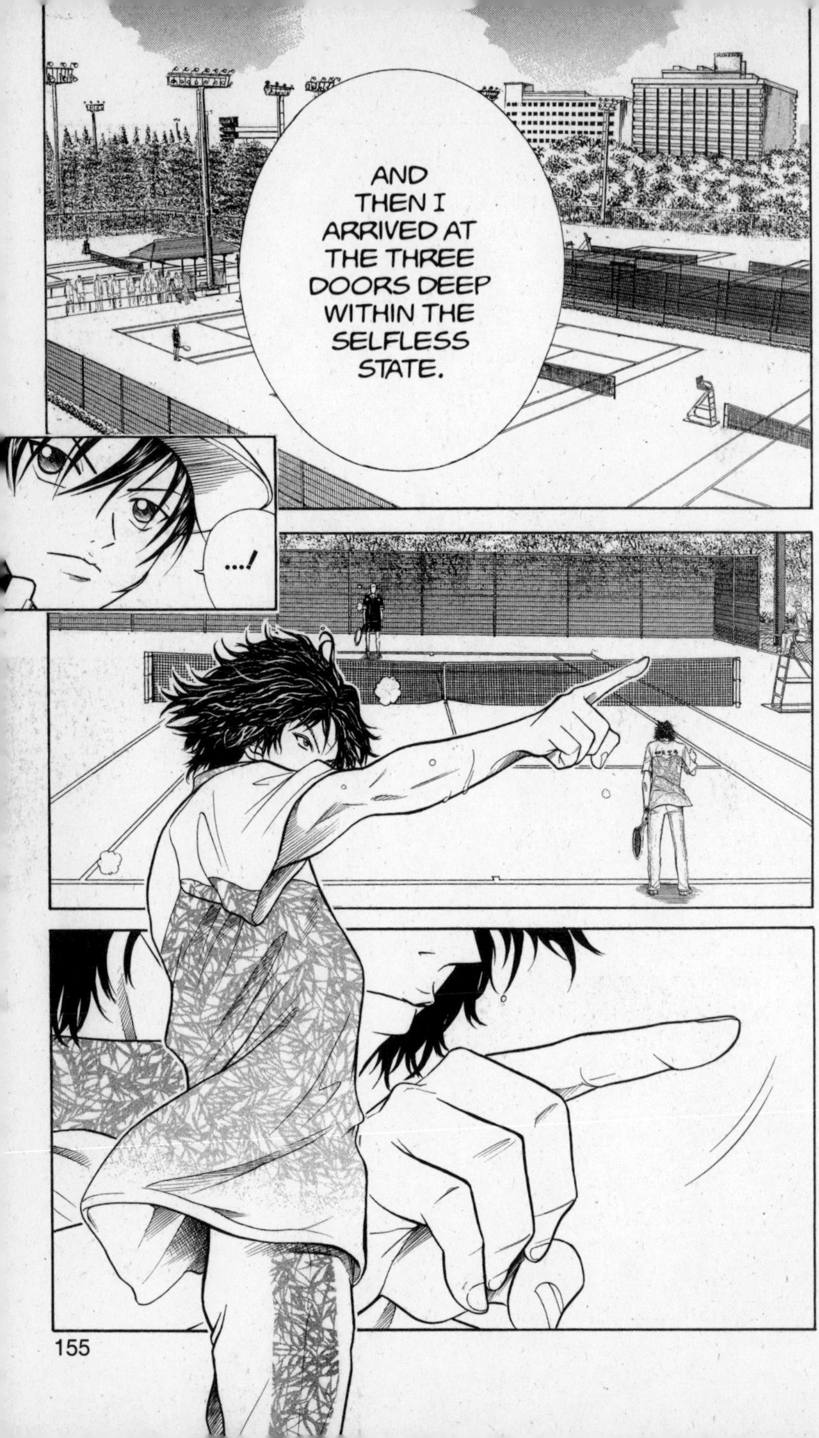
AND THEN I ARRIVED AT THE THREE DOORS DEEP WITHIN THE SELFLESS STATE.
...!

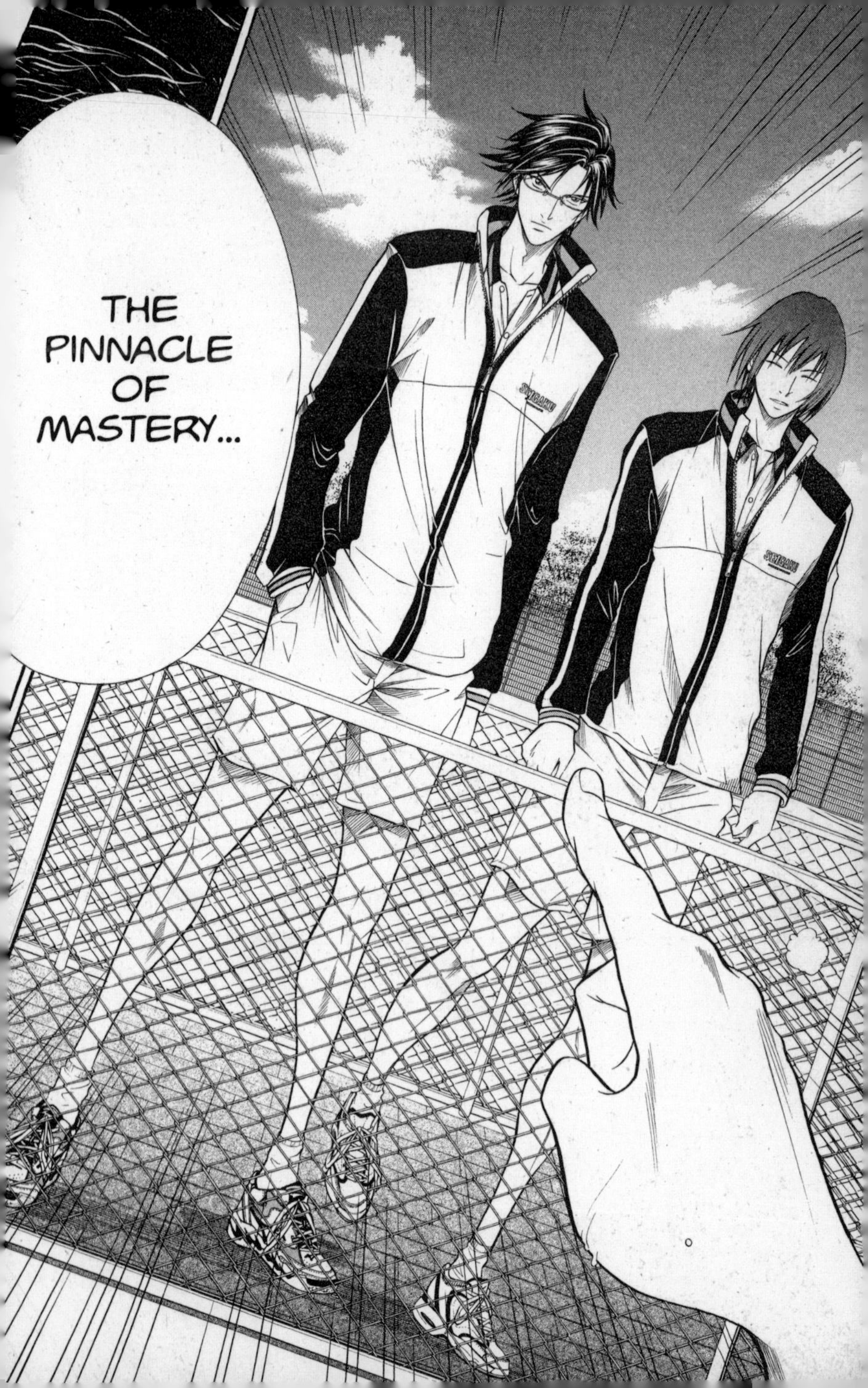
THE PINNACLE OF MASTERY...

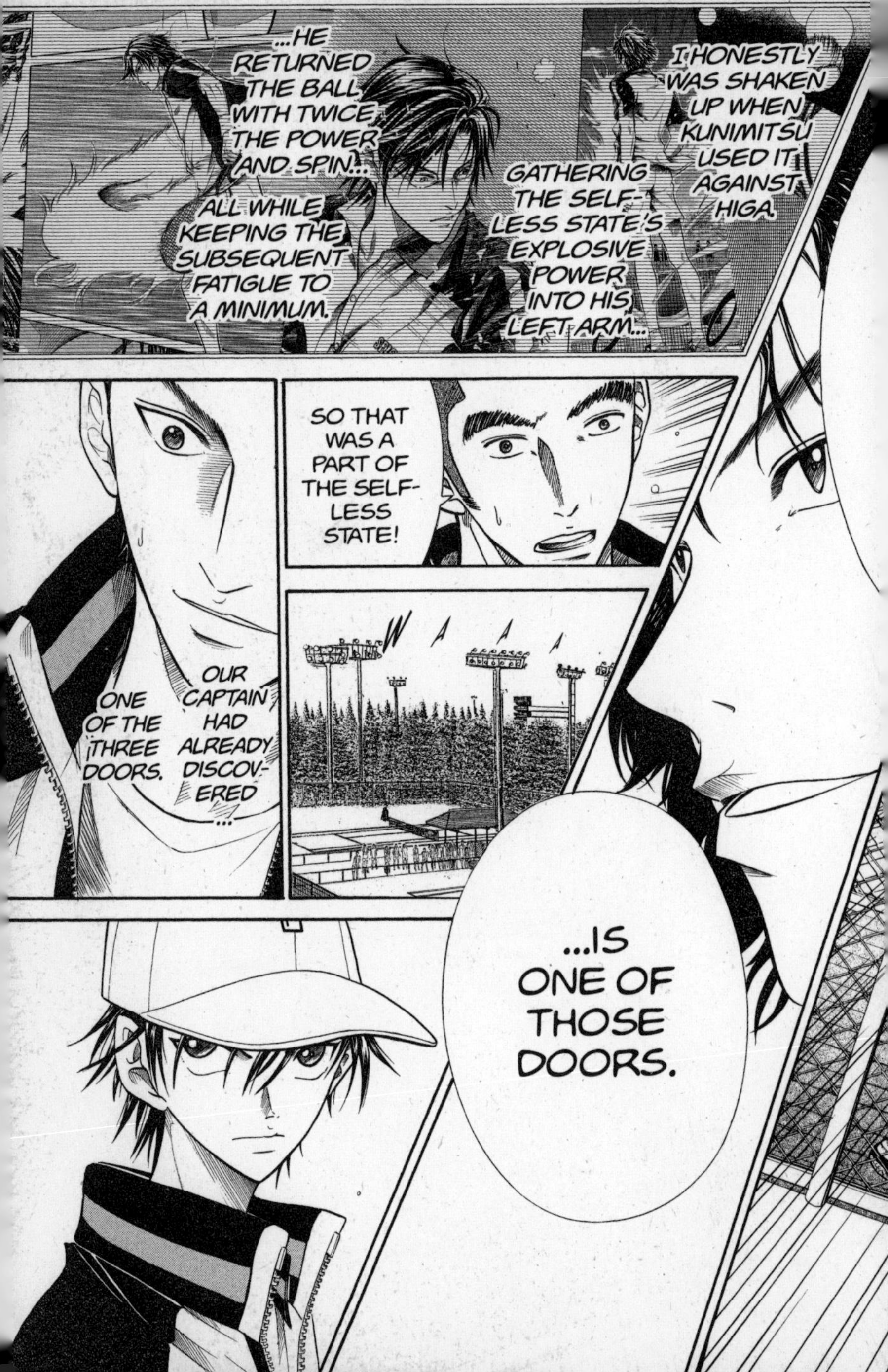
I HONESTLY WAS SHAKEN UP WHEN KUNIMITSU USED IT AGAINST HIGA.
GATHERING THE SELF-LESS STATE'S EXPLOSIVE POWER INTO HIS LEFT ARM...
...HE RETURNED THE BALL WITH TWICE THE POWER AND SPIN...
ALL WHILE KEEPING THE SUBSEQUENT FATIGUE TO A MINIMUM.
SO THAT WAS A PART OF THE SELF-LESS STATE!
WAAA
OUR CAPTAIN HAD ALREADY DISCOVERED...
ONE OF THE THREE DOORS.
...IS ONE OF THOSE DOORS.

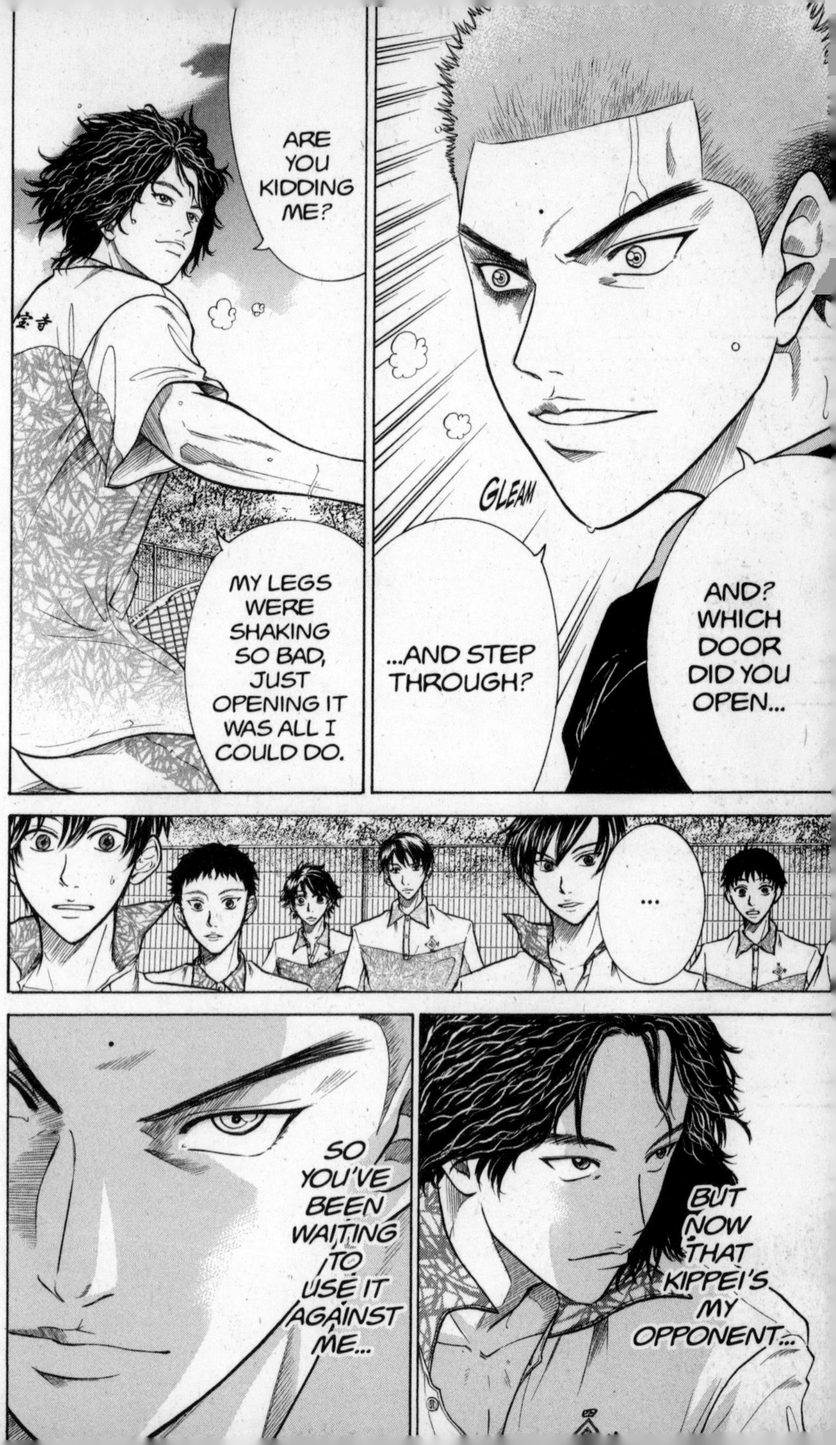
AND? WHICH DOOR DID YOU OPEN...
...AND STEP THROUGH?
GLEAM
ARE YOU KIDDING ME?
MY LEGS WERE SHAKING SO BAD, JUST OPENING IT WAS ALL I COULD DO.
...
BUT NOW THAT KIPPEI'S MY OPPONENT...
SO YOU'VE BEEN WAITING TO USE IT AGAINST ME...

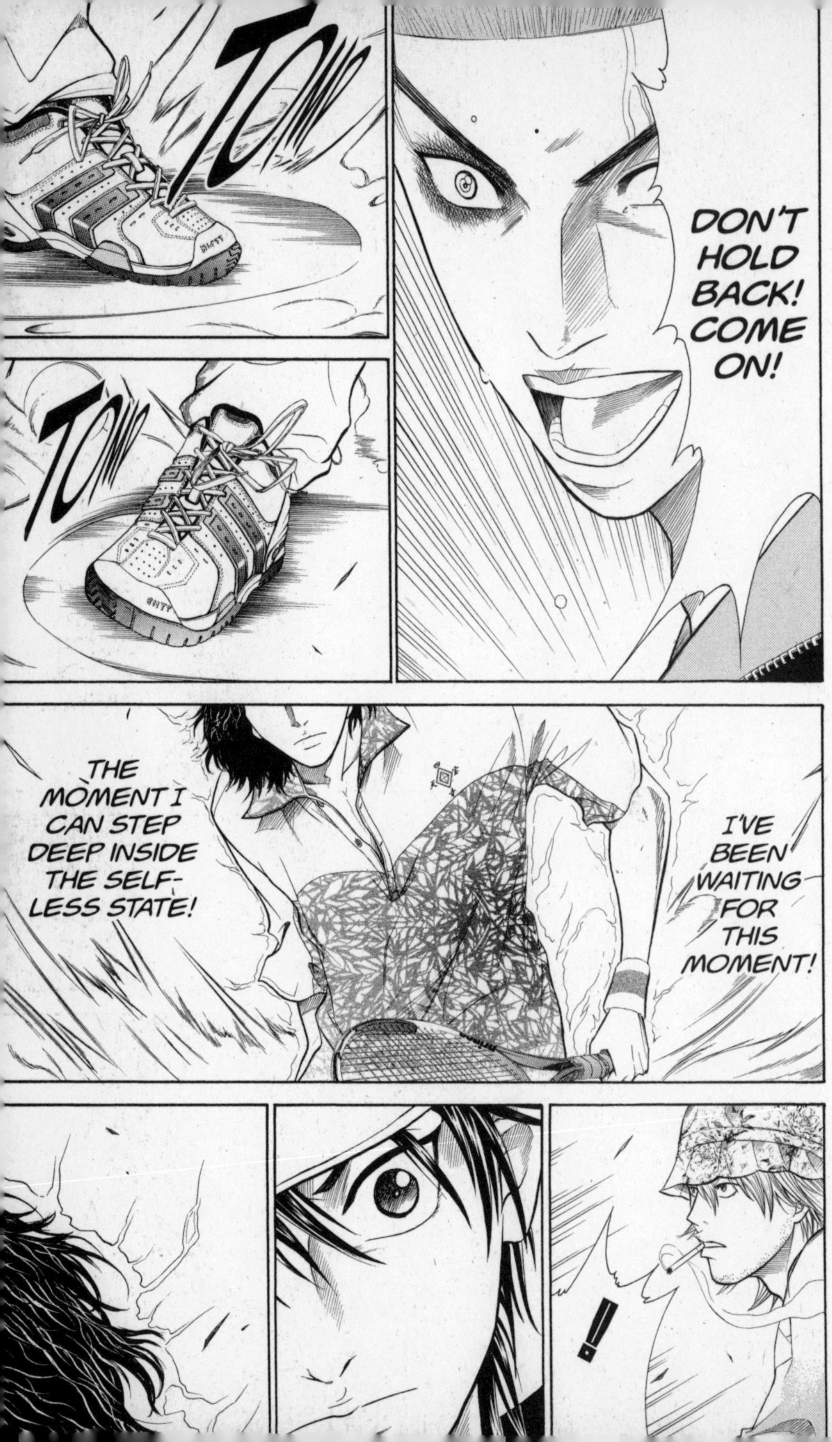
DON'T HOLD BACK! COME ON!
TOMP
TOMP
I'VE BEEN WAITING FOR THIS MOMENT!
THE MOMENT I CAN STEP DEEP INSIDE THE SELF-LESS STATE!
!

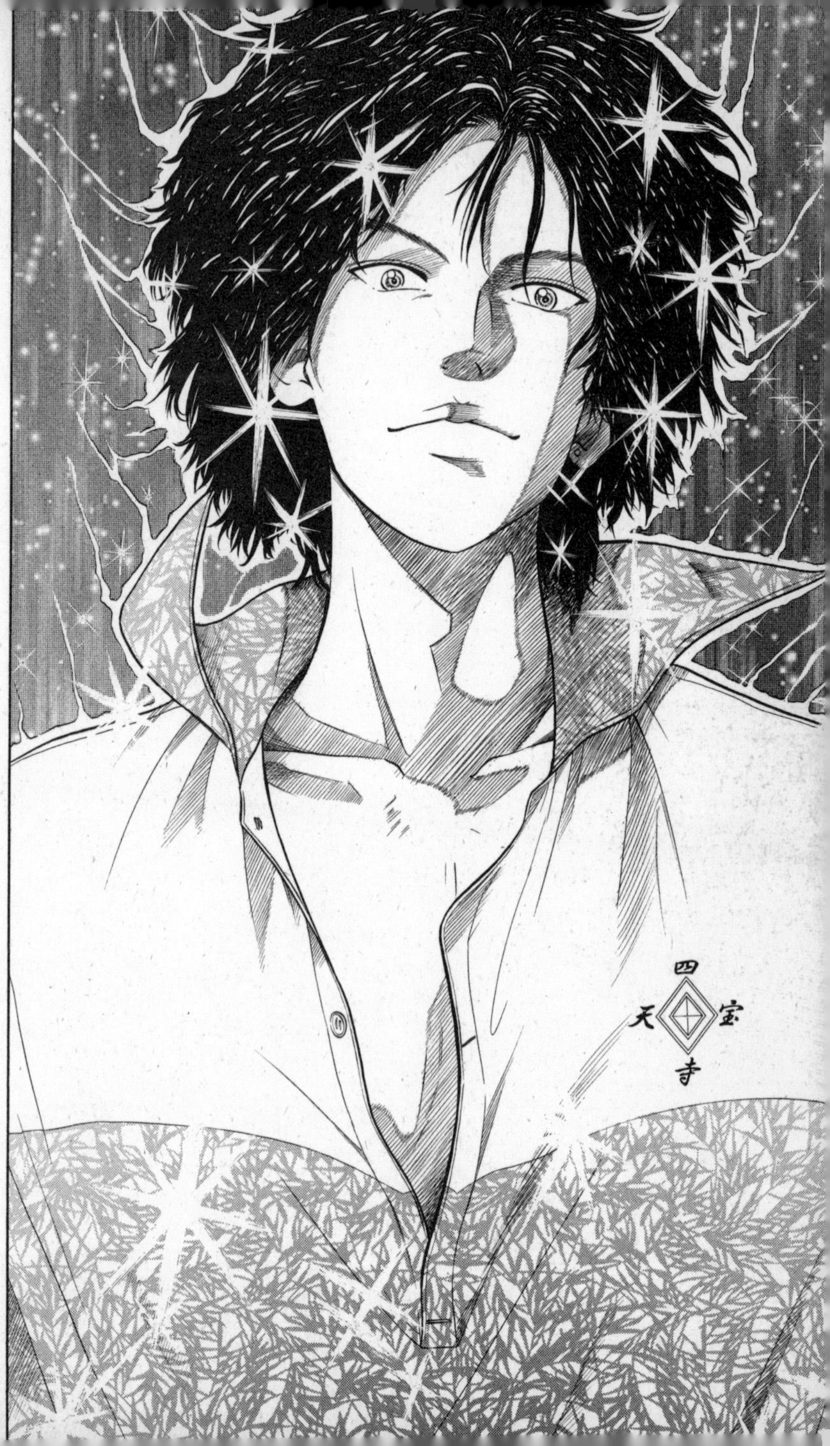
四天宝寺

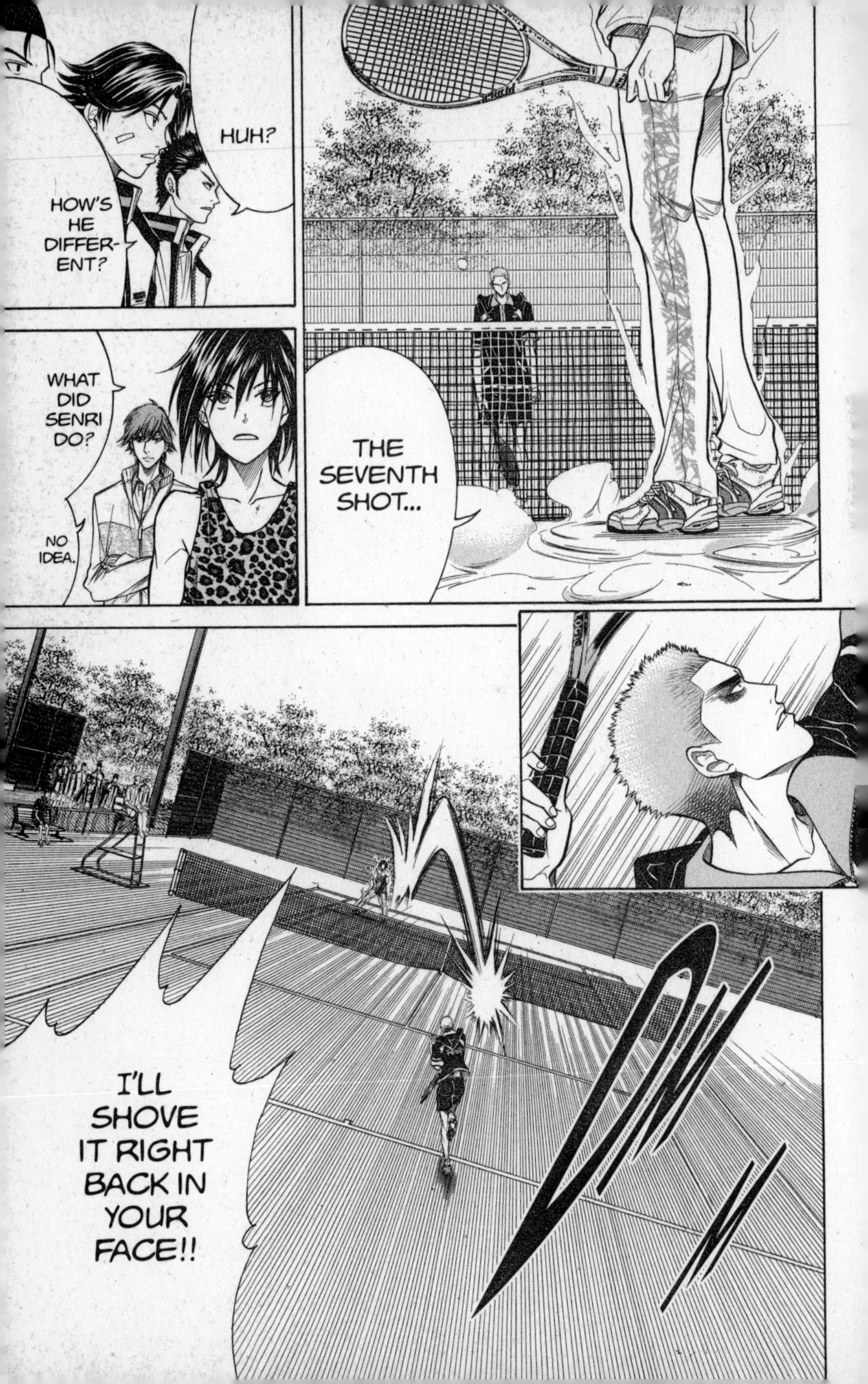
THE SEVENTH SHOT...
HUH?
HOW'S HE DIFFERENT?
WHAT DID SENRI DO?
NO IDEA.
I'LL SHOVE IT RIGHT BACK IN YOUR FACE!!

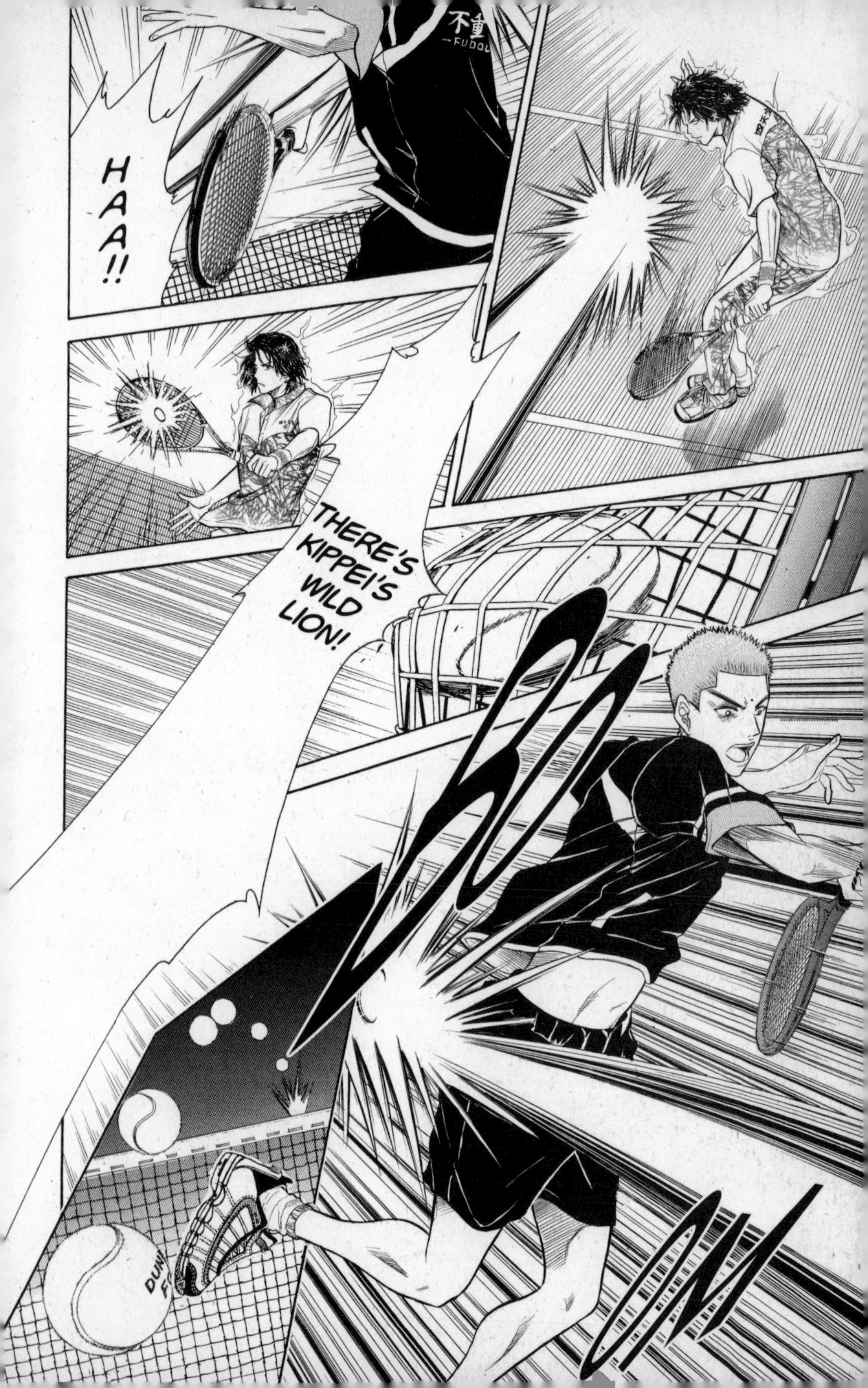
HAAA!!
THERE'S KIPPEI'S WILD LION!

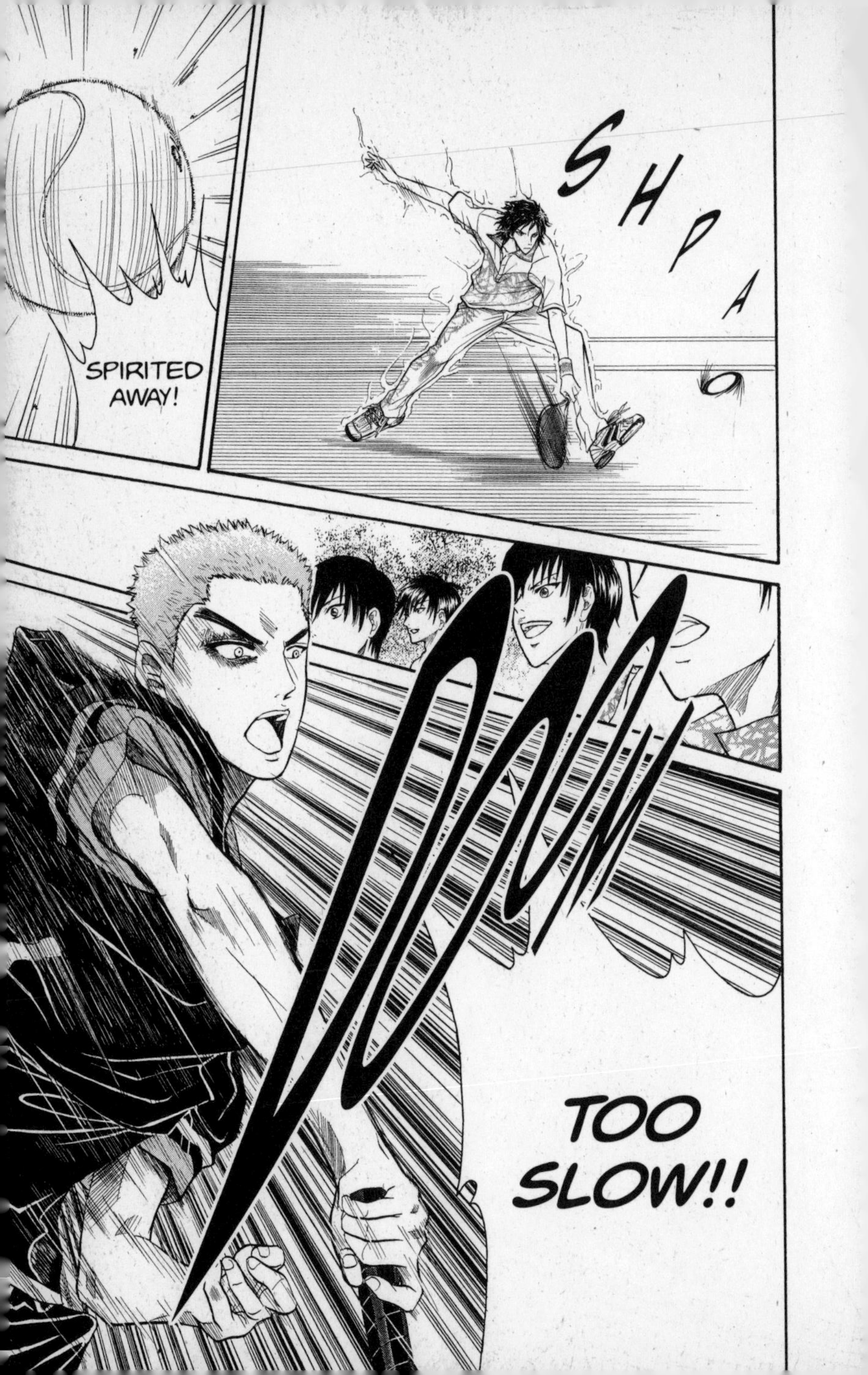
SHPAO
SPIRITED AWAY!
TOO SLOW!!

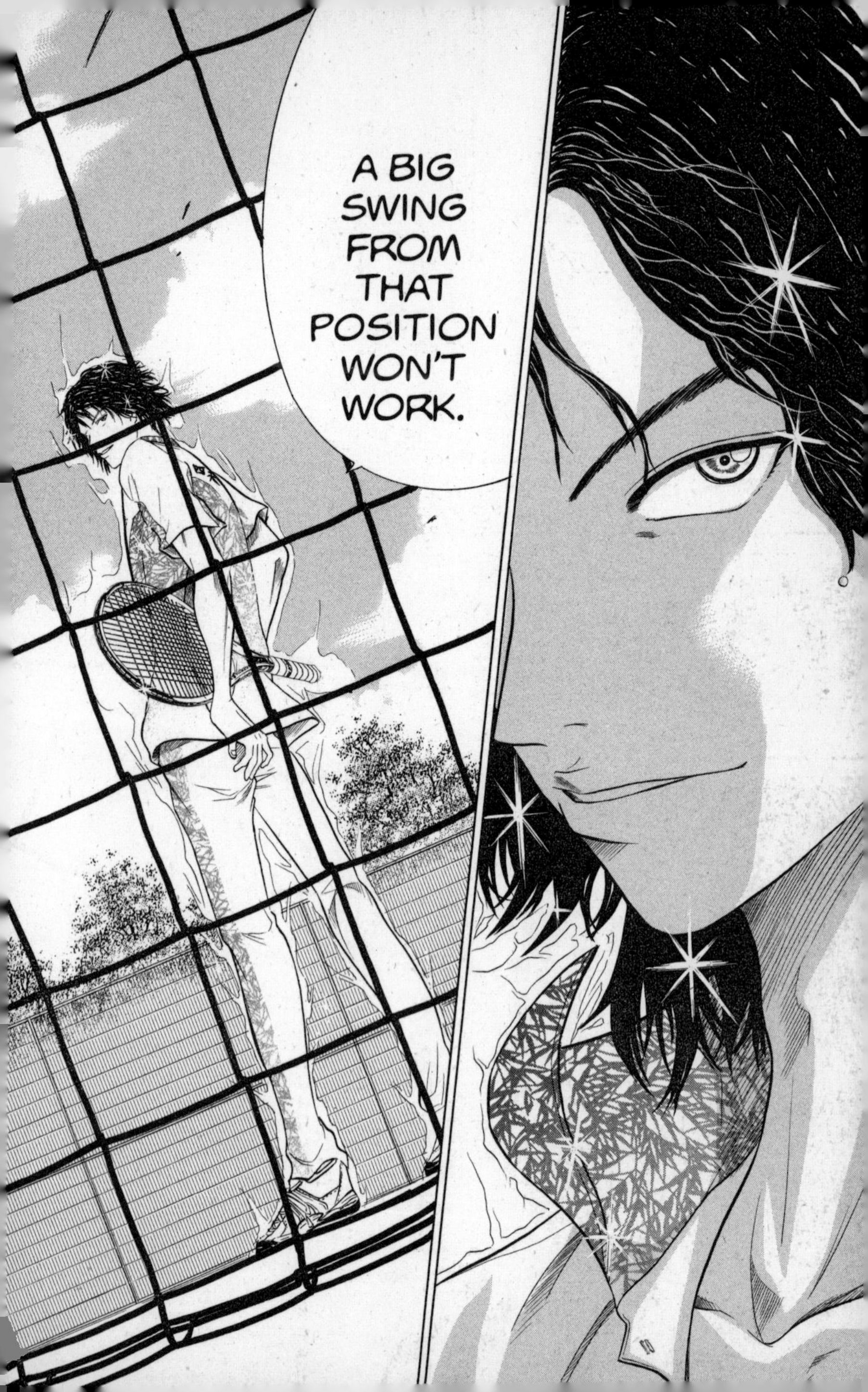
A BIG SWING FROM THAT POSITION WON'T WORK.

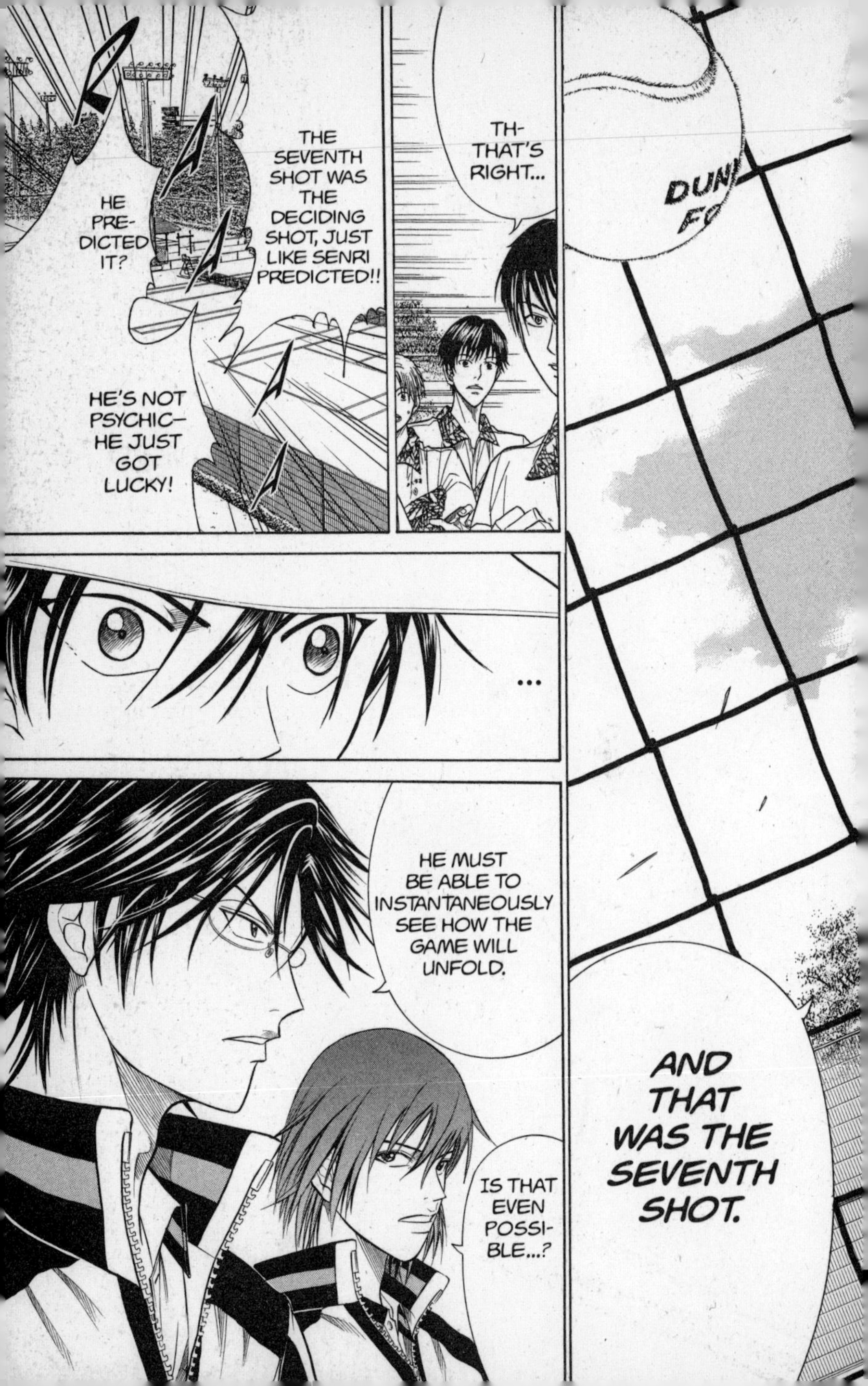
AND THAT WAS THE SEVENTH SHOT.
TH-THAT'S RIGHT...
THE SEVENTH SHOT WAS THE DECIDING SHOT, JUST LIKE SENRI PREDICTED!!
HE PREDICTED IT?
HE'S NOT PSYCHIC—HE JUST GOT LUCKY!
...
HE MUST BE ABLE TO INSTANTANEOUSLY SEE HOW THE GAME WILL UNFOLD.
IS THAT EVEN POSSIBLE...?

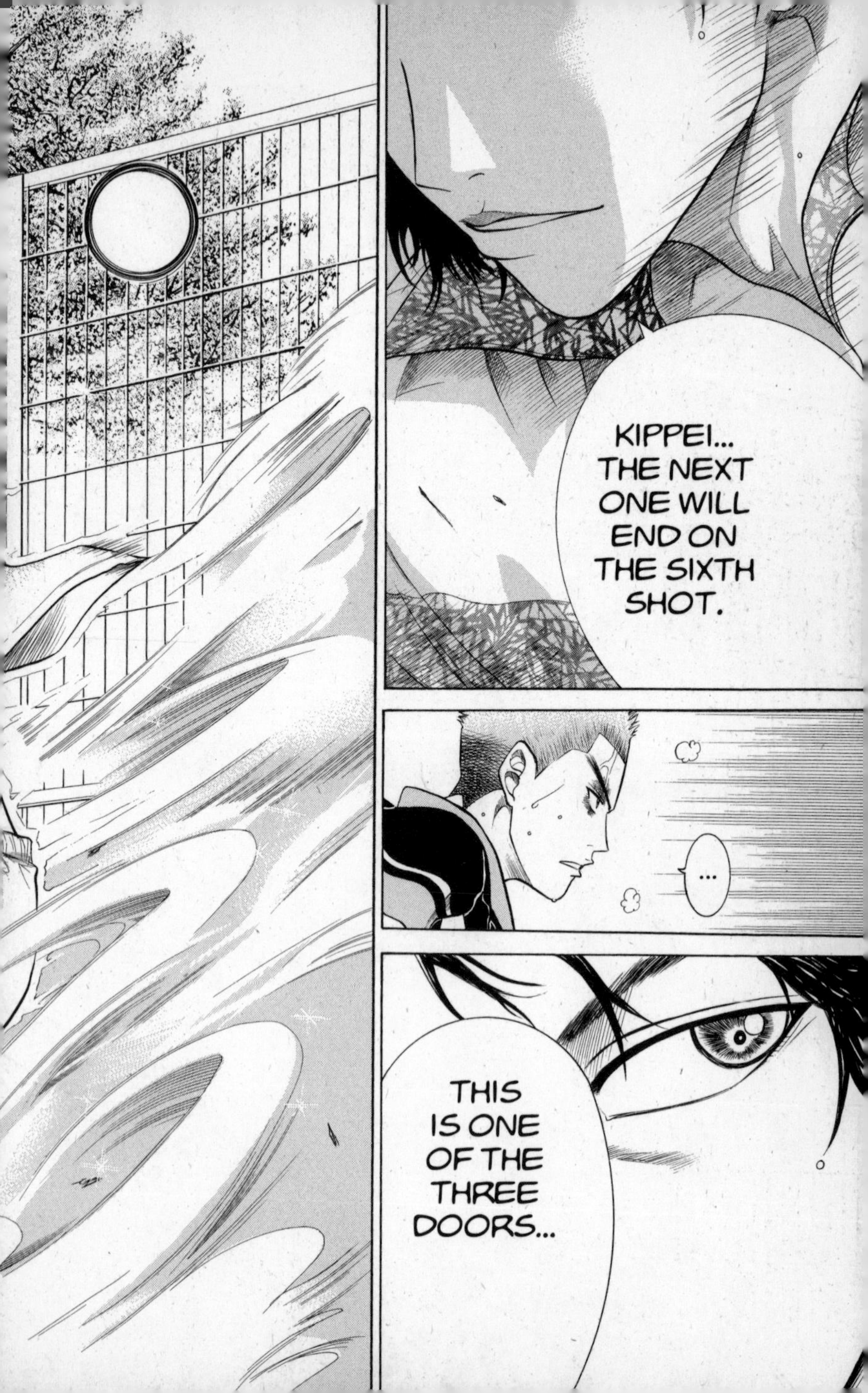
KIPPEI... THE NEXT ONE WILL END ON THE SIXTH SHOT.
...
THIS IS ONE OF THE THREE DOORS...

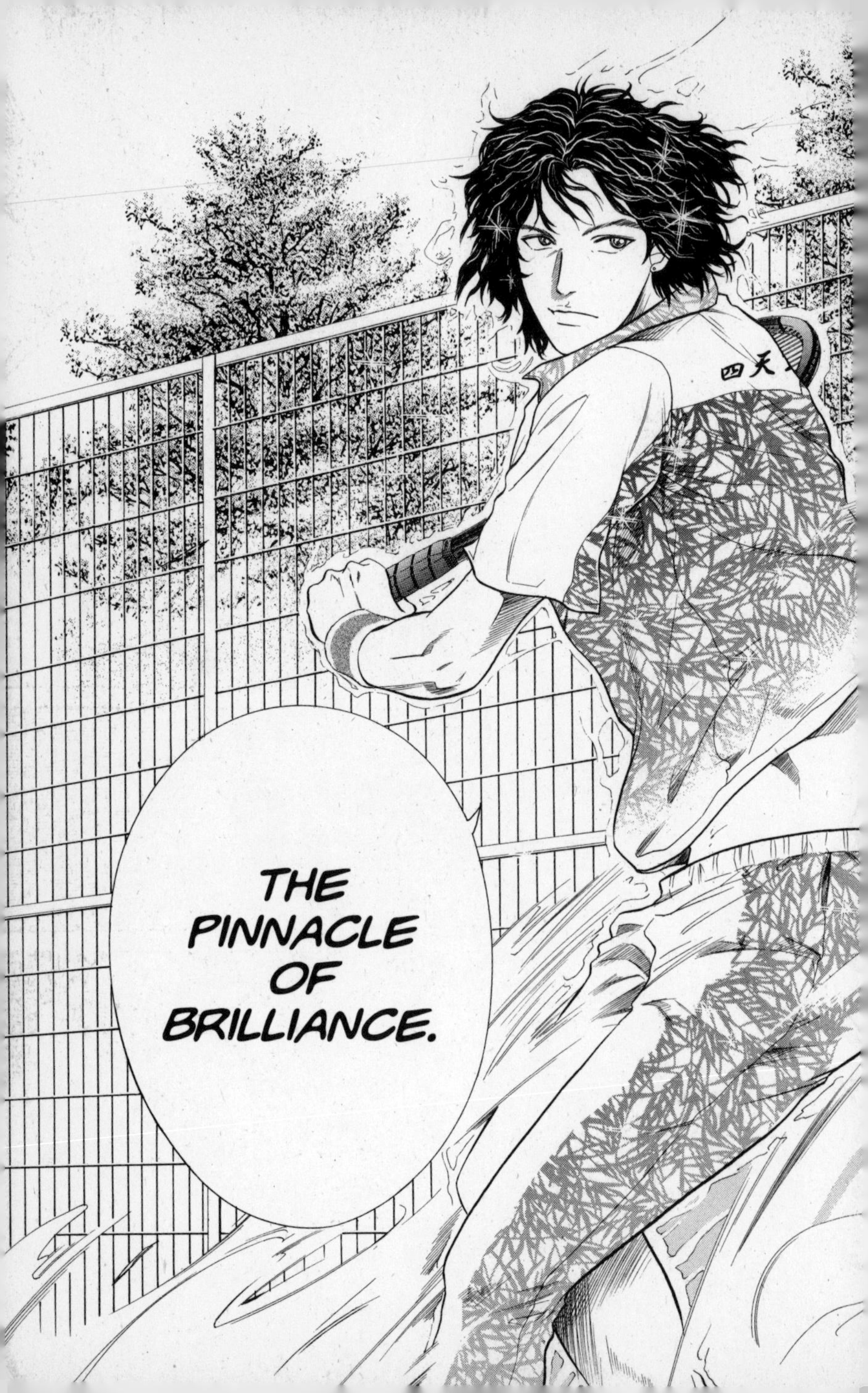
THE PINNACLE OF BRILLIANCE.
四天

テニスの王子様
THE PRINCE OF TENNIS

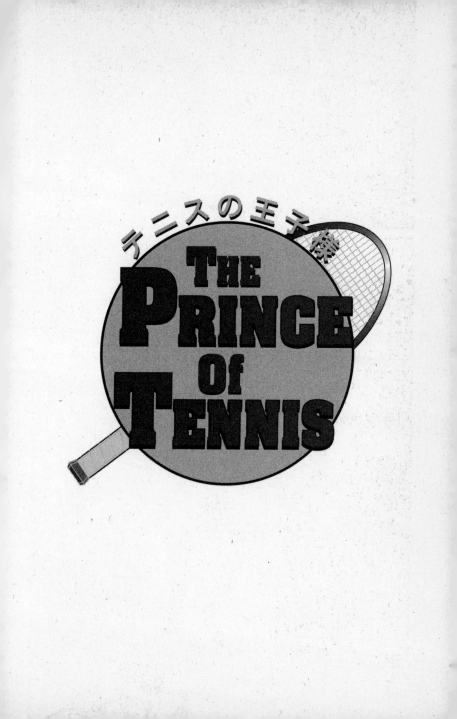

GENIUS 312: THE PINNACLE OF BRILLIANCE

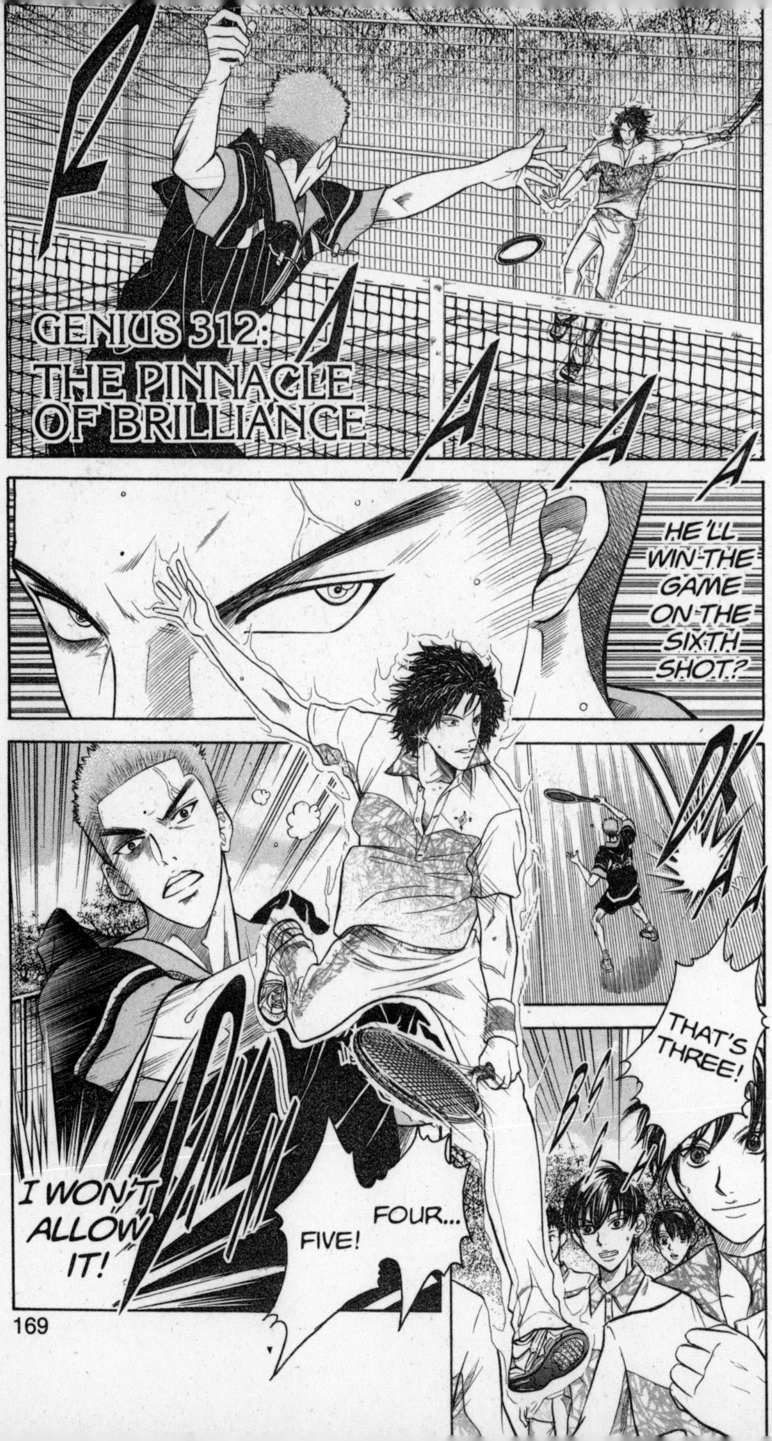
HE'LL WIN THE GAME ON THE SIXTH SHOT?
THAT'S THREE!
FOUR...
FIVE!
I WON'T ALLOW IT!

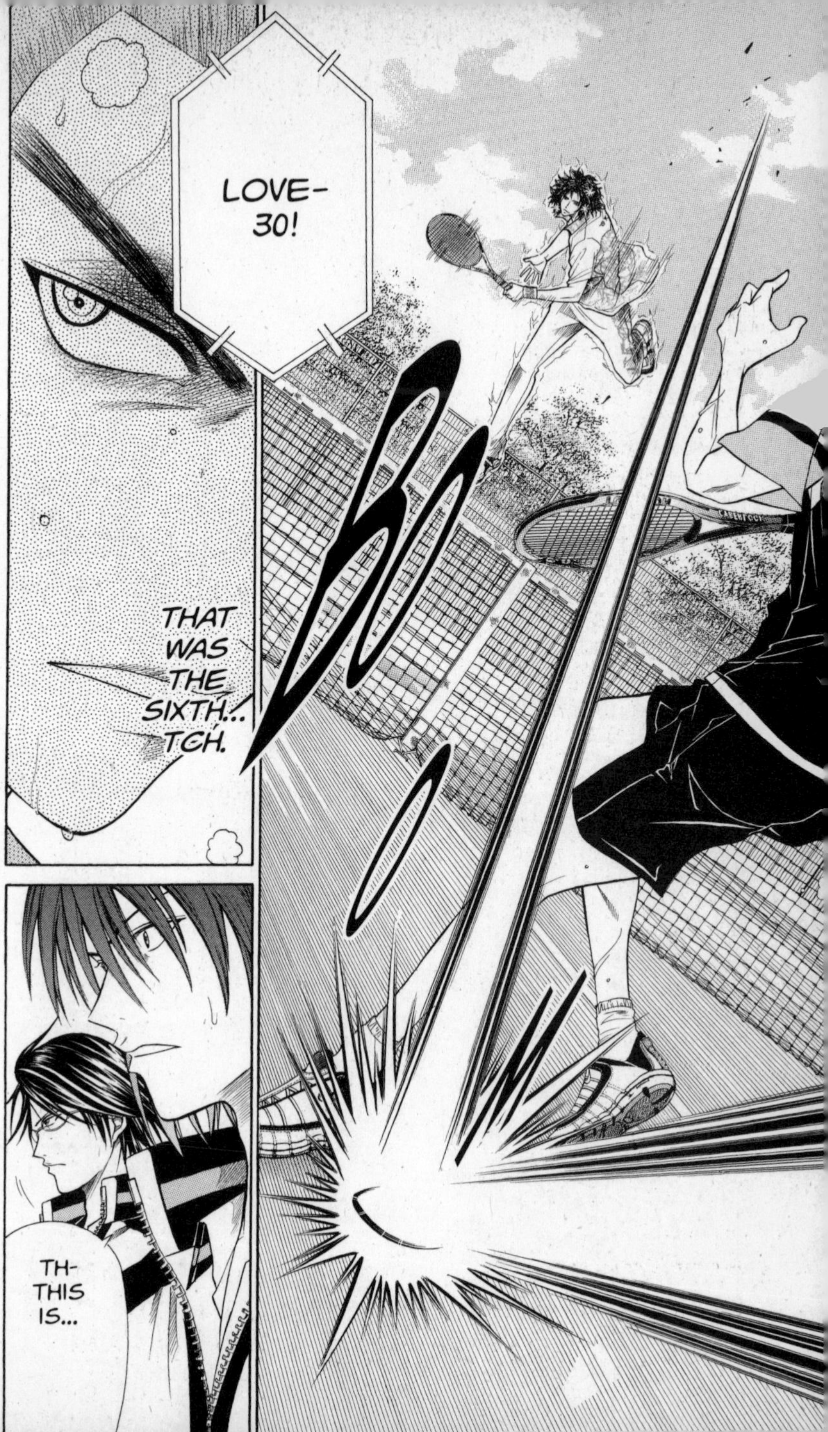
LOVE-30!
THAT WAS THE SIXTH... TCH.
TH- THIS IS...

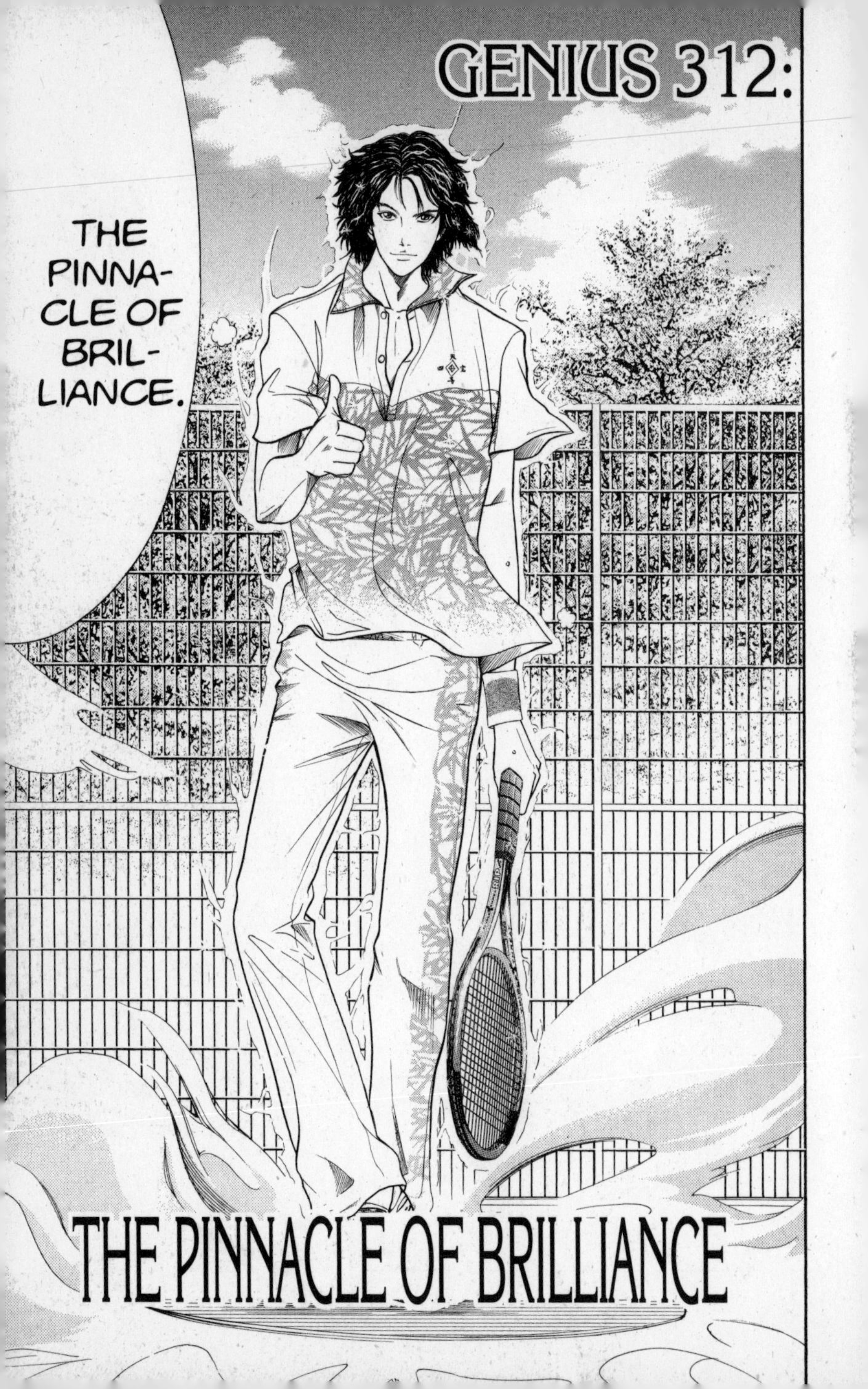
GENIUS 312:
THE PINNACLE OF BRILLIANCE.
THE PINNACLE OF BRILLIANCE

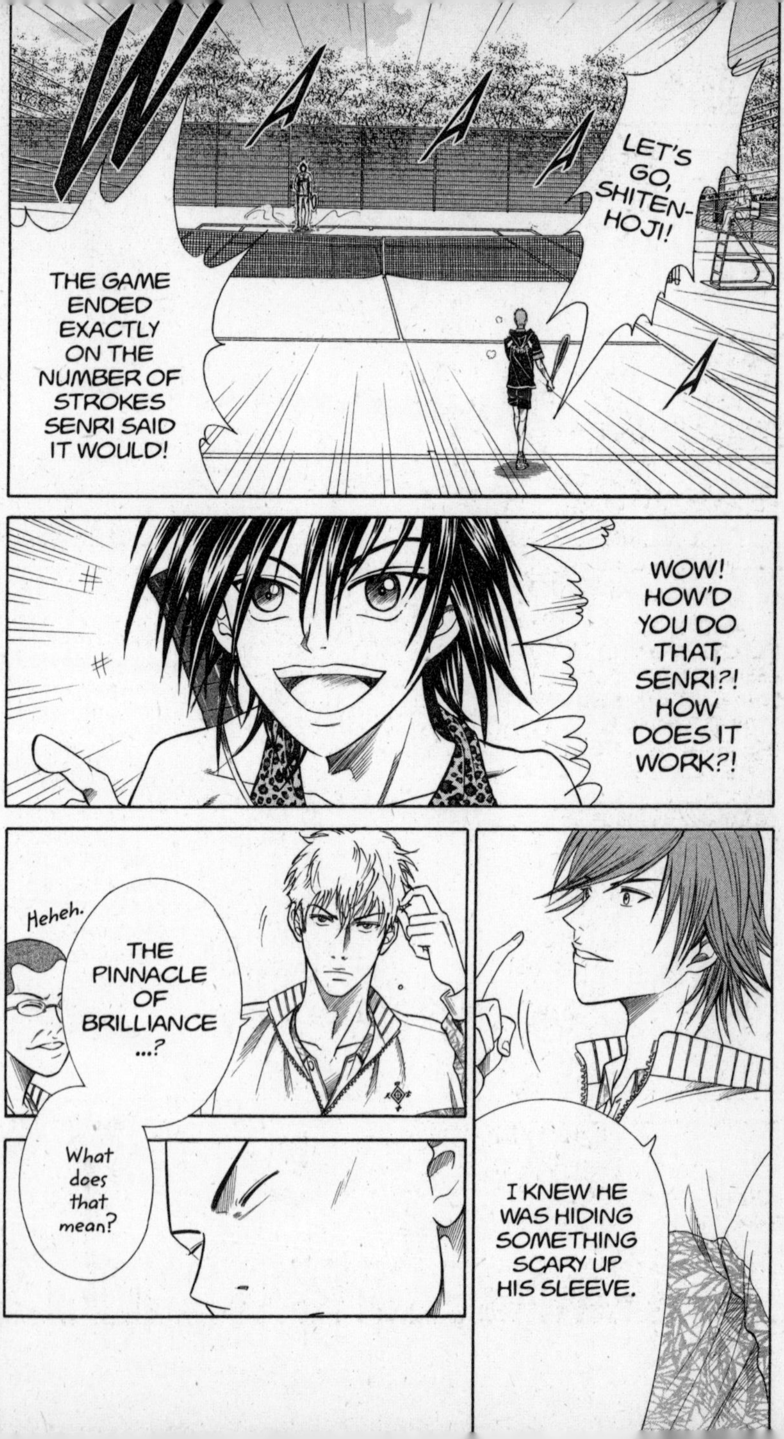
WAAAAA
LET'S GO, SHITEN-HOJI!
THE GAME ENDED EXACTLY ON THE NUMBER OF STROKES SENRI SAID IT WOULD!
WOW! HOW'D YOU DO THAT, SENRI?! HOW DOES IT WORK?!
I KNEW HE WAS HIDING SOMETHING SCARY UP HIS SLEEVE.
Heheh.
THE PINNACLE OF BRILLIANCE ...?
What does that mean?

READ THIS WAY

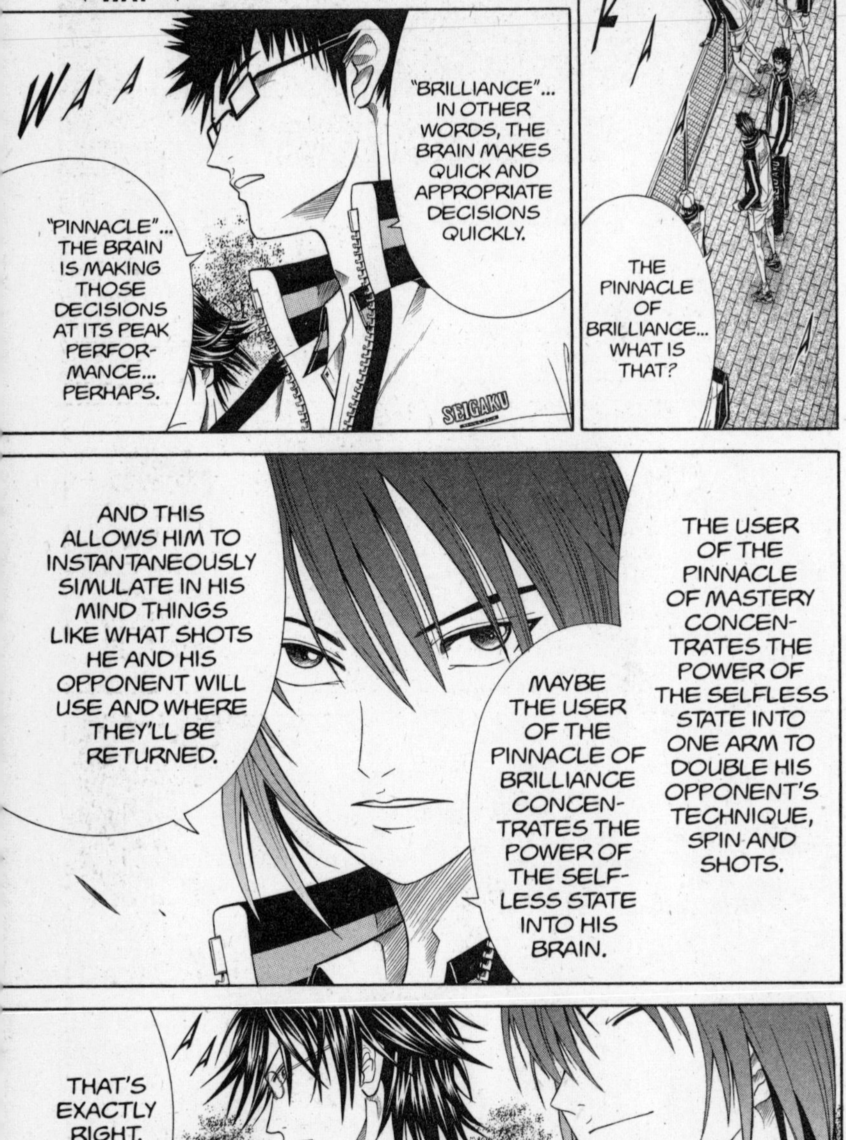
THE PINNACLE OF BRILLIANCE... WHAT IS THAT?
WAA
"BRILLIANCE"... IN OTHER WORDS, THE BRAIN MAKES QUICK AND APPROPRIATE DECISIONS QUICKLY.
"PINNACLE"... THE BRAIN IS MAKING THOSE DECISIONS AT ITS PEAK PERFORMANCE... PERHAPS.
SEIGAKU
THE USER OF THE PINNACLE OF MASTERY CONCENTRATES THE POWER OF THE SELFLESS STATE INTO ONE ARM TO DOUBLE HIS OPPONENT'S TECHNIQUE, SPIN AND SHOTS.
MAYBE THE USER OF THE PINNACLE OF BRILLIANCE CONCENTRATES THE POWER OF THE SELFLESS STATE INTO HIS BRAIN.
AND THIS ALLOWS HIM TO INSTANTANEOUSLY SIMULATE IN HIS MIND THINGS LIKE WHAT SHOTS HE AND HIS OPPONENT WILL USE AND WHERE THEY'LL BE RETURNED.
THAT'S EXACTLY RIGHT.

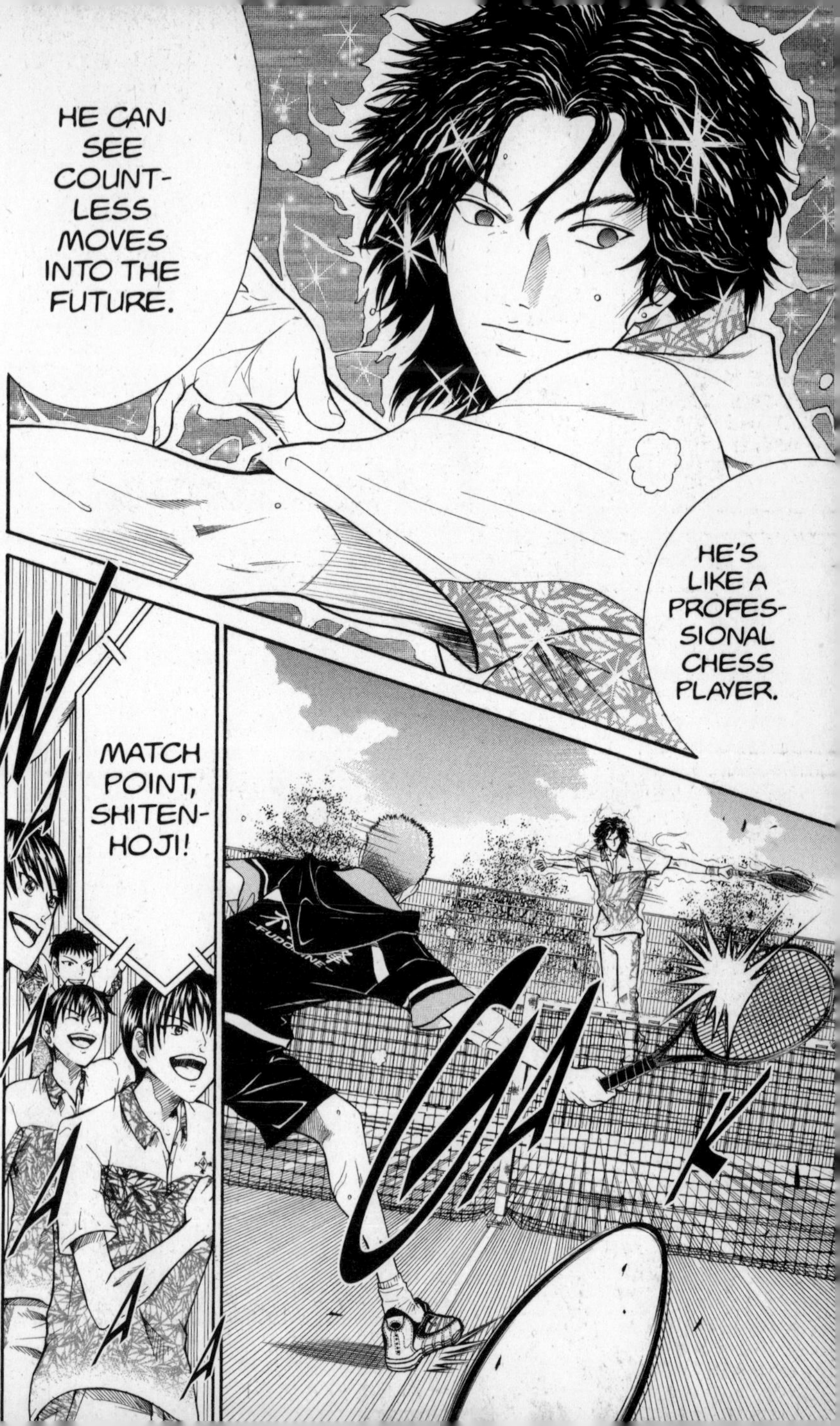
HE CAN SEE COUNT-LESS MOVES INTO THE FUTURE.
HE'S LIKE A PROFES-SIONAL CHESS PLAYER.
MATCH POINT, SHITEN-HOJI!

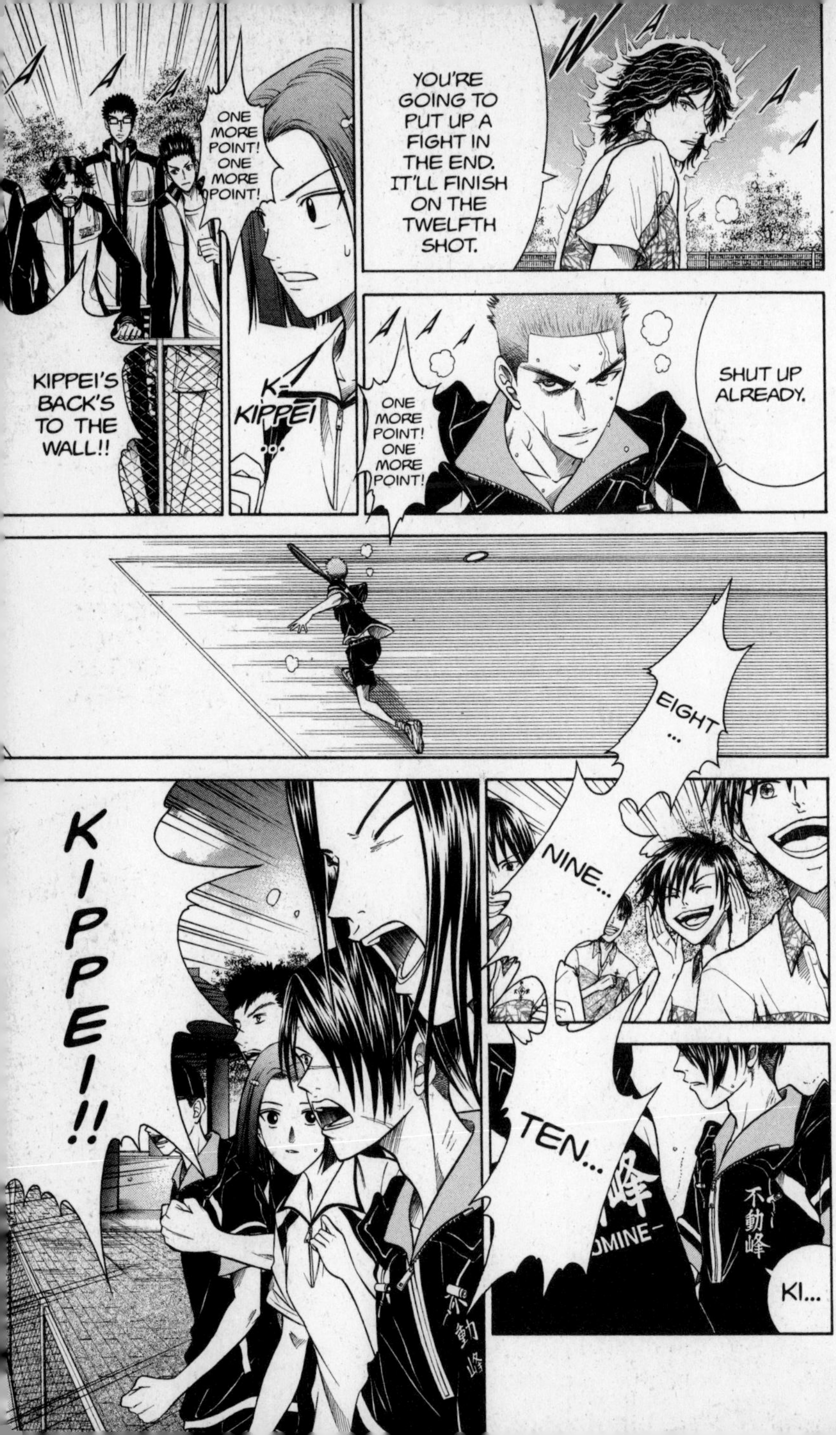
WAAAA
YOU'RE GOING TO PUT UP A FIGHT IN THE END. IT'LL FINISH ON THE TWELFTH SHOT.
SHUT UP ALREADY.
ONE MORE POINT! ONE MORE POINT!
ONE MORE POINT! ONE MORE POINT!
K-KIPPEI...
KIPPEI'S BACK'S TO THE WALL!!
EIGHT...
NINE...
TEN...
KI...
KIPPEI!!

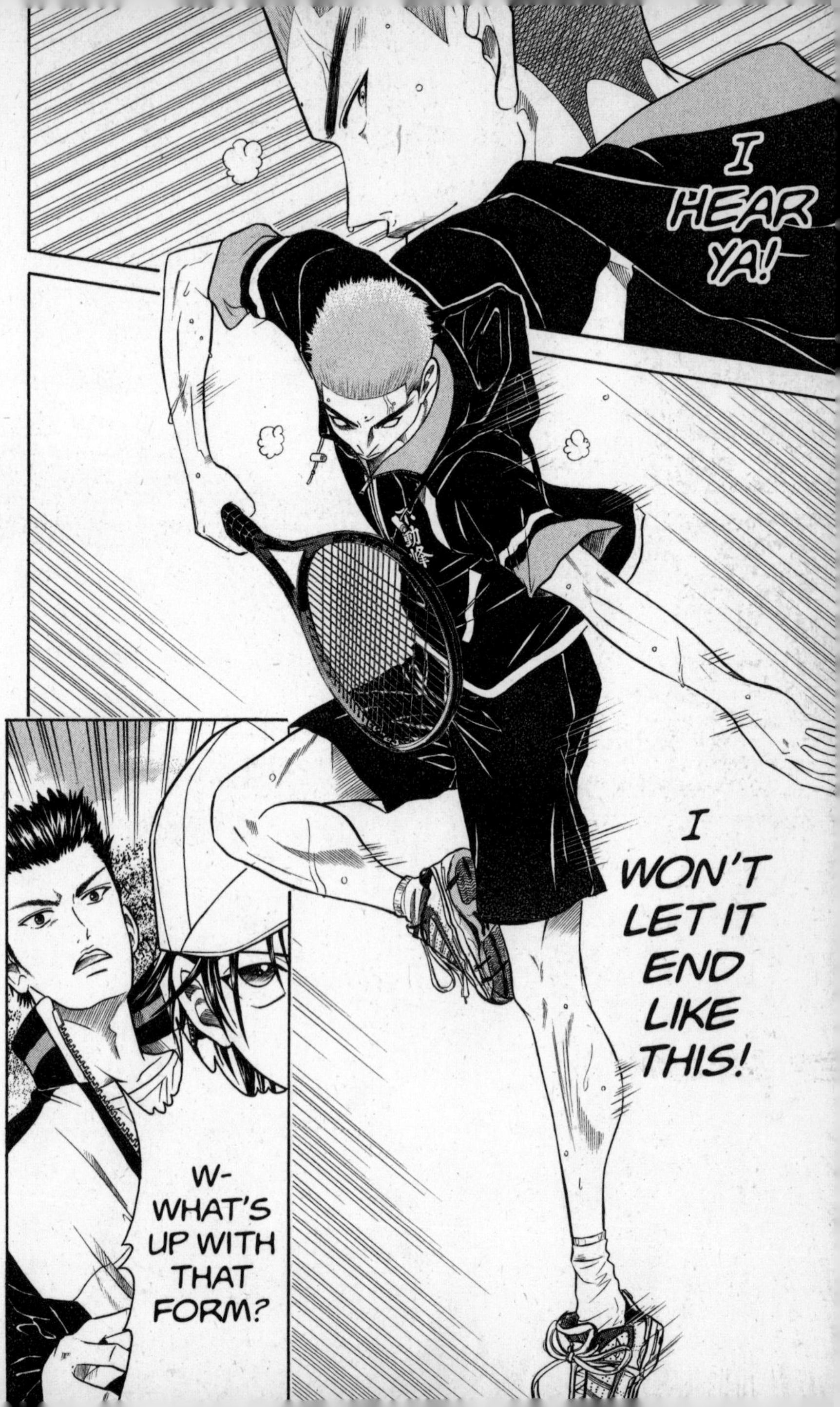
I HEAR YA!
I WON'T LET IT END LIKE THIS!
W- WHAT'S UP WITH THAT FORM?

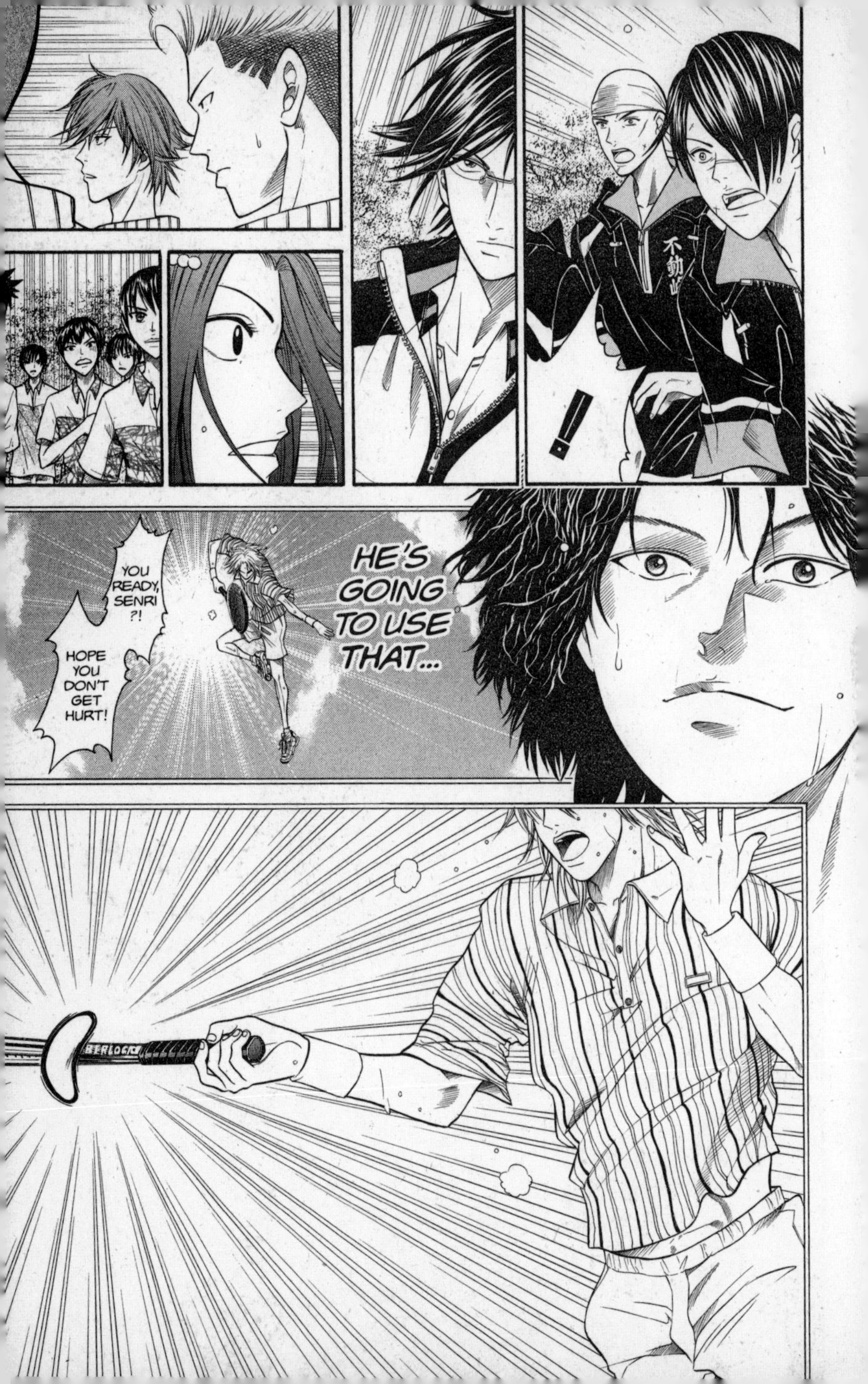
HE'S GOING TO USE THAT...
YOU READY, SENRI?!
HOPE YOU DON'T GET HURT!

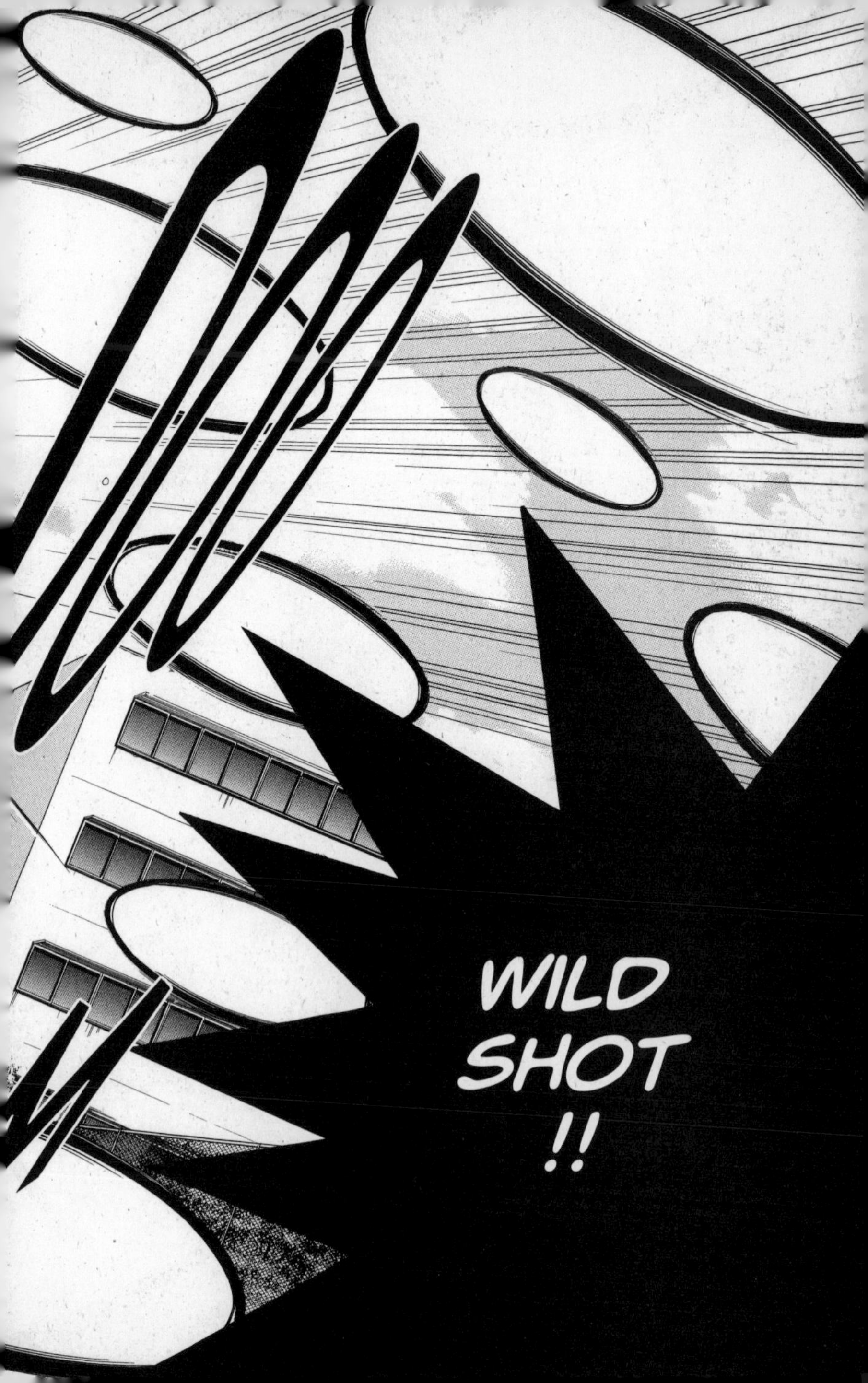
WILD SHOT !!

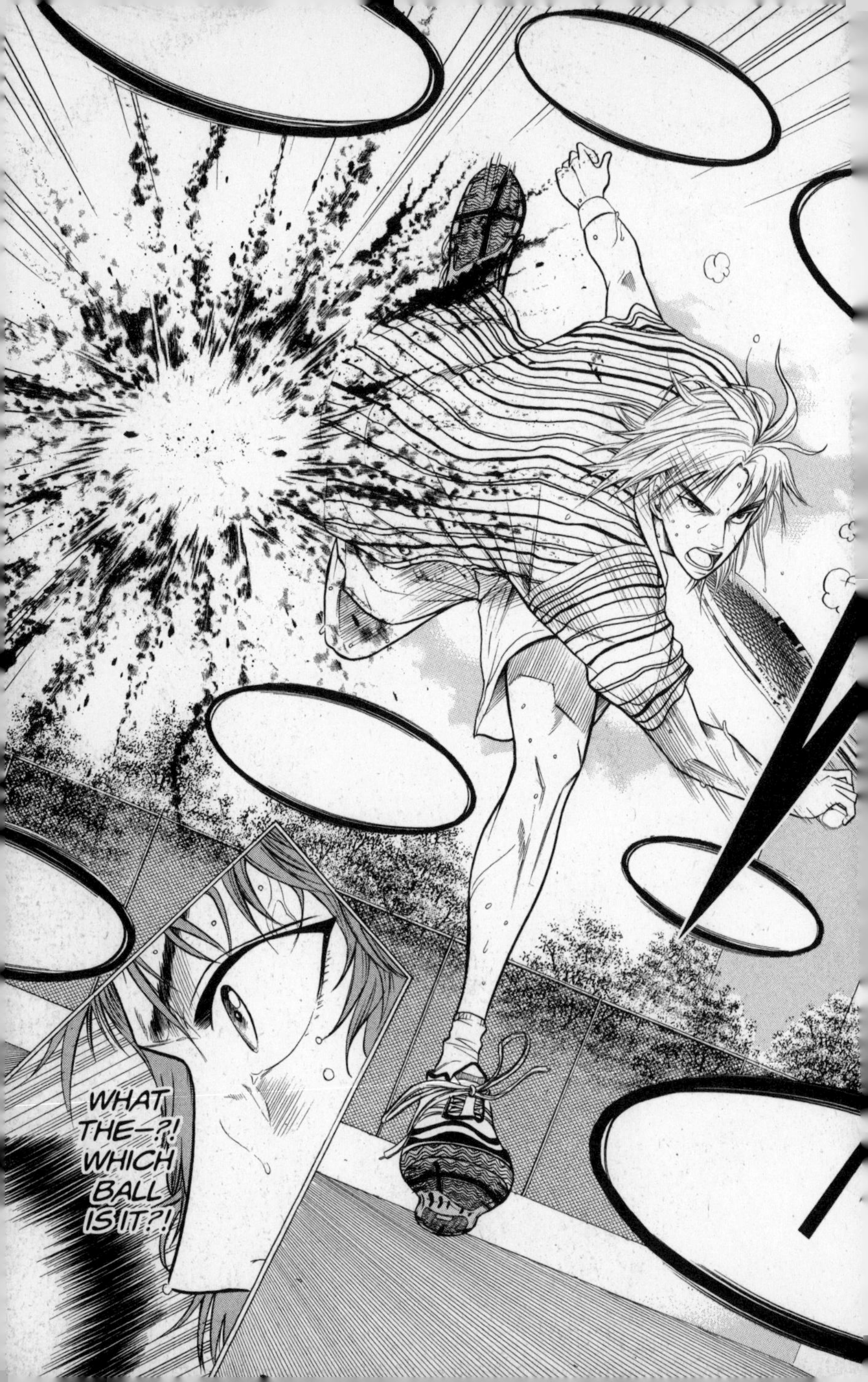
WHAT THE--?! WHICH BALL IS IT?!

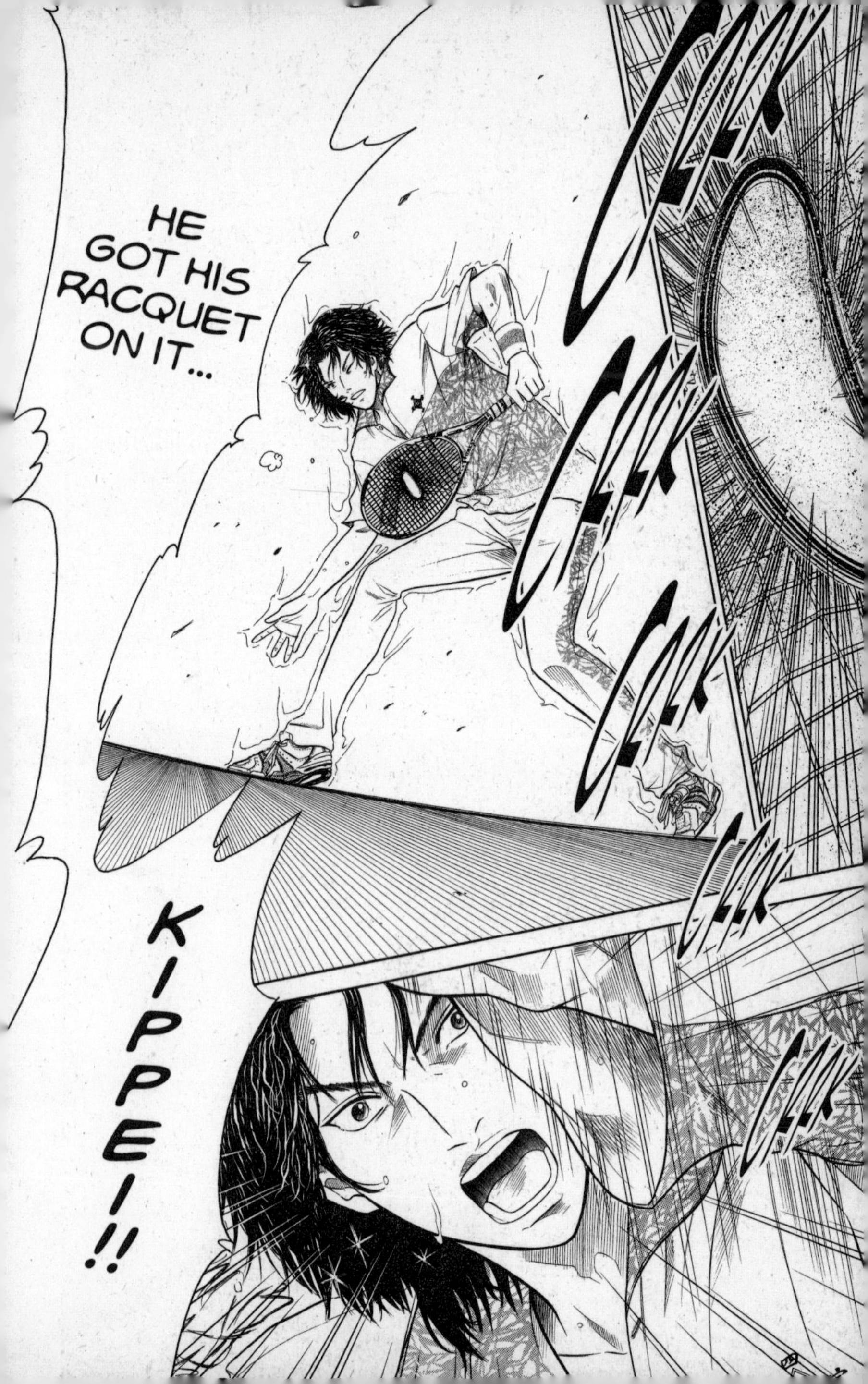

HE GOT HIS RACQUET ON IT...
KIPPEI!!

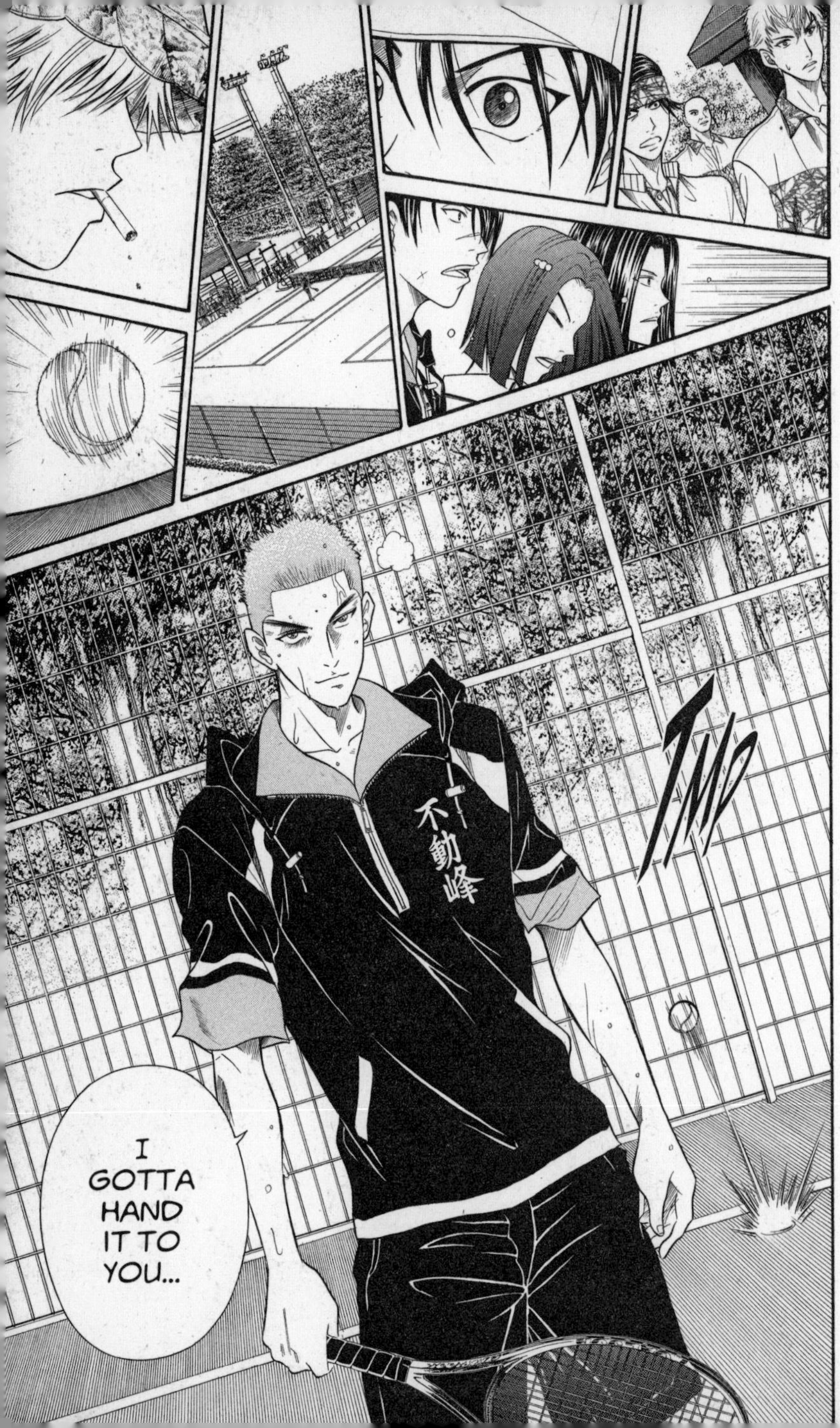
TMP
不動峰
I GOTTA HAND IT TO YOU...

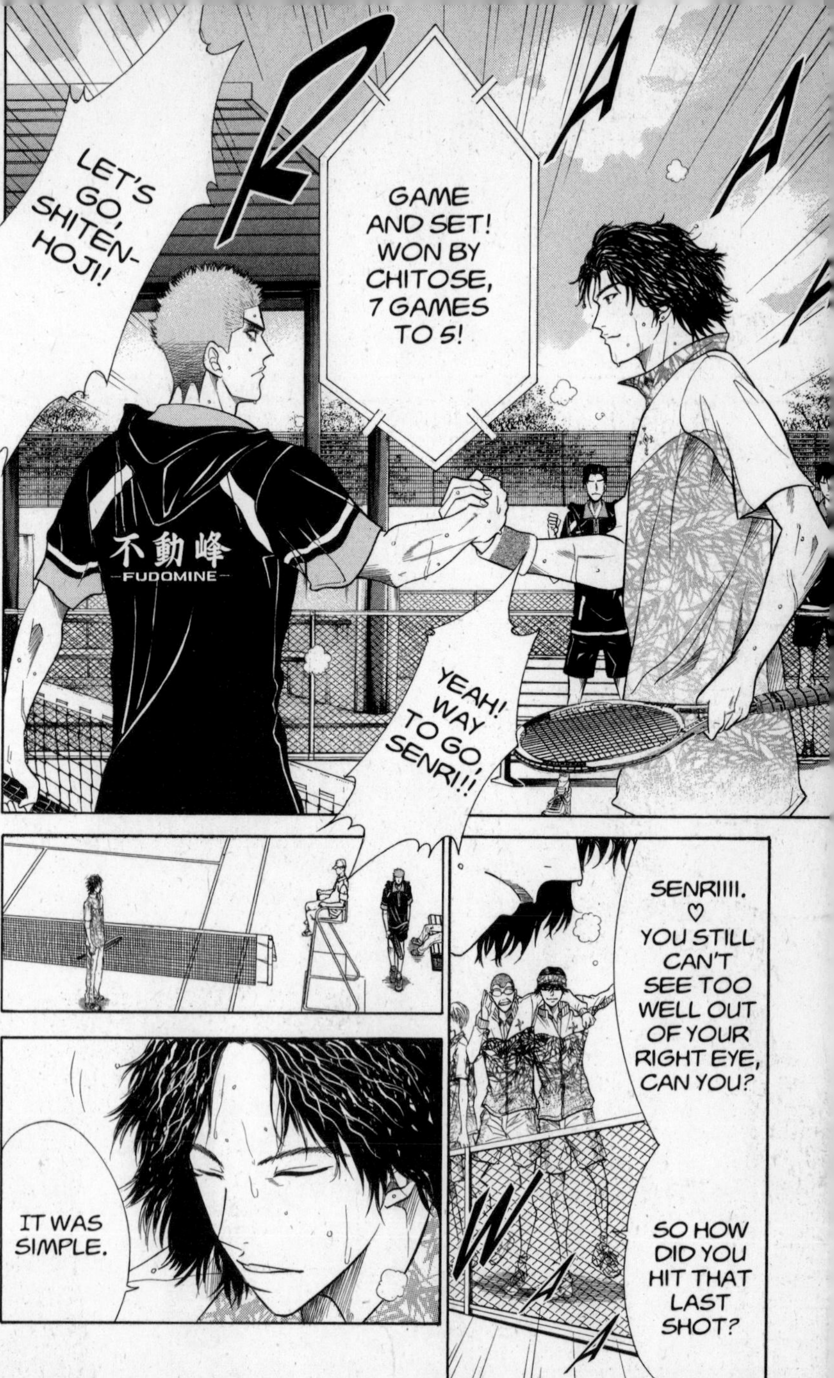
GAME AND SET! WON BY CHITOSE, 7 GAMES TO 5!
LET'S GO, SHITEN-HOJI!!
不動峰 —FUDOMINE—
YEAH! WAY TO GO, SENRI!!
SENRIIII. ♡ YOU STILL CAN'T SEE TOO WELL OUT OF YOUR RIGHT EYE, CAN YOU?
SO HOW DID YOU HIT THAT LAST SHOT?
IT WAS SIMPLE.

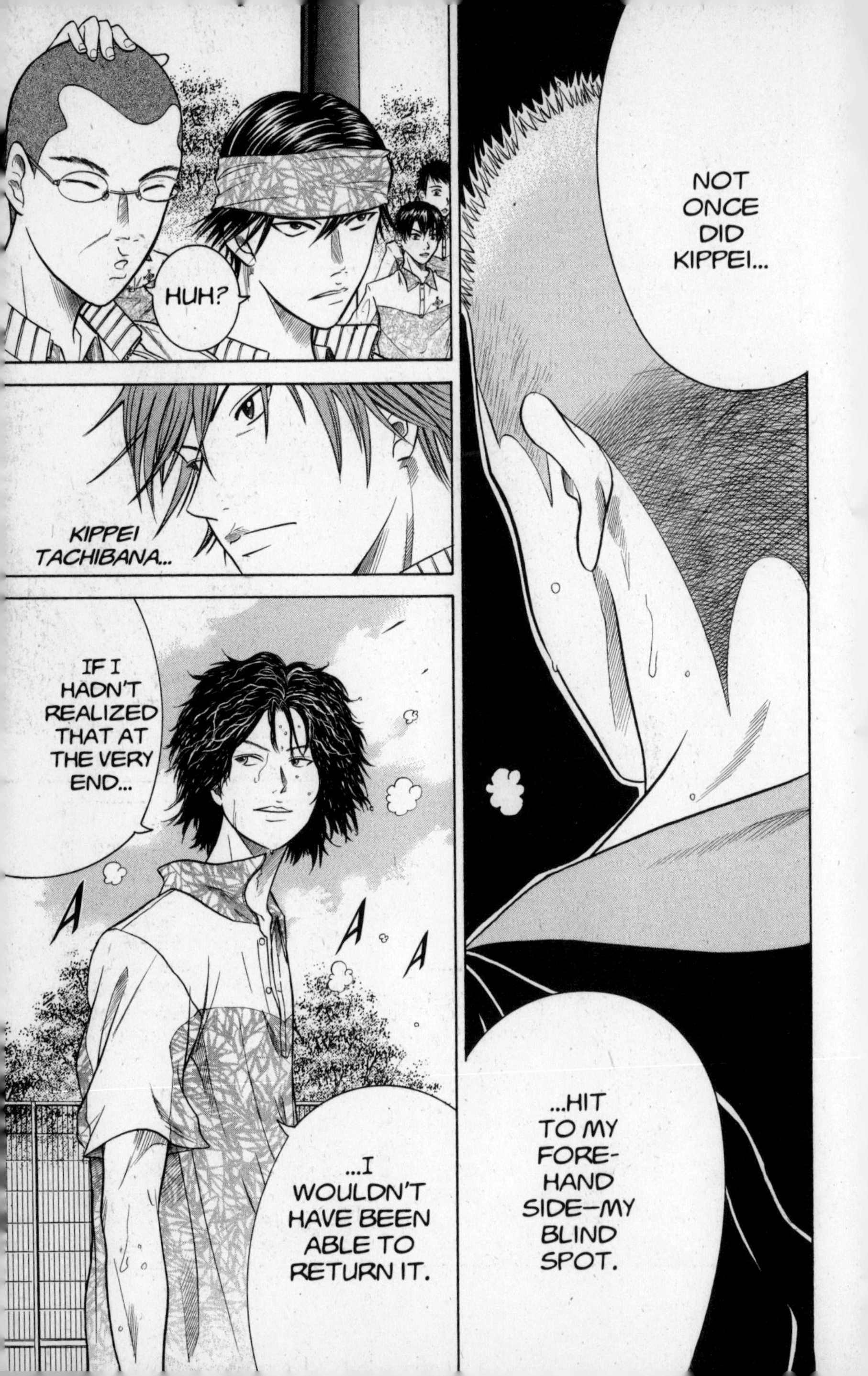
NOT ONCE DID KIPPEI...
...HIT TO MY FORE-HAND SIDE—MY BLIND SPOT.
HUH?
KIPPEI TACHIBANA...
IF I HADN'T REALIZED THAT AT THE VERY END...
...I WOULDN'T HAVE BEEN ABLE TO RETURN IT.

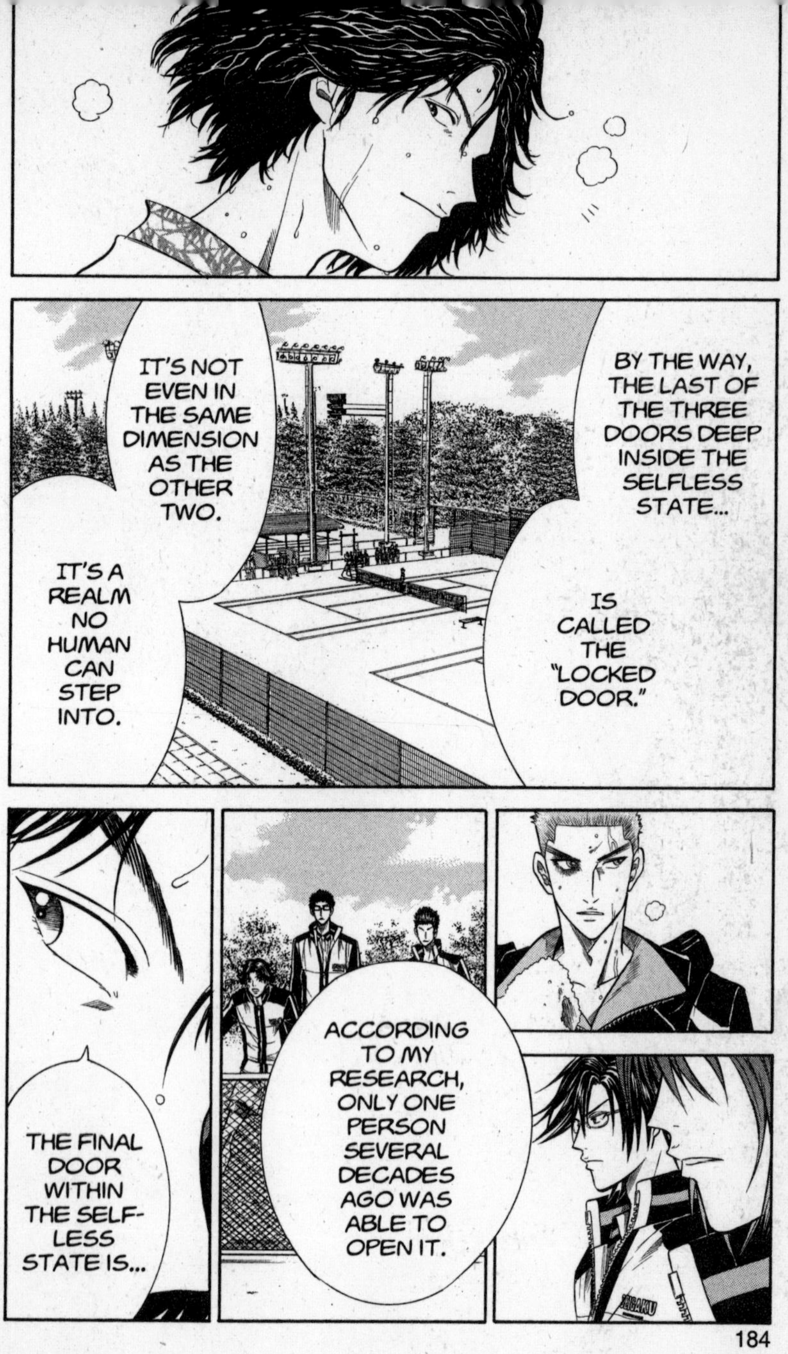
BY THE WAY, THE LAST OF THE THREE DOORS DEEP INSIDE THE SELFLESS STATE...
IS CALLED THE "LOCKED DOOR."
IT'S NOT EVEN IN THE SAME DIMENSION AS THE OTHER TWO.
IT'S A REALM NO HUMAN CAN STEP INTO.
ACCORDING TO MY RESEARCH, ONLY ONE PERSON SEVERAL DECADES AGO WAS ABLE TO OPEN IT.
THE FINAL DOOR WITHIN THE SELF-LESS STATE IS...

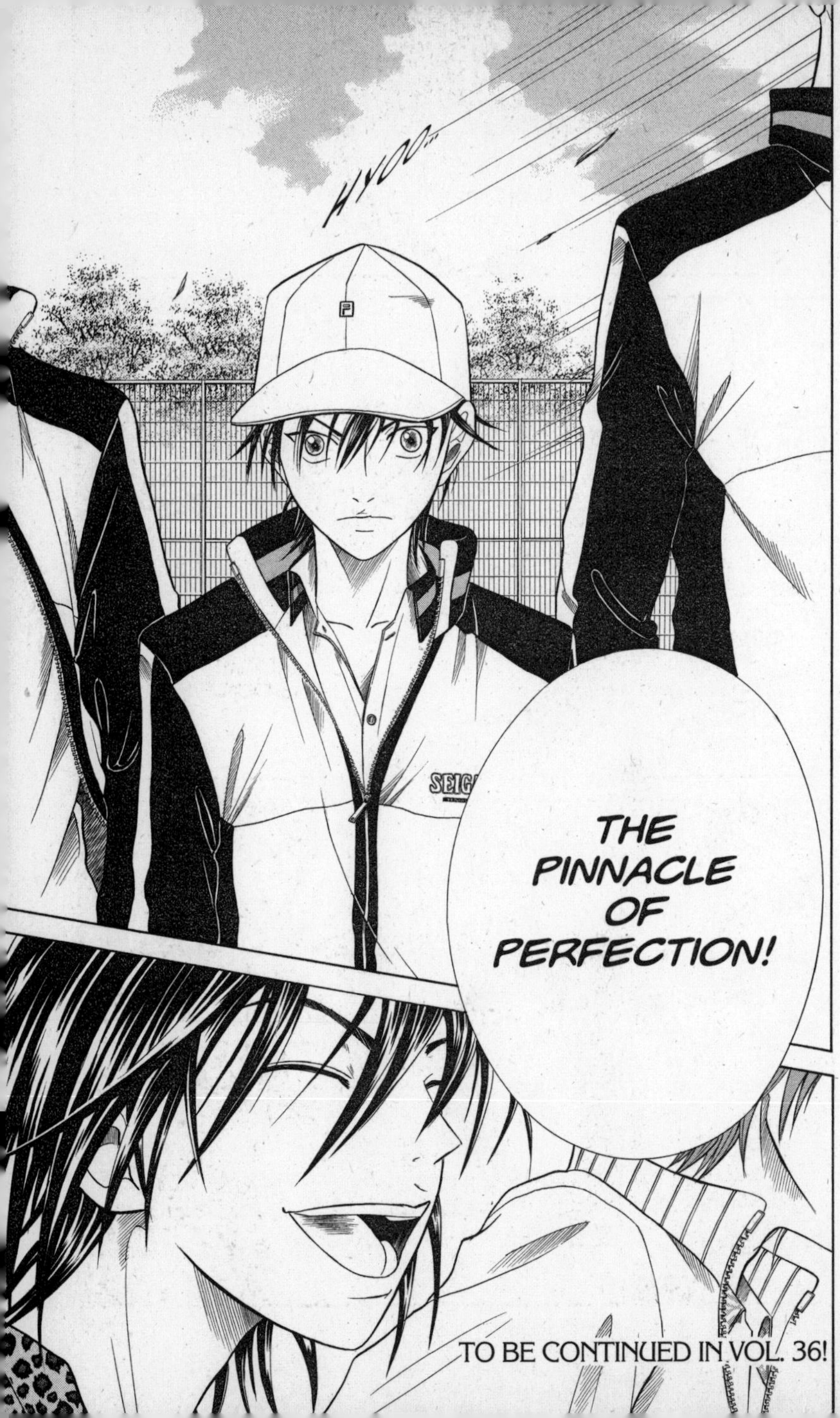
HYOO...
SEIGAKU
THE PINNACLE OF PERFECTION!
TO BE CONTINUED IN VOL. 36!

In the Next Volume...

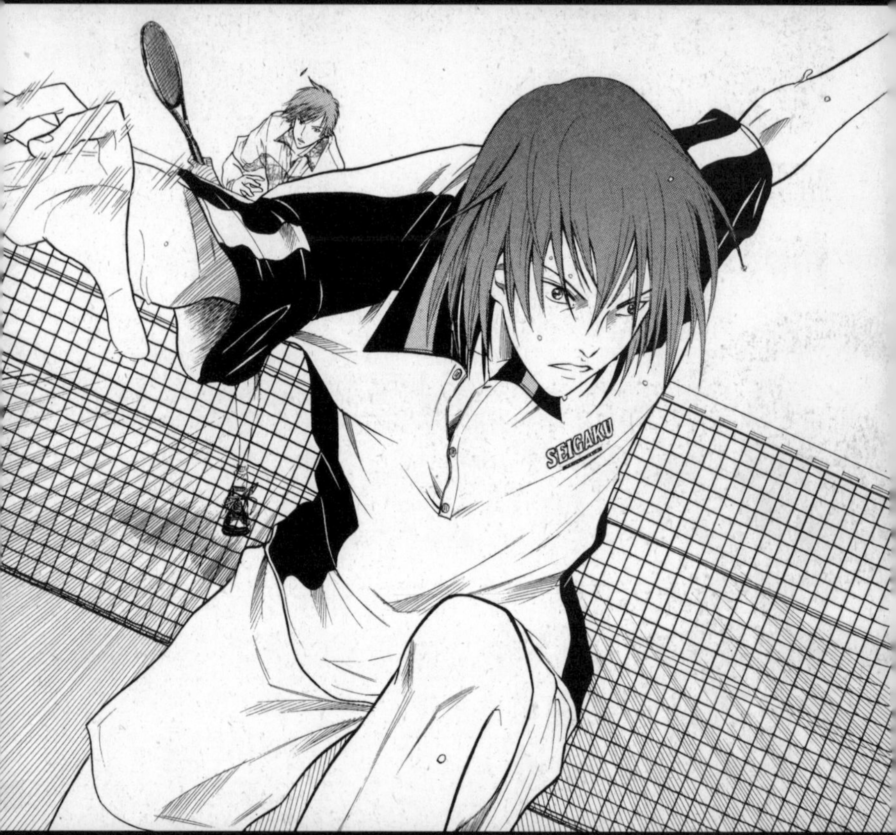
SEIGAKU

A Heated Battle! Seishun vs. Shitenhoji

The semifinals of the National Tournament begin! Seishun is pitted against powerhouse team Shitenhoji. The first match is No. 3 Singles, with Shusuke up against the Shitenhoji captain, Kuranosuke Shiraishi. Shusuke may be Seishun's resident "genius," but the mysterious Kuranosuke is rumored to play "perfect tennis," a game with no flaws.

Available March 2010!

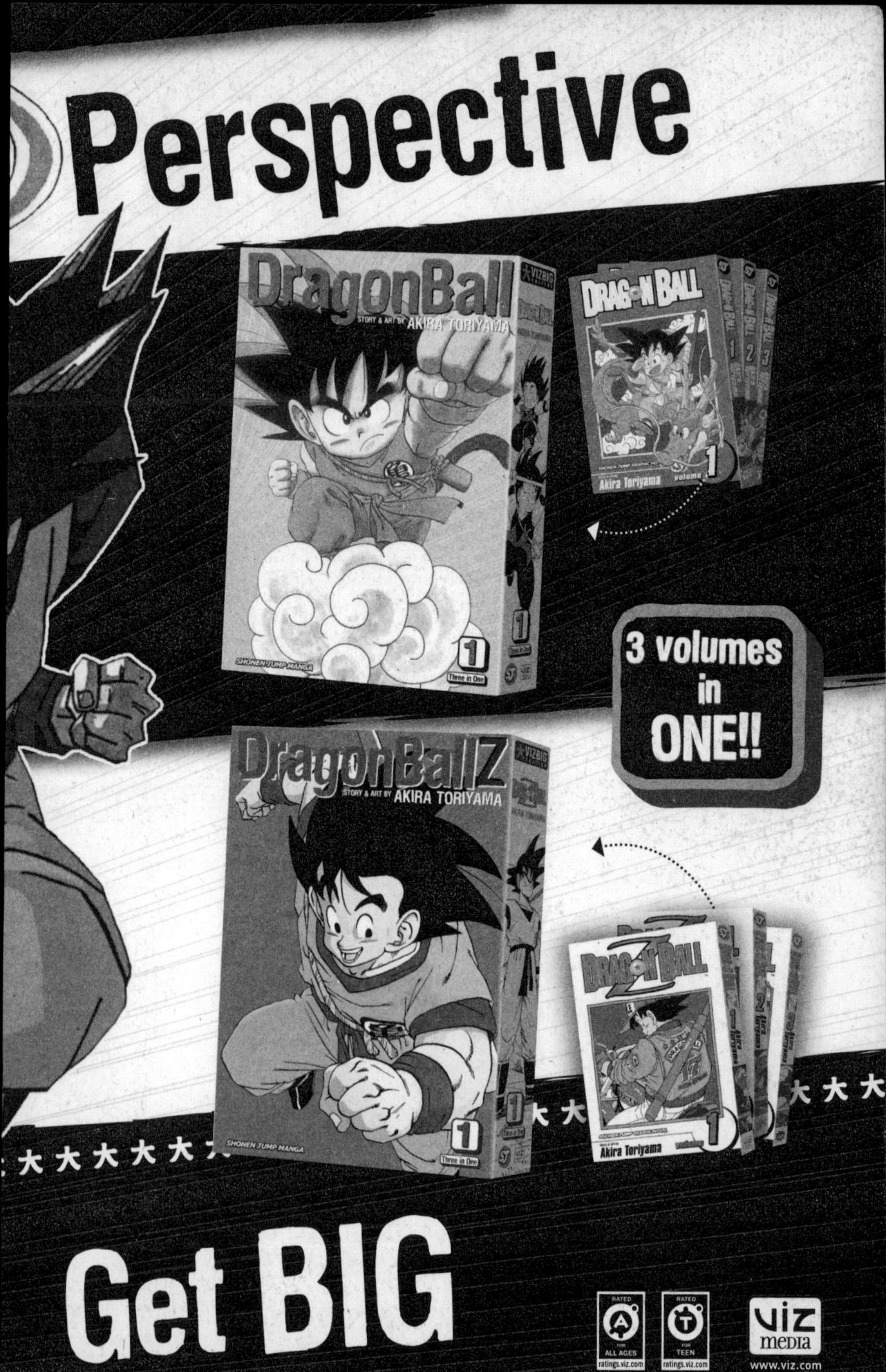
Perspective
DragonBall
STORY & ART BY AKIRA TORIYAMA
SHONEN JUMP MANGA
1
Three in One
DRAGON BALL
Akira Toriyama
volume 1
3 volumes in ONE!!
DragonBall Z
STORY & ART BY AKIRA TORIYAMA
SHONEN JUMP MANGA
1
Three in One
DRAGON BALL Z
Akira Toriyama
volume 1
Get BIG
RATED A FOR ALL AGES
ratings.viz.com
RATED T FOR TEEN
ratings.viz.com
viz media
www.viz.com

Change Your

From Akira Toriyama, the creator of *Dr. Slump*, COWA!, and SandLand

Relive Goku's quest with the new VIZBIG Editions of *Dragon Ball* and *Dragon Ball Z!* Each features:

- Three volumes in one
- Larger trim size
- Exclusive cover designs
- Color artwork
- Color manga pages
- Bonus content

And more!

✳ ✳ ✳ ✳ ✳ ✳ ✳ ✳ ✳ ✳ ✳ ✳ ✳ ✳ ✳ ✳ ✳ ✳ ✳ ✳

On sale at:
www.shonenjump.com
Also available at your local bookstore and comic store

Tell us what you think about SHONEN JUMP manga!

Our survey is now available online.
Go to: www.**SHONENJUMP**.com/mangasurvey

Help us make our product offering better!